WOODWORKING
MAGAZINE

ISSUE NOS. 8 THROUGH 12
2007-2008

Cincinnati, Ohio

Woodworking Magazine Issues 8-12. Copyright © 2009 by F+W Media. Printed and bound in China. All rights reserved. No part of this book may be reproduced in any form or by any electronic or mechanical means including information storage and retrieval systems without permission in writing from the publisher, except by a reviewer, who may quote brief passages in a review. Published by *Woodworking Magazine*, an imprint of F+W Media, Inc., 4700 East Galbraith Road, Cincinnati, Ohio, 45236. First edition.

Distributed in Canada by Fraser Direct
100 Armstrong Avenue
Georgetown, Ontario L7G 5S4
Canada

Distributed in the U.K. and Europe by David & Charles
Brunel House
Newton Abbot
Devon TQ12 4PU
England
Tel: (+44) 1626 323200
Fax: (+44) 1626 323319
E-mail: postmaster@davidandcharles.co.uk

Distributed in Australia by Capricorn Link
P.O. Box 704
Windsor, NSW 2756
Australia

 Visit our Web site at www.woodworking-magazine.com.

Other fine F+W Media Books are available from your local bookstore or direct from the publisher.

13   12   11   10   09   5   4   3   2   1

Library of Congress Cataloging-in-Publication Data

   Woodworking magazine : issues 8-12 / by the staff of Woodworking Magazine. -- 1st ed.
      p. cm.
 Consists of a compilation of issues 8-12 of Woodworking Magazine.
 ISBN 978-1-4403-0163-6 (alk. paper)
1. Woodwork. I. Woodworking Magazine. 8-12.
TT180.W6573 2009
684'.08--dc22
                            2008055088

Publisher: Steve Shanesy
Editor: Christopher Schwarz
Art director: Linda Watts
Senior editors: Robert W. Lang, Glen D. Huey
Managing editor: Megan Fitzpatrick
Associate editor for the web: Drew DePenning
Illustrators: Matt Bantly, Mary Jane Favorite, Louis Bois, Hayes Shanesy, Len Churchill
Photographer: Al Parrish

A Magazine Committed to Finding the Better Way to Build
Filled With Good Craftsmanship, the Best Techniques and No Ads

WOODWORKING
MAGAZINE

Traditional Workbench Rediscovered

19th-Century Design Outworks Most Wimpy Modern Benches

Flush-Cut Saws: Meet The $22 Tool that Rips the Competition

Better & Simpler Hand-Tool Rack

Pumpkin Pine Finish: Chemistry Adds 100 Years in a Day

Bore Better: Become a Human Drill Press

fw F+W PUBLICATIONS, INC.
US $5.99
CAN $7.99

woodworking-magazine.com ■ AUTUMN 2007

Contents

"The only really good place to buy lumber is at a store where the lumber has already been cut and attached together in the form of furniture, finished and put inside boxes."

— Dave Barry, columnist and author

1 On the Level
Is wood a precious natural resource that we should treat like gold, or is it something even more important for the woodworker?

2 Letters
Questions, comments and wisdom from readers, experts and our staff.

5 Shortcuts
Tricks and tips that will make your woodworking simpler and more accurate.

8 Holtzapffel Workbench
We revive a 19th-century bench that was designed just for cabinetmakers. This unique and simple bench blends the best features from German, French and English designs.

HOLTZAPFFEL BENCH: PAGE 8

24 Wall-hung Tool Racks
Toolboxes, chest and cabinets are ideal for storing your tools during transport, but they aren't convenient for the workshop. The classic solution is to build a simple rack above the bench. After experimenting in our shop, we found the best dimensions to create a simple rack that holds a wide array of tools.

27 Glossary
Our illustrated guide to some of the unfamiliar terminology you'll encounter in this issue.

28 Flush-cutting Saws
Is there a difference between a flush-cutting saw that costs $15 and one that costs $94? We tested seven and found significant (and surprising) differences among these no-set saws.

32 Discover Flush-cut Saw Techniques
Whatever you do, don't use your flush-cutting saw the way that the woodworking catalogs show you. You'll end up with a bent blade. Here's the right way to use these saws so they cut pegs and tenons flush without marring your work surface.

36 Be a Better Borer
Drilling accurate holes freehand is a skill worth learning. Our simple exercises will show you how to bore accurate and true with an electric drill or a brace and bit.

42 Pumpkin Pine
You don't have to wait 100 years for your pine to develop a beautiful amber glow. How about one day and three off-the-shelf products?

44 End Grain: Caught in the Act
Following the rules of woodworking can sometimes box you into a corner. We discuss how we go about bending or breaking the rules every day in our shop.

WALL-HUNG TOOL RACKS: PAGE 24

DISCOVER FLUSH-CUT SAW TECHNIQUES: PAGE 32

PUMPKIN PINE: PAGE 42

WOODWORKING MAGAZINE

Autumn 2007
woodworking-magazine.com
Editorial Offices 513-531-2690

Publisher & Group Editorial Director
■ **Steve Shanesy**
ext. 1238, steve.shanesy@fwpubs.com

Editor ■ **Christopher Schwarz**
ext. 1407, chris.schwarz@fwpubs.com

Art Director ■ **Linda Watts**
ext. 1396, linda.watts@fwpubs.com

Senior Editor ■ **Robert W. Lang**
ext. 1327, robert.lang@fwpubs.com

Senior Editor ■ **Glen D. Huey**
ext. 1293, glen.huey@fwpubs.com

Managing Editor ■ **Megan Fitzpatrick**
ext. 1348, megan.fitzpatrick@fwpubs.com

Illustrator ■ **Matt Bantly**
Photographer ■ **Al Parrish**

F+W PUBLICATIONS INC.
David H. Steward ■ Chairman & CEO
John Speridakos ■ COO/CFO
Barbara Schmitz ■ VP, Manufacturing
John Lerner ■ Executive VP, Interactive Media
Eric Svenson ■ Group Publisher, Interactive Media

F+W PUBLICATIONS INC.
MAGAZINE GROUP
Colin Ungaro ■ President
Sara DeCarlo ■ VP, Consumer Marketing
Tom Wiandt ■ Business Planning Director
Sara Dumford ■ Conference Director
Linda Engel ■ Circulation Director
Susan Rose ■ Newsstand Director

PRODUCTION
Production Manager ■ Vicki Whitford
Production Coordinator ■ Katherine Seal

Newsstand Distribution: Curtis Circulation Co.,
730 River Road, New Milford, NJ 07646

Back issues are available. For pricing information or to order, call 800-258-0929, visit our web site at woodworking-magazine.com or send check or money order to : *Woodworking Magazine* Back Issues, F+W Publications Products, 700 E. State St., Iola, WI 54990. Please specify *Woodworking Magazine* and month.

Highly Recommended

I'm often asked to recommend a book for people who want to learn hand tools. Here's my best recommendation: Robert Wearing's "The Essential Woodworker." It covers basic hand skills better than any other book. And it shows you how to put them to use to build a basic cabinet, table and drawer. You can find it used for $10 to $20.

— *Christopher Schwarz*

On the Level

Why I Waste Wood

No one told my eldest daughter that it would be difficult to make clothing by hand and by eye – without a pattern, a machine or even a lesson.

And perhaps because no one told Maddy that it would be hard, it wasn't. During the last three years she has made more than a hundred garments for her stuffed animals, from jogging suits to sequined disco pants to chain mail. She works entirely by instinct. Never measuring. Just cutting, stitching and improving.

Now, every parent will tell you that their child is remarkable, but I don't think that's the case here. I don't think Maddy is a stitching savant. I think that she simply is acting on an impulse and without fear of failure.

It would be easy (read: lazy) for me to now end this column with that same advice about woodworking: Don't be afraid; just get to it. But I know that the fear of failure can be crippling.

For example, last week I taught Maddy how to pump gasoline. Learning that common task was so stressful that by the end of the lesson, her hands were trembling a bit as she yanked the receipt from the pump. At first I was bemused by her trepidation. But then I realized the difference between pumping gas and pushing a sewing needle. It was the raw material.

Maddy has a lifetime supply of cloth in our basement, thanks to the women in my life who buy it for her. And when she needs more sequined fabric to make a disco jacket and floppy hat to match the pants, it will cost her a dollar or two for a supply that will last many years.

Now consider gasoline: It's precious, poisonous and explosive. So here's my real point: I think that wood is a lot more like cloth than it is like gasoline.

This statement might be hard for some of us to swallow at first. It was for me. I'm a conservationist at heart, and saving the trees always seemed like a good idea when I was growing up.

But home woodworkers aren't really the source of the problem when you talk about deforestation, which I know is a critical problem in some places on the globe. Several years ago I toured the hardwood forests of Pennsylvania with a group of journalists and watched loggers cut down enough cherry trees in an hour to last me more than 100 lifetimes of building furniture.

It was that trip that changed my view of the raw material we work with. Before that moment, I would squeeze every single part of a project out of the fewest number of rough boards, even if that meant compromising the design or aesthetics. I would allow myself to use a board with a less-than-ideal grain pattern in a face frame or door stile or stretcher. This, I argued to myself, was being a good steward of the forest.

Now I see things differently. I get only one chance to make each project. And the fate of that project – kicked to the curb or cherished by my grandchildren – depends on the choices I make today with regard to its design, grain, joints and finish.

I don't throw away tons of wood, but I'm not afraid to plow through lots of it to find the right board. I'm not afraid to make a lot of test cuts to get a tight joint. And I'm not afraid to make a lot of sample boards to get the right finish. My leftover pieces end up as interior parts for a future project, as kindling or as compost at the dump. So here's my confession: I now throw away more wood than I ever did before.

"Don't fear slow, only fear stop."
— Chinese saying

But here's how I rationalize that choice: The more wood I go through, the better my end result is. And wood is a renewable resource. We can get it almost anywhere, even rescuing it from the city dump if we so desire. Furthermore, wood is inexpensive when compared to the hours of labor invested in any piece of fine workmanship.

All this makes me bristle when I see companies hawking virgin plastic products under the guise of "saving a tree." Where do they think plastic comes from? It comes from petroleum.

So consider this: We can (and should) always plant more trees (or make more sequined cloth). Compressing dinosaur poop for a million years, however, is another matter. **WM**

Christopher Schwarz
Editor

Letters

ILLUSTRATIONS BY HAYES SHANESY

A Forecast for Successful Fuming

My nephew and I are constructing some quartersawn white oak frames to hold some Motawi tiles that my wife purchased.

We need some advice on fuming. (Yes, I know it's dangerous.)

My wife's family is in the seed and fertilizer business, and have about 7,500 gallons of NH3 on hand, which my brother-in-law tells me is 30 percent ammonia in layman's terms. I think it should work for fuming.

Our question is: Do we need to wait for warm weather (we live in Iowa) to fume?

We will wear respirators and eye protection when we place a small amount in a pie pan in the small plastic enclosure box that we are making for the frames. We will try a sample piece first.

We have read quite a bit about the fuming process, and we are fortunate to have the contacts to get a quart of the ammonia to use when we get the frames finished. We just need to know if the weather should be warm.

Greg Humphrey
Fort Madison, Iowa

Greg,
It sounds like you're going to be doing this outside (which is a good idea) and if that's the case, you'll have better results in warmer weather. The fuming process depends on the liquid ammonia evaporating, and as with water, the evaporation will go more quickly with a warmer temperature. If you're building a tent, a very small heater would also be effective.

The agricultural ammonia should work just fine. I get mine from a blueprint-supply company, and it's about 26 percent, so what you have will be slightly stronger, and should take a bit less time. Test some pieces and be careful.

Robert W. Lang, senior editor

Can a Leg Vise be Adjusted Without Losing Pressure?

The Roubo workbench you made (Autumn 2005) has inspired me to build my own. I plan to incorporate a leg vise, and I have a few questions.

I know that the farther away the parallel guide is from the vise screw, the more powerful its grip can be. However, I would like to place it higher up on the leg vise, so that when I do have to change the pin or put a block down there I will just have to bend over slightly rather than squat down. I plan on putting the vise screw 9" from the top of the bench like you did. So, how much higher do you think I could place the parallel guide and still maintain good, solid clamping pressure to hold pieces for carving and chiseling?

I was planning on placing the parallel guide 20" from the benchtop instead of placing it at the floor. Would this result in a significant decrease in clamping force?

Jason Wood
Ramsey, Minnesota

Jason,
You are going to be fine with your parallel guide at 20" from the benchtop. I went out to the shop and checked the pressure by using a small block of wood as a fulcrum at 20". I couldn't even tell the difference from what I normally get from the vise with the guide at the floor.

The real reason the parallel guide is at the floor is to make it easier to cut the open mortise in the leg for the parallel guide. Leg vises have power to spare.

Christopher Schwarz, editor

20" from benchtop is effective

Usual parallel guide location

Truck Restoration Finish Advice

I am restoring a 1957 GMC truck. The step-side bed has wood strips in it. There is a choice of kits with either pine or oak for new replacement wood. I am thinking of using the oak. However, I have two questions:

1) Is oak the better choice for an outdoor application such as this?

2) What type of finish would be good?

There are so many products out there, and I have seen some that have been exposed to the extreme heat and sun we get here near Las Vegas. They blister and peel in less than a year. In the truck bed there really is no way to reapply the finish once it is in place on the truck bed due to the steel supports and runners used to hold the wood in place.

Jack Sivertson
Henderson, Nevada

Jack,
I would definitely use oak and preferably white oak (which is actually more brownish in color). White oak is not only harder than red oak, but it's a wood that's actually good for outdoor use.

As to finish, buy the most expensive marine varnish you can find – the kind used on old Chris-Craft boats. It's expensive because it's a "long oil" and has ample ultraviolet (UV) light-resistance additive. The extra oil, making it a "long oil," keeps the finish more flexible, which helps with the expansion/contraction problem you'll get with high heat. The UV additives are like "sunglasses" for the wood. UV light degrades wood fiber and when this happens, the wood to which the finish is literally stuck degrades so the finish has nothing more to adhere to. That's when the blistering occurs.

Also, be aware that no varnish will be permanent in the sun. You're going to have to re-apply the finish in the future. When the truck's all done but the wood finishing, you could just send it my way and I'll take care of that for you. It might take a couple years though!

Steve Shanesy, publisher

Can Mortise Chisel Handles Take a Good Beating?

Your piece on mortising chisels (Spring 2007) was, for me at least, dead on-target. I had been considering the Ray Iles chisels, but was hesitating for two reasons. First, I have three sets of mortise chisels already (both Sorby's London Pattern and heavy-duty monsters from Two Cherries). Second, I was considering the Lie-Nielsen ones.

The one issue not addressed in your article is the longevity of the handles. So many authors have noted how common it is to find "pigsticker" pattern chisels with cracked handles. I have seen quite a few of these with makeshift repairs generally consisting of wire neatly and tightly wrapped around a cracked handle. For this reason, I was considering the Lie-Nielsens with their socket handles. However, after your glowing review, how could anyone resist purchasing the Iles' products?

Mind you, I'm still considering the Lie-Nielsens, but they're going to have to wait for next year's capital budget.

Also, the brace in the photo on page 19 of the Spring 2007 issue is quite substantial looking; I couldn't put my finger on the model or manufacturer. Would you mind sharing who the manufacturer was?

Larry Ewing
Chicago, Illinois

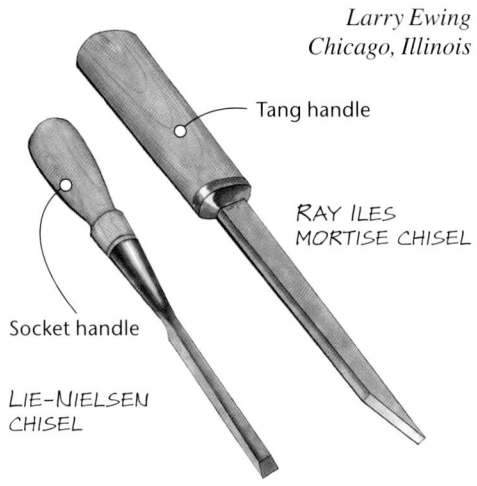

Larry,
The Ray Iles chisels take a heck of a beating. I have one of the first sets made, have used them quite a bit and am impressed. I don't think a home woodworker would ever have to worry about the longevity of the handles.

And the brace? It's the best brace ever made. Ever. It's a North Bros. Yankee brace. You can find them on eBay. Also, tool dealer Sanford Moss sometimes has some to sell: sydnassloot.com/tools.htm.

I can't say enough good things about the North Bros. It's the Cadillac.

Christopher Schwarz, editor

Benchtops and Bench Dogs

I would like to build my workbench so it is stout enough for handplaning activity and occasional mortise chopping. I can get a laminated maple top that is about 1¾" thick for about $150, which seems the route to go. I have a small shop, so 24" x 60" will do. I am concerned if 1¾" is thick enough, as I do not relish the task of laminating my own top to achieve more thickness. Will this be sufficient to prevent flexing?

I also like the concept of using the Veritas bench dogs and Wonder Dogs so as to eliminate the hassle of making a tail vise. The jaw of the Wonder Dog appears to be about ½" thick, so planing at that thickness or less will be problematic, right?

I am left handed so I assume I should put the face vise on the right end of the bench when facing it, correct?

Please also note that the nice Southern yellow pine you use is not available in my neck of the woods (Minnesota) but I suspect almost anything from the local big box stores can be used for the under frame of the bench.

Peter Borth
Maple Grove, Minnesota

Peter,
On workbenches: You should be fine with the commercial top. Maple is quite stiff, and you're only talking about a short span. When you mortise, simply work over the legs to avoid flexing the top. And you can use any wood for the base, even white pine.

The Veritas Wonder Dogs are actually ⅝" thick, which is their only real disadvantage. You can work around the problem with thin wooden shims if you need to.

And you are exactly right about reversing the face vise/end vise positions for a lefty.
Christopher Schwarz, editor

Wood-selection Woes

In one woodworking course that I took, the instructor said he no longer uses kiln-dried wood for his projects; instead he uses air-dried lumber. In another course, the instructor said that he only buys so-called "rough and ready" lumber for his projects. And, recently I read that one should not use S2S lumber. But, another of my woodworking instructors sees no particular issue with S2S stuff, as long as you buy it thick enough to "re-mill."

So, what's a fellow to do?

Dave Raeside
Norman, Oklahoma

Dave,
The question is a great one, but I'm afraid my answer won't be definitive. I think it is, for the most part, a white wine versus red wine question.

There is great advantage to using air-dried lumber in some cases. Some species, such as walnut and redwood, are often steamed during processing to migrate some of the color from the heartwood into the sapwood. The result is that the boards have less color overall. I think steamed walnut looks rather flat when you compare it to the stuff that hasn't been steamed.

However, air-dried wood is less likely to be stable and acclimated to its environment because of the unpredictable nature of the drying process. As a result, you need to be more careful when

> "Basically, I no longer work for anything but the sensation I have while working."
> — John Gay (1685-1732)
> English poet and dramatist

using air-dried wood and checking its moisture content to ensure you don't have any surprises ahead when you mill your material.

You also need to be more careful with air-dried wood when it comes to mold and fungus. Kiln-drying kills these organisms; air-drying does not. Also, when it comes to softwoods, kiln-drying will crystallize the wood's resins, making the boards less sappy and nasty on your tools.

As I see it, the rest is up for debate. The kiln-drying people say their wood will have fewer drying defects. The air-dried people say they can get the same yield when drying is done with care. The air-dried people say their wood is superior in that the kiln-dried stuff has a "dead" feeling. I've never experienced this, however.

I work with both. Instead of judging the wood by the process that dried it, I judge the wood on its grain, figure, defects and moisture content. If the boards meets all, or at least most of, my criteria, I'll buy it and use it.

On the subject of rough lumber versus S2S or S4S, this is a question that is more about your tooling and your time.

You'll save money if you buy rough lumber, but you'll need heavy-duty machinery to process it and allow more time in your schedule for processing. You'll also face more surprises with rough lumber (both good and bad) because beautiful figure and ugly figure can be obscured when the board is in a rough form.

If you buy surfaced stock, you'll be better able to judge the figure of what you are buying and it will take less time when you are processing it, but it will cost more and you do need to be more concerned about warping, twisting and bowing. Surfaced stock that has been poorly processed or stored will be more warped. So buying over-thick stock is a typical fall-back position.

So this debate comes down to judging the stock in front of you. If you are looking at rough stock, you need to develop an eye for picking out good figure in rough material. If you buy surfaced stock, you need to be acutely aware of twisting and warping. And, you have to consider the time factor and extra cost.
Christopher Schwarz, editor

In Search of the Perfect Tenon

I have been making a carcase using mortise-and-tenon joinery. I cut the tenons on my table saw using the dado blade and left a little extra to trim off for a good, snug fit. Then, I made the mortises using my drill press and squared up the mortise using chisel and mallet.

The problem I found with using a shoulder plane on the tenons to size each for its respective mortise, was that I frequently ended with the tenon tapering toward its end. I even clamped a good straight piece of oak on the piece I was working to keep me referenced square. I used the plane at waist height and used my body to try to get a nice fluid motion back and forth.

Any other hints for me? Also, my mortises were not perfect but I figure I will get better each time I do them. Should I switch to mortising chisels instead of bevel-edge chisels here?

Michael Schnurr
Ames, Iowa

Michael,
This is an interesting problem with many valid solutions. Here are a few that spring to mind.

1. When you hold your shoulder plane, focus the downward pressure directly over the bevel of the cutter to keep the tool in the cut and consistently cutting. I place my fingers right over the blade when grasping the tool.

2. Count the strokes you are making near the shoulder and near the end of the tenon. Be careful about overlapping the cuts as you get comfortable with using the shoulder plane. It is a finesse tool. Speed will come later.

3. Alternately, disregard all the advice above and embrace a tenon that has a slight taper. Some woodworkers swear that a slightly tapered tenon can be a good thing. They worry that a piston-fit tenon will scrape all your glue away from the mortise walls. A taper will help spread the adhesive evenly and a tenon has plenty of strength, even when tapered. I personally don't try to achieve a slight taper in my tenons, but if the end tapers a bit, I don't fret.

4. Try a different tool approach. You can use a router plane and a scrap of wood that is the same thickness as your tenoned piece to produce dead-perfect tenons. If you have a router plane, this is worth trying. If you don't have a router plane, I would keep practicing with the shoulder plane.

As to your chisel question, I used bevel-edge chisels for cleaning mortise corners for many years. That works fine. You don't have to have mortise chisels to cut mortises. They just make the job easier when hogging out material from scratch without drilling out material first.

Christopher Schwarz, editor

Details on the Shop Boxes

I am thinking of building the knock-down workstation in *ShopNotes* Vol. 15 Issue 87. The workstation includes a sort of I-beam in its design. However, I was recently looking at your blog on popularwoodworking.com and noticed the "I" beams you constructed for your shop. What

are the dimensions for those I-beams, and what would you consider the ideal length?

I already have some heavy-duty sawhorses and I think your I-beams and those sawhorses will do everything I need – and then some.

Richard D. Welsh
Washington, D.C.

Richard,
The I-beams, along with the boxes they sit on, were featured in the Autumn 2005 edition of Woodworking Magazine.

The three plywood pieces are ³⁄₄" thick x 4³⁄₄" wide. The top and bottom piece have a ¹⁄₄" dado for the vertical center piece, making the overall height 5³⁄₄". The set I have now were ripped from a full sheet of plywood, so they are 96" long. Depending on the work you do, a 4'-, 5'-, or 6'- length might be more manageable. I can't take the credit for these – they are a common item in cabinet shops in Cleveland, but I don't think I've seen them elsewhere.

Robert W. Lang, senior editor

Drawbore v. Pegs: Which Offers More Holding Power?

I tend to get *Woodworking Magazine* and read the articles as I find a need for the skill. This week, I am making frame-and-panel doors with hand-cut mortises, so I studied "Mortising by Hand" in the Spring 2007 issue. I hope I can end up with a ⁷⁄₈"- thick frame, and want a ⁵⁄₁₆"-wide mortise.

While reading the same issue, I came upon Glen Huey's article on pegged joints. I had planned to use drawbore joints as you described in the Autumn 2005 issue. I think I would get more holding power. Can you make a comparison?

Don Boys
Hope, Michigan

Don,
You raise an interesting question. I don't think that either method (simple pegging or drawboring) strengthens the joint in all cases. In fact, any peg has the potential to weaken it if the joint is subjected to sudden stress. That's because the peg can rip up the mortise and make the piece impossible to repair.

However, the peg can provide other benefits. A simple non-drawbored peg can keep an assembly together if the glue fails in the joint. If the assembly isn't subjected to sudden shocks, the joint will only become loose instead of falling apart. This can be an advantage in some cases.

A drawbored peg offers you other advantages. If the wood is a bit wet, it will keep the assembly tight as it dries. If your cheek fit is loose, it will tighten up the joint. If you cannot get a clamp across the assembly, it will pull up everything tight.

So – bottom line – I would leave the joint unpegged completely if you have a nice tight fit, are using modern glue and the assembly is unlikely to see much stress.

Christopher Schwarz, editor

Does Table Stand Test of Time?

I was thinking about building the trestle table from the Autumn 2006 issue. I was curious, now that some time has passed, have you been happy with it? Has it been stable? Do you like the size? Are there any improvements you would make if you were building another one?

Rob Parsons
Peachtree City, Georgia

Rob,
We've been very pleased with the table. It has remained sturdy and the design specs (based on classic formulas) make it comfortable for sitting. The only change I would make is that I wouldn't use through-chamfers on the post. I'd stop them. That would look more traditional.

The table also looks good without chamfers (as in the one I built for my home). **WM**

Christopher Schwarz, editor

HOW TO CONTACT US

Send your comments and questions via e-mail to letters@fwpubs.com, or by regular mail to *Woodworking Magazine*, Letters, 4700 E. Galbraith Road, Cincinnati, OH 45236. Please include your complete mailing address and daytime phone number. All letters become property of *Woodworking Magazine*.

Shortcuts

ILLUSTRATIONS BY HAYES SHANESY

Set a Miter Gauge or Sliding Table Perfectly Square

Setting a table saw's miter gauge or sliding table to make a perfectly square crosscut can be an endless cycle of cutting, testing and tweaking. I've found a quick and easy way to square my crosscutting devices using an inexpensive dial indicator with a magnetic base and a known square surface.

Here's how. Place your known square surface in position against your miter gauge or the fence of your sliding table. I use a machinist's square with a thick blade. You also could use a piece of MDF, UHMW (ultra-high molecular weight) plastic found in jigs, or even plywood. The key is to have a piece of work that has a square corner, smooth edges and is at least 1/4" thick.

Now stick your dial indicator to your table saw's top and place the plunger against one corner of your square. Zero out the needle of the dial indicator. Now push your miter gauge or sliding table forward, as if you were making a cut, and watch the needle on the dial indicator. If it moves off zero between the beginning and end of the cut, then your gauge or sliding table needs adjustment. Simply adjust your gauge or table until the needle stays on zero as you move the square past the dial indicator. (Actually, being a couple thousandths off won't hurt anything, but I like to shoot for perfection.) Then go to work. No test cuts are necessary to confirm the setting.

Kelly Mehler
Berea, Kentucky

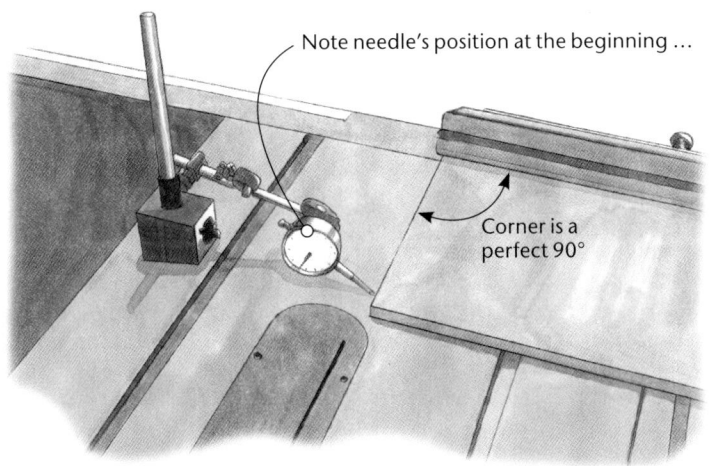
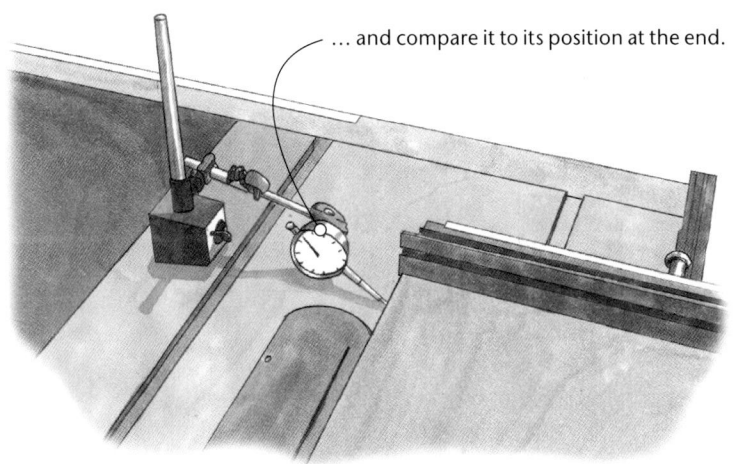

Sticks and Nails Slash the Time You Must Wait for a Finish to Dry

Whenever I finish a piece of furniture, I use my "finishing sticks" to cut in half the time I spend finishing a project. Here's how they work:

Make your finishing sticks from narrow and long offcuts. With a brad nailer, drive an array of 1 1/4"-long brads through the sticks. Use the same brad size, no matter what the thickness of your offcuts is.

Now lay these sticks out in your finishing area. When I spray lacquer I put a stick on top of each of my sawhorses. When I finish in the shop with a rag-on or brush-on finish I put an array of them on my bench.

When finishing furniture, almost every component has a show side and a non-show side. So begin finishing the non-show side with your work on the sticks. With the finish still wet, flip the work over onto the sticks and finish the piece's edges and the show side.

In almost all cases, the nail tips create only small indentations in the finish. These can easily be rubbed out so you can't see them. Or you can just leave them because they are barely noticeable and they will be on the underside of the shelf or the inside of a door.

This trick, simple as it is, cuts out a significant amount of time from your finishing process.

Christopher Schwarz, editor

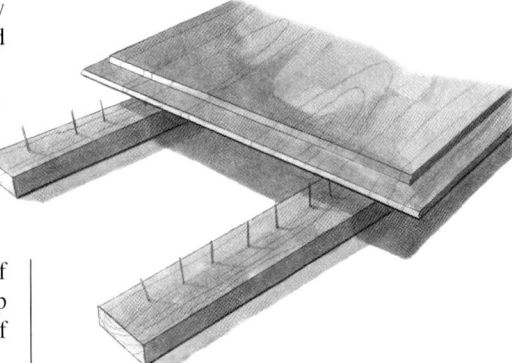

Two Quick Table Saw Tricks

■ The purpose of a zero-clearance insert on the table saw is usually seen as preventing tear-out on the bottom of the work and keeping thin pieces from falling through the blade slot. But it has another function that can increase accuracy and speed your setups. The kerf makes it incredibly easy to set the fence, a stop on the miter gauge, or a piece of wood to be cut at the exact location of where the blade will be when cutting. Just line up a pencil line on your work to the kerf in the insert instead of with a tooth on the blade.

■ The hollow, square tube that serves as the front rail of most rip fence systems is a great place to keep the arbor wrench, push stick or other small item in easy reach, yet out of the way. Some saws have a plastic cap on the end of the tube. Throw the cap in the trash and keep the wrench in the now-accessible space.

Robert W. Lang, senior editor

woodworking-magazine.com ■ 5

Trim Face Frames Flush With the Help of Some Scotch Tape

When building cabinets, I like to attach the face frame to the cabinet with a little bit of an overhang, then trim the face frame flush with the outside of the carcase. A bearing-guided flush-trim router bit works well for this, but if there are indentations on the carcase they will be transferred to the face frame, or sometimes I don't want to take the time to install the router bit just for one quick operation. Also, while the router is my favorite portable power tool, I do admit that it is a bit noisy.

I figured out a quick and easy way to use an edge-trimming plane as a flush-trimming plane, similar to a flush-trim router bit. The problem is that I run the risk of making some cuts into the carcase if I take off too much material. The solution I found was to put a piece of Scotch tape on the lowest edge of the plane in the positions shown in the drawing. The thickness of the tape is about the amount that the plane iron protrudes through the sole of the plane. (I didn't actually measure this.) The tape ends up being the equivalent of the bearing on the flush-trim router bit.

With the tape in place, I trim the face frame flush until the plane stops cutting. Then, the work is done.

Steven McDaniel
Humboldt, Tennessee

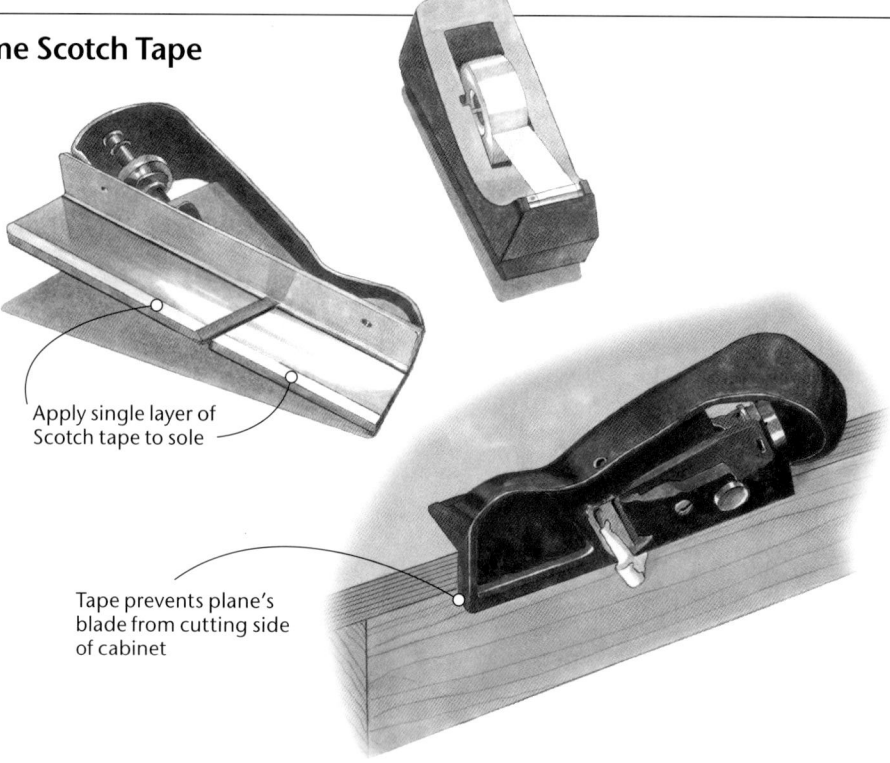

Apply single layer of Scotch tape to sole

Tape prevents plane's blade from cutting side of cabinet

Plane Irons are Good for More Than Just Planing

The plane iron in your block plane or bench plane is useful for many workshop tasks once you remove it from the plane's body.

I use a sharp block-plane iron to slice off runs and sags left behind when I apply too much finish to a workpiece. Be sure to let the finish dry before attempting this. Place the plane iron flat on the work and move it forward into the sag. The cutting edge will slice the sag off the surface of your work. Then you can re-sand the piece and apply the next coat. This trick is both faster and more effective than sanding out a run or a sag.

I also use my plane irons as scrapers. The iron from a smoothing plane or jointer plane works quite well as a scraper to remove localized tear-out. These irons typically have a slight curve to their cutting edge so the corners won't dig into your work when you scrape with them. To do this, hold the iron upright like a scraper and use the unbeveled side of the iron as the cutting edge. Because there's no hook – unlike what you find on a traditional card scraper – the scraper will take only light cuts. This can be a good thing.

I also use my plane irons like a wide paring chisel. Sometimes I need to remove a thin sliver of waste in a corner and need an accurate and clean cut; I'll use a wide plane iron instead of a chisel. This is ideal when surgically removing junk from a rabbet or tenon shoulder. The wide iron can remove the waste in one clean cut – a typical bench chisel will require several overlapping cuts, and you might not overlap them all perfectly.

Longer plane irons are also excellent marking and cutting knives. When I need to mark an accurate line across a piece of work with a recess, I'll lay a wooden straightedge across the work and run the unbeveled face of the iron against the straightedge and use a corner of the iron to mark the work. This gets me into places my other marking knife won't go because its handle gets in the way or the blade isn't long enough.

I'll also use a plane iron in a similar fashion to slice thin veneer strips. I'll lay the straightedge on my cut line on the veneer. Then I run the iron against the straightedge like a knife. The mass of the iron is an asset with this cut – you don't need to press down as hard as you would with a typical shop knife.

Christopher Schwarz, editor

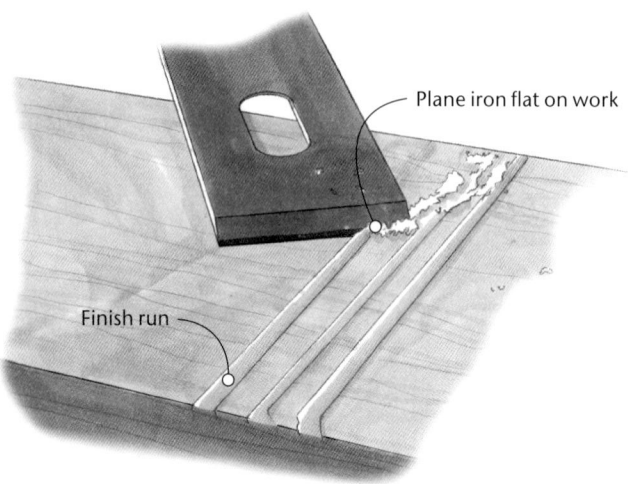

Plane iron flat on work

Finish run

Recess in work

Wooden straightedge

Change the Height of Your Benchtop in a Snap

A low workbench is great for handplaning and assembly, but it can be murder on older backs or when trying to do close-quarters work, such as inlay. You could build two workbenches at different heights, or you could make your bench convertible with this trick we picked up years ago from an English woodworking book.

This trick comes from English author Robert Wearing, who describes it as a solution used in the manual-training schools for dealing with children both young and old.

First decide how low you want your workbench to be for planing and build it to that height – our 6' 3⅝" editor finds that 32" to 34" high is right for him.

Then build simple risers that are the same width as your workbench and are as high as the height you want to add to your bench. Want to add 5"? Make the risers 5" high. Put the risers in place under your bench and attach the risers to your legs using a cabinet hinge – one hinge on each leg.

When you want to lower your workbench, simply lift up the top a little and fold each riser out from under the legs and set the bench's feet on the floor. When you want to raise the workbench, lift up the top and fold the riser in under the legs.

from the Woodworking Magazine *staff*

How to Make Any Size Dowel Using Your Table Saw

When working with dowels, it seems we never have the exact diameter we need for the task at hand. Or perhaps we need a truly odd-size dowel for an odd job.

Here's the fastest and easiest way to remedy that problem – and you don't need a lathe.

Get a dowel that is slightly larger than the diameter you require and is at least 24" long. Set the fence on your table saw to remove half of the waste. Here's an example: Say you have a ⅝" dowel and need a ½" dowel – you are going to waste away ⅛". Half of that is 1/16", so set your fence to 9/16". Raise your blade up high if you want a clean cut (don't forget the guard) or you can keep the blade fairly low if the final appearance of the dowel isn't important.

Turn on the saw and feed the dowel into the space between the fence and blade. With your hands safely away from the blade, rotate the dowel and feed it forward. I like to rotate it clockwise, but both directions work. The sides of the teeth of the sawblade trim the dowel to your finished diameter.

When you have fed enough dowel into the blade for the job you need, turn off the saw, let the blade stop then remove the workpiece. **WM**

Roger Amrol
Columbia, South Carolina

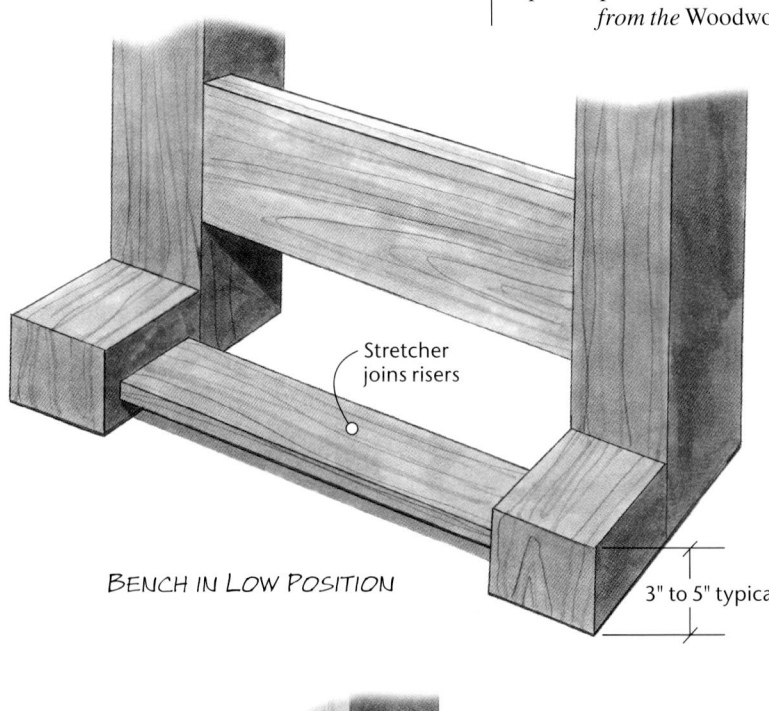

BENCH IN LOW POSITION

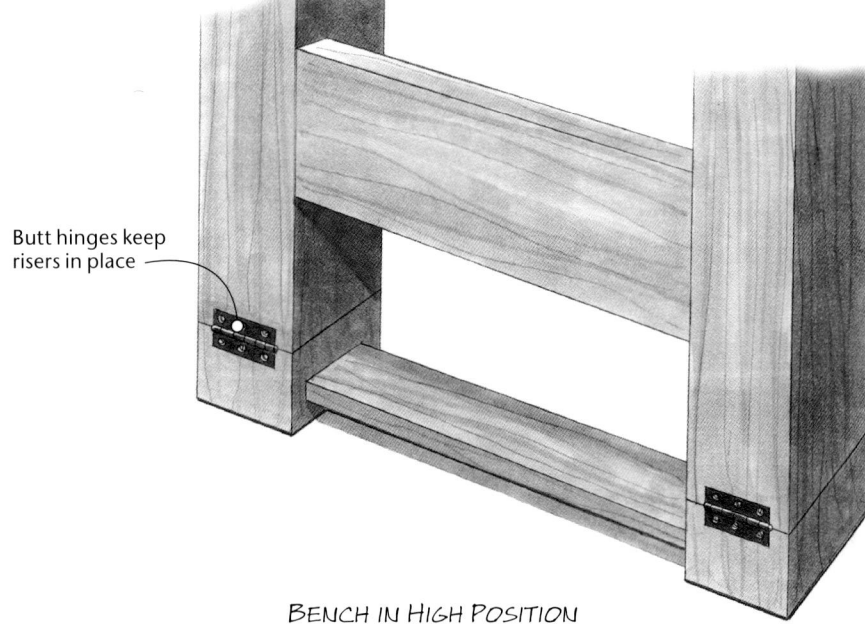

BENCH IN HIGH POSITION

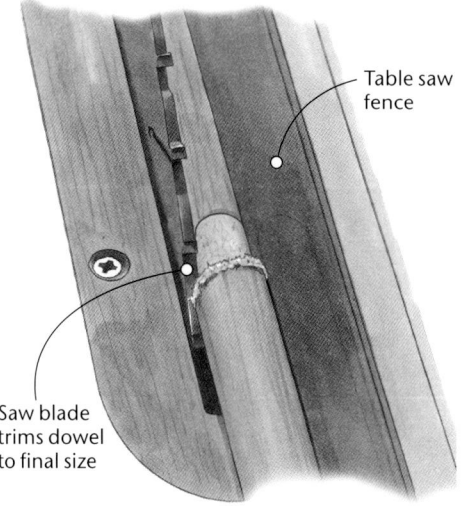

SEND US YOUR SHORTCUT

We will send you $25 to $100 for each Shortcut we print. Send your Shortcut via e-mail to shortcuts@fwpubs.com, or by regular mail to *Woodworking Magazine*, Shortcuts, 4700 E. Galbraith Road, Cincinnati, OH 45236. Please include your complete mailing address and daytime phone number. All Shortcuts become property of *Woodworking Magazine*.

The Holtzapffel Workbench

This 19th-century design is a bit German, a bit French and entirely ingenious. Plus, we came up with a way around the typical sagging tail vise.

The Industrial Revolution did as much harm as it did good to the world of woodworking and workbenches. The Industrial Revolution created machines that could make metal handplanes and handsaws in tremendous numbers, but it also created the woodworking machinery that made those hand tools obsolete.

The Industrial Revolution created the manual training movement (shop class) when good-minded people thought that children should learn to do something with their hands (what with the entire world becoming automatic and mechanical). And the Industrial Revolution created both the market for and the ability to manufacture workbenches to encourage the spread of the manual-training movement.

And this, in my opinion, changed the course of workbench design in the 19th and 20th centuries. The old-style craftsman-made benches were displaced by the modern manufactured form that is dominant still today.

But in 1875, when the world was balanced on a precipice with its rural past behind it and the modern age spread before it, this bench was published in an English book: "Holtzapffel's Construction, Action and Application of Cutting Tools Volume II," by Charles Holtzapffel.

This 19th-century workbench can be built with bolts to be knocked down, or it can be built as a permanent addition to your shop, as shown here.

It's a tremendous book even today and is crammed with details on working wood and metal with both hand and power tools.

The author was the head of Holtzapffel & Co. of London, a tool-making enterprise that is best known for its line of elaborate lathes but also manufactured everything from scissors to gardening equipment to exquisite miter planes.

I have doubts that Charles Holtzapffel actually designed or even advocated this particular bench. He died in 1849, and the edition of my book came out in 1875. I really should scare up an earlier edition of the book and see what sort of bench might be lurking there. But that could be an expensive whim. Original copies of the 1875 books can cost $1,500 a set. Earlier editions are even harder to find.

Why Build the Holtzapffel?

The Holtzapffel workbench is the third archaic workbench that I've built and put to use in a modern shop. Each of the three benches had a deep connection to the culture that developed it. The bench from A.J. Roubo's 18th-century books is as French as bernaise, strong coffee and berets (see the Autumn 2005 issue). The bench from Peter Nicholson's 19th-century "Mechanical Exercises" (visit our blog to see photos) is entirely British. The only other place this English bench shows up with any regularity is in the Colonies.

The Holtzapffel is a cultural mongrel. The Holtzapffels were Germans who settled in England. And the bench has features of both cultures that, in my opinion, create a bench that is outstanding for cabinetmaking.

From the Germanic tradition, the Holtzapffel has a traditional tail vise on the right side that most English cabinetmakers and joiners would sniff at as unnecessary. The skeleton of the bench – its base and top – are equal drams German and French. The massive legs are Gallic. The tool tray and knockdown bolts are German.

The workholding is also a melting pot of Stilton, Camembert and Butterkase. The bench shows holdfasts (trés French), a variety of planing stops (English and French), a twin-screw vise (quite British), and a leg pieced with holes for supporting long stock (fairly standard pan-European fare).

Usually when you start mixing and matching bits and pieces like this, you end up with something along the lines of catfish pizza. But all the parts of the Holtzapffel work together like, well, I'll spare you any more food metaphors.

About the Bench's Framework

The original bench has a French undercarriage that is joined using bolts in some places. The legs and stretchers of the benches are – for the most part – pushed out so they are flush with the front edge of the benchtop. This arrangement allows you to use the legs and stretchers as clamping surfaces, which is handy when working long boards and large frame assemblies.

I've built five or so benches using a bolt system and find it great for benches that will have to travel on occasion. For homebody benches, drawbored mortise-and-tenon joints are just as good. If you go with the bolt system, you can shorten the tenon on the stretchers to 1" long if you like. Leave it unglued, obviously.

If you go with the bolt system, you'll also want to modify the way the top of the bench attaches to the base. I went with the permanent old-school French method: drawbored mortise-and-tenon joints. If you want to knock down your bench, I suggest you add a second rail to the top of your end assemblies then use lag bolts (in slotted holes) to secure the top to the base.

My base is built using hard maple, though any heavy wood that is inexpensive and plentiful will do just as well. Yellow pine, Douglas fir and white oak are excellent choices.

About the Bench's Workholding

The top is made using some figured ash that was exquisitely dry, a bargain and easy to work with. Those three traits – and ash's weight and stiffness – made it an ideal choice for this benchtop. I implore you, however, to use what you have on hand. There is little magic in choosing a wood for a workbench; just go for stiff, heavy and cheap.

Far more important than the species of the wood is the selection of vises. All workbenches need some way to hold boards so you can work on their ends, long edges and faces with a minimum of Rube Goldberging. This bench is designed for a woodworker who builds typical furniture using both hand and power tools. It excels at working on panels with planes or sanders. And it is the best bench I have ever used for hand dovetailing.

Here are the details so you can decide if this setup is for you. The face vise is a massive twin-screw vise that offers 24" between the screws. This ensures that you will be able to clamp almost any case side, door or drawer in its jaws for dovetailing, sawing or planing. The wide spacing of the screws also allows you to clamp a 72"-long board on edge for handplaning with ease.

The holes in the leg under the vise are for holdfasts. These support your work from below and even allow you to clamp the work to the leg if the need arises. You can use two metal screws to make this vise, or you can use the commercial Veritas Twin-Screw vise for this bench. (I used wooden screws that I had been saving for some time.) Each strategy has pluses and minuses.

The wooden screws are more fragile than iron, though they are durable enough for normal workshop tasks. I like how they don't mark your work with grease, which is a common problem with metal screws. The wooden screws operate independently – this allows you to easily clamp tapered and odd-shaped pieces, but it forces you to pay more attention to advancing and retracting the screws in tandem and with two hands.

Using two independent metal screws is also a fine choice (see the Supplies box for a source for metal screws). You'll be able to clamp tapers, plus the mechanism is easy to install and inexpensive. But you can mark your work with oil.

The Veritas Twin-Screw Vise also is a good choice. It takes longer to install, but that is offset

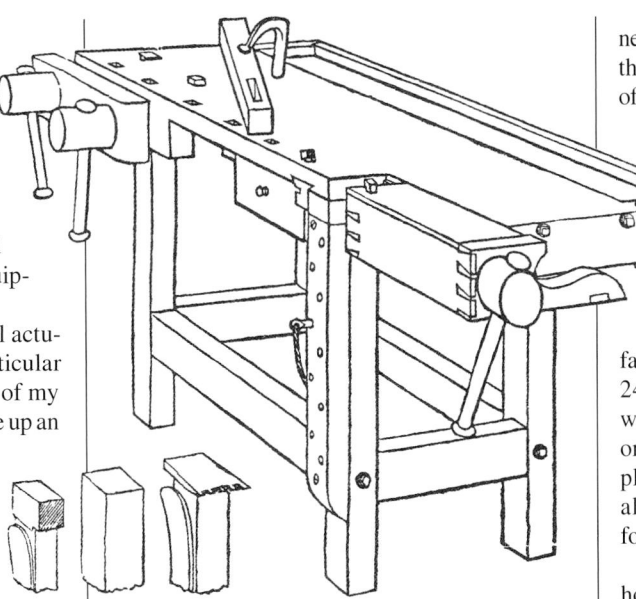

The Holtzapffel has old-world features, such as its tree-trunk legs. And it has elaborate workholding, such as its sexy-looking tail vise. Unlike some other benches of this era, the Holtzapffel blends several traditions to create an effective bench.

This wooden twin-screw vise has a tenacious grip. I can secure any board of any size and put my entire weight on the board without it slipping. That's good enough for me.

The Veritas Twin-Screw Vise takes about a day to install and adjust. But it offers many years of trouble-free service. I can't really say anything bad about it as a face vise.

by the fact that you can operate the jaws with one hand (the screws are connected by a chain drive). And it's more expensive than the other options.

If you never plan on dovetailing anything, you can replace the twin screw with another face vise, such as a quick-release iron vise. If you are an occasional dovetailer, I'd choose a leg vise for this position.

The end vise on this bench is a clever piece of work – it's my only real contribution to this venerable design. You see, I think the traditional L-shaped tail vise can be more trouble than it's worth. They are fussy to install. They tend to droop. And you cannot work on the vise itself. But the tail vise remains the dominant vise for the end because it offers great support for clamping panels and narrow boards on edge.

I wanted something easy to install, fast to use and as good as a tail vise. The arrangement I devised almost meets all three of these tough requirements. It's a quick-release metal vise with a big wooden chop (sometimes called a jaw). It takes a couple hours to install and will never droop. The quick-release function is quite handy in this position because it allows you to quickly switch setups for boards of different lengths – there's much less spinning of the handle than with a traditional tail vise.

The chop offers a lot of support for your work below, though I admit it's not as unerring as a tail vise. But what makes up for that is that I've spaced the dog holes in the benchtop less than 4" apart, so there's always less than 4" of open space below your work between the chop and the benchtop. And your work isn't going to sag or bow over that short a span.

There are also a few well-placed holes for holdfasts in the top to round out the workholding for the Holtzapffel workbench.

Another virtue of this bench is its utter simplicity. I built this bench in 37 hours of shop time, from surfacing the rough lumber to applying a second coat of finish. Other benches that have the same number of advanced functions are far more complex and have dovetailed skirts and tail vises for you to fuss with. This bench gets you straight on to the good part: building furniture.

Begin with the Legs (or the Top)

If this is your first workbench, that can change the order of the operations involved. If you don't have any form of workbench in your shop, then

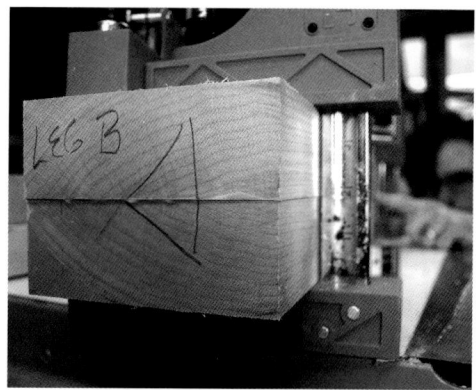

Once you choose the boards for the legs, mark the mates with a cabinetmaker's triangle across the joint. These triangles help prevent mistakes and guide your assembly operations. Face-glue the leg pieces together, then joint and plane the assembly.

Strategies for Squeezing the Maximum Thickness From Your Stock

In woodworking, it is usually the first steps you take in any operation that set the stage for success or failure. And wood preparation is no exception to this rule. How you treat your stock at the beginning of a project will determine if you have plenty of stock that is thick and wide enough. Or if you will limp along through a project with boards that are just a bit on the thin side.

One of the worst mistakes a beginner will make is to take an 8'-long board, joint one face and then plane the other. Then rip and crosscut the board into smaller pieces. This is a wasteful path to creating stock that is too thin.

Here are the strategies that we use to ensure we squeeze the maximum amount of thickness from our stock.

1. First lay out all the available stock for a project and try to mark out all the parts you need on the rough stock with a grease pencil or chalk. Give yourself some extra parts for joinery setups, messing up a few rails and stiles and even some extra stock for unexpected problems. Allow yourself an extra 1" in length and an extra ½" in width for each piece.

2. Mark out some rough cuts on these boards and try to group the cuts so that your boards are of middling lengths. About 24" long should be a good minimum for grouping short parts. Parts that are longer than that (36", 48" etc.) can be marked out for cutting by themselves. By grouping parts into these lengths you will defeat any bowing over the length of the boards by sharing the bow among several boards. Crosscut your boards in their rough state on a miter saw or with a handsaw.

3. With great care, rip out your parts. If your stock is true, you can joint one edge and rip your parts on the table saw. If the board has any corkscrewing to it, the band saw is a much safer machine for this. Ripping your stock in the rough defeats any cupping along the width of the boards by sharing the cup among several boards.

4. With your parts roughed out, proceed to joint one face and then one edge. Then plane the opposite face down and rip the board to its final width.

— CS

By ripping a cupped board into narrower pieces in the rough, you can get thicker stock. Simply face-jointing this entire board would result in a board that is thinner than I need.

10 ■ WOODWORKING MAGAZINE Autumn 2007

Cut the shoulders first. The shoulder is the critical cut so perform it first. The rest of the tenon involves just wasting away the excess stuff on the face cheeks.

Keep consistent downward pressure. A sled or a sliding table on your saw makes this operation safe and accurate. However, even with those nice features, the work will tend to rise up a bit as you are in the cut. Keep firm pressure down to ensure a consistent tenon.

Check your work. Dial calipers can be a crutch, and I tend to use them more than necessary. However, they do point out where the errors are in my tenons so this tool earns its keep.

Then the edge cheeks. Having a stop on your sliding table or table-saw sled is key to cutting tenons. Here I am cutting the ½" shoulders and edge cheeks on the tenons.

you should glue up the top first, put that on sawhorses and build the bench's base on that. If you have a workbench (or a Workmate, or a solid-core door on sawhorses), you can begin by building the base and then adding the top.

For this bench, I began by building the legs from 8/4 rough maple. Each leg consists of two layers of maple, face-glued together. First I face-jointed one face of each board and then glued the two jointed faces together with the rest of the wood still in the rough. Because I handplane almost every surface, I did my best to keep the grain running the same direction on both halves of each leg.

Then, when the glue was dry, I jointed, planed and ripped the assemblies to their finished size. This strategy reduces the time slaving over the planer and jointer by processing things twice.

If you plan to join your top and base with a mortise-and-tenon joint, then you need to cut a 1"-thick x 2" long tenon on the top of each leg. If you are going to join the top with lag bolts, simply cut each leg to 31" long and move on to the stretchers.

I went with the tenon option, a joint I prefer to cut using a dado stack on a table saw. The only other way I'd cut this joint is by hand. I don't own a shaper, most routers don't have enough juice and using a tenon jig on the table saw involves a dangerous balancing act to cut the stretchers and legs with them sticking up in the air.

First cut the shoulders of the joint. Then waste the face cheeks. Lower the arbor of your saw so the blades project ½" above the table and then cut the edge cheeks. Note that these edge cheeks are optional. You can cut the edge cheeks as shown in the photographs, or you can omit them, as shown in the illustrations at the end of the article. It's your choice.

Make Stretchers and Decisions

The tenons on the stretchers are thinner than the ones on the legs, but they are made in the same fashion at the table saw. The tenons on all the

With your tenons milled, you can clean up any stray tool marks on your legs to prepare them for joinery. Here I'm using a finely set bevel-up jack plane. Usually I'd finish up with a smoothing plane, but the gnarliness of the work demanded a high planing angle (about 62°).

woodworking-magazine.com ■ 11

stretchers are 5⁄8" thick, 4" wide and 3" long.

These tenons are wider than traditional tenons. The rule on width is the tenon should be two-thirds the width of the work, which would put the tenon at 3 3⁄8" wide. I bumped it up to 4" wide because these tenons aren't located anywhere near the fragile ends of the legs, where the tenon could blow out the ends when driven into the mortise. Plus, with a 4"-wide tenon, there is less material to remove when making the tenon and less end grain to pare to fit the joint.

With your tenons cut you should arrange the parts as they will be assembled and lay out your mortises in the legs.

Marking and Making Mortises

Use your finished tenons on the stretchers to mark out the locations of the mortises on the legs. Mark on the legs where the stretchers will go then place the shoulder of the stretcher's tenon directly on your work. Use your tenon like a ruler and trace its shape on the leg. The less you measure things out, the less likely it is that you'll make a mistake.

If you're a making a version of this bench that can be disassembled, don't forget to mark out the mortises for the additional stretchers that run at the top of the side assemblies. And be sure that you have at least a 3⁄4" shoulder on the tenons of these stretchers, or you will likely blow out the end grain at the top of the leg at the worst possible moment.

Cutting the 5⁄8"-wide mortises takes some doing. While there are 5⁄8" hollow-chisel mortising bits available, they are not common and they are expensive. They also are not needed for this operation. If you are careful, you can cut accurate 5⁄8"-wide mortises using a 1⁄2" hollow mortising chisel by overlapping your strokes.

If you don't do this with care, you can snap a mortising bit (I've done this a few times when I had a little too much vim, vigor or venom in the blood that day). After laying out your mortises, go ahead and bore out the mortises with a 1⁄2" chisel, which will leave you 1⁄8" of extra waste that has to be removed.

Reset the fence of the mortising machine and bore out the remaining sliver of waste. Take this cut slowly. If you pound through this cut you can deflect the chisel into the path of least resistance – the open mortise. If you deflect the chisel, then your mortise will get skinnier in its deepest depths. Or the chisel will bend. Or break.

Once you bore all your mortises, you can test-fit your joints and tune them up. Clamp up your side assemblies and fix any gapping at the joints' shoulders. Then do the same thing as you fit the long stretchers to the legs.

I use a couple strategies for fitting tenons. If there are problems, I'll undercut the shoulder near the tenon proper, leaving the outside of the shoulder. A chisel is the best tool for this job. Then I'll fit the outside of the shoulder with a shoulder plane until the gap closes tight.

This strategy prevents you from making the fit worse. By undercutting the shoulder first with a chisel, you leave just a small ribbon of wood to remove with the shoulder plane. This reduces the chance that you'll muck up the shoulder with the plane – it's easy to make the joint worse with a shoulder plane.

Assemble the Base

Though the original bench was bolted together, I decided to alter the bench joinery with some

Group your legs as they will be assembled to mark your joinery. Here I've bundled my legs so the front legs are facing up and the back legs are on the benchtop. This helps prevent layout errors.

Show the tenon to your leg and mark things out by using the tenon like a big ruler. Have you noticed how many of these photos are taken with the overhead lights off? That's not just to be moody (I'm moody enough as it is). The window light alone makes my marks easier to see. Fewer light sources equals better visibility.

Make your ⅝"-wide mortises with your ½" chisel. Begin by boring a ½"-wide mortise for the stretchers on all the legs. This is a deep mortise, so be sure to let your tooling cool a bit and lubricate it with canning wax or a fancy high-priced lube.

Reset the fence on your mortiser to remove the ⅛" strip of waste. First mortise the ends (the most critical parts) then fill in by removing the waste between your first cuts.

I tune up all my tenons, and not because I'm some sort of anal-retentive craftsman. No matter how careful I am at cutting my tenons and mortises, the joints will be a tad too tight if I've done everything to the print. Remove a few shavings to make the tenon fit well and to correct the location of the shoulder. You can shift the stretcher in and out of its assembly by removing material from the inside or outside of the tenon's cheek. That is real power.

Assemble the ends and clamp them up. Take a close look at each joint and note where the shoulder touches the leg and where it doesn't. The places where the shoulder touches is where you want to remove material. Mark those areas while the legs are clamped up, then use the marks as a road map to fixing the problems in the shoulders.

Not every joint needs to be massaged, but many big joints do. The first measure is to undercut the shoulder. Begin with the chisel about ⅛" from the outside of the shoulder. Push the tool in and remove a wedge-shaped piece of end grain that's about 1/16" thick at its most girthsome.

The shoulder plane will true up a lumpy shoulder and knock down a shoulder that is too high compared to the other shoulders. It's easy to overdo things and reduce the shoulder too far. I take three passes then check my work during a typical tenon fix.

woodworking-magazine.com

older technology: drawboring. I've written a lot about this traditional technique (see the Autumn 2005 issue), which involves driving a peg through a hole in the mortise and a hole in the tenon that are offset. The offset of the holes "draws" the "bores" together when you insert the peg.

I used $3/8$"-diameter white oak peg stock and a $3/32$" offset. This maple is tough and thick, so a brutish peg and serious offset are appropriate. I glued and clamped up each joint and drove two pegs through each joint. I removed the clamps immediately after driving the pegs.

Once the glue cures, trim your pegs flush (see Glen D. Huey's review of flush-cutting saws on page 28 for advice on this matter). Then plane all your joints flush, rout some stopped chamfers if you please and turn your attention to the top.

Build a Laminated Top

Workbench tops are a matter of some trepidation for beginning woodworkers. They tend to overdo things in the gluing one stick to another stick department. In general, I'm a fan of overdoing things, but I have limits.

You don't need to bolt your top together with massive all-thread rod. You won't hurt anything by doing this, but you will eat up precious shop time for little benefit. The glue by itself is plenty strong.

You don't need to use biscuits to align the boards in the lamination. Workbench tops are thick and are flattened regularly. So a few boards that are out as much as $1/32$" aren't going to change things much when it comes to the final and effective thickness of your top.

Here's how I've glued up many workbench tops with wild success. Glue up three or four layers – however many you think you can manage at once. After the glue is dry, joint and plane the assembly flat. Make a few more assemblies, and joint and plane them as well. Then start joining the assemblies together and try to get these joints as accurate as possible.

Once your top is glued up to its finished width (24" in this case), you should trim the ends to size. Good luck trying this on a table saw with a stock miter gauge. I prefer a handsaw or circular saw. And when I feel the need for extra precision, I'll make the cut using a circular saw and an edge guide.

Mortise the Top

Joining the top and base with a mortise-and-tenon joint seems intimidating, but it's quite simple. Here's the basic drill: Turn the top upside down

Drawboring the joints reduces your dependence on expensive long clamps. A clamp or two plus your peg are enough to hold the joint as the glue cures.

I have always liked stopped chamfers. They protect the fragile sharp edges from splintering and look darn good as well. You can do them by hand with a drawknife and chisel, but the technique that requires far less skill is to use a 45° chamfer bit in a handheld router. The short ramps where the chamfers stop are simply where I pulled the router away from the leg. Purists will balk that I didn't flatten the ramp with a chisel. But I'm not pure.

and hump the base into position on the top. Trace around the tenons and remove the base.

Bore out the mortises. Make the mortise at the rear of the bench 1/8" wider to allow the top to move (this is optional – old workbenches allowed the base to cast into an A-frame shape). Clean up the corners and join the base and top together with drawbored pegs.

So begin by getting the base in position on the underside of the top. After positioning it (take your time), trace around the 1"-thick tenons with a marking knife or marking awl. If you are aggressive with a knife, clamp the base to the top before you mark the locations of the mortises.

Chopping out the mortises can be tough work. These are wide, deep and long. I've done these entirely with a chisel and it's a lot of effort in hardwood. It's much more efficient to bore out the waste with a 1" Forstner bit and then clean up your work with a chisel. The tenons are 2" long, so make the mortises 2 1/8" deep. Don't go

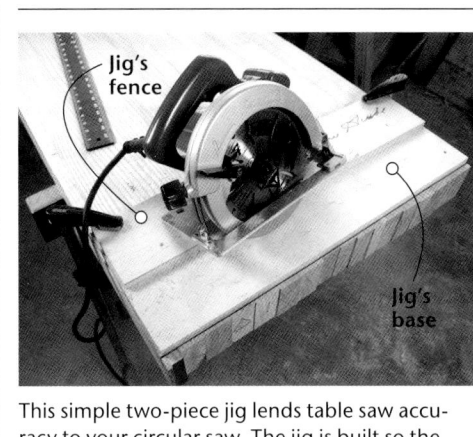

This simple two-piece jig lends table saw accuracy to your circular saw. The jig is built so the base and fence fill the space on the left side of the saw's shoe. You just lay the jig on your cut line, clamp it down and saw right on the line. It's hard to miss or mess up.

Three assemblies together: For this top, I glued up three boards for each sub-assembly. Then I jointed and planed each of those and glued them to their new neighbors. Even experienced woodworkers have trouble managing nine boards all at once. So don't think you are wussing out with this approach.

Jointing a big edge: Here I've got the two assemblies for the top nearly ready and am jointing the edges. Even though these edges were planed flat, they were distorted by all the clamping pressure during assembly.

Use a square to guide your efforts to shift the base in position on its mate. Focus your efforts on getting the front of the legs flush to the front edge of the benchtop. Don't fuss over the back legs as much.

woodworking-magazine.com ■ 15

Do You Need a Sliding Deadman on Your Holtzapffel Bench?

Long-time readers (and critics) will note that there is no sliding deadman on this bench. No, I haven't gone soft. After some calculations, I think I can get away without a deadman. The huge twin-screw face vise will handle long boards and the holes in the right leg will allow me to clamp doors and assemblies to the legs and stretchers. At least, that's the theory.

Just in case, I added the architecture for a sliding deadman on the bench. So if I go running home with my tail between my legs, it will be a 20-minute fix, instead of something that is cobbled together and bolted on. — CS

I cut two 45° bevels on the top of the front stretcher for my ghostly deadman.

A groove (or grave) for the deadman: After assembling the benchtop, rout a groove along the front edge of the underside of the bench for the deadman. Make it deep – 1" will do nicely – to give yourself flexibility when attaching the device to the bench.

The only cordless drill I'd recommend for this job is a brace and bit. (If you go that route choose a brace with a 12" or 14" sweep.) A cordless battery drill will balk at this task. Use a slow rpm and clear out the chips as best you can as you work.

too deep – you can blow through the top when mortising with the chisel.

For the mortises for the rear legs, I made this mortise 1⅛" wide. I bored out the 1"-wide mortise and then knocked ¹⁄₁₆" off each cheek of the mortise with a mortising chisel. The other option is to thin your tenon a bit, which is also a sound strategy with these sizable joints.

Then clean up the corners of the joint with a heavy-duty chisel such as a mortiser. Fitting these two assemblies together is no fun, so I recommend you take steps to avoid as much testing and tweaking as possible. Scrutinize your mortises before trying to assemble things. Undercut the shoulders of the tenons.

If you do have to take things apart a few times, spreader clamps are the best things to assist disassembly. Use the same gap-fighting strategy you used to assemble the base. Fit your joints, mark the problem areas on your tenons (these will be the high spots that touch the top) and work those until the gaps close.

Keep in mind that if your efforts don't seem to be producing predictable results, it could be the top that is out of whack instead of the tenon

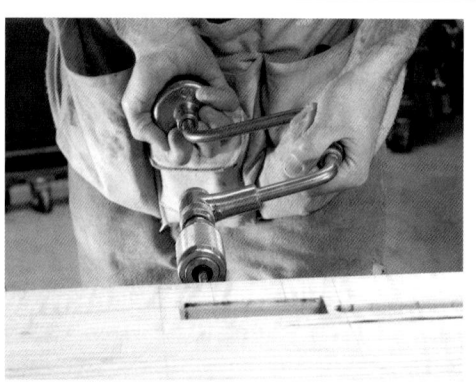

I use a brace and bit quite a lot when building a bench. With a little practice you will bore true with little effort. Until then, keeping a square handy to check your angle is a sound idea.

When cleaning rounded corners, make the cut in a couple steps. Cut away half the waste. Then remove the rest to your layout lines. This makes it easier for you to steer the cut – otherwise the wood will be doing most of the steering.

shoulders. So doing some preliminary flattening on the underside of the top can work wonders. When you have to fix a problem with end grain on a workpiece, consider if the problem could be fixed by dealing with face grain on its mate.

When you're ready to assemble the bench, consider drawboring the top to the base. I've found that drawboring is particularly effective when dealing with joints such as this one. Bore the holes for the pegs in the mortises (I used ⅜" pegs for this joint). Assemble the joint and mark the location of the hole in the mortise on the tenon

Early woodworking texts on drawboring say you should offset your holes by the thickness of a shilling. Old shillings are about a ¹⁄₁₆" thick, maybe a little more. After you make five or six of these joints, you'll stop measuring, start eyeballing things and stop worrying about it.

By making repeated kerf cuts in the notch, you'll make the resulting notch cleaner. The chisel will follow your kerfs and be less likely to dig into the benchtop. So if you can slit straight, you'll be in good shape.

Popping out the waste is like working on the world's largest dovetail socket. Use your chisel to pop out the waste halfway through the top. Then flip the bench on its feet and finish the job. This makes for cleaner results.

using the tip of the auger bit (or brad-point bit).

Then drill a hole through the tenon that is $3/32$" closer to the shoulder of the leg's tenon. Add glue, reassemble things and drive your pegs home. One quick tip on the pegs: I like to taper them with a pencil sharpener before driving them. The taper helps move the peg through the joint and prevents it from getting hung up or destroying things inside the joint.

Add the Vises

The end vise for this bench is a quick-release iron vise. And while I won't hold much work directly in its jaws, the occasion will come up. As a result, I decided to let the vise's rear jaw into the end of the benchtop. I first kerfed the entire notch with a dovetail saw (the saw's rip-tooth profile sped things up). Then I knocked out the waste with a mortise chisel and fit things with a paring chisel.

The Lee Valley quick-release vise needed a spacer between it and the benchtop to make the jaws flush with the top. My vise required a $5/8$"-thick spacer. This size of spacer actually put the jaw a little below the top of my benchtop, but that's a good thing. This allowed me to flatten the top with a handplane without running the risk of colliding with the vise's jaws.

I nailed the spacer to the benchtop and then began drilling $5/8$"-diameter holes for the $1/2$"-diameter, 4"-long stove bolts that would hold the vise to the benchtop. Some people use lag bolts, but lags will sag someday. Bolting through the top is the better way to go.

Then bore the holes in the top for the dogs. I have flirted with square dogs on some benches. And they are more trouble than they are worth in my book. The round dogs are easier to make and can also be used for a traditional holdfast – which is reason enough to use them. Keep your dogs close – I bored 17 holes on $3 3/8$" centers. This prevents you from having to move your vise much and reduces the amount of stock that will be unsupported by any setup.

I made a jig for boring the dog holes, but it is an unnecessary crutch if you have any experience with a brace. After drilling two holes with the jig, I threw it aside and drilled the remainder

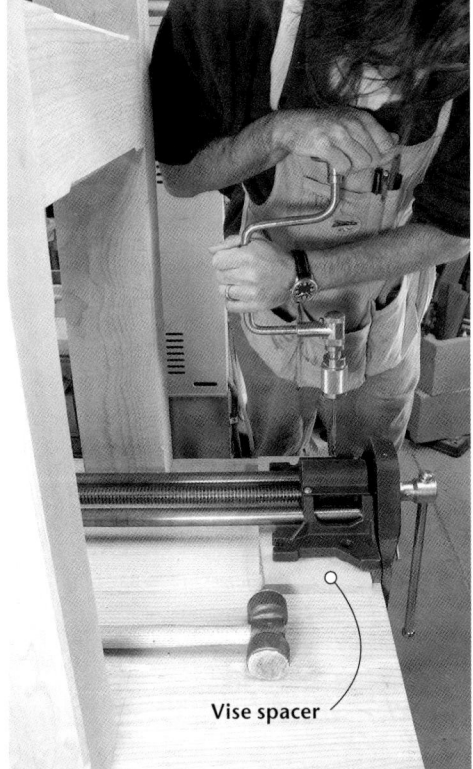

Vise spacer

With the vise in position, I drilled $5/8$"-diameter holes though the spacer and top. As soon as the lead screw of the auger broke through the top of the benchtop, I stopped boring.

I used the hole left by the lead screw of the auger as a guide to bore the counterbore for the bolt heads on the top of the benchtop. Be sure that your counterbore is big enough to hold the washers you picked out at the hardware store.

This jig helps locate the dog holes. The additional hole in the jig allows you to position it right over your layout lines. The notches in the jig's face allow you to get a clamp right where you want it. After two holes, this jig was as good as firewood to me. Freehand drilling is much faster for me.

Sometimes it's hard to get a finger under the bench dog to push it up for action. A notch in the chop is a big help.

freehand. They came out great and the work went quickly. After drilling the holes in the top (see the illustrations for details) go ahead and drill the holes in the legs for holdfasts.

The other part of the end-vise setup is the big wooden chop screwed to the moving jaw of the quick-release vise. This chop ended up 2¾" thick, 4⅛" wide and 13½" long. I bored a ¾"-diameter hole through the chop for the bench dog (the metal dog on the vise isn't ideal). Then I cut a 1"-wide access notch in the bottom of the chop. This notch lets me push the dog up and down with great ease.

Then I routed the ends of the chop with a large beading bit for a traditional look and screwed the jaw to the iron vise, which has holes just for this purpose.

The Twin-screw Vise

There's not much to say about the twin-screw. It's an easy vise to install as long as you do the steps in the correct order. Here they are: Begin by building the chop. Create the 3"-thick chop by face-gluing up a few pieces of thick maple. Rout the ends to match the chop for the end vise then lay out the location of your holes for your vise screws.

Bore these holes and install the two screws in the chop.

You'll have two blocks that will house the threaded portion of the vise's screws. Run these onto the screws through your chop and tighten them up against the chop. Now place this whole assembly in position on your benchtop. Mark where the vise's blocks should go on the underside of the benchtop then bolt these blocks to the benchtop with through-bolts.

Depending on the screws you select, you might need to fit some support blocks between the screws and the underside of the benchtop. These supports will prevent the screws and chop from sagging. My wooden screws required ½"-thick support blocks that I simply nailed to the underside of the bench.

Flushing and Finishing

Now you can flatten the benchtop and flush up the chops with the benchtop so everything lines up. I use a jointer plane and diagonal strokes to

Installing the face vise is best done with the bench on its back. Gravity holds everything in place and you get access to both the benchtop and the underside of the top. It's also a good way to drill the holes in the legs for the holdfasts.

true things up. If you were careful when gluing up your top this should be a 45-minute job on the outside.

Once the diagonal strokes flattened the benchtop, I switched to strokes that ran with the grain. How do I know when to switch my strokes? Winding sticks tell me that the top is flat and not in wind, and getting shavings from all points of the top tells me that the low spots on the benchtop are gone. That's when I switch.

The real evidence that the top is flat is that your work behaves predictably on your bench as you work it. If you have trouble planing things flat on the bench, one of the problems could be that your top is too far out of true.

When the benchtop is flat and the chops are planed flush to the top, I recommend you apply a layer of sueded leather to the moving jaw of the face vise. The leather is kind to your work and helps grip it fiercely. You can attach the leather with yellow glue. Put down the glued leather, roll out a layer of wax paper then close the vise until the glue is cured.

As to finishing a bench, less is better. (Some say that no finish is better.) For a workbench, I like a little protection from spills and stains. I like a finish that isn't slick or shiny. I like a finish that is simple to apply and renew. I like a finish that I can do in one day. Bottom line: I like an oil/varnish blend, usually sold as a "Danish oil."

These common finishes are boiled linseed oil with a little varnish resin in them and some paint thinner to make them easy to apply. Rag it on and rag off the excess. Apply another coat later that day and rag off the excess. When that layer is dry, you are ready to go to work.

I've already built several projects on this workbench during the last few months and I have been thrilled by the bench's workholding. The face vise is a monster when it comes to dovetailing. I am glad that I added the holes for holdfasts in the left leg. I tend to use these to support my work from below there because the vise takes two hands to open and close. That's a small price to pay for a vise that will hold a board up to 24" wide with little effort.

However, the quick-release vise in the end vise position has been the real surprise. Why I didn't do this earlier I'll never know. I'm both enthused and disheartened by this revelation. I'm thrilled because the vise works well beyond any expectations I had for it. And I'm disheartened because this surprise means there are probably other surprises ahead for me with this bench that I'm now blind to. **WM**

— *Christopher Schwarz*

Supplies

Lee Valley Tools
800-871-8158 or leevalley.com

1 ■ Quick-release Steel Bench Vise, large vise
 #10G04.13, $129

2 ■ 4⅜" Bench Dog
 #05G04.01, $11.95 ea.

1 ■ Twin-Screw Vise, up to 24" centers
 #05G12.22, $198

1 ■ Veritas Hold-Down
 #05G14.01, $59.50

Woodcraft
800-225-1153 or woodcraft.com

2 ■ Economy bench screw (a metal substitute for wooden screws)
 #144959, $29.99 ea.

Stephen Fee
sfee13@verizon.net

2 ■ Wooden screws, 2½" diameter, 24" length, $125 ea.

Tools for Working Wood
800-426-4613 or toolsforworkingwood.com

1 ■ Gramercy Holdfasts
 #MS-HOLDFAST.XX, $29.95 pair

Prices correct at publication deadline.

Wooden screws show up for sale from time to time on the Internet and at sales of old tools. When you see them, snatch them up. Or you can buy them from the supplier listed at right.

Holtzapffel Workbench

	NO.	PART	T	W	L	MATERIAL	NOTES
❏	1	Top	3	24	72	Hardwood	
❏	4	Legs	3½	5	33	Hardwood	1"-thick x 2"-long tenon on top
❏	2	Long stretchers	1¾	5	44	Hardwood	⅝" x 4" x 3" tenons
❏	2	Short stretchers	1¾	5	23	Hardwood	⅝" x 4" x 3" tenons
❏	1	Face vise chop	3	6½	34	Hardwood	Wide, plane to fit
❏	1	End vise chop	2¾	4⅛	13½	Hardwood	
❏	1	Spacer for end vise	⅝	6	10½	Hardwood	Sized for Lee Valley vise
❏	2	Supports for face vise screws	½	2	11	Hardwood	Prevents screws from sagging

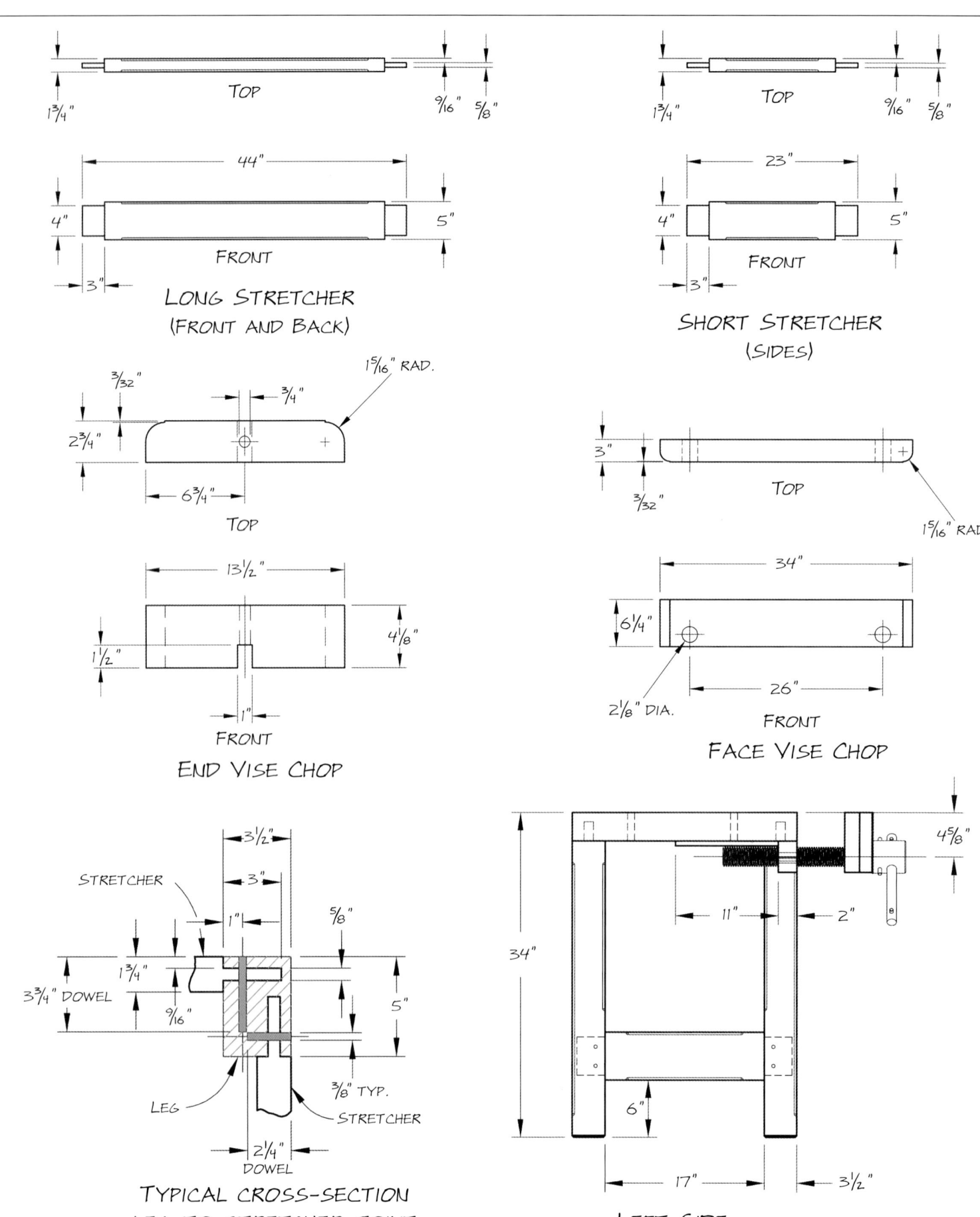

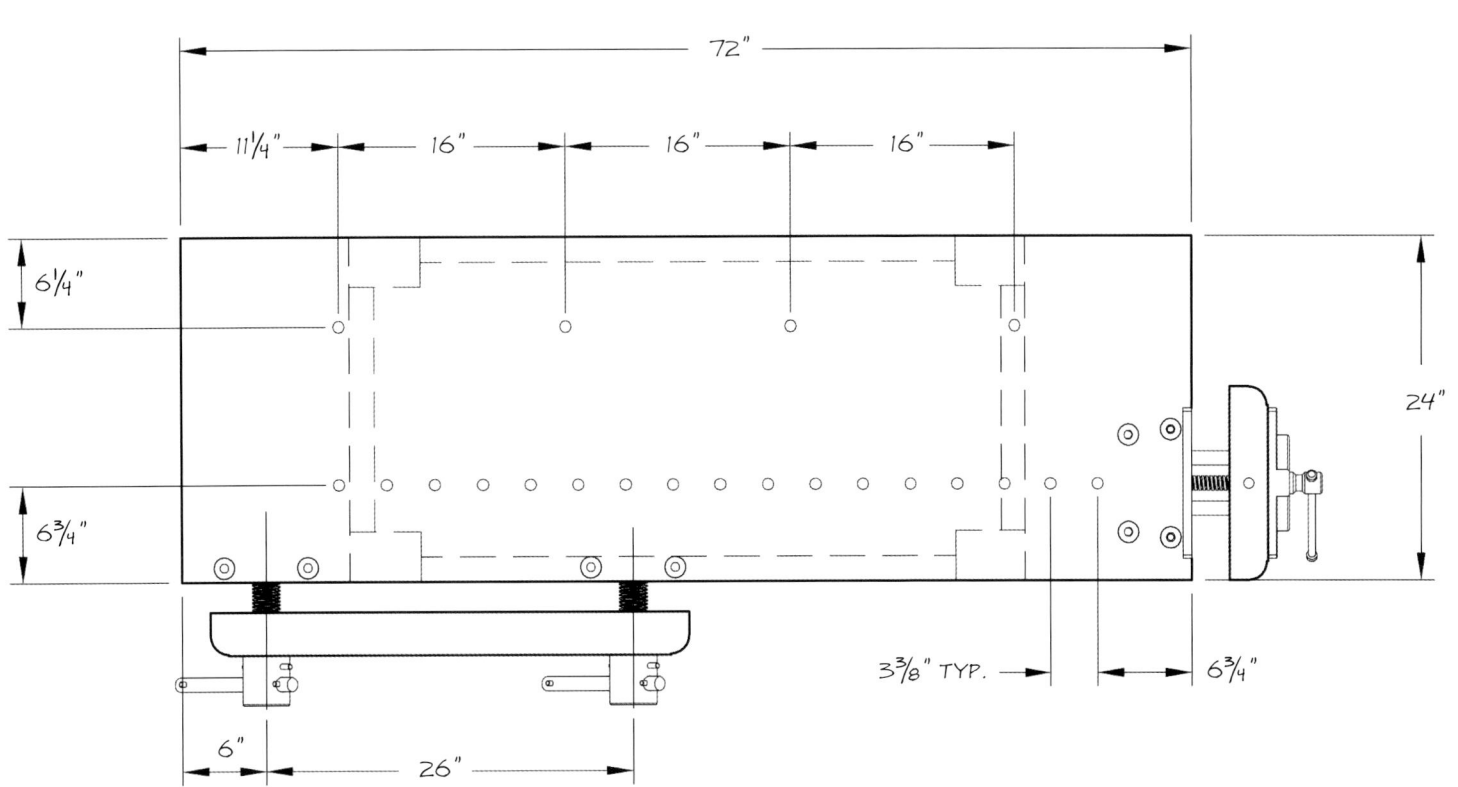

TOP VIEW

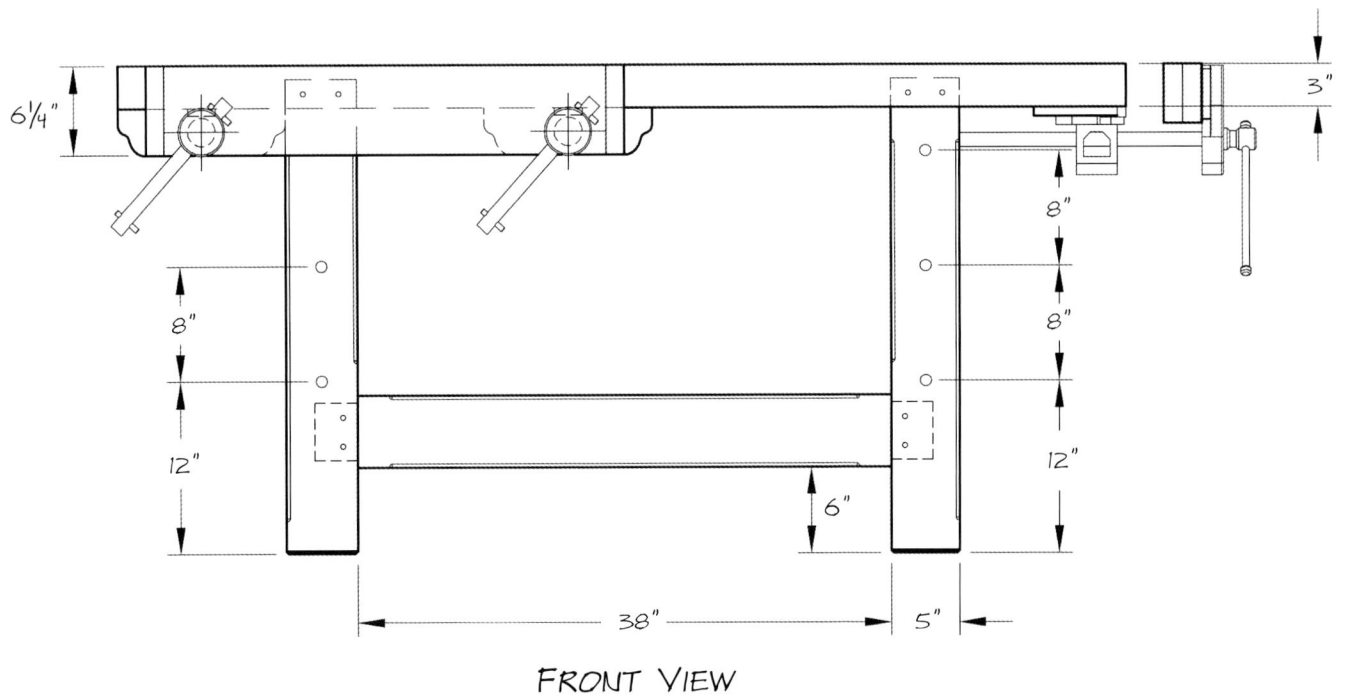

FRONT VIEW

BACK LEFT LEG

BACK RIGHT LEG

STOPPED CHAMFERS 3/16" X 3/16" AND 2¼" FROM ALL INTERSECTIONS

FRONT LEFT LEG

FRONT RIGHT LEG

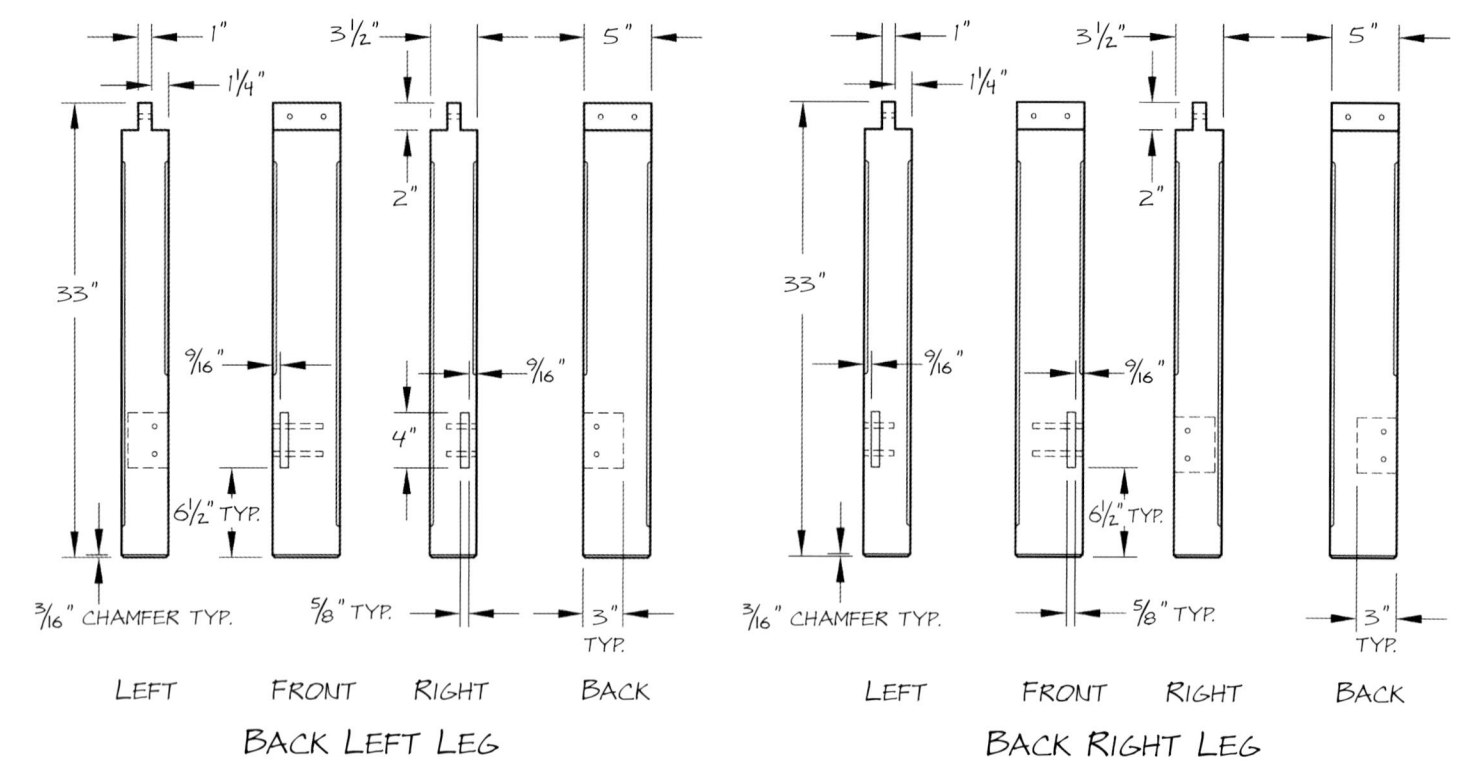

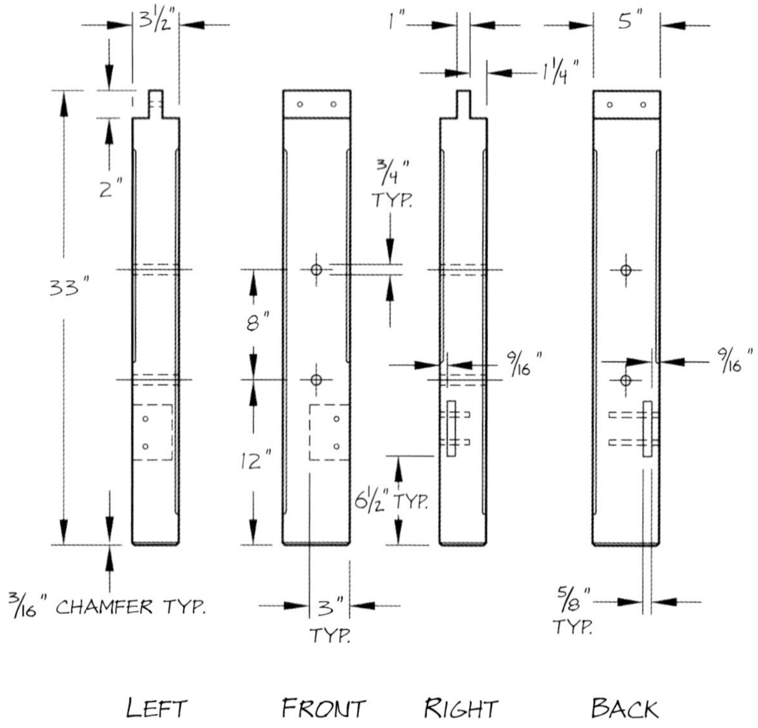

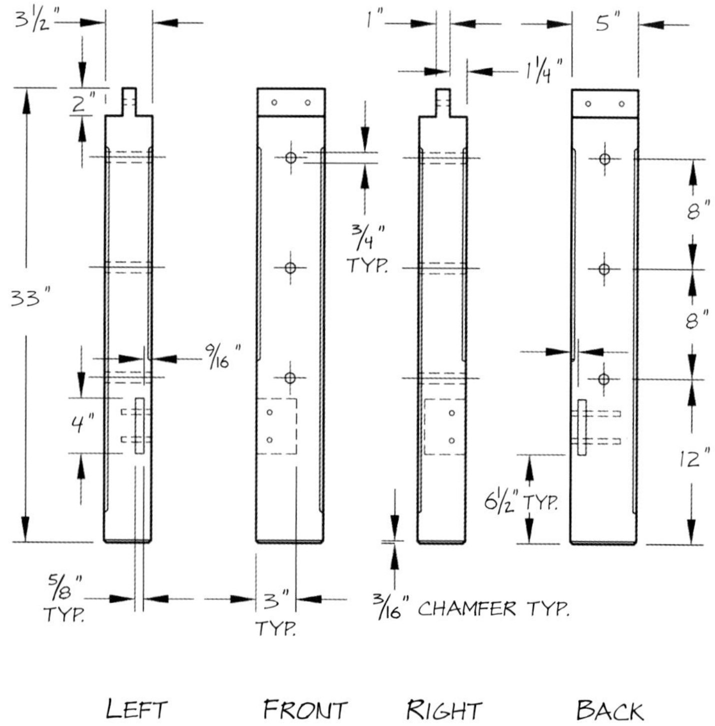

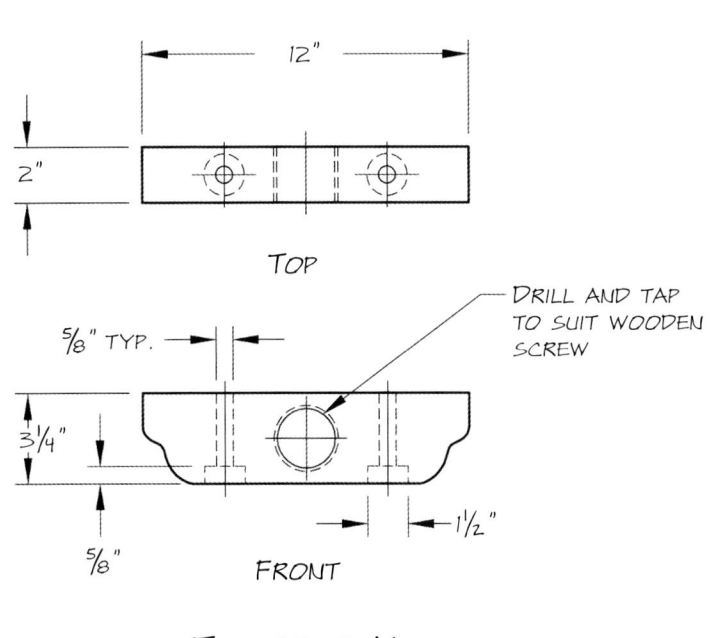

THREADED NUT
(2 REQ'D)

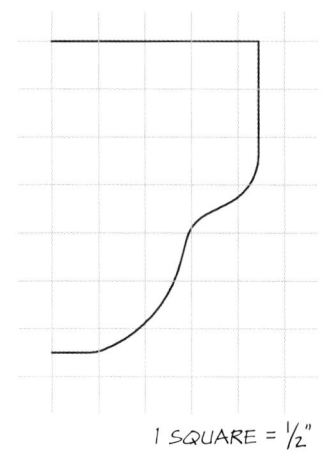

1 SQUARE = 1/2"

THREADED NUT END PROFILE

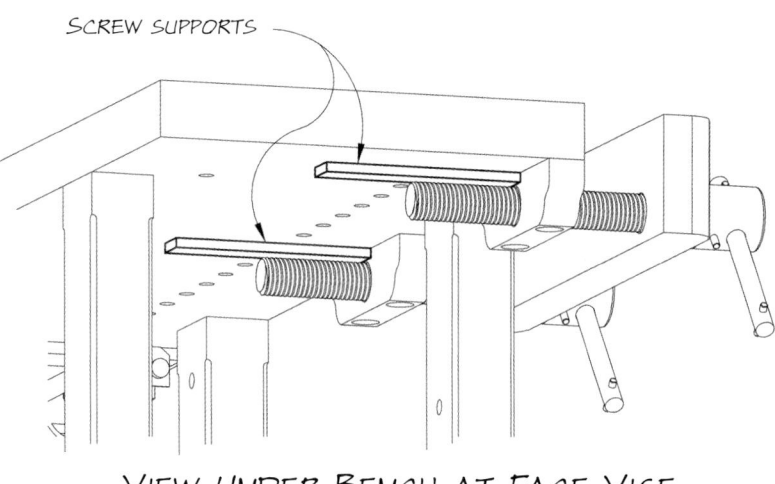

VIEW UNDER BENCH AT FACE VISE

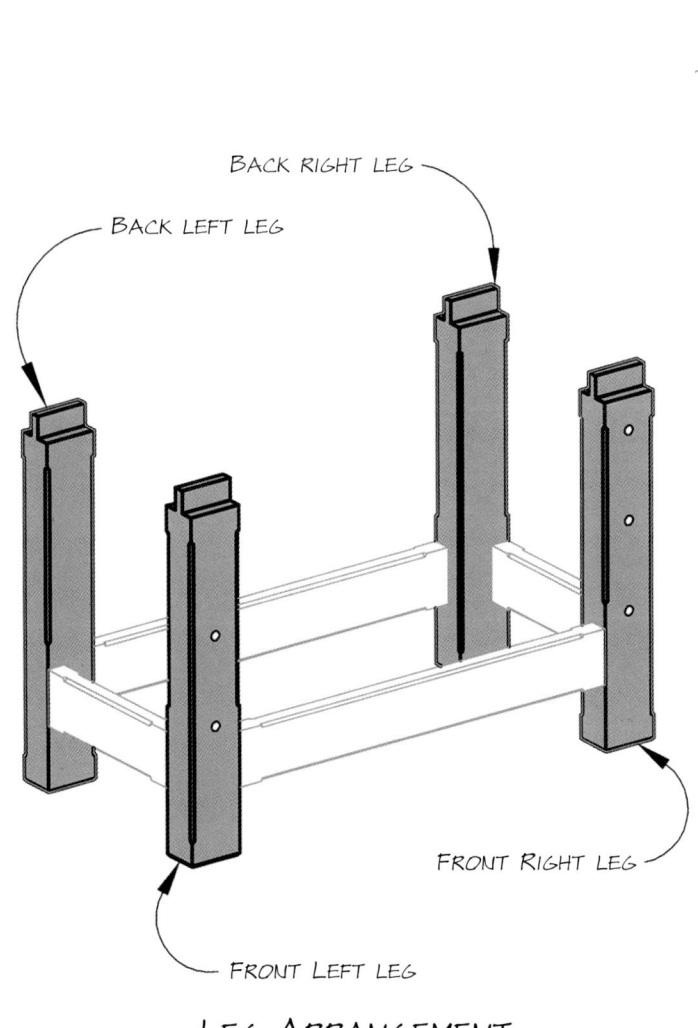

LEG ARRANGEMENT

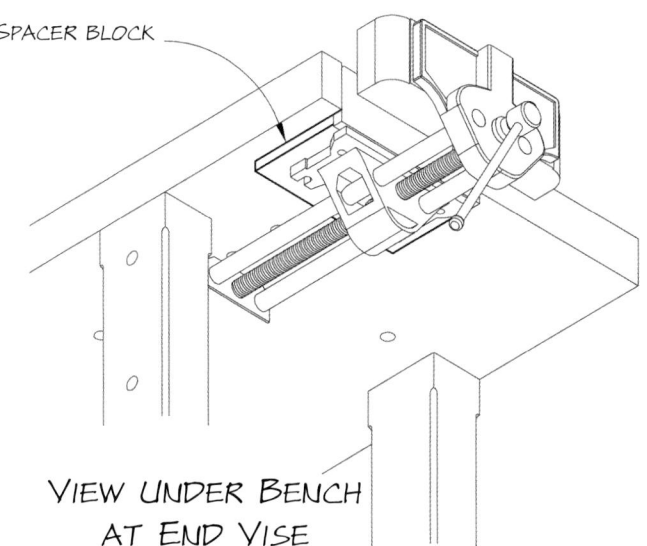

VIEW UNDER BENCH
AT END VISE

Wall-hung Tool Racks

Tool storage out of the box: A flexible system takes root and grows on the walls of our shop.

I used to keep my hand tools in drawers in machinists' and mechanics' tool chests. My tools were organized and protected, but it wasn't very convenient. Edge tools rattled against one another as drawers opened and closed, and my layout tools were never at hand. During projects, tools stayed on the bench where they could be found, but soon were buried as my work, shavings, scraps and more tools piled up.

When I opened my first shop, I decided to make a wall-hung tool chest. Two wide doors opened off a cabinet. I designed the doors around the tools I used regularly, and in between the doors were shelves and a bank of dovetailed drawers. It changed the way I worked. The tools had a place to live and were right at hand. If I started to see too much empty space in the inside of the doors, I knew it was time to take a break and clean up.

While the wall-hung chest functioned well, I never quite completed it. I intended to put in a latch and lock mechanism to keep the doors closed, but after a few months, I realized that I rarely closed the doors. It was like a television cabinet in most homes – the doors are functional but if the TV is always on (or the tools always being used), the doors really aren't needed.

When I came to work at *Woodworking Magazine*, I planned to bring in my tool chest and hang it on the wall. My plan had to be aborted when I recognized that our shop's biggest blessing, an abundance of windows, didn't allow the 6' of wall space I needed. I was back to tools in drawers

Waiting in line, ready to be used. A rack of tools directly above the bench keeps them out of harm's way and makes them easy to locate.

and odd boxes, and I pondered how to add a wall without losing any windows. I wanted the accessibility, safety and organization of the chest, but I was developing an impractical plan.

One day as I walked into the shop, I glanced to the left as I almost always do. Most of the time there will be some interesting project or part of a project or esoteric tool on Editor Christopher Schwarz's bench. What caught my eye that morning was his simple and elegant solution to the same problem I faced. He had installed a simple rack across the window directly above his bench and it held more tools than I would have thought possible.

Recognizable as leftover baseboard, two ¾"-thick boards, about 3½" wide, were held ½" apart by wood spacers in between. The back board was a few inches longer than the one in front, allowing it to be easily mounted to the wall, or in this case the wood casing on our window. By that afternoon, I was loading a similar rack across the window above the bench in my corner of the shop.

I was delighted at how well this simple solution solved a problem. My only reservation about hanging my tools was securing them so they wouldn't fall. When I made my tool chest, I made French-fit holders for individual tools. With the new rack, most would fit neatly within the slot between the two boards. They were handy, in sight and out of danger. A few didn't fit between the slots, so I drove a few screws and nails to hang them on the outer part of the rack.

Organization came in time. Instead of planning where each tool should go ahead of time, I started using the slotted rack as I worked, putting tools in a slot as I completed typical tasks. Before long, an organizational scheme emerged that works better than I would have planned. I also found that the slots were good for many tools, but not everything fit quite the way I wanted.

Above the bench at the other end of the shop, Shaker pegs began to appear on the outside of my shop mate's rack. First, a few near one end, then an entire row with hammers hanging from them. A day or two later, another row of pegs appeared above the first rack, holding more than a dozen saws. Not being a collector, I didn't need that

The simple start is two pieces of wood, ¾" thick x 3½" wide, of a convenient length. The back piece is longer than the front by a few inches to allow fastening to the wall. The rack is wide enough to hold tools securely, and provides a place for Shaker pegs for hanging tools.

The two pieces are separated by ½"-thick spacers, and tools drop into the space. This was a "sweet spot" for our tools and can be varied to accommodate your tools.

Screws and nails aren't as attractive as Shaker pegs, but function well – especially in tight spaces and for tool-specific hanging.

The flexibility of using the slots gives you freedom to change the overall arrangement as your tools, needs, habits or projects change over time.

woodworking-magazine.com ■ 25

much space – I only have four saws and five hammers, but my tool rack did need some improvements and additions.

My first addition was a simple shelf, about 4" wide that rests on band-sawn brackets. This provided a place for planes and a few other tools that I didn't want to hang, but needed at hand. The remaining problem to solve was the chisel chaos. They fit between the boards of the rack, but because they're top heavy with wide handles, they wouldn't hang straight. It bothered me to see them leaning against each other like a gang of out-of-work loafers. I wanted them standing straight – at attention and ready for action.

My solution was another shelf, held in notched brackets with a series of holes that fit the chisel handles. I experimented with some different-sized holes and various chisels and found that a ⅞" diameter worked for almost all of them. I also wanted a slot at the front of the hole so I wouldn't need to lift a chisel its entire length to get it in or out of the rack. A little more experimentation and a couple test-fittings later, and I had my final dimensions; the holes were drilled with the edge of the hole ⅛" back from the front edge of the 2"-wide board. A center-to-center distance of 1⅛" provided room to reach each handle individually.

After marking off the series of equally spaced centerlines, I stepped off one-fourth the diameter from each side of the centerlines and sawed slots from the front edge of the shelf to each hole, leaving a ⁷⁄₁₆"-wide slot connecting each hole to the edge. I used a rasp to chamfer the edges of the holes and slots, connected the shelf to the brackets, and mounted them in place. Wider chisels need a bit of a turn as they go in and out of the rack. Narrow ones slide right in. They all are held securely.

More concerned about function than decoration, I made my racks out of scrap hardwoods and didn't use a finish. A light sanding and a coat of shellac, lacquer, oil or wax would make them look nicer, but I rarely bother with doing that on something for the shop.

I considered doing some decorative carving on the brackets, but that reminded me that my carving chisels still live in canvas rolls in drawers in a nearby cabinet. I'm not a collector, but I will need a rack for 40 or 50 of them, and while I'm at it, I may as well start gathering the 30 or 40 more carving chisels that I really need. Maybe I can clear some space on the building column to the left of my bench for a row of them.

The great thing about these racks is that they are adaptable and made easily and quickly. As happened to me, once you start, you'll need another two or three as the list of necessary tools grows, and the way you work and the things you work on change. If you cross the line to "collector," you might need many more than that. **WM**

— *Robert W. Lang*

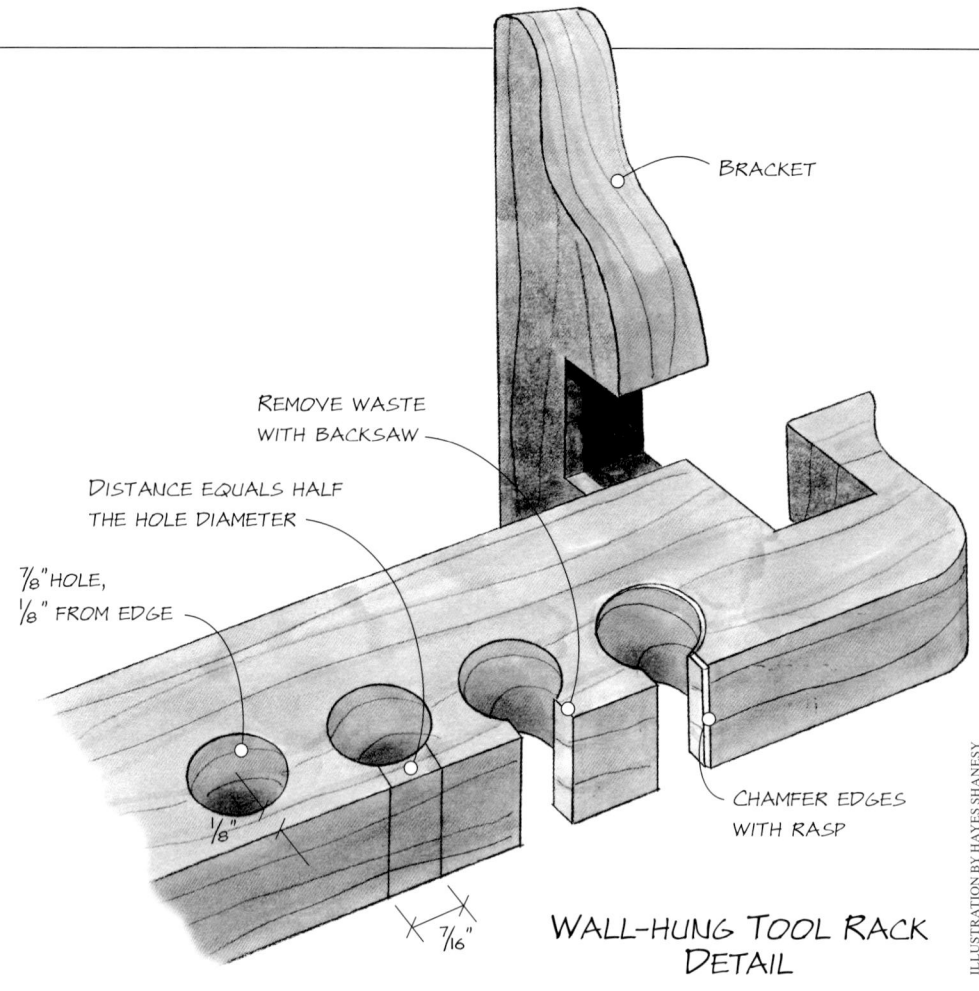

WALL-HUNG TOOL RACK DETAIL

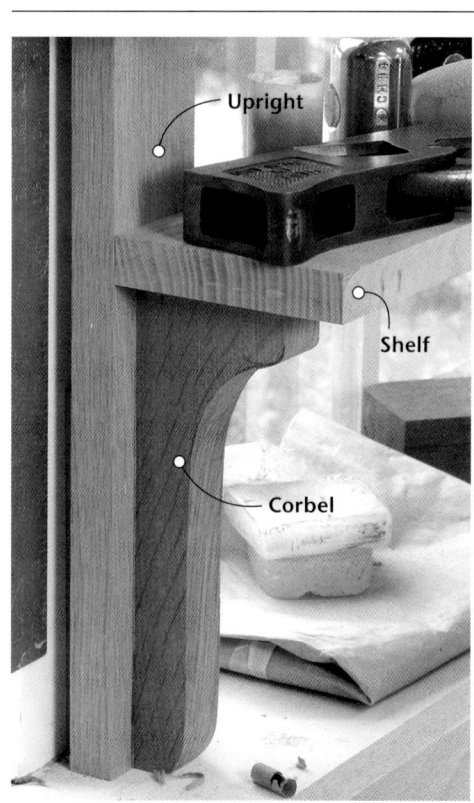

This rack has uprights at both ends and in the middle. These provide a place for brackets and corbels that can support shelves.

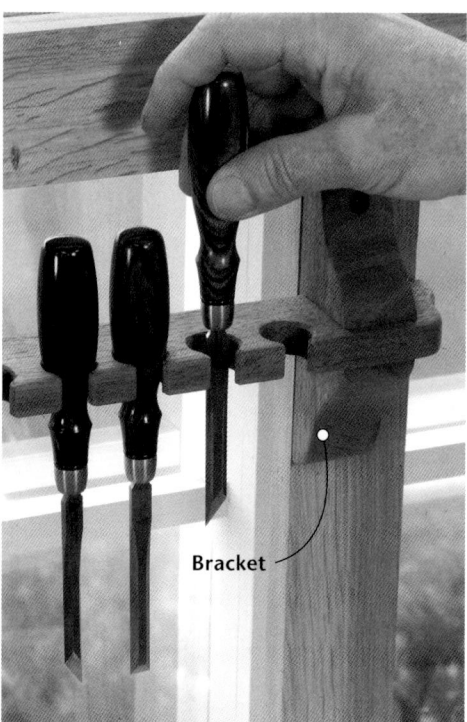

A ⅞"-diameter hole, ⅛" in from the edge of a 2"-wide shelf holds a variety of handle sizes. The sawn slot connecting the hole and edge allows you to hold a chisel with a blade that is wider than the handle diameter.

Glossary

"Rule of thumb: Always finish the job with the same number of fingers you started with."
— anonymous

Woodworking's lexicon can be overwhelming at times. The terms below are from this issue. Check out woodworking-magazine.com for an expanded and searchable glossary.

4/4 stock (n)
Wood sold in the rough is referred to in terms of thickness, in quarter-inch increments. Thus 4/4 rough stock is 1" thick, 5/4 is 1¼" thick, 6/4 is 1½" thick and so on. Surfaced wood is not referred to in these terms.

S2S and S4S lumber (n)
The first "S" stands for "surfaced," the second "S" for "sides." So S2S is surfaced on two sides; S4S is surfaced on all four sides.

brace and bit (n)
A brace is a boring tool that holds bits. Pressure is applied to the head on top, and the tool is rotated with a U-shaped grip, which is part of a type of crankshaft. Many braces have a three-position ratchet on the chuck.

cabinetmaker's triangle (n)
A triangle drawn atop the pieces of a project that designates the front, back and sides of any assembly.

chop (n)
On a vise, the chop is a block of wood that acts as a jaw.

crochet (n)
The French word for "hook," this is essentially a planing stop for working on edges.

cutting lips (n)
The sharp beveled horizontal edges at the end of an auger or bit that levers waste out of the hole.

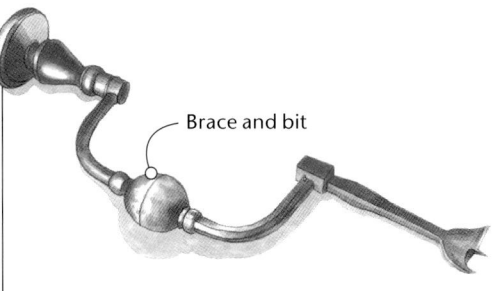
Brace and bit

dado stack (n)
A nested set of table saw blades and chippers that cut a variable-width dado; the dado width depends on the number of chippers stacked together on the arbor for the cut.

dial indicator (n)
A precision measuring tool. A dial indicator has a plunger that moves in and out from the body of the indicator, which in turn moves the measuring needle on the dial face. Typical dial indicators usually have a 1" or 2" range, and are calibrated in increments of .001".

drawbore (n)
An early woodworking technique for reinforcing mortise-and-tenon joints with a wooden peg. Before assembly, a hole is bored through the mortise. Then an offset hole is drilled in the tenon. A wooden peg is driven into the holes, pulling the joint tight.

Planing stop
Crochet

French fitting (n)
The use of the outline of a tool (or other item) to make a pattern. The pattern is then used to create a perfect tool-shaped nest for the tool to fit into. Very fussy, but offers excellent protection.

planing stop (n)
A piece of wood or metal (we recommend wood) that can be moved up and down in your benchtop, for workpieces to push against as they are planed.

sliding deadman (n)
Sometimes called a board jack, this panel slides horizontally across the front of a workbench and is pierced with holes to offer support of long boards or assemblies.

spurs (n)
The sharp beveled vertical edges at the end of an auger or bit that score the diameter of the bore.

tail vise (n)
A vise fixed at the end of a bench, usually bored with multiple dog holes. These holes work with dog holes in the workbench top so that it can adjust to grip workpieces of varying sizes.

twin-screw vise (n)
A vise with a long chop (usually 16" at least) that is secured to the bench with two adjustable screws, allowing a wide unobstructed area between the screws for clamping.

wash coat (n)
A thin sealing of protective film of any finishing product.

winding sticks (n)
Two perfectly true lengths of wood or metal used to divine whether a surface is flat. The sticks are placed at opposing ends of the surface and sighted across. Surface irregularities prevent the sticks from lining up in your field of vision. **WM**

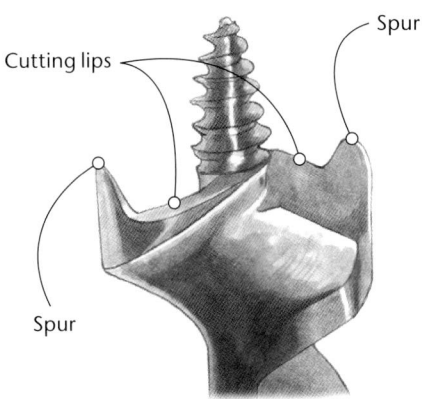
Cutting lips
Spur
Spur

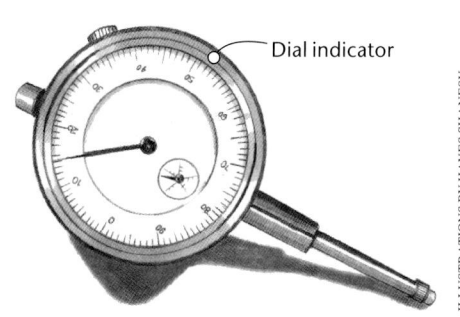
Dial indicator

ILLUSTRATIONS BY HAYES SHANESY

Choosing a Flush-cut Saw

Wide or narrow? Thick or thin? Aggressive or fine? All these qualities influenced our choice for top saw.

Until now, my flush-cut saw has had an air hose attached to the back of it with a 5" abrasive disc as the teeth. I'd cut pegs with my dovetail saw – one that had just passed its usefulness for cutting dovetails – then grind the surface with my Dynabrade random-orbit sander. In other words, I sanded any pegs flush to the surface before finishing. While I now know that a flush-cut saw is capable of trimming more than just pegs, there was once a time when that's all I thought a flush cut saw was for.

A long time back, I owned this type of saw, used it once or maybe twice and pitched it in the garbage can. That's because my cut was anything but flush. In fact, it was so not flush, that there was a distinct gash that required I sand even more than normal. Instead of smoothing the peg to the surface, I had to level the surface to the peg. After a couple harrowing experiences like this, you can see why the saw ended up in the dust bin.

Now I've been enlightened to the idea of using the saw to trim wedged tenons – my power sander used to have that covered too, when the need arose. And, I've heard mention that you can trim the height of inlaid dovetail keys.

As you may have guessed, I had a great deal to learn about the flush-cut saw. I needed to first learn how they work and how the brands differ, then I needed to learn how to use them correctly. (See the related article on flush-cut saw techniques on page 32.)

So I ordered a number of saws from different suppliers and delved into them to see what differentiates an ordinary flush-cut saw from a great one. The saws I received were priced from a high of $94 to a low of $15. Admit it; right now you suspect that the expensive saw is the best and contrarily, the least expensive is not. I began with the same convictions. The question is: Did I end up feeling that same way?

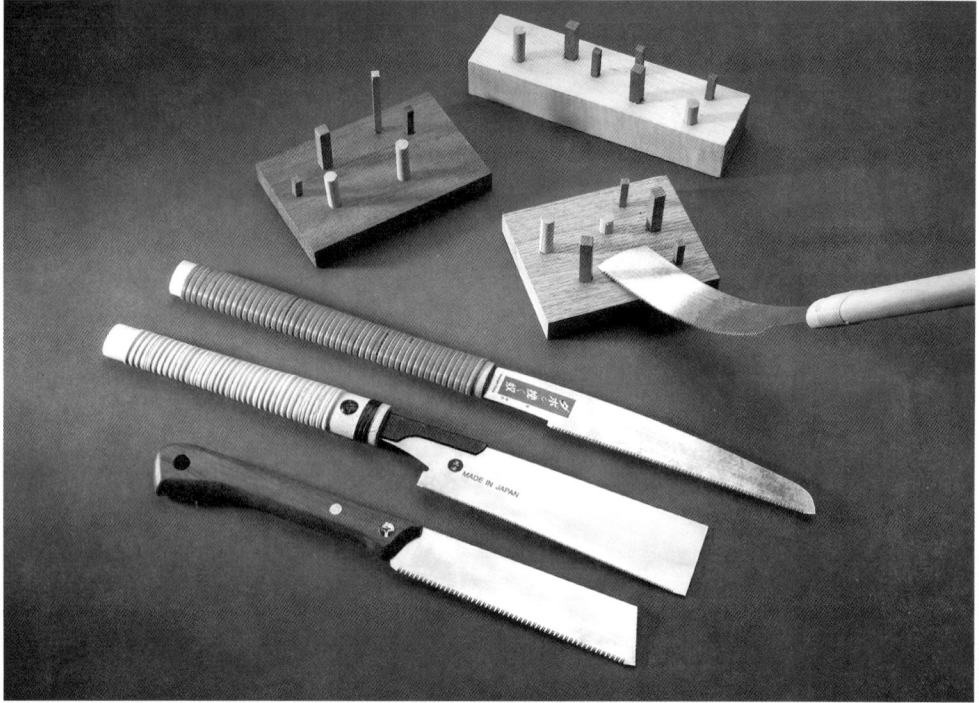

Flush-cut saws are available in many shapes, sizes and designs. The blades of these saws are flexible. While the sawing technique shown above isn't standard, it comes in handy in tight situations.

And in This Corner ...

I began with a few ideas as to what to test in these saws, and after I got some saws in-house, I developed a few more things at which to look. I studied the teeth per inch (TPI), the length of the blade and the thickness of the blade. In addition, I checked the width of the blade. Surprisingly, this characteristic came to be of some importance. Finally, I looked at the aesthetics and ergonomics of the handle as well as the actual cut.

I tested saws from most major suppliers. Included were two saws from Lee Valley (the kugihiki and the Japanese flush-cut saws), two saws from japanesetools.com (the Kaneharu and the Maruyoshi; call Harrelson Stanley at 877-692-3624 for specific order information) and the Bridge City Tool Works JS-4. In addition, I examined the flush-cut saw from Robert Larson (available at Amazon.com) and the Nakaya kugihiki from thebestthings.com.

I also brought in three other saws that simply aren't worth discussing. Two, the Lynx and Pax, had round wooden handles with very narrow blades. Neither made the final testing because my cuts with these two resulted in a divot on the surface – as with the one I tossed in the trash years ago. Also, flush-cut saw teeth should be able to cut with either side of the blade flat on the work surface. This is where the Veritas flush-cut saw dropped the ball. These three aren't the saws to be buying in my opinion.

Saws That Bite

Studying the teeth on a typical handsaw leads you to look at the TPI as well as the set of the teeth (the amount the teeth are bent out). But, flush-cut saws are inherently different from most handsaws. There's no reason to check the set of the teeth; there should be no set because these saws are designed to lie flat on the surface and cut without marring that surface.

That left only the TPI for my study. The TPI on these saws ranged from a low of 17 to a high of 32. Which is better? This is an area of debate. Harrelson Stanley, of japanesetools.com, says the more teeth per inch, the finer the cut, so you'll notice a smoother cut through hardwood. The results should be a finer cut than something designed to whack off a heavier amount, but the cut takes longer to complete. Stanley is a hand-tool enthusiast. He's looking to get the finest cut so the next step is just a quick stroke with his plane (if necessary at all). If you work exclusively with hand tools, then you might want to test drive one of the saws with a higher TPI.

However, I like the quicker cut. I'm looking to remove the peg end and get into the finishing of the project. I'm a power-tool guy and my projects are going to involve sanding. That's what I do.

I also believe that the longer you have the saw against the surface while making those multiple strokes, the better chance you have to twist your wrist and introduce the teeth to the surface. That potential nick means additional sanding (or planing). That's d thing.

A quick glance at the chart on page 31 shows the TPI for all saws. The kugihiki from Lee Valley is my choice. With 17 TPI, I found the cut to be quick – decreasing the length of time the saw was on my project – and nearly as smooth as the finer TPI saws.

All About the Blade

As I set up the testing for these flush-cut saws, I figured that the length of the blade would come into question. I likened this to the length of the handle of a hammer. When most of us start working with a hammer, we grab the handle just below the head and gingerly tap the nail into the wood. As we gain experience, we move our hands down the handle and start to swing the head properly as we make contact with the nail.

I've seen woodworkers act in this manner with regular saws as well – short, choppy strokes until they feel comfortable, then long, strong strokes as their confidence builds. They cut using the entire length of the blade. But flush-cut saws are different for me and most others I've seen use them. Because of the very nature of what we're cutting, the stroke is short. We are generally cutting a small area on a small width, and that requires

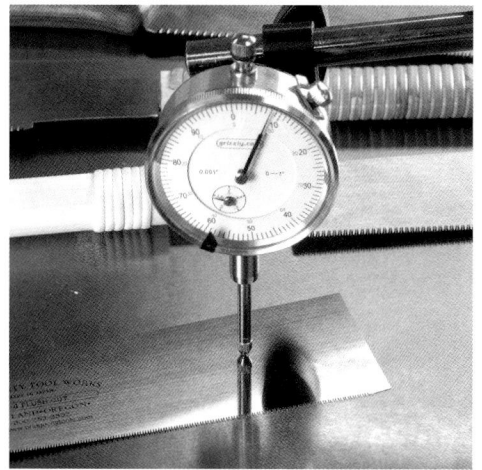

The thickness of the flush-cut saw's blade is a factor in its use. The thinner the blade the more likely you are to "flex" the blade while cutting.

This is a blade "flexing." Because these saws cut on the pull stroke the flexing occurs during the forward thrusting. Flexing can cause the teeth to slash into the surface.

short, deliberate strokes. As a result, blade length isn't much of an issue and the lengths of the tested saws are not much different – ranging from the shortest at 5¾" to the longest at 7⅛".

What turned out to be most interesting, and the consideration I felt really made a difference in the usability of the saws, was the thickness of the blades. I immediately noticed that some blades exhibit an almost whip-like feature whereas others seem very stiff. How to get accurate measurements of thickness was my charge.

My fractional calipers were of no use. The variations in thickness were much finer than they could measure. So I grabbed the dial indicator that we use to set the blades for our machinery.

I tested using a table saw top (a known flat surface) as the platform. I set up the indicator with the magnetic base locked in and set the needle to zero. Next, I lifted the plunger and slid the saws in for a reading. The range was from .008" (very flimsy) to .021" (somewhat stout, comparatively).

What does this indicate as to the workability of the flush-cut saws? Let's start with the technique of using this type of saw. If you look at most catalogs, or even the picture at the beginning of this article, you'll see the saws flex to the point of risking permanent bend. I guess it's acceptable when you're in extremely tight quarters to work this way. But how often does that happen? The method that most use in cutting with these tools is to lay the blade flat on the work and place fingers on the blade to keep it flat (see "Flush-cut Techniques" on page 32 for more instruction).

So here's my take. As I used these saws I noticed that my fingers hold the saw flat and as I saw back and forth to make the cut, my drive hand (the one on the handle) tends to wander either upward or downward. As this happens, I begin to put force on the blade that causes the

Having no set in the teeth allows the blade to lay flat during use and cut without marring the surface of your project.

The number of teeth per inch (TPI) influences the saw's cut and varies from saw to saw. One way to find that number with really fine saws is to tap the blade into wood and count the holes in any given inch.

woodworking-magazine.com ■ 29

"Truth is immortal; error is mortal."
— Mary Baker Eddy (1821 - 1910)
author, founder of Christian Science Movement

thinner blades to bend slightly on the push stroke. On the pull stroke, the saws remained flat. This caused me to raise my fingers and lose that flat contact between the blade and the surface. Marring is more apt to occur during this sequence of events. The thicker blades didn't show signs of this happening.

Obviously, there's a direct correlation between bending and the thickness of the blade stock. I'll take a thicker blade – remember we're talking a difference of .013" – for my flush-cut saw. I found it easier to keep the thicker blade flat.

Wider is Better

You've heard it before I'll bet. I think it was a car commercial. Wider is better. While I'm not so sure about a wider body on a car, I do think this is fact when working with flush-cut saws. The wider the blade, the better able you are to keep the blade flat. Narrow blades allow you to twist the blade across the cut.

Two major things can happen when the blade doesn't stay flat to the surface. First, the cut wanders down into the surface. You know that causes problems from above. Do you want to level the surface to the peg? No. The second result of blades not staying flat is the cut of the dowel or peg is proud. Is that what we are aiming for with this entire exercise? No again.

Interestingly, the two widest blades in the test, the Bridge City Tool Works JS-4 and the Nakaya kugihiki from thebestthings.com, were also the thinnest blades in the test. I think that one characteristic offsets the other.

Also, none of the saws are impulse hardened to keep the teeth sharp. And, there's a golden sheen on two of the saw blades. This is a simply a result of factory processing and adds no benefit.

Test Drive for Looks, Comfort and Cut

There can be no doubt that the Bridge City saw is the most handsome. It will take any award for looks, hands down. The handle is wrapped in a burgundy thread-like material that is secured with showy brass bands. That material is actually line used for shark fishing.

The next tier for looks includes the Maruyoshi from japanesetools.com and the Nakaya kugihiki from thebestthings.com with the handles wrapped with raffia. Following closely is the bubinga handle on the kugihiki saw from Lee Valley. The balance of the saws have fairly nondescript handles.

If a tool is uncomfortable to hold, I doubt you'll reach for it when you need that job done – unless it's the only tool that can do that job. Given all the saws and the many different handles, I had to find one that was comfortable to use – even though I don't plan to use a flush-cut saw as often as I do my dovetail saw.

Of all the saws, only two did not have a typical Japanese-handle design. The Lee Valley kugihiki saw and the Robert Larson saw both have an oval handle with a flared end. I found these handles very comfortable and they felt secure in my hand during use.

The All-important Cut

No matter how the saws stack up in the looks department, the telltale of purchase-worthiness is the cut. It might be a great-looking saw, but if the cut is not right, you don't need it in your toolbox or hanging on your wall.

In order to make cuts that I could look at closely, I planed a walnut board by hand, installed $5/16$" dowels and made a cut with each saw. I was looking for two things. The first was if the teeth left any indication that they were there (that gnarly gash). The second was the resulting cut. Was the dowel flush with the surface? Did the saw tend to float up or move down as it cut? This would tell the story.

The Lee Valley kugihiki is the winner. This saw brings everything from an aggressive cut to a shapely and comfortable handle to the table. Not the most expensive – just the best saw for your money.

None of the saw cuts slashed into the walnut, however a few did leave ever-so-slight lines: the Nakaya kugihiki, the Kaneharu and the Maruyoshi. Not a problem really, just a calling card. With the other four saws I saw no lines in the grain.

The peg cuts of the Kaneharu, Maruyoshi and the Lee Valley kugihiki saws left a smooth top on the dowel and the finish was flush with the walnut. The Nakaya kugihiki, the Robert Larson and the Bridge City JS-4 saws rolled uphill as the cut progressed, leaving a slight elevation at the back edge of the cut. The Lee Valley Japanese saw was humped in the center of the dowel.

Where I'll Place My Money

These are not saws that you quickly wear out, but what if you break a tooth on these saws? Are they trash? There are four saws for which a replacement blade is available: the Nakaya kugihiki, the Maruyoshi, the Lee Valley kugihiki and the Bridge City JS-4. If they are used appropriately, I wouldn't expect that you'd go through three saws of this type during your woodworking days.

So, how do they stack up? Make a list of the important features of a flush-cut saw and you'll find what I think is the best saw for your hard-earned money. Choose thicker blade stock with a more aggressive cut, a wide enough blade to allow two-finger hold down and to help eliminate any potential for twisting, and a nice-looking tool that fits and is comfortable in the hand. Finally, it must have the right cut. That's a cut that is flush with the surface without leaving scratches, stays flat across the entire peg width and leaves the finished surface of the cut smooth.

At the beginning of this story, I mentioned the costs of the saws and wondered if I would choose the most expensive one. I didn't. For my money, I'll select the Lee Valley kugihiki with the bubinga handle. It fits all the requirements for a great flush-cut saw at the reasonable price of $22. This flush-cut saw fits nicely into any tool arsenal. **WM**

— *Glen D. Huey*

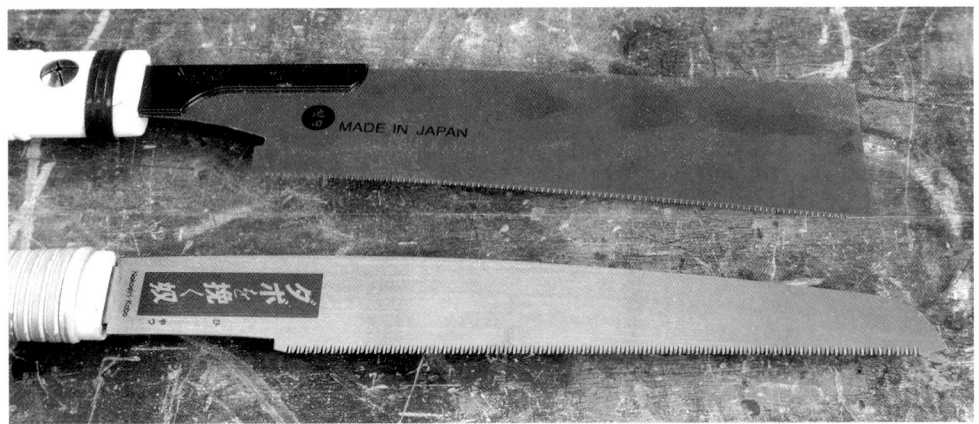

Wide blades give more support while cutting, reducing the chances of twisting your wrist and driving the saw teeth into the surface.

Flush-cut Saws

BRAND	PRICE	TPI	BLADE THICKNESS	BLADE LENGTH	OVERALL LENGTH	AVAILABLE FROM

Highly Recommended

Lee Valley kugihiki (60T06.20)*	$22	17	.021"	6¼"	13½"	leevalley.com or 800-871-8158

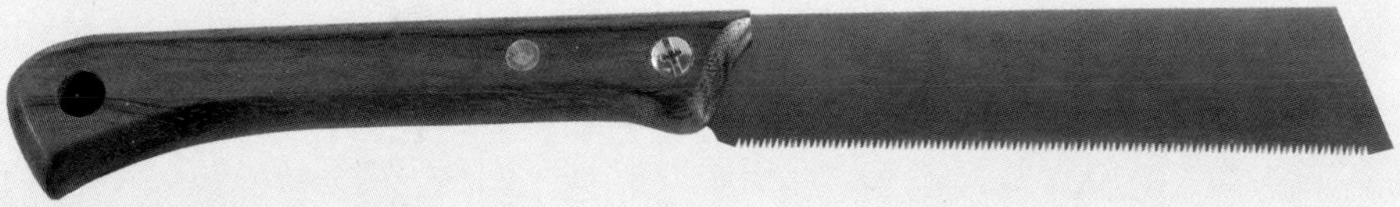

The comfort of the handle, the thickness of the blade as well as the aggressive TPI make this the pick saw. The cut was nearly as smooth as higher TPI saws.

Recommended

Bridge City JS-4 (#1101-170)*	$59	32	.008"	6⅝"	16¼"	bridgecitytools.com or 800-253-3332

By far the most elegant saw in the group. This saw has a thin and wide blade. Cutting is very fine given the TPI. Overall a good choice.

Kaneharu	$94	26	.012"	7⅛"	17⅛"	japanesetools.com or 877-692-3624

A very nice saw. The blade thickness lessened the chance of flexing while the cut of the peg was dead flat. Light scratch lines appeared on the surface after the cut.

Lee Valley Japanese (60T1901)	$27	22	.011"	6¼"	16¼"	leevalley.com or 800-871-8158

The thin and narrow blade makes this saw susceptible to reacting to wrist movements. Those movements have a negative effect on the cut.

Maruyoshi*	$56	23	.014"	7"	18¼"	japanesetools.com or 877-692-3624

With the excellent fit and finish, this saw's only downfall is the narrow blade. The cut is smooth but fine scratches showed up on the surface.

Nakaya kugihiki (K-180G)*	$35	32	.008"	7"	16½"	thebestthings.com or 800-884-1373

The flimsiness of the blade is offset by its wide profile, which gives it more area to hold flat to the surface. More strokes are needed due to the high TPI.

Robert Larson	$15	19	.021"	5¾"	12"	amazon.com

The least expensive saw in the group. The stout blade makes using this saw easy and the fit of the handle makes it comfortable. Worthy of being in the test.

* replaceable blades

Discover Flush-cut Saw Techniques

Trim the fat from flush-cut saw techniques. With proper practice your finished cuts will be extra-smooth.

When I began building furniture I bought a flush-cut saw. Knowing that I was going to build Shaker-style furniture and that square pegs were used in nearly every project, I was certain the saw would be one of the most-used hand tools in my shop. With saw in hand, and willing to spend some time testing the cut, I loaded a few pegs into a chunk of wood and started at it.

Having no formal woodworking education – I'd last received lessons in junior high shop class – I made the flush cuts. I wasn't sure how to correctly handle the saw or even if I had my hands in the right position. Was there a proper method to using these saws? Pictures of the saws in woodworking catalogs show the blade of the saw bent just short of a 90° angle. I always wondered if this was the correct sawing position.

I positioned the saw flat to the surface while I sawed back and forth, allowing the saw blade to slide over the surface of the wood. Some cuts were acceptable, some weren't. Eventually I found more cuts weren't acceptable. The blade dug into the wood and my overall sanding time escalated as I found myself leveling the surface to remove the gash left in the wood. The saw was causing too much repair work. And so I pitched it into the garbage. Was I doing something wrong? Was my technique bad?

I then adopted a new technique of cutting close to the face of my project with a regular backsaw, then sanding the pegs flush with a random-orbit sander. Sometimes I'd place a piece of laminate or a business card over the peg and trim as close as possible then sand everything flush. I worked this way for years.

Recently I brought a number of flush-cut saws into the *Woodworking Magazine* shop to test and to select the best saw (See "Choosing a Flush-cut Saw," page 28). At the same time I thought I would get some first-hand experience using this type of saw. I'd refine my technique. So, I loaded some pegs into a block of wood in order to perform a couple dozen cuts and complete the tests.

Seeing the momentous number of advertisements and pictures of these saws being used with that huge bend, I again wondered if I was approaching this cut in the correct manner. Not wanting to miss an opportunity to learn, I bent the saw to that extreme angle and began to cut. It wasn't a good thing. At that angle, the saw cut worse than if I'd just taken a small hatchet and chopped at the peg. I couldn't keep the saw flat on the surface and the cut was ragged at best.

Practicing a few times with the same results, I began to think that I just wasn't going to be capable of using this technique to cut flush. So, I enlisted the help of editors Christopher Schwarz and Robert W. Lang to help uncover my problem. Was it me or were all those photos and advertisements wrong?

"Trust your gut instinct." "Your first thought is probably correct." Do these sayings sound familiar? They do to me. I contemplated these truisms as I watched Chris and Bob step to the bench one at a time. I didn't let them know what I was looking to find, only that I needed them to cut the peg with a flush-cut saw.

Much to my relief, they both approached the peg with the saw flat on the work and didn't bend the blade as they worked. I now knew I had the basic technique correct. What I needed was to refine the procedure and make the saws work for me instead of against me by leaving that huge gash in the wood.

"Is it the saw or operator error?" That question arises in discussions about problems using flush-cut saws. Learning proper technique puts half that question to bed.

The Technique, Step by Step

I needed to start at the beginning, so I mulled over the process of using the flush-cut saw. First things first: Position the blade flat on the surface of the project. There shouldn't be any set in the teeth of a flush-cut saw so placing the saw to either side of the peg is acceptable. I'm right-handed, thus you might think it's correct to begin with the blade on the right-hand side of the peg. However, if you're right-handed it's best if you begin with the saw on the left side of the peg. This requires that you rotate your wrist 180° or change your grip on the handle.

As we determine the correct placement of the left hand, you'll see why this saw positioning is so important. Two fingers of the left hand should hold the blade flat to the surface. This keeps the blade flat, minimizing the chance of it lifting from the surface, which would result in a proud peg. And, it prevents the teeth from diving into your nearly finished surface and causing those nasty gash lines, which would be worse.

Your fingers act as a hold-down for the saw as you stroke the saw back and forth, allowing the blade to slide between your fingers and the surface. Make sure that you hold your wrist so the blade remains flat. If you twist forward you place additional stress at the front of the blade increasing the chances of digging into the surface. If you twist back you'll place that stress at the rear of the blade and your cut won't be flat and smooth across the peg. Using a saw with a wide blade provides you a better chance to remain flat to the surface. A wide blade helps obtain a better cut.

And here is the importance of setting your hands properly: As you finish the cut through the peg the saw blade isn't traveling toward your hand. If you've cut with your hands positioned differently – moving the blade toward your stationary hand – when you finished the cut I'll bet you jabbed the blade into your hand. I've seen this happen on more than one occasion in the classes I've taught. I'll let you in on a secret: I've done this a time or two to myself (third time's the charm.) If you haven't made this mistake, consider yourself lucky, as well as warned.

Location Dictates the Direction

What happens when you need to make a cut with the blade positioned on the right-hand side of the peg because there isn't enough room on the left side of the peg for you to place the blade flat on the project?

If you're a left-handed woodworker the procedure is as described, only mirrored. If you're a right-handed woodworker, the process requires a repositioning of the stationary (or left) hand.

Now, in order to keep your stationary hand out of the line of fire as you complete the cut, it's necessary to reach across the peg to place your fingers on the blade. (See the top-left photo on page 34.) This position may feel awkward but rest assured, you will not cut your hand as the saw slices through the peg.

Making the Flush Cut

With hand positioning covered, how do you cut? I've seen people try to make this cut using surprising techniques. One such technique was to slice through the cut by starting at the back end of the blade and zipping completely past the front end of the blade – all in one swift motion. This action was repeated numerous times until the cut was complete – each time introducing the blade to the peg and the surface of the project.

Basic handsawing techniques suggest that you start the cut with a few short strokes in the

Bad technique or a bad saw? Either way this is not good. The only recourse from here is to level the surface to the gash left by the saw.

This cut started on the right. Rolling the wrist caused the blade to ride upward as the cut progressed, which resulted in a higher left side. Additional work is needed to flush the peg. Holding the wrist level results in a smooth cut.

This is ideal hand placement. My fingers keep the blade flat on the surface and once the cut is finished the hand is clear of danger.

This cut is wrong in so many ways. The blade is not held flat, it's not supported through the cut and the blade has direct access to the stationary hand. This is an accident waiting to happen.

woodworking-magazine.com ■ 33

When having to cut toward your stationary hand make sure to raise the wrist and other appendages out of harm's way. Maintain two fingers on the blade for support and guidance.

The number of teeth per inch (TPI) influences the time required to make the cut. More teeth keeps the saw at its job longer and that increases the chances for mistakes.

direction that is opposite of the tool's cutting motion. On Western saws this would indicate a cut on the pull stroke. On the Japanese design, which includes most flush-cut saws, the cut would begin with a push stroke. Once the cut is begun and the saw is nestled into the kerf and running smooth you should use full and complete strokes of the blade.

Using the entire blade does two things. First, it allows for better waste removal. When the gullets between the teeth fill up with dust, the saw stops cutting. Using full strokes helps empty the gullets. Second, using full strokes allows all the teeth to cut, which keeps the blade sharper longer. If you only use a small sampling of the teeth, those teeth wear faster.

One area of particular interest when using handsaws, especially thin-bladed saws such as the flush-cut saw, is the amount of pressure you exert as you saw. In working with any saw, the more force you use, the more apt you are to veer from the line. This happens (in part) because the blade bends or warps under the force.

Continuous sawing as the blade bends causes the kerf to drift. This is not acceptable when using the flush-cut saw. If your blade moves off the flat surface you'll end up with a cut into the project or a cut that is nowhere near flush. In extreme instances it's possible to actually kink the blade of flush-cut saws.

Allow the blade to cut with minimal pressure. If the length of time it takes to make the cut seems long, it's probably because the saw isn't sharpened correctly or the teeth per inch (TPI) count is high. The higher the TPI, the finer the cut – and the slower the cut is made. Lower TPI saws are more aggressive.

About the Cut
Should you perform the cut from only one direction, or do you start the cut on one side of a peg and then move to the second or opposing side to complete the operation?

The simplest method is to start the cut and saw through the entire peg. That's fine if all you're looking to do is hack away waste material. Much of the time this is exactly what you're after. But, problems surface if you catch the second-to-last stroke wrong. As you return to make the last stroke, it's possible to break the remaining material before it's cut by the teeth. Because the break is at the outer edge of the peg, it's conceivable that the fibers of the wood will tear down the peg side versus simply breaking off. That can leave a jagged finish to the peg that will require additional work or a nasty visible area that has to be addressed. This is same reason why tree loggers make a relief cut on the back side of the trunk as they fell trees.

Creating a cut on one side prior to completing the cut from the opposing side reduces this possibility. If something does happen, say the peg breaks as the two cut areas intersect, the peg will not rip down the outer edge, but break somewhere in the interior of the peg. If material is left protruding from the surface, it's much easier to pare the center of the peg with a chisel without damaging the project surrounding the peg.

A Final Note
In most woodworking if you're trimming pegs, chances are you've installed them using some type of glue. Glue is the enemy of flush-cut saws (and saws in general). The teeth are small and the glue easily becomes lodged in them. Within a short time the saw becomes useless or untrustworthy as it cuts. Either scenario is something to avoid. Make sure to clean any glue remnants as soon as they're discovered.

Develop correct cutting methods and a flush-cut saw will reap huge rewards in your woodworking. These saws are delicate with fine teeth, but will last a lifetime if cared for properly. WM

— *Glen D. Huey*

Starting the cut on one side and finishing on the opposing side reduces any chances of ripping the grain down the side of the peg. A faux pas such as this shows in a finished project.

The main use for flush-cut saws in my woodworking is to trim pegs. Those often have been glued into position. The glue fills the teeth, rendering the saw useless. So you must clean the teeth well on a regular basis.

Flush-trimming Router Base: Pare Your Pegs With Power

There is always more than one way to perform any task in woodworking. For flush-trimming pegs, here's a motorized method for tackling this task.

A trim router equipped with a mortising bit would be ideal for flush-trimming pegs, were it possible to set the bottom of the bit even with the bottom of the router base, while at the same time push the base over a protruding peg. This simple, 10-minute modification to the trimmer base does just that.

Two 3/8" x 3/8" pieces of smooth hardwood are attached to the base plate with double-stick tape. The exact location will depend on the width of the piece; narrow stiles and rails require the pieces be placed close together. It's a balancing act; they should be as far apart as possible while leaving both on the surface.

The best router bit to use is sold as a mortising or dadoing bit. The key is that the bit is designed to leave a flat-bottomed cut and has a carbide cutter on its end.

Set the bit height with a straightedge spanning the two wood runners. Start with the cutter a hair below the straightedge and make a test cut. Lower the cutter and repeat the test cut until it will trim a peg flush without marring the surrounding wood. If dead flush makes you nervous, the peg can be left a wee bit proud, then sanded or scraped flush.

This method works best when the router is doing the least work possible, so don't leave much of the peg exposed, 1/8" to 1/4" works well. The only real risk in this method is allowing one of the runners to fall off an edge, tilting the base. Move the cutter in slowly over the peg, and remove it in small nibbles by rotating the tool.

— Robert W. Lang

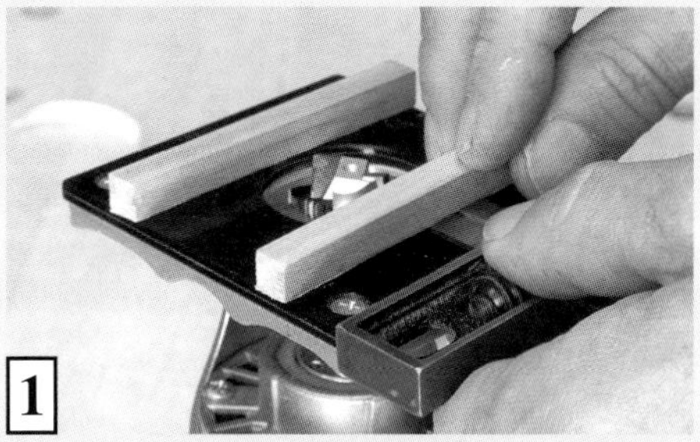

1 Adhere two small strips of wood to the router base plate with double-stick tape. Space them as far apart as possible, but less than the width of the surface they will be resting on.

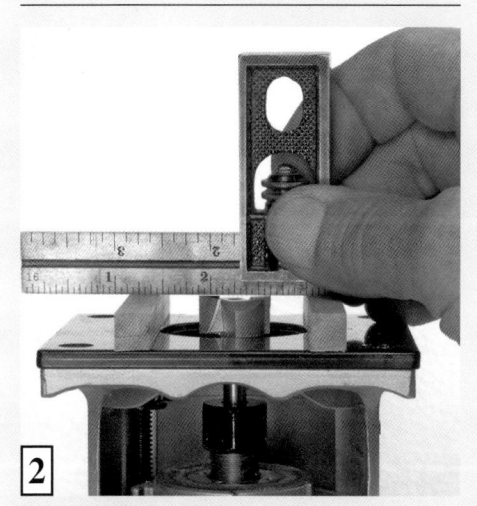

2 Set the bottom of the mortising bit even with the bottom surface of the wood runners.

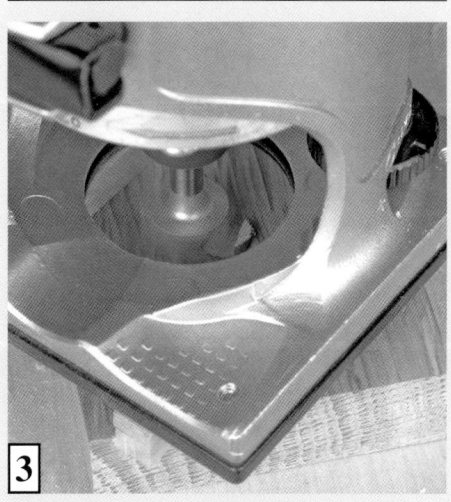

3 After making test cuts to set the depth of the cutter correctly, trim the pegs by slowly moving the spinning cutter across the protruding peg.

4 Keeping the wooden runners in contact with the surface is essential. If one runner falls off an edge, the base will tilt and the router bit will dig into the wood surrounding the peg. A bit of paraffin on the bottom of the runners will allow them to glide across the surface.

Become a Better Borer

Drilling clean, accurately placed holes is essential to good woodworking. Learn to become a human drill press with our simple exercises.

Modern woodworkers tend to look at making holes as merely one small step toward crafting a joint. We bore out waste to make a mortise to hold a tenon, or we drill a pilot hole for a screw. But for centuries, it was the holes themselves that were the height of high-technology joinery.

In many pieces of early Egyptian and American Indian furniture, the only joints were holes that were then lashed together with leather strips. I've seen beds, coffins and household goods such as buckets built using this system.

This skill didn't disappear with the Pharaohs. The skill – sometimes called marlinship – survived through the Victorian era. Even the Wright brothers' early airplanes were lashed together using some of these principles.

Today we lean on the drill press when we need an accurate hole, and we use an electric drill when accuracy is second to speed. And when we need a hole at an odd angle or in an odd place, we end up building complex jigs and guides that can consume hours of valuable shop time.

I worked this way for years until I took a chairmaking class. The only boring tools in the chairmaker's shop were the brace and bit. The entire time I was taking the class, I made mental notes about how I could develop a drill-press jig to make the difficult compound bores involved in building Windsor chairs. But by the end of the week, I'd abandoned my plans for jigs.

"I try not to anthropomorphize my tools. They hate that...."
— Tom Bruce
Akbar 'n' Jeff's Tool Hut
(www.workingtools.biz)

The trick to boring accurate holes isn't years of practice (though that always helps). Instead, you need to understand the goal of your hole, and the role each of your hands must play in the boring saga.

That's because somewhere after about 30 or so holes, I found I could bore as straight as a drill press with a brace and bit. What was the trick? Well, the practice helped – it always does – but more important was understanding the proper body position for boring and thinking through the goal at hand.

Excited, I took my new-found love of boring back home, and during the airplane ride I contemplated throwing away my cordless drill. The batteries weren't holding a charge, anyway.

That turned out to be a cockamamie idea as well. Cordless drills are a gift from the gods when speed can trump accuracy. Plus, I found that my new-found brace skills spilled over to using the cordless drill as well. In other words, I was an all-around better borer.

You can be one, as well, with just a bit of practice. The first step is to understand the tools and what they're used for. Let's begin with the brace itself.

Brace Yourself

Before braces were invented, holes were bored with a bow drill, according to old paintings and drawings. What's a bow drill? Picture a drill bit held in place at the end of a long wooden handle. Then the string of a bow – much like a bow for arrows – is wrapped around the wooden handle. Each stroke of the bow rotates the bit. It's a fairly inefficient and low-torque way to make holes.

On the other hand, the brace – even in its most primitive form – is a marvel of mechanical advantage, courtesy of the 15th century. The bit is held in a chuck. One hand grasps the top of the tool. The other hand cranks a U-shaped handle. With this simple tool you can develop torque that only large-horsepower motors can achieve.

I stumbled on this revelation while drilling ¾" holes in 3"-thick yellow pine with an auger bit. The task drained a cordless drill's battery after one or two holes. So I switched to a corded drill. After two holes, that drill caught fire. But the brace with the same sharp auger breezed through the wood, and I barely broke a sweat.

Here's an anatomy lesson of a brace, and a discussion of its most important features.

■ The Head or Nave: The round knob at the top of the brace is properly called the head, though you will see other names for it, such as "pad." It is made of metal, wood or a composite material and should spin freely around. When you pick up a vintage brace, one of the first things you should check is how well the head fits. A wobbly head is an indicator that the tool is worn or poorly made. The wobble will make it difficult to bore straight.

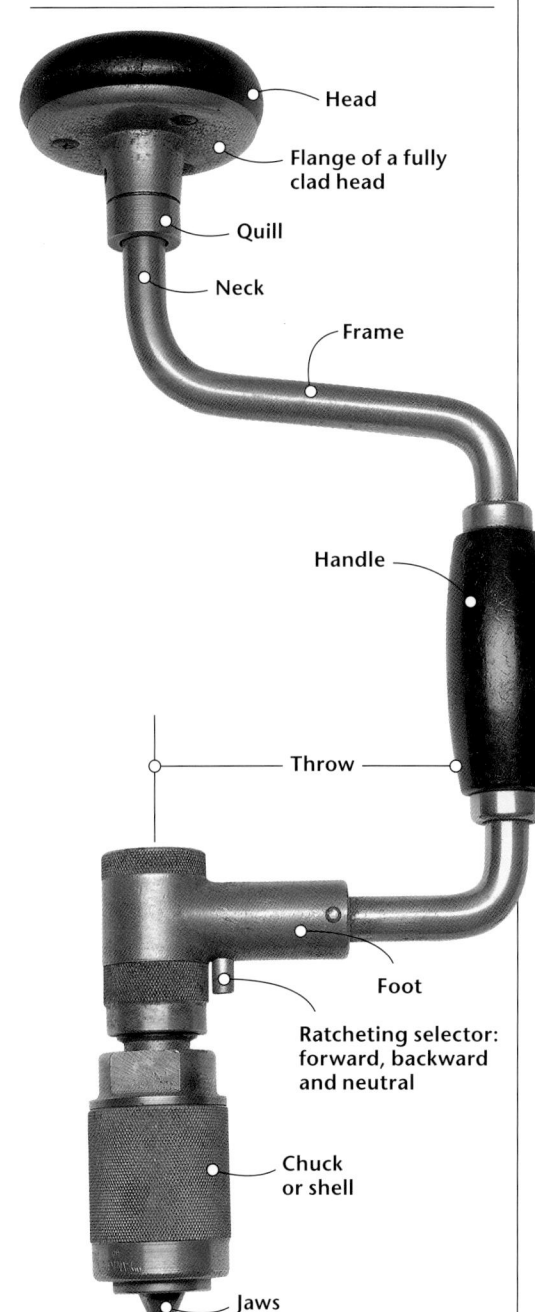

■ The Frame: The U-shaped section of the brace is called the frame, though sometimes it's called the crank. The part where the frame joins the head is called the neck. The part where the frame joins the chuck is called the foot. The place you grasp the frame is called the handle. What's important about the frame is how much the handle is offset from the head and chuck of the tool. Braces commonly have an offset from 3" to 7" – this offset is called the throw. Tools with more throw can generate more leverage with less effort, but they require more space to work. If you take the amount of throw and double it, you've calculated the sweep of the tool. The sweep is essentially the diameter of the circle created by turning the handle one revolution. The sweep is the number that tool merchants use to describe the tool's size. The most common sweeps are 8" and 10". The 6" size is good for small bits in tight spaces; the 14" sweep is good for holes that are larger than 1" diameter in tough woods.

■ The Chuck: The part that holds the bit is the chuck, and it is the biggest variable in a brace. There are probably hundreds of different designs. Most of them work fine for holding the tapered, rectangular tang designed for braces. But some chucks also will hold standard round twist and brad-point bits, which is handy. The most important thing to look for is that the jaws of the chuck close tightly and don't flop around inside the chuck, sometimes called the shell. Floppy jaws are usually a sign that the spring inside the chuck is broken or dislocated. I'd pass on a brace with a broken chuck.

Many chucks have a ratcheting feature, which is a lot like the three-position switch on a socket set. You can set the brace to turn the bit only on the forward stroke, only on the reverse stroke or during both forward and reverse. While some woodworkers think the ratchet is as unnecessary as socks on a squirrel, I disagree. The ratchet allows you to bore easily in tight spots where you can only move the handle through part of its arc, such as in a corner. Also, the ratchet allows you to easily rotate the handle in one part of its arc that is comfortable or requires less effort. One example: When working with the brace horizontal, it's easier to push the handle to the floor (gravity is your helper), and the ratchet allows you to work in that narrow band.

The ratchet does add some weight to the tool, which some people dislike. But I don't mind the weight. Most boring at the bench is done with the brace vertical, so the weight isn't an issue.

The ratchet should move smoothly and click (just like a socket set) when engaged. In vintage braces, the ratchet mechanism can get gummed up. On some tools it's easy to clean and lubricate these. On others (particularly the fine brace made by North Brothers of Philadelphia) re-assembling the ratchet requires an engineering degree and an extra hand.

Basic Brace Use

Braces aren't difficult to use. To load a bit in the chuck, here's the basic drill: With the chuck pointing up to the ceiling, grasp the chuck with one hand and hold the tool's handle with the

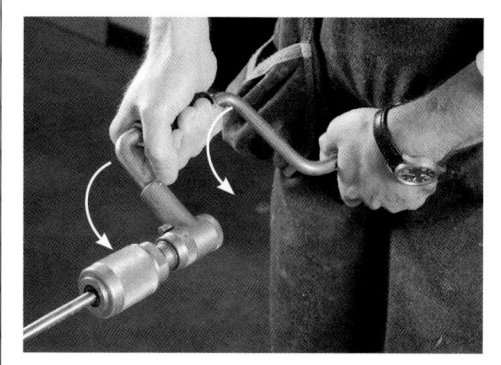

When boring large-diameter holes you can fatigue one set of muscles on the arm that is holding the handle. Instead, engage the ratchet and work only in the narrow area where gravity is working with you.

Cranking the jaws closed by using the handle is faster than simply spinning the shell with one hand. Plus, you can get the jaws tighter on the bit with less effort by adopting this technique.

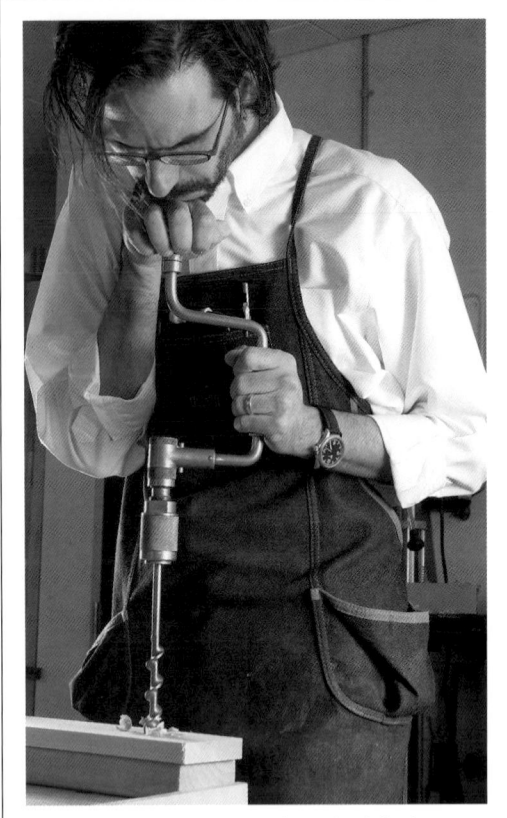

Keep your body as close to the axis of the brace as possible and focus your downward pressure on the head of the tool. Note that the hand on the handle is employing a loose grip.

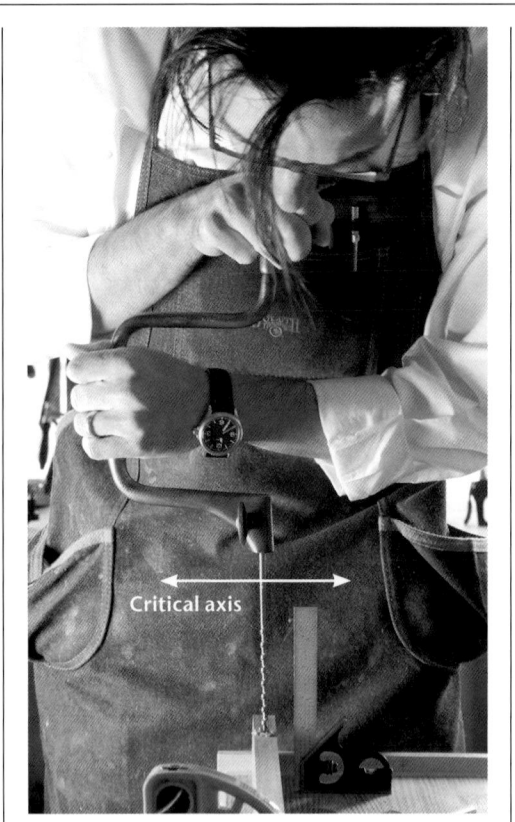

With many holes there is a critical axis that requires attention. If I stray left or right here, this door stile is as good as firewood.

Here's the non-critical axis. If I stray forward or back then it's no big deal. That can be corrected with the next hole.

other hand. Set the ratchet (if there is one) to the middle position so it is disengaged. This is like the neutral position on some ratchets in a socket set. Now crank the handle clockwise to open the jaws. Insert a bit between the jaws and close the jaws until they just barely hold the bit. Wiggle the bit until its rectangular shank finds its nesting place in the jaws. Now crank the handle until the jaws close tight.

To make a hole, place the tip of the bit in position. If you are boring with the tool vertical, then do your best to get your body over the tool as much as possible. I'll frequently perch my chin on the head of the brace. This increases accuracy.

If you are working horizontally, brace the head of the tool against your stomach or chest (whichever is more convenient).

Now you want to begin boring. I like to assign separate jobs to each of my hands. My dominant hand typically goes onto the head and grasps tight. That hand has only one job: Steer straight down. My off-hand goes on the handle – lightly now – and has only one job: Travel in a circle.

Mastering this basic stroke and approach to the work is the first step to getting an accurate result with a brace. The other tricks have to do with all forms of boring, whether they are powered by electrons or empanadas.

Learn Plumb; Learn Level

While growing up, we first learned good posture by balancing textbooks on our heads and then walking around the classroom. To learn to bore accurately, there are a couple good crutches to lean on until you get the feel for the tool. These rules apply no matter what sort of boring tool you have in your hands.

Most boring is done at 90° to the work, so you can teach yourself to bore true by sighting your work against a try square positioned on your work or your bench. You also can sight your bit against any layout lines scribed on your work, such as when you've marked out a mortise on a stile. What's critical is to figure out which axis is more important to observe, and to then position your body (and try square) to take advantage of that knowledge.

Here's a classic example: Let's say you are boring out the waste in a mortise in a door stile. The stile is sitting on your bench and you are standing at the end of the board. The critical axis for this job is left and right. If you lean left or right as you bore, the mortise will not be straight – or you might even bore through the face of your stile. The non-critical axis is forward and back. If you lean too far forward or too far back, it's no big deal. The next hole (or your chisel) can correct that error. In some cases the error doesn't even need to be corrected.

So remember this when you bore: It is easier to sense whether you are listing left or right than it is to tell if you are leaning forward or back. That should tell you where to stand and where to place your square as you are training yourself to work at 90°.

But what about when you must bore at an odd angle? That is, anything to do with a chair or a stool? You might not be able to train yourself to hit 17.5° off of 90° in your sleep, but you can train

> *"The more a guitar is played, the better it will sound; it needs to get used to being an instrument and not a chair, so it's difficult when some musicians expect a guitar to play itself. That's why I think most good luthiers would make great shrinks: It's usually not the guitar."*
>
> — Frankie Montuoro
> guitar technician for the band Wilco in
> "The Wilco Book" (DAR)

In critical boring operations, you can use a block of wood that's cut to your desired angle and press the flutes against the block.

Extend your index finger when drilling, hammering, sawing or planing. Your finger will help bring the rest of your body in line.

yourself to stay consistent once the cut has begun. Just remember that one hand steers and the other hand cranks, and you'll get the hang of it.

When boring odd angles, you can use a sliding T-bevel as a guide, which is a help. But you also can use a friend to act as a spotter. Whenever I get ready to bore something on the odd side, I'll take one of three approaches.

If it's an angle that has to be dead-on, I'll position a T-bevel along the critical axis and have a friend or co-worker spot me as I begin the hole. (Once the cut has commenced, you're committed and it's probably better not to have people watching.) If I'm alone in the shop, I'll begin the hole with the lead screw of the auger only and try to get the bit lined up against the blade of the T-bevel before I commit to burying the bit's cutting spurs into the work.

The third option involves the miter saw. Set the saw to make a cut that matches the angle you're seeking. Cut a piece of 2x4 scrap at that angle. Then clamp or screw that scrap so the flutes of the bit ride the angle as you bore. This final approach isn't as fussy as building a complex boring jig, but it does increase your accuracy dramatically. And remember, if you measure the angle from the underside of the stool or chair you can screw your guide block directly to the work because any holes from that process will be hidden.

The above guidelines aren't just for braces. They work with cordless and corded drills as well. When dealing with drills that have a pistol-grip (corded or cordless), there is an additional trick to learn. When you grip the handle of the drill, point your index finger out so it's in line with the chuck of the tool – don't use your index finger as the trigger finger. That's the job of your middle finger.

This little trick works with any tool that requires guidance (especially handsaws and jigsaws). Sticking your index finger out to point the way is a cue to your body to straighten out and head the direction of the pointer finger. This might sound like bunk. I swear it is not.

Most early tools were designed for a three-finger grip and encouraged the user to extend the index finger. Modern woodworkers who pick up these old tools usually assume that the reason the handle hurts their hand is that it was designed for people back in the day when they had smaller hands. That's just not the case. Study the old books that depict hand-tool use and you'll see immediately that extending the index finger is common. And, in fact, people weren't that much smaller in the 18th century. Not to belabor the point, but if you're interested in this myth, The Plimoth Plantation in Plymouth, Mass., has an engaging article on this topic on its web site: plimoth.org/discover/myth/.

Watch the Spurs

Once you have the confidence to leave the try square behind as you bore (and your head has been cleared of images of our forefathers being tiny people), then try this other trick to check your work as you begin boring. When using an auger bit, the first part of the bit to bite the wood is the lead screw. It's a simple cone and can't help you

Supplies

Tools for Working Wood
800-426-4613 or
toolsforworkingwood.com

- Nicholson 7" Auger Bit File
  # ST-AUG, $9.80

Brass City Records and Tools
203-574-7805 or
brasscityrecords.com

- Walt Quadrato is an excellent source of vintage braces and auger bits at fair prices.

Sydnas Sloot
sushandel@msn.com or
sydnassloot.com

- Sanford Moss's excellent web site is a wealth of information on braces. Sanford also sells a fair number of braces and other vintage boring accessories.

When you are boring a critical hole, begin the cut cautiously so you can see if the spurs are entering the wood at the same time, which is a good sign. With this wayward bore, there's still time to correct the angle.

with anything except making sure your bit starts at the right point. Whether or not you are plumb isn't the job of the auger's lead screw. Instead you need to pay attention to the spurs – the football-shaped cutters that rim the bit and score the outside diameter of the hole. These spurs travel the entire circumference of your hole, and you can use that to your advantage.

As the lead screw begins to bury itself into the work, watch the hole and advance slowly. Watch to see if both spurs hit the wood's surface simultaneously. If the bit is angled off 90°, one spur will contact the work before the other spur – assuming your spurs are filed to the same height.

If one spur plows across the wood before the other, then stop boring, release the brace and step back to see where things are going awry. It should be fairly obvious to your naked eye. If not, get out a square to see where you are leaning. With just the lead screw engaged, it's fairly easy to make a slight adjustment and get on track. But once both spurs and the flutes of the bit are engaged, you're fairly committed to cutting that angle.

But not always. Chairmakers commonly use spoon bits to allow themselves some wiggle room before committing to a particular angle. A spoon bit looks like someone split a metal pipe along its length and ground one end to a rounded spoon shape. The rounded end allows the woodworker a fair amount of time to change angles as the cut begins. I'm personally not fond of spoon bits for a few reasons. One, they're somewhat rare. They cut slower than an auger. And the inexperienced borer is just as likely to wander off of a correct angle as wander onto the correct one.

Engage the Autopilot

There are other tricks to drilling holes with precision that don't involve a drill press. Whenever I have a hole to bore that must be located precisely or involves combining bores of different diameters, such as when drilling for a bolt and its washer, then I almost always rely on a narrow pilot hole to guide all of my bits.

A pilot hole is a good idea for a couple reasons. One, a small-diameter hole is easier to drill in a precise manner than a large-diameter hole. With small bits you can focus almost all of your effort and attention on boring true without worrying about swinging your arm wide and throwing off your angle.

Once you get a pilot hole drilled, you can use that to guide all of your other larger bits. The lead screw or brad point of your bit will always want to follow the pilot hole because it's the path of least resistance through the wood.

How big should a pilot hole be? You need to use some judgment here. Use the smallest-diameter bit possible for the thickness of the work you are drilling. Thicker woods will require bits that are bigger and longer. For ¾"-thick work, I'll usually choose a ³⁄₃₂" bit and work up from there.

Once you get your pilot hole drilled, you should drill the largest-diameter holes first – usually these are the counterbored recesses for the washers, the nut or the head of a bolt or screw. For these counterbores, always pick a bit that has some sort of well-defined point, such as a Forstner, brad-point, auger or center bit. Garden-variety twist bits (designed for metalworking) don't follow a pilot as well. Their blunt tips can be difficult to start without first using a centerpunch on your work to dimple the wood.

Place the point of the bit in your pilot hole and drill your counterbores on the entry and exit points of your pilot.

With the counterbores complete, you can then drill the hole that connects them. Again, choose a bit with a well-defined point. Place the tip in the pilot hole in the middle of the counterbore and bore the through-hole. If it's a particularly deep hole, you can work from both entry and exit holes to increase the chance that your holes will line up just right in the end.

How you stop the cut is almost as important as how you begin it. When you bore through a piece of work, you can blow out the far side of the workpiece as the bit exits the work. You can prevent this blow-out by backing up the exit hole with a piece of scrap. But sometimes that's not practical, such as when boring into the middle of a board. So here's another approach.

Drive the bit into the work until the lead screw just begins to poke out the far end of the work (mark your bit with tape so you'll know when you are close to the final depth). Remember this: Stop boring as soon as you can feel the bit on the exit side. You want the exit hole to be really small. A small hole will make the next hole you make easier to bore accurately.

Remove the bit from your first hole then move over to the hole's exit side. Place the lead screw of the bit into the small hole on the exit side and advance the bit. It will cut a clean exit hole that's lined up with your first hole.

Clear a Path

Don't, however, confuse pilot holes with clearance holes. Their names give away their jobs in the shop. A pilot hole is designed to lead the way for something else that will then cut into the walls of the pilot hole – perhaps it's another bit, a wood screw or a cut nail.

A clearance hole, on the other hand, is supposed to clear a wide path for something to follow behind, such as a bolt or a piece of hardware. The difference is important. A clearance hole should be wide enough so the hardware doesn't cut significantly into the walls of the hole. Whereas a pilot hole should be small enough that the hardware can bite into the walls of the hole but big enough to prevent the hardware from jamming and breaking.

The most common (but misunderstood) application of pilot holes and clearance holes is when using a screw to fasten two pieces of wood. Let's say you are going to screw a top piece to a bottom piece. The best form of this joint is where you first drill a pilot hole through the top piece and

When you need a hole that's dead-on or stepped in size, consider making a pilot hole first to guide your future drilling efforts.

The pilot hole helps guide all subsequent boring operations. For the counterbore, place the lead screw in the pilot hole.

When the lead screw poked through the exit side of this hole I stopped turning the handle, removed the auger and began the cut on the exit side. This eliminates the grain from blowing out as the bit clears your work.

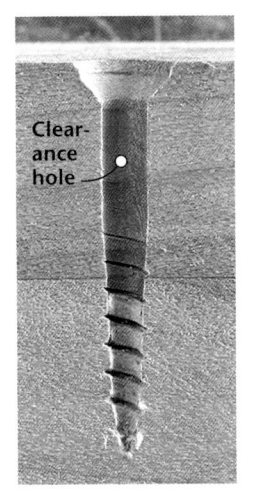

In this cutaway, you can see how the pilot, clearance hole and countersink all work together to ensure that the screw will pull the work up tight (left). And you can see an example of what bridging looks like with the screw removed.

into the bottom piece. The pilot hole should be the same diameter as the shank of the screw (the metal part minus the threads). This is sometimes called the "minor dimension" of a screw.

Then drill a larger-diameter clearance hole in the top piece only. The clearance hole should be slightly larger than the entire diameter of the screw (this is sometimes called the "major dimension" of the screw). Drill a countersink for the head of the screw if necessary then drive your screw. This arrangement of holes will allow the screw to do its job: The threads will bite into the walls of the pilot hole and pull the head of the screw down – pulling the top piece onto the bottom piece. If you don't drill a clearance hole in the top piece, the screw's threads could bite into the top piece and prevent the joint from closing. This is called bridging.

With these basic skills in hand you will be prepared to move into one of the great unexplored realms of woodworking: boring holes. Open any old tool catalog or book from the 19th century and you will be stunned by the wide variety of bits that were available to the woodworker.

And though all the different types of bits might be bewildering, they all work on the same principle. Take heart in that when Joseph Moxon penned the first English text on woodworking in 1678, he barely made mention of the brace, which he called a "piercer."

"Its Office is so well known, that I need say little to it," Moxon wrote. "Only, you must take care to keep the bitt straight to the hole you pierce, lest you deform the hole, or break the Bitt."

That's all you get in the first-ever English book on the craft. According to Moxon, the whole world of hole knowledge is widespread and shallow. But I actually think it goes a bit deeper. **WM**

— *Christopher Schwarz*

The Care and Feeding of Auger Bits

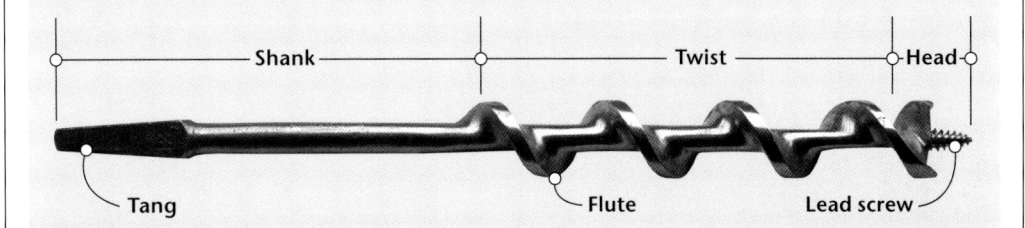

Auger bits are wondrous, efficient bits of tooling. When sharpened, they eat through wood with little effort. Sharpening them is simple. The first rule is to sharpen them as little as possible. Mimic all the angles present on the tooling and take as few strokes with an auger bit file as possible. Here are the important parts of the auger bit and how to care for them.

- **The Lead Screw:** If this is clogged, the bit will not advance into the work. You don't have to sharpen the lead screw, but you do have to keep it clean. If it's gunky, I'll soak it in some mineral spirits and then clean the threads of the screw with some dental floss. If the threads get worn or broken I pitch the bit and reluctantly spend another 25 cents on a replacement at the flea market.

- **The Flutes or the Twist:** These carry the shavings out of the hole. If they are rusty, the bit is more likely to clog. You can polish up the flutes with fine sandpaper if things aren't too bad. Or you can spend another quarter. Keep the flutes as shiny as possible. Wipe down the flutes with a little WD-40 or light machine oil when you are done with the bit for the day.

- **The Spurs:** These football-shaped cutters score the diameter of your hole. You file them on the inside only. Filing the outside will shrink the diameter of the circle that they score and the auger will jam. Game over. Take a few strokes with an auger bit file and mimic the gentle radius of the spur.

- **The Cutting Lips:** These two wedge-like parts of the bit act like levers. They wedge themselves under the waste that's defined by the spurs and force it up the flutes. File their bevels, which face up toward the flutes of the auger. Five or six strokes will do.

— CS

To file the cutting lip, brace the bit against a piece of scrap and rub the file against the lip. A few strokes should produce a fresh edge.

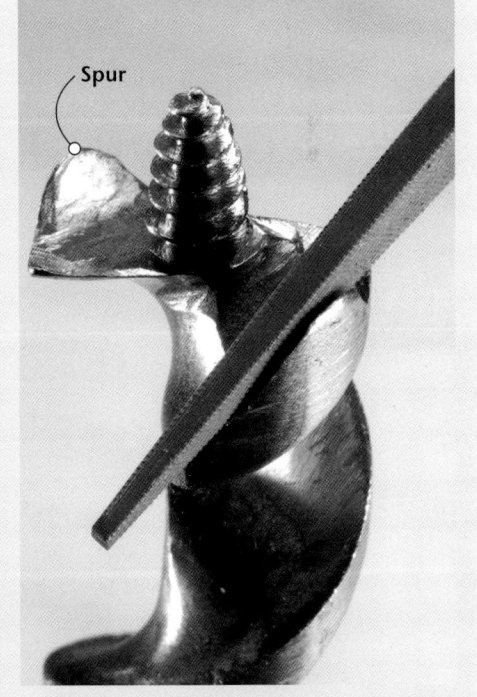

To file the spurs, clamp the auger upright and gently file the radius of the spur. Never file the outside diameter of the bit. Work the inside only.

Carving out a Pumpkin Pine Finish

We experimented to find the perfect recipe for this most-requested finish for pine – and it's as easy as pie.

Pumpkin pine is a developed patina that glows a warm orangy color similar to – you guessed it – a pumpkin.

Ask woodworkers what finish they want to replicate when using white pine as their primary wood in a project, and you're likely to hear two words: pumpkin pine.

A real pumpkin pine finish has many years of age. Begin with heartwood from Eastern white pine then allow a century of wax, grime and exposure to daylight, and you'll start to see a patina that displays a golden-orange hue.

Old Growth v. New Growth
Back in the day, Eastern white pine or yellow pine was sought after by woodworkers. It was easy to work, available in very wide boards, had tight growth rings and developed a rich warm patina over time. Who wouldn't want to use this type of lumber to build furniture – especially with the abundance of white pine in New England and yellow pine in the South.

Today, we don't often have the opportunity to work with old-growth material. It is salvaged occasionally from sunken logs and old buildings that sacrifice their beams to be resawn into lumber. But for the most part, we use new-growth lumber for woodworking.

Preparing to Finish
Most pine bought today is dimensioned lumber from retail stores. This S4S lumber is sent through sharp knives on jointers and planers at a high feed rate. As a result, milling marks are evident. These marks won't be completely erased unless you start the sanding process with #120-grit sandpaper. With pine, it's best to sand to #220 grit, which will help reduce its tendency to blotch. Because pine is a softwood, the progression of each sanding step is quick. It's also necessary to step through each grit because it becomes evident if grits are skipped when stain is applied. Scratches stand out after applying color.

The most sought-after pine finish is a one-day, three-step process. Finding a sample to copy (such as this antique firkin) is a good strategy. See the Contents page of this issue for a color photograph.

Three Steps to Pumpkin
With the enlisted aid of my local Rockler salesperson – where the products with which to experiment are close at hand – I began mixing ingredients and ideas to arrive at the pumpkin pine finish.

One of the biggest roadblocks in using pine is how the finish blotches because of variations in grain density. To combat blotching, you could add a wash coat of shellac (shellac thinned with alcohol). If the wash coat is too heavy, new problems are created; the stain won't penetrate the surface. If the wash coat is too thin, the end result after staining would still be blotchy.

Finding a reliable way to control the blotching caused by the stain is the task. For that, we used a water-base clear stain.

The Pumpkin Pine Formula
The pumpkin pine finishing process begins with a coat of natural stain (no pigment present), then a second layer of pigmented stain that adds color, then two coats of shellac as a topcoat. It's easy to complete the process in one day.

The formula begins with a coat of General Finishes wood stain in Natural (generalfinishes.com). Don't be surprised when you open the can. The stain starts as a paste-like goo but dries clear. This product has enough resin in it to partially seal the pine against color penetration, like a wood conditioner. And because it is water-based, it dries faster than oil-based conditioners. The sealing action of this product allows some coloring near the surface of the wood, but it prevents the color from penetrating deeply and blotching.

Simply apply a coat onto the surface of the project with a clean cloth then immediately wipe away the excess stain as you rub the goo into the wood. Remove as much as possible when wiping clean, then allow the piece to dry. Drying takes from two to four hours under ideal conditions. And if conditions aren't ideal, small projects can be forced dry with a hair dryer or heat gun.

The next layer of stain is also a pasty goo, but with color added. We liked the look of General Finishes Shaker Maple water-based stain. Brush on a coat and rub the stain into the wood by twisting the brush bristles. The twisting action pushes the stain into any small scratches to create a uniform color layer.

Let the pigmented stain sit on the surface for about five minutes then wipe away any excess. Don't be tentative. This isn't like a glaze where you wipe selectively to create faux effects. And we're not trying to even out any mis-matched coloration. Wipe as much stain off as possible and allow the stain to dry for two to four hours.

The Shaker Maple stain adds two important colors. First, it develops the brown shade necessary to present the aged look. Second, it casts a reddish hue onto the piece.

Why do we need the reddish hue? Remember those school days when you studied the primary colors? Yellow and red make orange – or pumpkin, in our case.

The amber shellac delivers the yellow.

Shellac: Is it the Right Stuff?
Shellac isn't the most durable topcoat, and you should always consider how your project will be used before choosing a topcoat. If you're finishing a tabletop or an area that will experience a lot of wear, a tougher finish is probably called for. Add a more durable topcoat after the pumpkin finish is achieved – but test it first to make sure that it doesn't affect the pumpkin pine color.

Before applying the first coat of shellac, use a maroon non-woven abrasive pad to knock down any fibers that raised after applying the first coat of water-based stain.

Zinsser's amber shellac, ready to use right out of the can, is the topcoat. (I said it was easy.) Check the date of manufacture while at the store. Outdated shellac – it's definitely good for a year after the date printed on the can – shouldn't be used because it won't dry.

You can brush the shellac onto the piece or apply it with a cotton rag. With either option watch for runs or sags in the finish. A run or sag is actually another layer that increases the color build. Because shellac adds color with each layer, any imperfections such as those will show.

Lightly sand the surface with #400-grit sandpaper once the shellac is dry; don't sand through the earlier finish.

The next coat of shellac delivered the exact look for our pumpkin pine finish and the surface was thick enough to level to a smooth finish.

You might need a third layer to build the shellac and ensure a smooth finish. If this is so, use a clear shellac because it adds to the thickness without affecting the color. Apply a third coat directly over the previous coats and remember to sand lightly in between.

Once both the color and the thickness of the finish are reached, sand the piece again with #400-grit sandpaper and apply a good coat of paste wax.

Three readily available products with a one-day stretch in the shop, and you'll have a finish that comes as close to aged pumpkin pine as anything I've tried or seen. WM

— *Glen D. Huey*

Apply the "Natural" stain with a cotton cloth. Pad it into the pine and wipe away any excess. The stain dries clear.

Apply the pigmented stain making sure that it's worked into the surface. On small pieces, swirling as you apply the stain works best.

The pumpkin pine color becomes apparent after the second coat of shellac is added. Scuff the surface between shellac coats. If you need an additional coat to build the surface, use a clear or super blonde shellac. Notice the even tone of the stain. This is a result of the first layer of unpigmented stain.

End Grain

Caught in the Act

Knowing when and how to break the rules can keep you from getting locked up.

I am caught breaking the rules on a regular basis. When you do woodworking and publish the results for a few hundred thousand woodworkers, it comes with the territory. When readers respond to something I've written or said, the questions begin one of two ways: "I thought you were never supposed to …" or "I thought you were always supposed to …." And so I admit that, yes, I broke the rule, but here are the reasons the rule doesn't apply in this particular case.

The rules are the rules, usually based on decades or even centuries of experience. But even with a sound basis for most of them, the words "always" and "never" never always apply.

There is a comfort in rules, especially when trying something new. The expectation is that the rule will make up for a lack of experience, and the logic of the rule will prevail and keep us out of trouble. The dilemma in woodworking is that the rules are narrow while the material and situations they apply to are wide and ever-changing. Traveling a city street is not the same as hiking a mountain trail; rules for one may not apply to the other, even though the principle behind the rule, going from point A to point B, is the same.

New woodworkers are inundated with rules: "Feed the wood into the jointer cupped side down"; "Feed the wood into the jointer bowed length down"; "Feed the wood into the jointer so the cutter doesn't lift and tear out the grain."

Some of my best thinking is done while performing mundane woodworking tasks, and all of this came to mind, as you might guess, while I spent an afternoon milling a lot of lumber at the jointer. In nearly every piece I was trying to straighten, following one rule required breaking another. I didn't want to spend the day dissecting the structure of each piece to make the right decision, so I was left with something other than following the rules.

It's not that the thinking behind the rules is flawed; they became the rules because they are correct. The problem is that each piece of wood we work with is an individual with a distinct set of inherited character traits, and something very close to a personality.

Building furniture with solid wood is like being a Cub Scout leader or a second-grade soccer coach. There is a potential in each piece, but to join them in a successful whole requires getting to know each piece's strengths and weaknesses and fitting them in a place where the strengths are seen and the weaknesses are (hopefully) hidden forever.

Woodworking is an art of relationships. How well does the worker know his material, his tools, his strengths and weaknesses, and his willingness to take a risk? The rules we hear and repeat are the foundation for developing these relationships, but in the end, the nature of the parts of the equation affect the rule more than the rule dominates the parts.

When we face a paradox of conflicting rules, and discover a resolution that works for us, we tap into the part of woodworking that moves it beyond a pastime and into a way of life.

An understanding of the rules is vital, but so is the knowledge of when they should be bent, broken or ignored. This comes from experience – from following rules to successful work and from following the rules to sometimes-flawed or failed work.

When you find yourself at the jointer, with a piece of wood with rising and falling grain that bows one way and cups another, you can stand there paralyzed trying to decide which rule trumps another. Or, you can make your best guess, give it a try and see what happens. If it works it works. If it doesn't work, try something else.

If you catch me breaking a rule, or ask me to explain the best or right way to do something, be prepared for an answer that begins with, "Well, it all depends …." **WM**

— *Robert W. Lang*

Extras

"It is a curious and sad fact that although most machines are developed not to cheapen quality but to lessen cost, this is precisely what usually happens."
— Graham Blackburn, "Traditional Woodworking Handtools"

Questions About *Woodworking Magazine*?

What is *Woodworking Magazine*?

Woodworking Magazine teaches the fundamental knowledge necessary for good craftsmanship. Our goal is to make you an independent, mindful and competent woodworker by filling the inevitable knowledge gaps left by teaching the craft to yourself. To ensure our magazine is of the highest quality, we challenge woodworking's conventional wisdom to find the techniques, materials and tools that work best. Every operation and tool in *Woodworking Magazine* has been tested time and again by our staff of professional and enthusiastic woodworkers in our shop in Cincinnati.

Why is there no advertising?

To ensure that *Woodworking Magazine* is free of bias – or the perception of bias – we don't accept any outside advertising from the manufacturers or sellers of woodworking tools and equipment.

Who publishes this magazine? And who are the editors?

Woodworking Magazine is owned by F+W Publications Inc. F+W publishes a wide variety of magazines and books for the enthusiast on topics that include hunting, scrapbooking, gardening, writing and woodworking. The editors include a staff of professional journalists and woodworkers who also work on a sister publication, *Popular Woodworking*. Their names, phone numbers and e-mail addresses are listed on page 1, as well as online.

New! PDF Downloads Now Available for All Eight Issues of *Woodworking Magazine*

If you're missing an issue of *Woodworking Magazine*, or bought the five-issue CD and need the remaining issues, we now have an inexpensive and quick solution. Downloads of single issues of *Woodworking Magazine* are now available at our bookstore for just $6 each.

All you need to view and print these fully searchable electronic versions is Adobe Acrobat's free reader (and if you don't have it already, you can download it at adobe.com).

To download, visit woodworking-magazine.com/backissues.

Coming Soon: *Woodworking Magazine* – the Book

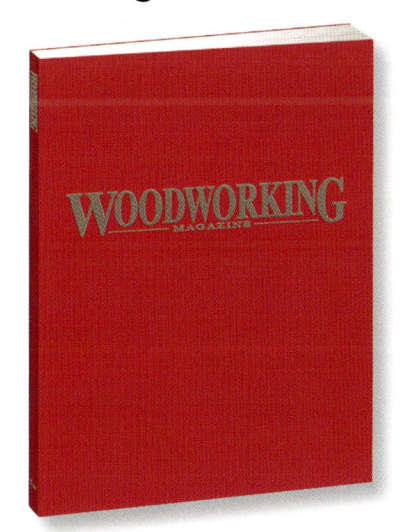

Though we now offer digital versions of all eight issues of *Woodworking Magazine* … we have an affection for the printed word. So, at the request of readers, we've also collected the first seven issues of the magazine and bound them into a book.

This hardcover book features a sturdy, deep red cover with a foil-stamped title on the cover and spine, as well as heavyweight interior matte-finish pages and colored end papers. This book belongs in your permanent collection.

Woodworking Magazine – The Book will be available on our web site (woodworking-magazine.com/books) on or before Sept. 1, 2007, for $30. It's a perfect way to ensure your collection will last for years to come … not to mention it's a great holiday gift for a fellow woodworker. Order yours today – quantities are limited!

IMPORTANT SAFETY NOTE

Safety is your responsibility. Manufacturers place safety devices on their equipment for a reason. In many photos you see in *Woodworking Magazine,* these have been removed to provide clarity. In some cases we'll use an awkward body position so you can better see what's being demonstrated. Don't copy us. Think about each procedure you're going to perform beforehand. Safety First!

Discover In-depth Information at *Woodworking Magazine*'s Weblog

Our magazine's weblog (some people call it a "blog") allows you to explore in further depth the projects, tools and techniques in the printed version of the magazine.

Updated weekly, our weblog discusses what we're working on for future issues, answers questions from readers about projects we've published, and discusses the techniques we're testing right now. To visit our weblog, go to woodworking-magazine.com/blog.

CONTACT US

We welcome letters from readers with comments about this magazine, or about woodworking in general. We try to respond to all correspondence.

To send us a letter:
- E-mail: letters@fwpubs.com
- Fax: 513-891-7196
- Mail carrier:
  Letters • *Woodworking Magazine*
  4700 E. Galbraith Road
  Cincinnati, OH 45236

Woodworking Magazine | Sandpaper | Autumn 2007

Garnet
- Natural abrasive
- Not friable
- Cuts slowly, wears quickly
- Produces a smoother finish than aluminum oxide of the same grit

Aluminum Oxide
- Highly friable – abrasive creates new, sharp edges as it wears
- Lasts longer than garnet papers

Silicon Carbide
- Wet/dry paper
- Useful for wet sanding with lubricants
- Friable on metal, but not on wood
- Wears quickly

Lubricated
- Treated with lubricant to glide over film finishes
- Useful for sanding between coats of finish

Ceramic
- Hardest of all currently available abrasives
- In woodworking, generally used only for hogging off material
- Most commonly found on sanding belts

How Friable Abrasives Work

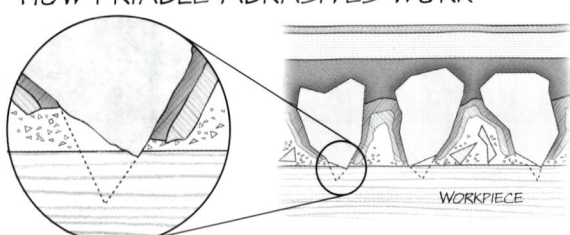

As mineral particles are worked during sanding, they fracture.

Fractured tops break off, revealing new, sharp facets that cut more aggressively.

Backing Materials for Sandpaper

- **Paper**
Inexpensive. Easy to work with. Tears easily. Moisture causes curling and decomposition. Graded A (extremely flexible), C (moderately flexible), D (moderately stiff), E (very stiff) and F (extremely stiff).

- **Wet/Dry Paper**
Coated with latex. Stronger than regular paper. Often of silicon carbide. Used for wet-sanding applications. Graded A and C.

- **Fiber-reinforced Paper**
Heavyweight paper with cloth fibers. Used on heavy-duty abrasives such as coarse grits for machine sanding.

- **Cloth**
Offers strength and durability. Often used on sanding belts. Graded J (thin, very flexible), X (moderately flexible) and Y (thick, fairly stiff).

- **Film**
Expensive. Extremely flat and even, so it yields a consistent scratch pattern. Good for final sanding and for leveling finishes.

Adhesives Used in Sandpaper

- **Hide Glue** – Inexpensive, flexible. Allows for grit deflection under pressure, so hide glue papers result in a finer scratch pattern than resin-bond of same grit.

- **Resin** – Greater resistance to heat and is more durable than hide glue, but less flexible and can leave harsher scratches than hide-glue papers of same grit.

Different Grit Scales

In the United States, there are two common grit-grading scales: Coated Abrasives Manufacturers' Institute (CAMI) and Federation of European Producers (FEPA). CAMI papers often are marked with just the grit number; FEPA papers often precede that number with a "P."

FEPA papers have a larger number of particles that are close to the stated grit, resulting in a more consistent scratch pattern. Up to #220 grit, the difference between the two scales is slight; above #220, the grading diverges.

So how do you know which scale is being used? European manufacturers (Mirka, Klingspor) use the FEPA system, but only Mirka adds the P. Norton's 3X papers use FEPA grading, but the P is printed only on the packaging. 3M has both FEPA and CAMI papers, but distinguishes between them by adding a P on FEPA products.

Recommended Grits

- **#100** – Removes machining marks
- **#150** – Refines scratches enough for a clear film finish
- **#180** – Finest grit to use when finishing with dyes (otherwise they may not penetrate correctly)
- **#220 and higher** – For oil finishes only

Closed-coat v. Open-coat

- Surface completely covered with abrasive. Must be cleaned often, and run more slowly on power sanders to reduce loading and burning.

- Surface covered only 50-70 percent with abrasive.
- Spaces provide clearance for dust so paper won't clog as quickly. The best choice for most woodworking.

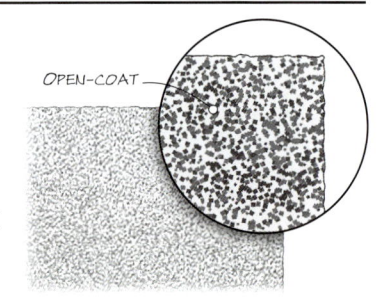

Anatomy of Sandpaper

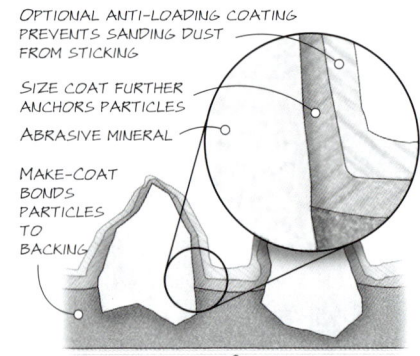

- Optional anti-loading coating prevents sanding dust from sticking
- Size coat further anchors particles
- Abrasive mineral
- Make-coat bonds particles to backing
- Backing material
- Back treatment

Approximate Equivalencies of the Two Common Sandpaper Scales

CAMI (U.S. Standard)	FEPA (European Standard)
800	P2000
600	P1200
500	P1000
400	P800
360	P600
320	P500
280	P400
	P360
240	P320
	P280
	P240
220	P220
180	P180
150	P150
120	P120
100	P100
80	P80

Illustrations by Matt Bantly

A Magazine Committed to Finding the Better Way to Build
Filled With Good Craftsmanship, the Best Techniques and No Ads

WOODWORKING
MAGAZINE

Authentic Stickley Tabourets

Master 3 Classic Joints As You Build These Sturdy, Stylish Tables

3 Simple Tricks to Learn the Forgotten Art of Handsawing

Cut Perfect Circles Without Pricey Jigs

Glazing: The Pro Trick To a Better Finish

Western Backsaws – Back From the Dead

POPULAR WOODWORKING PRESENTS

F+W PUBLICATIONS, INC.
US $5.99

Display until May 26, 2008

woodworking-magazine.com ■ SPRING 2008

Contents

"Without craftsmanship, inspiration is a mere reed shaken in the wind."
— Johannes Brahms (1833 - 1897), composer

1 On the Level
Woodworking Magazine began on the back roads of Ohio in 2002, with a small disagreement as to the best route to take.

2 Letters
Questions, comments and wisdom from readers, experts and our staff.

4 Shortcuts
Tricks and tips that will make your woodworking simpler and more accurate.

6 A Tale of Two Tabourets
The theory behind this story was to build one table entirely by hand, and the other using only power tools. But sometimes, theories change in the actual doing.

A TALE OF TWO TABOURETS: PAGE 6

14 How to Saw
When it comes to sawing, practicing won't help if you're practicing a poor method. These 10 rules and three tricks will have you sinking your teeth into perfect saw use.

20 Understanding Western Backsaws
The Western backsaw has almost vanished. But a few toolmakers are trying to turn back the clock to when this venerable tool was in every woodworker's toolbox.

24 Cutting Circles
Circles are a perfect geometric form – but they can be perfectly beastly to create. We tested the various popular methods, and came up with a plan and a jig that promises success.

28 Circular Cutting Board
Bring your woodworking into the kitchen with this simple, circular maple cutting board. The feet of contrasting wood brings the design to a new level – and makes it easy to pick up.

30 Glazing for the Ages
Sandwich a stain between two layers of finish, and you've found the best (and simplest) way to add age, blend tones and highlight carvings on your projects.

32 End Grain
All too often, we're seduced by tools that promise to make us better, faster, stronger ... then they sit in our shop corners gathering dust.

CIRCULAR CUTTING BOARD: PAGE 28

HOW TO SAW: PAGE 14

GLAZING FOR THE AGES: PAGE 30

WOODWORKING MAGAZINE

Spring 2008, Issue 9
woodworking-magazine.com
Editorial Offices 513-531-2690

Publisher & Group Editorial Director
■ **Steve Shanesy**
ext. 1238, steve.shanesy@fwpubs.com
Editor ■ **Christopher Schwarz**
ext. 1407, chris.schwarz@fwpubs.com
Art Director ■ **Linda Watts**
ext. 1396, linda.watts@fwpubs.com
Senior Editor ■ **Robert W. Lang**
ext. 1327, robert.lang@fwpubs.com
Senior Editor ■ **Glen D. Huey**
ext. 1293, glen.huey@fwpubs.com
Managing Editor ■ **Megan Fitzpatrick**
ext. 1348, megan.fitzpatrick@fwpubs.com
Illustrator ■ **Matt Bantly**
Photographer ■ **Al Parrish**

F+W PUBLICATIONS, INC.
David Nussbaum ■ Chairman & CEO
John Speridakos ■ CFO
Barbara Schmitz ■ VP, Manufacturing
John Lerner ■ Executive VP, Interactive Media
Mike Kuehn ■ Director, IT

**F+W PUBLICATIONS, INC.
MAGAZINE GROUP**
David Blansfield ■ President
Sara DeCarlo ■ VP, Consumer Marketing
Tom Wiandt ■ Director, Business Planning
Sara Dumford ■ Conference Director
Linda Engel ■ Circulation Director
Susan Rose ■ Newsstand Director
Michael Kushner ■ Director, Digital Media Solutions
Debbie Thomas ■ Production Coordinator

SUBSCRIPTION RATES: A year's subscription (4 issues) is $19.96. In Canada: Add $5 for postage & handling (includes GST/HST). Outside the U.S. and Canada: Add $10 for postage & handling and remit payment in U.S. funds with order.

NEWSSTAND DISTRIBUTION: Curtis Circulation Co., 730 River Road, New Milford, NJ 07646

POSTMASTER: Send all address changes to *Woodworking Magazine*, P.O. Box 420235, Palm Coast, FL 32142-0235. Canada GST Reg # R122594716.

SUBSCRIPTION SERVICES: Subscription inquiries, orders and address changes can be made at woodworking-magazine.com (click on "Customer Service"). Or by mail: *Woodworking Magazine*, P.O. Box 420235, Palm Coast, FL 32142-0235. Or call toll-free 1-800-283-3542 or 386-597-4322. Include your address with all inquiries. Allow 4 to 6 weeks for delivery.

BACK ISSUES: Back issues are available. For pricing information or to order, call 800-258-0929, visit our web site at woodworking-magazine.com or send check or money order to : *Woodworking Magazine* Back Issues, F+W Publications Products, 700 E. State St., Iola, WI 54990. Please specify *Woodworking Magazine* and issue date.

fw
©2008

Highly Recommended

I've long been a fan of the 6" Starrett 4R ruler, but after continued use, I now like the Bridge City SR-6 ruler better. The SR-6 ($16.95, bridgecitytools.com or 800-253-3332) reads left-to-right on one face and right-to-left on the other. That's nice for adjusting your machines when you need to set a fence. The ruler has gradations on each end, and I think it's easier to read than the Starrett.

— *Christopher Schwarz*

On the Level

Back Roads Are Better

The story of the magazine you're holding begins with a car ride through the back roads of Ohio in 2002 and a small disagreement.

Publisher Steve Shanesy and I were driving to West Virginia to a woodworking show and we were at odds about the route to take. I'd mapped out a path on the interstate, but Steve had other ideas. His finger traced a twisty path on my atlas that relied on small towns and two-lane roads.

This, I thought, was going to be a long trip.

As we forged into the wilds of Ohio, the conversation turned to how frustrating it can be to teach yourself to build furniture. Without formal training, many of us tend to develop our skills to match the project at hand.

For example, if we want to build a dovetailed blanket chest, we decide it's time to learn to cut dovetails, even if we've never picked up a dovetail saw or used a dovetail jig. And so we buy a bunch of tools, chew up a lot of good wood and end up with something that is OK, but took twice as long as it should have.

There are better ways to learn the craft.

First you need to learn how handsaws work, how to pick the right tool and how to hold it. Then you start by sawing a board in half, cutting some tenons and half-lap joints and learning exactly where the kerf of each of your saws will fall so you can split a knife line.

If all those tasks sound difficult, you've probably never done them. Cutting simple joints with a sharp saw is easy and satisfying work. You just have to know where to begin. And once you begin in the right place, the path is easy to follow.

It's like being on an interstate instead of poking through the back woods, I reminded Steve (who smirked at my remark).

As we drove on, we tried to figure out what we could do to help beginning woodworkers learn the craft in an orderly way, and to help intermediate woodworkers fill in the astonishing gaps in their knowledge because they are self-taught. So Steve and I decided to start this magazine. And after more than a year of thinking and plotting, we published our first experimental issue in early 2004 with the help of the entire staff of *Popular Woodworking*, the magazine that is our day job, for a lack of better words. We published *Woodworking Magazine* without a dime of marketing money. Without fanfare. Without additional staff. We wanted to see if the woodworking community would support a magazine that had no advertisements, that focused on building important skills, and that featured projects that are highly refined yet simple in their construction.

This is not the way most companies launch a magazine. Usually you start with a bang. You try to grow your circulation to a ridiculous level to get the attention of advertisers. You lose money for a long time in the hopes of it paying off big in the end.

I'm proud to say that *Woodworking Magazine* started life in 2004 by making a modest amount of money thanks to a passionate group of supporters. And we have continued to make money and grow slowly during the last three years, even though we've only been publishing twice a year (another thing that's never done in this industry).

But now, thanks to you, we are ready to move into the next phase. With this issue, we are now a quarterly magazine, and we are now happy to sell you a subscription (call 800-283-3542 or visit woodworking-magazine.com).

It has been a bit of a twisty path for all of us these last few years, but we've ended up in the right place at the right time. It is a lot like that fateful trip I took with Steve in 2002. Despite all our trekking on the back roads, despite all the four-way stops in tiny towns, we made it to our destination in West Virginia and shaved nearly 45 minutes off the time it would have taken us on the interstate.

Steve had been down this road before. **WM**

Christopher Schwarz
Editor

> *"The significant problems we face cannot be solved at the same level of thinking we were at when we created them."*
> — Albert Einstein (1879 - 1955)
> theoretical physicist

Letters

ILLUSTRATIONS BY HAYES SHANESY

What are the Pitfalls to Working in an Unheated Shop?

Today was a balmy -20° Celsius (-4° Fahrenheit) up here in northeast Alberta, and I was sanding a bit of plywood in my unheated garage. My question is: Can you properly sand wood in that type of environment and then bring it indoors for finishing, or should it all be done in a heated environment?

Derek West
Cold Lake, Alberta

Derek,
Well, it's unlikely that plywood will be a problem there, but solid wood will likely give you fits.

And not so much from the changing temperature, but from the changing humidity. Projects that are assembled in an unheated area (assuming your glue will work at that temperature – mine won't) and then brought into a heated area will shrink (or expand) and possibly distort badly. Tops can split. Joints won't be flush, etc.

Plywood, however, doesn't change as much with humidity, though it can warp.

Christopher Schwarz, editor

Why are the Striking Faces of Woodworking Mallets Sloped?

Mallets seem like a simple thing; you just hit things with them, right?

I started to look for a mallet recently and thought it was going to be a quick purchase. As I looked around, however, I noticed there were many types and styles. It seems there are two main types: the hammer-looking wooden mallet, which seems like it would be unwieldy, and the cylinder type, which I am leaning toward.

Here's my question: Both of these styles of mallets have sloped striking faces. Why? It seems like this would cause a glancing hit on the top of a chisel. I was thinking about how you would hold a mallet as opposed to a hammer. When I use a hammer (with a flat striking face) my arm is perpendicular to the top of the chisel. When you use a mallet, do you drop your arm/elbow down?

Michael Lingenfelter
Bothell, Washington

Michael,
I've always used the square-head mallets. Not because of some functional advantage, just habit. Other guys in our shop use both kinds and report there are no real differences in the tools (except that one will roll off your bench sometimes).

However, the sloped head is indeed important on both tools because it prevents you from delivering a glancing blow off your tool, forcing the tool away from you. The sloped face is necessary because our arms travel in arcs like a windmill, and not up and down like a jackhammer. When you use a mallet to strike a chisel, your arm is higher in this arc than when you use a hammer to drive a nail. (Chisels are longer than nails.) The slope on the striking face helps ensure your striking force will be directly down when you bring the mallet onto the tool.

Christopher Schwarz, editor

Hand-cut Mortises vs. Machine-made Mortises

I've noticed that you have a mortise machine in your shop. Knowing that you are a big fan of hand-tool work, I was wondering how often you cut mortises by hand versus machine. I have been contemplating the purchase of a mortise machine, and was wondering if there are certain features that you would consider important.

Trevor Saunders
Cobourg, Ontario

Trevor,
I have a mortising machine because I like Arts & Crafts furniture. Making that style by hand is (as you might imagine) a lesson in insanity.

If I made post-modern furniture (whatever that is) or 18th-century furniture as a historical re-enactor, there would be little need for the machine. It's really driven by the style of work.

As far as important features go, I think it's worthwhile to spend the extra money for a unit with a sliding table. Also, the 1-hp machines stall a lot less than the smaller units.

Christopher Schwarz, editor

Can You Use Butcher Block To Build a Workbench Top?

I would like to know if I buy a $1^{7}/_{8}$"-inch thick butcher-block countertop, will it be good enough for a workbench top?

Leonard Ross
Castleton, Vermont

Leonard,
I think you'll be OK as long as you have some support from below the slab and it's not true butcher block, which is where the end grain faces up. Those require significant support below.

My personal inclination would be to purchase two of those tops and glue them together to make a $3^{3}/_{4}$"-thick top, however you also could add stiffness to the top by laminating a sheet (or two) of plywood below it.

Christopher Schwarz, editor

Building the Perfect Workbench On an Imperfect Floor

I am currently designing a workbench and have a couple questions.

I have a basement workshop. As with most basements, the floor is slightly sloped to provide drainage. Most garage shops will have a similar drawback. If I make all the workbench's legs the same length, I'm concerned that this will introduce a low spot at one corner which will cause my top to warp. I could match the legs to the floor, but if the bench is moved it will then create the warping problem again. If add levelers to the legs to get a perfectly flat top, I feel that this may make the bench more liable to slip when I am actively working on it. Are these valid concerns, and do you have any suggested remedies?

"If trees could scream, would we be so cavalier about cutting them down? We might, if they screamed all the time, for no good reason."

— Jack Handy
Saturday Night Live

My second question concerns the joinery of the legs to the base. I am considering either a drawbored mortise-and-tenon joint or a wedged tenon. Is there an advantage either way for base joinery?

Alan Graham
via e-mail

Alan,
Your question is a good one, though it's not really about bench building. It's a broader truth about cabinetwork.

With bench-building and furniture-making pursuits, you almost always build your piece level and square – even if it is going to be installed in a house that is clearly not those things. Then you alter the environment to suit the finished piece. With a built-in cabinet, this is done with scribe strips, cabinet levelers and shims.

With a workbench, this is done primarily with wedge-shaped shims on the floor. Leveler feet with workbenches are generally not a good idea. These benches (for whatever reason) tend to scoot around our shop. So shim your bench at the floor to get the top level wherever it sits.

As to the joinery for the base-to-top connection, I like both options – they are both overkill. Either will work. Do which one suits your skills, tools or interest.

Christopher Schwarz, editor

How Accurate Should Motorized Sharpening Systems Be?

I'm having some trouble with the Veritas Mk. II power sharpener I recently ordered and wondered if you could give me some perspective. The plates I received with the machine caused my block-plane blade to come out rounded on edge. I checked the flatness of the plates with a machinist's straightedge and they were out. Lee Valley sent me some new ones, and those are out .003" in some places.

So my first question is, how flat should flat be? What kind of tolerance will give good results? I bought the Veritas instead of the Work Sharp because it was supposed to be quieter and more powerful. However, you guys seem to like the Work Sharp pretty well. How is its glass plate? Is it flat? Is it noisy in use? I know I need to get sharp tools, but I'm intimidated by sharpening for some reason. And I don't like the mess, sound or gritty feeling of traditional waterstones.

Erich Buehler
Arden, North Carolina

Erich,
I've worked with several powered sandpaper systems including the Work Sharp and they all are going to be less precise than hand-sharpening. I would not consider your plates to be defective.

With machines there are just a lot of moving parts and factors involved. It's like trying to get .001" tolerance out of a table saw. It's just not going to happen. So I use them as an outstanding grinder and refine the edge with waterstones.

I personally own the Lee Valley system and have been using it for a long time. I can honestly say that even though it is a machine, it requires some finesse. Your edges will definitely improve over time if you practice. Like hand-sharpening, machine operation can be subtle.

Christopher Schwarz, editor

Are Joinery Floats Useful?

While perusing the Lie-Nielsen Toolworks web site, I came across their "joinery floats." While I have heard of "planemaker's floats" used in traditional wooden planemaking, I can find no reference to joinery floats. Are these something new, simply adaptations of the planemaker's tools, or are they indeed traditional? Can you direct me to any references on them?

That being said, what, if any, is your experience with them? Lie-Nielsen's web site touts them as useful for mortise-and-tenon work, but is that their only application? Can they be used with other joints? Also, why would I want to use these tools when there are at least three other methods of refining mortises and tenons with more common tools (rasps/files, shoulder planes and chisels)?

From my standpoint, these are fairly expensive tools that appear to be limited in their application. Are they worth the price for their resulting finished product?

John Leko
Huntsville, Alabama

A planemaker's bed float can be used to clean up tenon cheeks

A mortise float for joinery

John,
Floats are indeed a traditional joinery tool. I've seen them referenced in a couple old books. There also is an entry about them (page 197) in R.A. Salaman's "Dictionary of Woodworking Tools" (Astragal Press) with drawings that are very similar to what Lie-Nielsen makes.

I use the floats for cleaning up mortises, tenons and lap joints, and I think they work brilliantly for that – especially through-mortises. I also use them like a rasp for rough-shaping material.

I don't consider them to be tools that you absolutely must have (unless you make side-escapement planes), but they are one option for cleaning up mortises that is more accurate than a chisel.

Christopher Schwarz, editor

Can Anything be Done to Prevent Wood from Warping?

I recently handplaned some walnut and maple that I've had in my garage shop for two years to make some winding sticks and bench hooks. After all that time, I figured it would be acclimated to my shop's environment. I squared all these pieces, but the next day I checked them with a straightedge and found them to be warped, bowed and cupped in the same way the pieces were when I started planing them.

Why did this happen? It seems to me it defeats the purpose of planing wood square if it is going to warp again. Or maybe you have to plane the wood, cut the joints and assemble it all in one day before it warps again the next day. I'm new at woodworking so please help me on this matter.

Mike Nelson
Glasgow, Kentucky

Mike,
It might be the moisture content of the wood. Flip the boards over for a few days and see if the boards return to flat. However, my best guess is that your wood was in tension. This tension can develop in several ways – perhaps the tree was on a hillside, or grew crooked, or the wood came from near or from within a branch. It also can occur if the stock is poorly dried at the kiln.

When the wood is in tension, it distorts when you plane it by machine or hand as these internal stresses are released. There is nothing much you can do about it, really.

These boards can be usable if the parts are small enough, but usually this sort of wood is just too ill-behaved for fine furniture. **WM**

Christopher Schwarz, editor

HOW TO CONTACT US

Send your comments and questions via e-mail to letters@fwpubs.com, or by regular mail to *Woodworking Magazine*, Letters, 4700 E. Galbraith Road, Cincinnati, OH 45236. Please include your complete mailing address and daytime phone number. All letters become property of *Woodworking Magazine*.

Shortcuts

ILLUSTRATIONS BY HAYES SHANESY

The Better Way to Turn Razor Blades into Detail Scrapers

One of the first tricks I learned in woodworking was that single-edge razor blades make excellent scrapers for detail work. You can take them right out of the package and they will take a light, dust-like shaving without any more prep work. They work great like this for cleaning up small bits of tear-out, leveling joint seams that are slightly out and for removing drips of dried finish.

But if you invest about 30 seconds to tune them, you can transform that razor blade into a much more versatile tool.

Step 1: Permanently bend the spine of the blade. This curves the cutting edge of the razor so the corners will never dig in. You can do this with your fingers with the cheap blades. Some of the expensive blades have stiffer spines and require you to use pliers. You don't need to bend it much – a $1/16$" to $3/32$" bend in the middle is plenty.

Step 2: Burnish a quick hook. Take the scraper in one hand and hold a burnisher in the other. Rub the burnisher at 80° across the blade. Use light pressure – razor blades are soft steel (low 50s on the Rockwell C hardness scale).

After a pass, maybe two, you will have a tool that will take a plane-like shaving in hardwoods. Plus, you won't have to bow the scraper (always nice) and you won't have to use much downward pressure because the tool has an aggressive hook.

Christopher Schwarz, editor

Improve Your Vision When Sighting Across Winding Sticks

When looking at winding sticks on a board to detect twist, it is essentially impossible to hold the near and the far stick in focus simultaneously, and, for those of middle age, to even focus on both sticks through one eyeglass lens power. Thus, one really is comparing two blurry edges – or at best one clear and one blurry edge – to make the critical estimation of twist using the winding sticks.

There is a very simple solution to this that I have been using for many years.

Take a piece of brass sheet about $1/64$" thick, about 4" x 2". *(Editor's note: We used the lid of an Altoids tin, which worked extremely well.)* Drill a row, across the narrow dimension, of about seven $3/64$" holes, $5/32$" apart on center. The row should be about $1 1/2$" from the top edge of the sheet. Round the corners of the brass sheet. Hold the sheet with its length perpendicular (the row of holes is thus horizontal) up to your eye. It matters little, if at all, what glasses (reading/distance/etc.) you use. Sight the winding sticks. Both the near and far sticks' edges will be in focus and visible along their full lengths. It's really surprising to see once you try it. Use good lighting.

It has been suggested elsewhere to use a single pinhole. This does not work well because the restricted width of field forces you to use head movement to sight the full length of the sticks. This movement will invariably not be perfectly horizontal and confounds the accuracy of the process. (I will leave out the technical explanation as to what is actually happening in each of these two methods.)

In experimenting with this method I have found I can reliably see a .004" deviation at one end of my 30"-long winding sticks. Since the stick length amplifies the twist deviation in the board, errors of .002" in an 8"- to 10"-wide board can be detected.

Rob Porcaro
Medfield, Massachusetts

Get Your Waterstones Wet With a Solution from the Garden

Keeping your waterstones wet while sharpening is one of the keys to working quickly and accurately. The water floats away the sharpening swarf so the stone can abrade the steel.

Many woodworkers use a spray bottle – such as one that holds a household cleaner – to keep their stones wet during sharpening. The triggers on these bottles can wear your hands out if you have more than one tool to sharpen. By far, the best solution I have found is to purchase an inexpensive ($10) plant mister from any home center or garden store.

The chief advantage of the mister is that it is pressurized. You pump up the pressure like on a bicycle pump, then it will squirt water for a long time every time you pull the trigger. You'll use more water, which will keep your stones wetter and your sharpening will be easier.

Harrelson Stanley
Pepperell, Massachusetts

"Hey, let's not forget what's important! A plane is just a holder for a blade. Without a blade, it's a hammer. And with a good blade, it's still a hammer (after you get sufficiently p****d-off)."

— Ron Hock
founder of Hock Tools

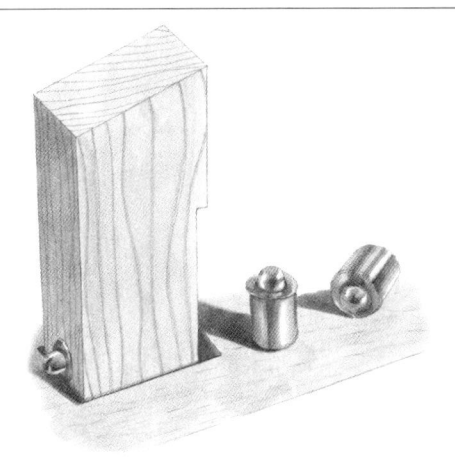

Use a Bullet Catch to Make Quick, Adjustable Bench Dogs

I picked up this trick many years ago in a book, magazine or from a fellow woodworker.

If you make wooden dogs for your workbench, there's an easy way to make them hold their position when you raise and lower them in their holes: Use a bullet catch from the hardware store. A package of eight costs about $6. First make your bench dog (it can be round, square or rectangular). Then bore a hole in the bench dog (the bullet catch is ³⁄₈" in diameter; you can use a ²³⁄₆₄" bit for a press fit) and epoxy the bullet catch into the hole. You're done.

*Carl Bilderback
LaPorte, Indiana*

Protect Tools Under Your Bench From Dust With a Curtain

We have a lot of workbenches and worktables in the machining room at The Windsor Institute. And we store a lot of tools and jigs in the open storage areas below the tops. The problem we had – that I'm sure many woodworkers have – is that the dust from machining operations tends to cover everything in the entire room.

Not only is this untidy, it's also unhealthy for your steel tools. Dust absorbs moisture from the air and can encourage your tools to rust.

The solution is simple. We purchase inexpensive plastic sheeting and attach it to the underside of the worktables. The plastic drapes over the openings below the tables to protect the contents below. The plastic is easy to push aside if I need to quickly grab one item, or I can easily flip the entire curtain up on the benchtop if I need to fetch several things.

*Michael Dunbar
Hampton, New Hampshire*

Use a Piece of Granite to Sand Small Parts With Precision

Here's a trick to sanding small parts (something I do quite a bit of). Attach your sandpaper to a piece of granite or flat glass and rub the parts on that. You can attach a series of grits across the granite if you like.

And you don't have to buy sticky-back sandpaper for this trick. You can use spray adhesive and stick any sandpaper to the granite.

One final note: You don't have to buy a machinist's granite plate for this operation. My granite plates are used in construction and come from job sites or home centers. WM

*John Hutchinson
Delaware, Ohio*

Almost Every Tool is a Measuring Device

We tend to grab a try square if we want to see if something is square. Or a straightedge if we want to see if an assembled panel or individual board is straight. But I tend to see all of my tools as having these functions built in.

When I'm undercutting the shoulders of a tenon, I use the unbeveled face or the long edges of my chisel to gauge my progress. Place the chisel across the joint and look for light peeking under the tool. If you see a hump under the tool, you have more work to do. If you see a slight valley there, your joint is properly undercut.

I don't own a fancy 24"-long machined straightedge. Well, actually, I do. It's my 24"-long jointer plane. I use the tool's long edge of the sole as an accurate straightedge. It might not be accurate enough for a machinist, but it is more than accurate enough for woodworking.

Similarly, I use a lot of my tools as squares. A well-ground chisel can easily judge the squareness of inside corners – such as checking to see if a dovetail pin is indeed square to the floor of the joint. I can sneak a chisel in almost anywhere to check a corner because chisels come in a wide variety of sizes.

Christopher Schwarz, editor

SEND US YOUR SHORTCUT

We will provide a complimentary one-year subscription (or extend your current subscription) for each Shortcut we print. Send your Shortcut via e-mail to shortcuts@fwpubs.com, or by post to *Woodworking Magazine*, Shortcuts, 4700 E. Galbraith Road, Cincinnati, OH 45236. Please include your complete mailing address and daytime phone number. All Shortcuts become property of *Woodworking Magazine*.

A Tale of Two Tabourets

One built by hand. One built with power tools. Well, that was the plan, at least.

Some of the best lessons in constructing cabinets actually come from building small tables.

In many ways, tables are like skeleton versions of complex casework pieces, which stymie beginning woodworkers with their many parts, complex joints and the way the two come together to make something that's stable and beautiful.

When you build a small table, there is far less wood involved than with a case piece, there are fewer joints and the overall structure is less complex and easier to master. But the real lessons for casework are there. Here are a few examples:

■ The mortise and tenon: This joint is the foundation of table construction – it joins the legs to the aprons and stretchers – and the joint is critical to master when building the frames necessary to make casework. Think: Doors, face frames, drawer dividers and dust panels. When

When I show these tables to people, I ask them to guess which one was built primarily with hand tools. Everyone gets it right, but none can say why.

you build one of the tables shown here, you'll use the mortise-and-tenon joint to join the legs and the lower stretchers.

■ The half-lap: Many small tables (such as these examples) have a half-lap joint where the stretchers overlap. Half-lap joinery requires a surprising amount of precision to do well. You are joining two surfaces that have 10 mating surfaces that must be in perfect alignment. If any of those surfaces is off, the joint will show a gap, be unacceptably loose or the parts won't mate flush. Mastering the half-lap – by hand or machine – is a great basic lesson for developing your fine-fitting skills.

■ The dovetail: Many tables great and small incorporate a dovetail where the stretchers meet the top of the legs. And while well-executed dovetails are the foundation of casework carcases and drawers, a table-style dovetail is remarkably forgiving and easy to make. It consists of one tail and one socket. Even poorly executed, this joint is remarkably strong. And here's the nice thing: The joint will be hidden from view thanks to the tabletop. In this table, you'll use a dovetail to join the upper stretchers to the legs.

■ The tabletop: Gluing up an attractive and strong tabletop is key to learning to glue up the wide carcase sides and door panels that are the skin of a typical cabinet. Yet, when you glue up a tabletop, there is much less at stake because the way the top interacts with the base of the table is fairly simple when compared to the complexity of a cabinet's side and its interior parts.

So building a couple small tables with traditional joints will definitely improve your casework skills – no matter what your abilities are at the moment. To prove it, we set out to build two different versions of the Gustav Stickley 603 tabouret – one using power tools and the other using hand tools. The idea was to show you the choices available so you could pick and choose the techniques right for you.

By Hand and By Power
Things, however, did not turn out as planned. I have built dozens of little tables during the last decade for the magazine and for sale. And during the last 11 years I have tried every method imaginable to cut these joints. Plus, with the help of the other woodworkers in our shop, I've refined these methods so they're simple, accurate and don't require complex tooling.

So when faced with the prospect of cutting a joint with a technique I'd set aside years ago, I balked in a few cases and simply refused. Sometimes this meant turning my back on my table saw, and sometimes it meant dismissing my chisels. At almost every step, I found myself forced to justify the tools and processes I employ in the shop. And that struggle to balance speed, simplicity and enjoyment is the heart of the following article.

Stock Selection and Preparation
People ask me all the time to show them how to process rough lumber into boards suitable for fine furniture with hand tools only. I'm happy to show them, and I'm fairly quick about it. It takes longer to explain than it does to actually do when you have the right tools.

But preparing rough lumber for furniture is something I do in the shop only when the boards are too wide for our power equipment. It's not a difficult skill to master, but it requires stamina and physical strength to do well. So when faced with the prospect of preparing the lumber by hand or with a powered jointer and planer, it was no contest.

"I respect a man who knows how to spell a word more than one way."
— Mark Twain (1835 - 1910)
American author and humorist

Stretchers of the Same Length
The four stretchers in the table might not be the most visible parts in the finished product, but they do some critical tasks. They join the legs and top together. And they decide if the base is square or out of kilter. So your first concern should be that each stretcher is the same thickness and width as its mate, and that the distance between the shoulders of all the pieces is the same: 11¾".

Note that I didn't say that your stretchers all had to be the same length. They can be, but they don't have to be. For the table with power-tool joints, I crosscut the stretchers to a consistent length with a table saw equipped with a crosscut fence and a stop. Then I marked the shoulders of all the tenons and dovetail joints with a marking gauge pushed along the end grain of the parts.

For the other table, I left the boards at their rough-cut length. Then I grouped all the stretchers together and marked out the shoulders in one fell stroke using a knife and a square. I found the location of the shoulder by measuring out from the center of the stretchers. After I cut the joinery, I trimmed up any ends that were a little long. The ends are buried in the legs, so their exact lengths are insignificant. Just make them sturdy and to fit.

Both layout approaches are valid ways to work in a modern shop. There are times when you cannot get a really long board on your table saw for an accurate crosscut, so marking out your joinery from a centerline will allow you to skip that machine process.

First Crisis: Cutting Mortises
For the power-tool table, I cut the mortises with a hollow-chisel mortiser using a ¼" mortising chisel. The mortises are about 1⅛" deep to house the 1"-long tenons on your stretchers.

Traditional joint design here would dictate a tenon that's ¼" thick and 1¼" long (tenon length is typically five times the tenon thickness). But a 1¼"-long tenon is risky in a 1½"-square leg. You need to make the mortise a little deeper than necessary to accommodate glue and inevitable junk at the bottom of the mortise, and so there is a real risk of boring all the way through the leg when making the mortise.

So a 1"-long tenon allows you to reduce the risk and maintain most of the strength. Sometimes you have to bend the rules.

After rule-bending and mortise-boring, I picked up my mortising chisel and mallet to cut the mortises by hand for the other table. Now, I'm fairly good at mortising by hand and don't think it's any big deal. But with the mortising machine just sitting there – set up and ready to go as it always is – I put down the chisel.

Most of my hand mortising occurs when the mortiser won't handle the task, such as angled or compound joints, or when the mortises are in a difficult spot, such as the middle of a case side or

Group your legs together as they will end up in the table (note the diagonal end grain, which ensures the legs will show the same face grain on all four faces) and mark a cabinetmaker's triangle. This triangle ensures your parts will stay in the same orientation throughout construction.

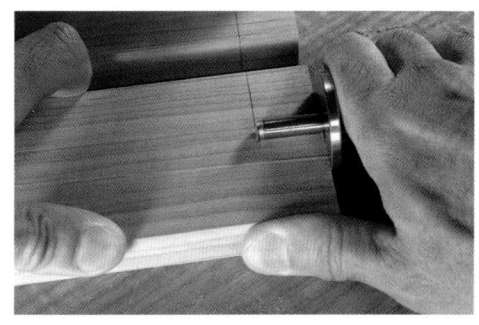

When your stretchers are all the same length, you can mark the shoulders for the joinery from the end grain as shown. This trick works best when you have the precision and repeatability of a machine.

A hollow-chisel mortiser is an essential machine in a shop that constructs traditional (or bulletproof) furniture. There are many methods for making mortises, but none is as simple or effective as a machine dedicated to this all-important joint.

A tenon cheek is a second-class saw cut (see "How to Saw" for details). Note that I'm advancing my cut on the end grain and the edge grain simultaneously. This helps keep the cut straight. When my kerf touches my shoulder line, I'll turn the tenon around and saw the other edge on the diagonal.

in a very thick part. But when it comes to straightforward mortising, I choose the machine.

Tenons Two Ways

When it comes to cutting tenons, however, I don't have a dedicated setup on my table saw, so I'll switch freely between hand and power methods. Setting the table saw to cut four tenons is as time-consuming as cutting four tenons by hand.

To cut the tenons by hand, mark out the face cheeks, edge cheeks and shoulders. Saw the cheeks with a tenon saw that is filed for rip cuts then saw the shoulders with a carcase saw that is filed crosscut. This technique is covered in detail in the "How to Saw" article on page 14.

When you cut tenons with power equipment, you have myriad choices. I use a dado stack in my table saw. Here's why I avoid other common methods: I've found that routers don't have the guts to make these cuts in one pass; you're removing ¼" of waste on each cheek and that's a big bite. So you end up making a few passes to make each tenon, and that's a lot of work for the small prize of a perfectly smooth tenon cheek.

I also shy away from tenon jigs on a table saw. They are faster than a router table, but they require a shop-made or commercial jig and they also require two tooling setups for each cheek and shoulder: One setup for the cheek and one for the shoulder. Plus, it can be unwieldy to balance long pieces of work upright on your saw's table.

A dado stack has the advantage of being able to make the cut in one pass (assuming your table saw isn't one of those with a motor that should be measured in "puppy power" instead of horsepower). Plus, there is only one tooling setup for cutting a cheek and shoulder. No special jigs are required. And you can work with your parts flat on your saw's table.

Cut the cheeks and shoulders of the lower stretchers. Then, using the same setting on your fence, cut a ¼"-deep (⅜"-deep if by hand) notch on the underside of your upper stretchers. This notch relieves the underside of the upper stretcher a bit and makes the dovetail easier to cut and fit.

Accurate Half-laps

Making good half-lap joints is a challenge. Years ago I made a series of sitting benches that were based on the work of Nicolai Fechin, and each bench had about 40 half-laps. So I became pretty good at fitting this joint. Here's how.

Begin with components that are the same size. And I mean exactly the same size, especially in thickness. The best way to do this is to handplane the pieces simultaneously on their thicknesses and on their widths. In fact, it's best to do everything you can to get your components nearly ready to finish at this stage. It's a common error to cut

A dado stack is ideal for cutting tenons. Work with your piece against a stop and all your tenons will come out the same length.

Stickley Tabouret

	NO.	PART	T	SIZES (INCHES) W	L	MATERIAL	NOTES
❏	1	Top	1	18 dia.		Cherry	
❏	4	Legs	1½	1½	19	Cherry	
❏	2	Upper stretchers	¾	1½	13¾	Cherry	1"-long dovetail, both ends
❏	2	Lower stretchers	¾	2⅞	13¾	Cherry	1"-long tenon, both ends
❏	4	Pegs	⅜ dia.		2	Oak	Oversized, trim to fit

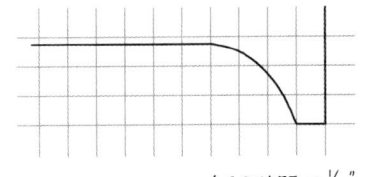

Corbel Stretcher Profile
1 SQUARE = ½"

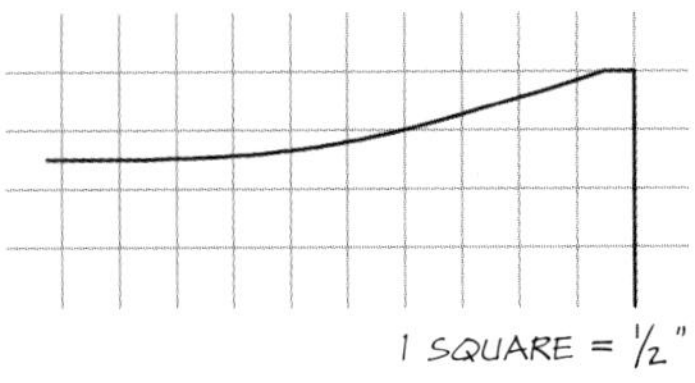

Trumpet Stretcher Profile
1 SQUARE = ½"

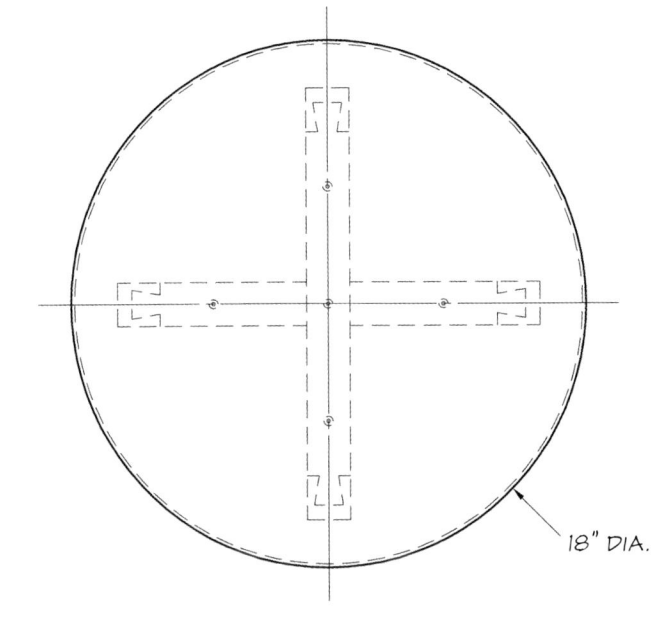

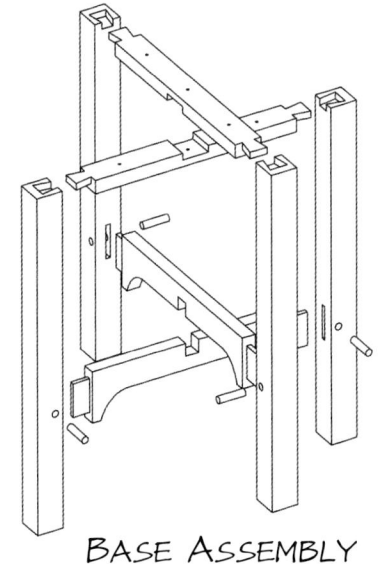

Base Assembly

Top View
18" DIA.

Corbel Stretcher
(2 REQ'D, ONE AS SHOWN AND ONE WITH NOTCH ON TOP)

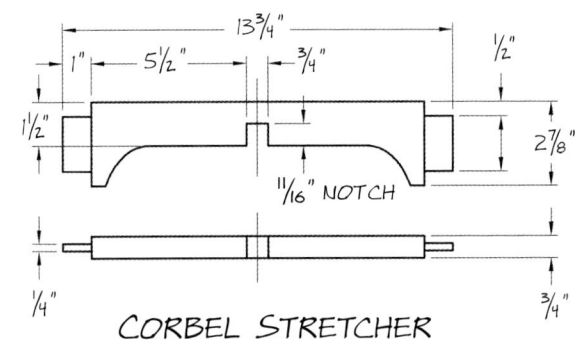

13¾" · 1" · 5½" · ¾" · ½" · 1½" · 2⅞" · ¹¹⁄₁₆" NOTCH · ¼" · ¾"

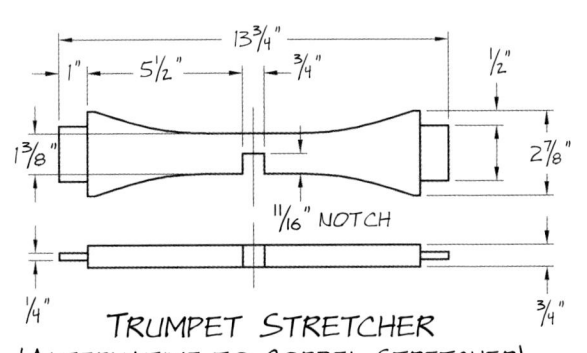

Trumpet Stretcher
(ALTERNATIVE TO CORBEL STRETCHER)
(2 REQ'D, ONE AS SHOWN AND ONE WITH NOTCH ON TOP)

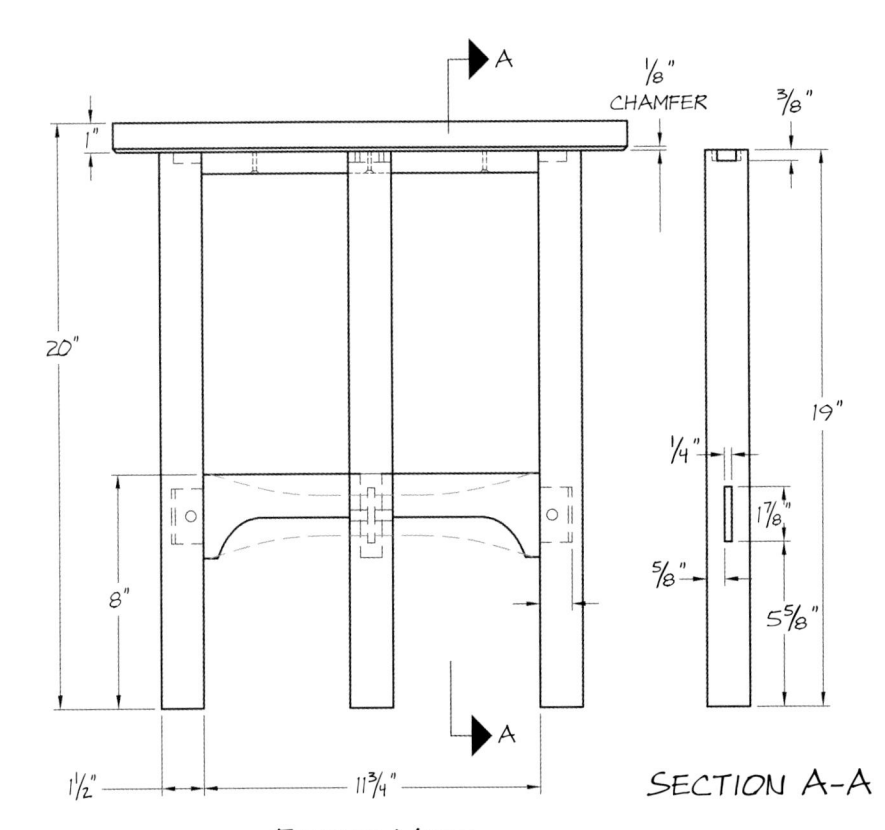

13¾" · 1" · 5½" · ¾" · ½" · 1⅜" · 2⅞" · ¹¹⁄₁₆" NOTCH · ¼" · ¾"

Front View
20" · 8" · 1½" · 11¾" · 1" · ⅛" CHAMFER · ⅜"

Section A-A
19" · ¼" · 1⅞" · ⅝" · 5⅝"

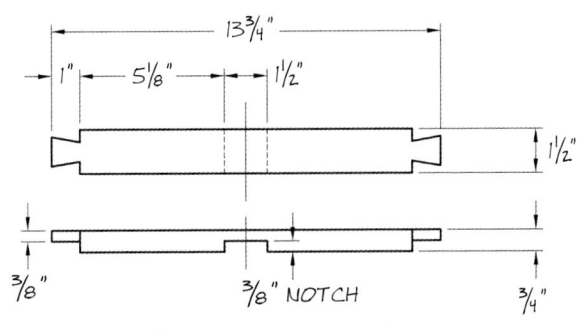

Top Stretcher
(2 REQ'D, ONE AS SHOWN AND ONE WITH NOTCH ON TOP)

13¾" · 1" · 5⅛" · 1½" · 1½" · ⅜" · ⅜" NOTCH · ¾"

ILLUSTRATIONS BY LOUIS BOIS

woodworking-magazine.com ■ 9

Whenever I need parts to be the same size, I "gang plane" them against a planing stop, as shown here. This is a quick way to ensure that the parts are identical in thickness and width. Remember: What's important is they be identical, not some arbitrary number.

Here I'm using the mating piece to mark the shoulder of the joint. Eliminating measuring during operations like this improves your accuracy.

In high-tolerance work I will take the chisel and pop out a wedge-shaped piece of waste to create a V-shaped trench for my handsaw. It works brilliantly.

A router plane can smooth the floor of the joint and prepare it to be fit to its mate. Remember: Router planes don't take a big bite. Small bites will reduce tearing. Also, work from your edges and into the center to reduce tearing.

To get an accurate shoulder, I deepen the knife lines with a light tap on my chisel. Note the bevel of the chisel faces away from my waste. This will drive the chisel back into the waste area a bit, which is what you want.

Any fine crosscut backsaw is good for sawing the shoulders. Here I'm using one of my older Japanese dozukis. If this table were made using oak, I'd use a Western saw with more robust teeth.

the joint and then plane or sand the components, making the joint loose and sloppy.

To lay out the joint, first mark one shoulder with a combination square and knife. Then lay the mating piece up against your combination square and mark the other shoulder of the joint by using this mating part as a ruler. Carry those shoulder lines down the edges and mark the floor of the half-lap, which is half the thickness of the work.

With the joint laid out, you can then decide if you want to cut it with hand tools or power tools. For the power tool-route, I chose a band saw and removed all the waste down to the floor of the joint. Then I cleaned up a little waste with a chisel.

Unless I'm cutting 40 half-laps, I'll use a band saw because it's quicker than a dado stack and doesn't require wasting any test pieces. If you have a lot to do, definitely fire up the table saw.

The hand-tool route is also good for doing just a couple joints. For the hand-tool table, I sawed out the shoulders, removed the waste with a chisel, then cleaned up the floor of the joint with a router plane.

With one side of the joint prepared you can try to press its mate into the lap. First trim up the shoulders if they are uneven. But if the shoulders are straight and nice, your better bet is to reduce the width of the mating piece with a handplane. It's easier to plane face grain than end grain.

Then press the mating piece into the lap joint. Knock it home. Then use a knife to trace the shape of the mating joint on the workpiece. Take the

If I have to choose between working end grain or face grain to fit a joint, I always try to choose the face-grain route. End grain is difficult to trim accurately.

With the two pieces pressed together, scribe the intersection of one onto the other. Take the stretchers apart and cut the second half of the joint the same way you did the first.

Mark the waste with little Xs (yes, I do this for every joint), then saw the cheek of your dovetail's notch like you would saw out a tenon cheek.

Here I'm sawing out the edges and shoulders of a dovetail joint on my band saw. On a well-tuned machine, this is a pleasure to do with excellent results. If your blade is dull (as ours is), the cut will be rough.

When marking any joint with a knife, resist the temptation to use a lot of downward pressure. You are better off using light strokes and making several passes. The knife is much less likely to wander away.

This bevel-edge chisel will clean out most of the waste, but there will still be a little left that you can tease out with a skew chisel or by simply turning your bevel-edge chisel on its side.

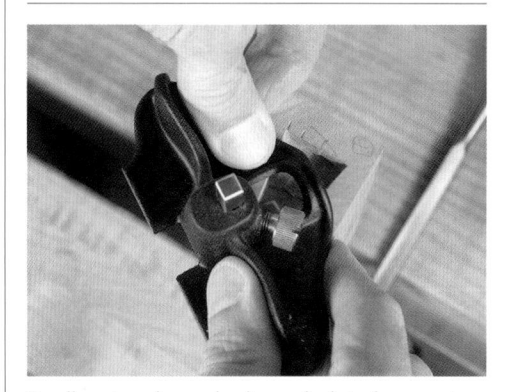

Small router planes don't need a lot of support to do their job really well. The thumb of my left hand is pressing the tool down. The fingers of my right hand are swinging the tool forward to remove waste.

stretchers apart and cut the other half-lap in the same fashion as you did the first part of the joint. Fit the two pieces until they are flush and tight.

Easy Dovetails In a Weekend (Really!)

The upper stretchers join the legs in a lapped dovetail joint that will be obscured by the tabletop in the completed project. The thickness of the dovetail is not the entire thickness of the stretcher – this makes the joint easier to fit into the leg (and it reduces the amount of brutal chopping).

You can cut the dovetail by hand or with a band saw – I find that a dovetail saw leaves behind a smoothr surface than my band saw (your tools may be different), and so the handsawn dovetails are easier for me to fit.

Mark out your dovetails on all your stretchers. The tails are 1" wide at the top and are the same length as the tenons (1"). The slope of the dovetail isn't critical as long as it's not too severe. Saw out the edges of the dovetail.

If you are doing this by hand, you'll need to notch out the underside of the dovetail (power-tool users already cut their notch on the dado stack while making the tenons on the stretchers). To make things simple, I cut the notch so it's half the thickness of the work.

The Dovetail Socket: More Failure

With all your dovetails cut, you need to hog out the waste in the top of the leg to make the mating socket. And here again is where I could not do one table by hand and one with power tools.

Cutting one of these sockets is such easy work by hand: Saw out the edges, chisel out the waste and clean up the floor with a router plane. (Note: The router plane is the secret weapon. It ensures the floor is the same depth on all four legs.) Doing this operation with power tools is inefficient.

When I've done these with a trim router, the usual method is to make a quick platform around the top of the leg to support the trim router. (The quickest and dirtiest way to do this is to clamp the leg in your vise with the top of the leg flush to the top of your benchtop.) Then you mark out the joint and freehand the cut, getting as close as to your lines as you dare. Oh – and be sure to make a couple passes or your trimmer will flame out or your bit will snap.

woodworking-magazine.com ■ 11

A card scraper worked quite well on the shallow curve of the trumpet-shaped stretchers. Use a thick scraper and try not to bow it as you work. This will keep your edges at 90° to the face. Bowing the scraper will hollow out the middle of your stretcher sandwich.

If you make the corbel-shaped stretchers, the long flat section can be trued up with a long rasp, as shown here.

An oscillating spindle sander is ideal for the curved section of the corbel shape, but not so good for the flat section. Use whatever combination of tools you have.

For the half-laps made by hand, I cut the shoulders with a carcase saw and chiseled out the waste. For the power-tool version, I did all the cutting and trimming with my band saw.

Once you put glue on everything, it's going to tighten up the way the joints fit. First get a clamp on those two half-laps. Then worry about the dovetails. I like to drive my dovetails into their sockets with a little scrap of wood.

Then you come back with a chisel and clean out the rounded corners. This entire process is difficult to do quickly. The visibility stinks while routing. And the clean-up work can be significant if you become a bit chicken while routing.

In the same time it takes to cut one joint with a trim router, I'll have most of the joints done by hand. So let's take a close look at that process.

Place your dovetail on top of its mating leg and scribe around it with your knife. I put the unbeveled part of the knife flat against the dovetail (as shown). Other woodworkers I respect turn the knife around and rub the knife's bevel against the dovetail. Try both approaches; both work.

Mark your waste and chisel a notch for your saw to run in (this is a second-class saw cut – see "Learn to Saw"). Define the socket without crossing your layout lines. If you do, it's not the end of the world. Then make a couple extra saw cuts in the waste to make it easy to pop it out.

Then put the leg down on your bench. Brace the foot of the leg against a bench dog and clamp the leg down with a holdfast. Chisel out the waste. Drive down until the chisel stops cutting. Then use the tool to pop out the waste by chiseling into the end grain of the leg.

Chisel out all four sockets. Then use a small router plane to clean up the floor of the dovetail socket. Use a chisel to get any waste in the corners and fit your dovetails in your sockets. Now fetch your lower stretchers and prepare to shape them and cut their half-laps.

A Nice Shape; Another Half-lap

You might have noticed that these two tables have lower stretchers with different shapes. Both the trumpet and corbel shape are historically correct and are taken from Gustav Stickley's drawings. The staff (and my family) was split on which one looked better, so we decided to present both.

I made several extra stretchers to get the shape just right, and I made the shapes with both hand and power tools. For fun, I cut one of the stretchers with a bow saw. It certainly worked, but the band saw is easier (if easy is your thing).

You can refine these shapes using a variety of methods. Rasps, scrapers and sandpaper were a good combination. As was simply firing up the oscillating spindle sander. The real trick, no matter how you do it, is to keep the stretchers adhered together with double-stick tape as you shape them. This makes their appearance consistent.

Now clean up the stretchers as best you can and try to get them to the same thickness. It's time to cut the half-lap that joins the lower stretchers. Make this joint the same way you made the half-lap for the upper stretchers. Make one notch, then use that notch to mark out its mate.

Assemble the Base

There are a couple ways to assemble the base, some of which will turn your table base into an M.C. Escher piece of sculpture. To avoid confusion, assemble the legs first to the lower stretchers alone. Make two separate assemblies.

Then peg the tenons if you like. I used $3/8$"-diameter pegs and drilled the hole $7/16$" from the edge of the legs. Then I drove the peg into the hole with a little glue. Always make a couple sample joints before you work on the real stuff. Your drill bits and dowels might not match in diameter. And the run-out on your drill (or your brace and bit) might make the fit even sloppier. Sometimes you need to use a drill bit that is $1/64$" smaller or you need to find some beefier dowels.

With the two leg assemblies complete, glue the two assemblies together at the lower stretcher and drive in the upper stretchers. Add a couple small clamps on the half-laps, check your angles with a square and walk away.

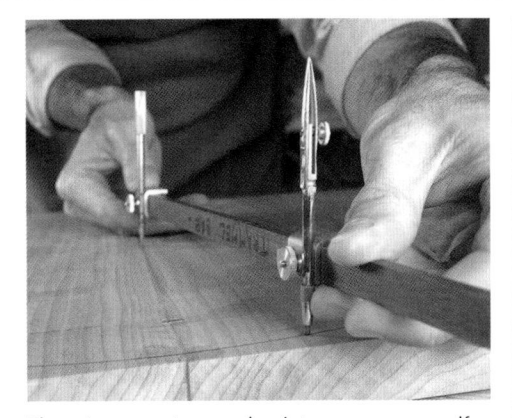

These Japanese trammel points were my grandfather's, and I look for any excuse to trot them out, such as a magazine article. Any trammel points will do. Or you can bore a couple tiny holes in a yardstick. Put a nail in one hole and a pencil in the other.

To make the workholding easy, I clamped a block on my bench and affixed the top to that block with some double-stick tape. Note that the face side of the tabletop is getting taped down to the block.

Around the Top

The top is a simple 18"-diameter disc with a small $1/8$" x $1/8$" chamfer on its underside. When gluing up these panels, I made one with edge joints using our power jointer. The other top was made with spring joints made with my jointer plane. Spring joints are edge joints that are a tiny bit hollow in the middle so the top is clamped in tension.

Both techniques worked equally well for me. How will the tops fare in the long haul? Call me in 20 years and I'll let you know.

After cleaning up both panels, I marked out the circle with a pair of trammel points. Note that I did this from the underside of the top so that the hole from the trammel point was hidden.

I cut both tops to rough size on my band saw. There was little point in dulling the blade on my nice bow saw for this rough operation. Then I came to another fork in the road when deciding how to make the top perfectly round.

Making something round by hand is a challenge. I've made a couple tabourets with round tops by hand and spent a long time fairing the top so it looked round instead of blobby and Schmoo-ish. So when Senior Editor Robert W. Lang showed me his router compass, I decided to use that for both tops. The jig is featured in this issue on page 24 and works quite well.

I screwed the arm of the compass to the underside of the top and routed off the ragged waste left by the band saw. This can be a tough cut and your grain might blow out where it changes direction around the edge. My best advice is to take light cuts. I had great luck sneaking up on my final diameter with two light passes.

After routing the top to shape, I routed a small chamfer on the underside. This isn't a historically correct detail. But I like chamfers and these tables look better when the tops look a little lighter.

Then it was time to clean up the edge to make it presentable. I've done this part with power tools (including an ill-fated circle-sanding jig on our disc sander), but I think there's more chance to botch the edge with a power sander. So I turn to scrapers and a little hand-sanding.

The last step is to prepare the top for finishing. Grasping round work can be a trick. Even if you have a fancy dog-hole setup you risk marring the edges of your top. So I converted the offcuts from band sawing my top into clamping cauls that I fit over my bench dogs. This works brilliantly for sanding or for handplaning.

Attaching the Top; Applying a Finish

The top is attached with screws that pass through clearance holes in the upper stretchers. Be sure to ream out the screw holes in the stretchers that extend across the width of the top. This reaming allows the top to expand and contract.

The finish is simple. I ragged on a coat of boiled linseed oil and allowed the tables to sit in the sun for a day. This oil and tan accelerated the aging process in the cherry. After the oil had cured completely I sprayed on two coats of lacquer, though any film finish will do.

Though the experiment to build one table by hand and one by power was a bit of a failure, the resulting tables looked nice, and there was still a lesson buried in there for me about the importance of following your gut. It's captured by a quote from chairmaker John Brown (a quote we published in our first issue in 2004):

"By all means read what the experts have to say," he wrote. "Just don't let it get in the way of your woodworking."

That's good advice – both for the readers and the editors of woodworking magazines. **WM**

— *Christopher Schwarz*

Rout the circumference with a spiral bit in your plunge router. Try to keep your motions fluid and quick to create a smooth and burn-free cut. Then get out your rasps and scrapers.

These cauls take a minute to make. Fetch your waste from shaping the top and run it through your thickness planer a couple times. Then bore a hole in each caul to fit it over your bench dogs.

How to Saw

Practice won't help if you are practicing a poor method. Here are 10 rules and 3 tricks to improve your sawing.

Let's begin at the end: dovetails.

If you don't cut dovetails by hand, chances are that you aspire to. That's because to the modern woodworker, dovetails are like teeth. A couple rows of tight and tidy dovetails make a good first impression – just like a mouth full of pearly whites. (Similarly, furniture mouldings are like our lips. We use these to hide our snaggle-tooth dovetails and orthodonture.)

And so for many woodworkers, their first handsaw purchase is a dovetail saw. Then they read every magazine article ever written on all the different methods of making the joint. (Well, they attempt to read every article. It's actually impossible to do this in just one lifetime.) And perhaps they take a class in cutting the joint by hand at a local woodworking store.

Despite all this effort, their dovetails still look like a mouthful of gappy teeth from a dental hygienist's darkest nightmare. Why is this joint so difficult? Here's my theory: I think most woodworkers go about learning dovetails all wrong.

I'm not talking about cutting pins-first or tails-first, I'm talking about tenons-first. Or how about cutting straight lines first? Then maybe cutting some slanted lines? Cutting dovetails, you see, is all about learning to saw. If you saw correctly, the chiseling part is easy.

The problem is that most woodworkers don't know how to saw. We make sawing harder than it has to be. We hold the saw incorrectly. We work too aggressively. We stand in the wrong place. And we don't know (or don't use) the tricks to make straight and clean handsaw cuts.

Once you master these details, you'll be on your way to cutting dovetails. But you also will have achieved something far more important: freedom. Being able to cut to any line – angled, compound, you name it – is the most liberating experience I know of in the craft. Suddenly, you can escape the tyranny of 90° – the always-right angle encouraged by our machines. Chairs, with their compound angles, won't seem so daunting. Plus, you'll build fewer jigs for your machines.

Sawing intimidates many woodworkers because one mis-cut can ruin the workpiece. But if you know how to stand and know how to start the cut, your accuracy will quickly improve.

10 Rules of Sawing

There's a lot to learn about sawing, from the tools themselves to the techniques for using them. I think the place to begin is to understand how to wield the saw in any cut, whether you are making joints or just breaking down rough stock to get it in your car in the Home Depot parking lot. Here are the 10 principles I've compiled from books, other woodworkers and my own experience.

1. Use a relaxed grip on the tote of the saw. Clenching the handle will push you off your line.

On a Western saw it's always best to extend your index finger out along the tote. Saws are designed for a three-fingered grip.

On Japanese saws, the advice is mixed. Some people saw with their index finger out. Others extend the thumb.

This is what a good sawing stance looks like. All the parts of my body are lined up so my sawing arm swings freely. The rest of my body is positioned in such a way that it encourages me to saw straight. Note how my toe touches the bench.

One of the most common mistakes beginning sawyers will make is they will keep their elbow tucked against their torso when sawing.

Constant vigilance is required here. As you saw, if you feel your elbow touching your torso, you're doing it wrong. Stop and adjust.

If you can see the line you can cut the line. So never let the sawblade obscure your line. Sometimes this involves moving the saw (or planning how to hold your work). Sometimes it involves moving your head without violating the rules on proper body stance.

Someone once told me that when you hold your saw you should pretend you are holding a baby bird and that you are trying to keep it in your hand without crushing it. You want to hold your tool with just enough force to keep it from flopping around and getting away from you. And this is something that you will be reminding yourself of for the rest of your life. It's easy to forget.

2. Extend your index finger out on the tote. A good Western saw handle is designed for a three-finger grip. Mashing your four fingers into the tote will make sawing difficult and your hand sore. Extending your index finger is good to do with any user-guided tool because it is a reminder to your body to perform that operation in a straight line. Try extending your index finger on your cordless drill, your jigsaw, your handplane.

That said, this rule is somewhat troubling when it comes to Japanese pullsaws. I've seen grip recommendations that violate this rule from people who get tremendous results. In fact, I grip my dozukis with my thumb extended out along the straight handle of the saw. I suspect that extending my thumb has the same effect as extending an index finger. In fact, early writings on hammers – which have a straight handle similar to that of a dozuki – offer the same advice about extending the thumb for precision nailing. (Yes, there is such a thing.)

3. Always work so your sawing elbow swings free like a steam locomotive. Now we're getting into body position – a critical point. Don't ever work with your arm rubbing your body. And don't move your arm at an angle that's not in line with the back of the saw – your arm and the saw should all be one straight line. This involves positioning your body so all your parts line up with your cut and all your moving parts swing free.

4. Use proper footwork. This rule works in conjunction with the rule above. If you position your feet correctly, chances are your sawing arm will also end up in the right place. Here's the drill: If you are right-handed, stand so your left foot is forward and your right foot is behind you. (Reverse this if you are left-handed.) Your feet should be almost perpendicular to one another, as shown in the photograph above. I like to place my left toe up against the leg of my workbench because I can then feel how my workbench is behaving when sawing. If my workbench is unstable, then I'll feel it in my left foot.

5. Whenever possible, work so you can see your line. First, position your work so that the line is visible throughout your entire cut. If you are right-handed, this means you should try to have the sawblade cut on the right side of the line whenever possible. (Again, reverse this if you're sinister.) If you cannot position your saw this way, you need to move your head and peer over the sawblade so you can see the line. Never

Here, I'm cutting a tenon cheek. I begin with a diagonal cut, then tip the saw to extend the kerf down the edge of the board (left). Then I use that kerf to guide the sawplate to extend the kerf along the end grain (right). Note that I'm peering over the saw's back to watch my lines.

let the blade of the saw obscure your line. If you cannot see the line, you cannot follow it.

6. Use minimal downward pressure when sawing. Western backsaws have a heavy back for two reasons: One, to stiffen the blade. Two, to give the saw some weight to carry it down into the cut. A sharp and well-tuned saw should require almost no downward pressure during the cut. When teaching the act of sawing, I tell students that their job is to move the saw forward and back. Gravity takes it down into the cut.

Using excess downward pressure almost always will drive you off your line. It is impossible (for me, at least) to force the saw through the cut with accuracy. Don't worry about the speed of your cut if it seems slow. As your skills pick up your strokes will be faster. Plus, remember this: It takes a lot to effort to correct a cut that has gone awry. So rushing a cut will only slow your overall progress.

This cut leaves behind too much waste. People are timid about sawing, so they saw far away from the line and leave some waste to pare away with a chisel or plane. Be bold (it's easier, too). Saw right up on the line or split the line.

7. Always imagine the saw is longer than it really is. I picked up this mental trick from a book a long time ago, and it has served me well. This bit of self-deception will fool you into using longer strokes, which will allow you to saw faster and wear your saw's teeth evenly. Most beginners use about half of the teeth in their saw, mostly the teeth in the middle. You should aim to use 80 to 90 percent of your teeth.

8. Whenever possible, advance your cut on two lines. This trick always increases your accuracy when sawing. There are lots of ways to make this trick work to your advantage. For example, when cutting tenons, I like to start the cut diagonally on a corner. Then I extend the kerf a bit down the edge of the board. Then I use that accurate kerf to guide my sawplate as I extend the kerf along the end grain. I'll work back and forth this way, using the existing kerf to guide my saw.

9. Always work right against a line. This rule is true with all saws, whether they are powered by electricity or by Ding Dongs. Try to avoid sawing a certain distance away from a line. It's hard to saw a consistent distance away from a line. Sawing on a line is always easier. Sometimes you will want to leave the entire line intact and sometimes you will want to split the line, depending on the joint you are cutting. But what's important is that you are on the line at all times.

10. Lifting the saw a tad on the return stroke clears your line of sawdust. This isn't a rule as much as it is a tip for catching your breath. If you lift up your saw on the return stroke, less sawdust will sprinkle onto your cut line and obscure it. As a result, you don't have to huff and puff your line clear with every stroke (there will always be some huffing, however).

This also relates to the proper rhythm and sound that result from efficient sawing. You can always tell a veteran carpenter from a newbie by listening to them saw. New sawyers drag the tool back through the kerf, making an unpleasant sound. Plus, they use short strokes because they are using only the teeth in the middle of the sawblade. The old pros make most of their noise on the cutting stroke only. Plus, their strokes are longer. And, as a bonus, they're not out of breath from puffing the line as well.

How to Start a Sawcut

While those 10 rules above will help you make a sawcut, they don't help much with the hardest part of sawing: Starting a kerf with your saw. In sawing (as with most things in hand tools) how you begin the cut is critical to how well the rest of the cut proceeds.

If you start correctly, you are much more likely to hit your line all the way down. If you start poorly, you'll spend your first few strokes trying to correct your cut, making your kerf unacceptably wide and fighting the saw the entire way.

There is a good deal of advice on how to begin a cut, some of it conflicting. One old chestnut is to begin a kerf with a few strokes of the saw that are in reverse of the tool's normal cutting action. That is, if you have a Western saw that cuts on the

Here, I'm about to break down some rough stock with a full-size 26"-long handsaw. Unlike when you use a backsaw, it's good practice to begin this cut with a few strokes of the saw that are the reverse of the tool's normal cutting action. The small notch shown in the photo is a boon to starting a cut with a large handsaw.

The thumb positions the work. Nudge the saw to the right by pinching your finger and thumb, which swells them both a bit. Move the saw to the left by relaxing your fingertips a bit and scooting the sawplate against your thumb.

push stroke, you should begin your kerf by making a few strokes on the pull stroke. These strokes make a little notch for the saw to ride in.

This is how I was taught to use a full-size handsaw on sawhorses as a boy. The advice shows up frequently in old texts on carpentry, and I think it's good technique when working with the big 26"-long handsaws or rip saws.

However, the older texts are mostly silent on beginning a joinery cut with a backsaw, such as a dovetail, carcase or tenon saw. So many modern woodworkers have assumed that the same rules for carpentry apply to making furniture cuts.

I'm not so sure they do.

For many years I used this trick with my backsaws, and many times it didn't seem to help much. Yes, it made a notch for the saw to begin in, but the notch wasn't the shape I wanted. This trick made a sizable V-shaped cut, with part of the V chipping across my line and into the part of the work I wanted to keep.

After I abandoned this trick when using my backsaws, my results were more consistent. So here's how I start a backsaw cut when I'm cutting to a pencil line.

After I draw the line, I place the sawblade on a corner of the work so I can see the line. With my off-hand (which is my left), I pinch the edge next to my cut line and use my thumb to nudge the sawplate left or right until I am exactly where I want to begin.

(A quick aside: Determining exactly where to begin requires you to instinctively know how wide your saw's kerf is. Once you have a gut feeling for that, you will place the tool right where you want it. This is also a good reason not to work with six different dovetail saws with six different-size kerfs – you'll never master them all.)

Now check the position of your sawplate in the reflection of your sawblade (assuming you have a shiny saw). If you are sawing a line that is square and plumb, then the reflection of your board should line up perfectly with the actual board. This trick works no matter where your head or eyeballs are located.

Correct a Wandering Cut

How do you get back on your line when you stray? There are two techniques that I employ. If the correction is needed early in the kerf, I'll twist my wrist for two strokes (and no more) to English the tool back on line.

Most people botch this technique because they twist their wrist for too many strokes so the saw wanders across the line in the other direction. Then they twist their wrist to correct that mistake and they wander back over the line again. After a couple cycles of that foolishness, the kerf looks like it just failed a drunk-driving test. If the error is particularly bad, the sawplate can jam in the wobbly kerf.

Remember: Just like working with a band saw, handsaws have a bit of delay when steering them. So make a couple strokes with your wrist twisted, then relax to your normal sawing position. Make a couple more strokes and see if you are moving back on line.

If the error occurs deep in the cut and I've done a good job up to that point, I'll use a different trick: I'll "lay down" the saw. When I do this, I lower the angle of the sawblade to about 20° to so I can put as much of the blade into the good kerf as possible. Then I take a few strokes. The good kerf guides the tool back on line. — CS

Here I'm laying down the saw into its previously cut kerf to correct a saw cut that is starting to drift across my line. Make a few strokes with the saw in this position and then return to your normal sawing position.

Trust your eyes here. We have an innate ability to sense plumb and square, which is perhaps why we like our houses and furniture made that way (instead of something out of a surrealist painting). If it looks square, it probably is.

This is a good argument for keeping your saws shiny and free of rust – the reflective qualities of the sawplate are an important feature. Also, a shiny saw tends to move more smoothly during a cut, and a rust-free saw will be easier to resharpen – you'll never lose a tooth to a bit of pitting on your sawblade. That's why I wipe down my saws with an oily rag after every use.

Now check your body position and ensure your sawing arm will swing free. Push the saw forward with your fingertips still on the board and against the sawplate (you won't get cut, I promise). After two strokes or so like this, you should begin angling the saw to start laying a kerf all along one of your layout lines. Now let all the other rules above kick into full gear as you make your cut.

You can judge if your saw is plumb and square by looking at the work's mirror image in your sawplate. Here you can see a cut that is slightly off square (left) and one that is slightly off plumb (right).

And here is the sawplate positioned correctly.

woodworking-magazine.com ■ 17

The Three Classes of Saw Cuts

The above advice and techniques are good for fairly accurate work, but not for high-precision sawing – such as cutting the shoulders of tenons. Most beginning sawyers ask too much of themselves and of their tools, sort of like expecting to be able to cut dovetails with a chainsaw.

There are lots of techniques to improve the accuracy and appearance of your saw cuts. But Robert Wearing's book "The Essential Woodworker" (now out of print and quite hard to come by) organizes all those tricks in an orderly fashion and shows you how to apply them to your work in a way that makes sense.

In his book, Wearing divides all saw cuts into three classes:

■ Third-class saw cuts, where speed is more important than either accuracy or the final appearance of the work. This is a rough cut designed for sizing stock before processing it further.

■ Second-class saw cuts, where accuracy is more important than speed or the final appearance of the work. This is for joinery cuts where the joint will not be visible in the end.

■ First-class saw cuts, where both accuracy and appearance are critical.

Each type of saw cut has a different set of procedures to prepare your work for sawing. Let's begin with third-class saw cuts for rough work. For me, the interesting thing about third-class sawcuts is that the technique for this lowly saw cut is a lot like what modern woodworkers use for all their sawing – so it's no wonder people love their table saws.

Third-class Saw Cut

The third-class saw cut is fast, rudimentary and useful when breaking down rough lumber into manageable pieces. I use it only when the board is going to be refined further by shooting the ends with a plane or crosscutting the board to a finished length with a powered saw or finer handsaw.

Begin by marking the cut line on the face and edge of your board with a sharp pencil. I like a carpenter's pencil that has a sharp chisel edge on its lead when working on rough stock, or a mechanical pencil when working on boards that have been surfaced.

Place the teeth of your saw on the waste side of your line and use your thumb to keep the saw positioned as you make your initial strokes to define your kerf. Advance on the face and edge

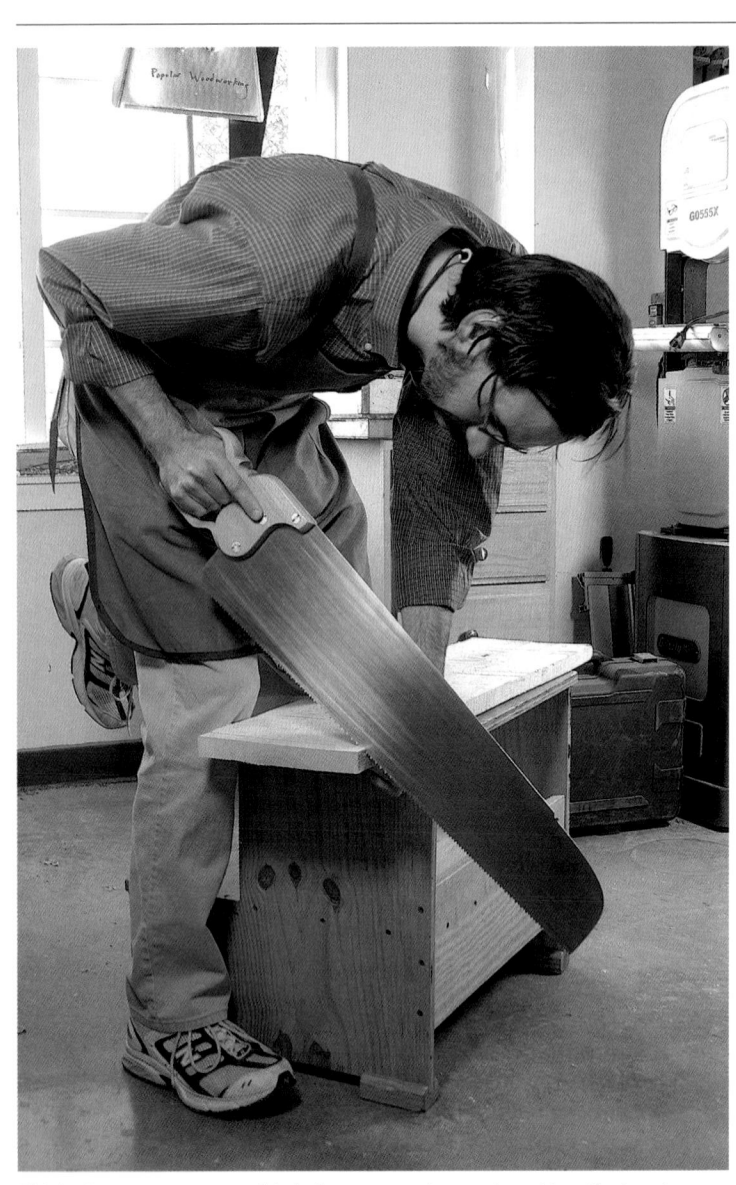

This is the most common third-class saw cut in my shop. Here I'm breaking down rough stock into manageable lengths to work (either by hand or by machine). If I stray from the line, it's OK because the stock will be refined further during construction.

Here, I'm making a second-class saw cut. You can see how a cutting gauge incises a line that has one flat face and one beveled face. Try to put the sloping part of the V on your waste side.

Here you can see the notch I've made with a chisel to begin my second-class cut. The flat side of the notch helps funnel the sawblade into the waste side of the work.

Tenon cheeks are an ideal place to employ a second-class saw cut. The cheeks must be sawn as closely to the line as possible without going over. If you saw too wide, you'll have a tenon cheek that requires a lot of work with a shoulder plane, chisel or rasp. If you saw over your line, you'll have made some pretty firewood.

of your board simultaneously to increase your accuracy. Saw rapidly through the board until you get near the end of your cut. Then use lighter and shorter strokes to cut the waste away cleanly.

This is the sort of cut I'll use with a full-size handsaw on my sawbench. Or when cutting wooden pins to rough length before pounding them into a drawbored joint.

Second-class Saw Cut

A second-class saw cut is used when accuracy is important, such as when sawing the cheeks of a tenon or a lapped dovetail joint inside a case piece. The results of your cut will be buried in the mortise or in the dovetail socket, so appearance isn't of primary importance. But if you wander too much in the cut, your joint won't fit its mate.

Begin a second-class saw cut by marking your cut line with a knife all around your work. You can use a marking knife and a try square; some woodworkers use the corner of a chisel to make this mark. When marking tenon cheeks I'll use a cutting gauge – essentially a marking gauge with a knife in place of a pin. One common commercial example is the Tite-Mark.

All of these types of marking devices make a line that is almost V-shaped. One edge drops directly down at 90°; the other comes in at an angle – the result of the bevel on the tool.

Now, you can get a little too fussy here, but I try to always put the sloped part of the V on the waste side of my line. This fine point is more important when it comes to first-class saw cuts, but it's a good thing to be thinking about as you make second-class ones as well.

Now, at the corner where you will begin your cut, place a chisel in your knife line with the bevel of the chisel facing the waste. Press the chisel into the work, remove the chisel and then come back and pare a triangle of waste that leads up to that corner.

Now place your saw in this notch and begin cutting. The notch ensures you begin the cut correctly. One of the nice things about this notch is that it actually is just like the little notch made with a full-size handsaw when you draw the tool backward for a couple strokes. The cutting begins at the bottom of the V. The difference here is that the V is shaped differently to guide your saw more accurately.

I use a second-class sawcut whenever I'm working on a joint that won't see the light of day. Nobody cares if the corners of your tenon are a bit ragged as long as the joint fits tightly.

First-class Saw Cut

First-class sawing is reserved for parts of the joint that will be visible on the finished piece, such as the shoulder cut on a tenon or half-lap joint. It requires a couple of extra steps, but the results are worth it.

First mark your cut line with a marking knife

The chisel here is deepening the line made by my marking knife for a first-class saw cut. You might be concerned about the chisel walking backward when you rap it, like what happens when chopping waste from a dovetail. However, the shape of my knife line and the shallow depth of the chisel cut keep your line in the same place.

on all surfaces that will be cut, just like you did for your second-class saw cut. Then take a wide chisel and place the tool's edge into your knife line with the bevel facing the waste. Rap the handle of the chisel to drive it into the knife line all around the joint. It only takes a couple raps. You don't want to drive too deeply.

Remove the chisel, then pare away a wedge-shaped piece of wood on the waste side, working up to your now-widened knife line. The second chisel cut must be deep enough so that the set of your saw's teeth falls below the surface of your workpiece.

Secure your work to the bench. Place your saw into the chiseled notch and make the cut. By using a chisel to define the kerf of your saw, you eliminate the common problem of the saw's teeth tearing up the surface of your work.

Here's why: You actually used your chisel to cut the part of the joint that will show; the chisel cut created the tenon shoulder. The saw cut began

"The highest reward for your work is not what you get for it, but what you become by it."

— John C. Maxwell (1947 -)
author

With a first-class saw cut you remove a wedge-shaped piece of waste all along your cut line. The chisel ends up making the critical part of the joint that shows.

below the surface thanks to the trench you chiseled out. That's how you get crisp shoulder lines with a handsaw – you use a chisel instead.

What About Dovetails?

So which class of cut is the dovetail? That's a tough question. The 18th-century woodworker would argue that the dovetail is probably a third- or second-class saw cut because the resulting joint would be covered in moulding. The goal (then, at least) was to remove material quickly with some accuracy.

But many modern woodworkers like to show off their dovetail joinery in a piece of handmade furniture. So the dovetail really encompasses more aspects of the first-class saw cut. Yet no one I know would ever chisel out the marked lines of a every pin and tail.

Instead, we work this joint more like it is a third-class saw cut. What allows us to do this is the dovetail saw, which was developed specifically for this joint. Its teeth are finer than other joinery saws. And the small scale of the saw allows us to get our eyeballs on our work to see what we are doing.

So while I still treat the dovetail like a third-class joint when marking it, I use a first-class tool. (And sometimes, when things get hairy, I'll even use some second-class notches to start a critical cut or two.)

So here we end where we started – still vexed about dovetails and how to cut them correctly and with skill. And while I cannot tell you everything about how to cut dovetails, I can tell you this: If you use the above techniques to saw and practice the three classes of saw cuts, then dovetails will suddenly become much easier.

Sometimes practice counts. **WM**

— *Christopher Schwarz*

Understanding Western Backsaws

The Western backsaw has almost vanished. But a few toolmakers are trying to turn back the clock to when this saw was in every toolbox.

The backsaws that built nearly every piece of antique English and American furniture almost became extinct, thanks to the universal motor and the Japanese obsession with quality.

A basic kit of at least three backsaws – a dovetail, carcase and tenon saw – were in the toolbox of every English-speaking cabinetmaker and joiner in the 18th, 19th and early 20th centuries. But after World War II, the manufacturing of these venerable saws went into steep decline with the rise of inexpensive portable routers and saws that were powered by the compact and cheap universal motor.

Handsaw giants such as Disston and Atkins faltered. Their enormous factories were shuttered, and the remnants of these companies began churning out low-quality saws with chunky handles and poorly formed teeth.

But it wasn't portable power tools that delivered the coup de grace to Western handsaws. That occurred at the hands of Japanese sawmakers. As Western saws became worse, the high-quality Japanese saw became more attractive to the woodworker who still needed a backsaw or two for joinery.

Thanks to Japan's thriving carpentry trade that still requires handwork (a result of their traditional timber-frame construction), outstanding manufacturing acumen and a general respect for traditional ways, Japanese saws were inexpensive and worked extremely well.

This was the opposite of the pricey and snaggle-toothed Western saw, which barely cut wood. And so the Japanese saw – which was once the laughingstock in the West as the tool that cut backward – became the best-selling style of saw in North America in less than a generation. And it is, by far, the dominant form today.

Western backsaws come in a dizzying array of sizes and tooth configurations. Add to that some confusing nomenclature (sash saw? carcase saw?) and it's no wonder people are confused. We help you choose the three backsaws you need for hand-cut joinery.

Two Guys Revive a Dead Patient

And if it weren't for two tool collectors, that might have been the final word: Either buy antique Western saws or new Japanese ones. But thanks to Pete Taran and Patrick Leach, the Western saw is today experiencing a revival. The two men had technical backgrounds in engineering and software, but that didn't stop them from becoming sawmakers in 1996. They founded Independence Tool and started making a maple-handled dovetail saw based on an early 19th-century example.

The saw, which was made with an incredible amount of handwork, became a cult classic among woodworkers on the Internet, and the saw began appearing in tool catalogs alongside the pages and pages of Japanese saws.

The Independence saw itself was a technical success. I've inspected and used pristine examples of these saws and I can personally attest that they were a revelation when compared to the chunky, lifeless and dull Western backsaws I used in my first woodworking class.

But the company was short-lived. Leach left Independence Tool and went on to become a full-time tool dealer (his site is supertool.com), and Taran announced in 1998 that he wasn't able to do his day job and still make saws at night. It looked like quality Western backsaws were about to disappear off the market again.

But then Taran sold Independence Tool to Lie-Nielsen Toolworks, which was cranking up its production of handplanes but wasn't yet making saws. (Taran isn't entirely out of the saw business. He now sells restored antique saws at vintagesaws.com as a side job.) Shortly after the sale, Lie-Nielsen began offering a dovetail saw – branded with both the Independence and Lie-Nielsen names – and then the company began selling other patterns of Western saws.

Recently, others makers have entered the Western saw market, including Adria Tools, Wenzloff & Sons, Gramercy Tools and a host of other small makers. And while these companies are making just a dent in the market share commanded by the Japanese sawmakers, it is now possible to purchase an entire kit of quality Western backsaws that work right out of the box. And that is a milestone.

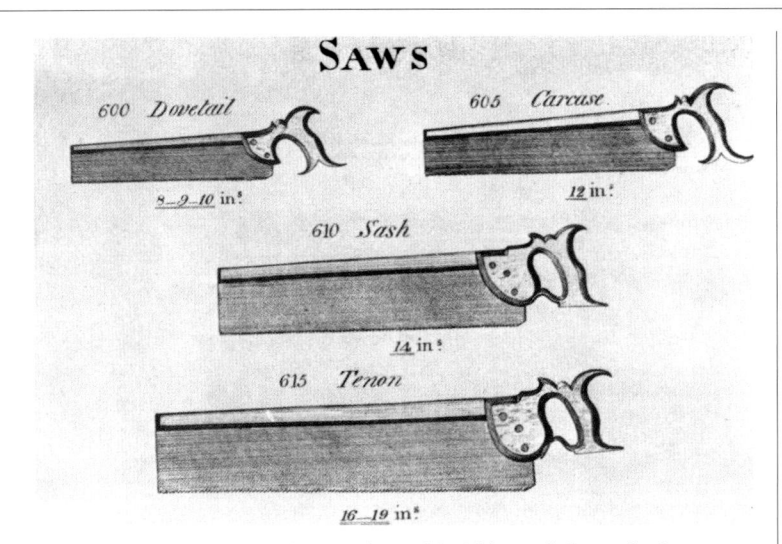

One of the earliest tool catalogs we have, "Smith's Key," shows the four types of backsaws available in 1816 from makers in Sheffield, England. Note how this tool catalog shows the blades as tapered – they are narrower at the toe than at the heel. There's a likely reason for that.

The saw on the bottom is a typical pistol-grip dovetail saw from sawmaker Mike Wenzloff of Wenzloff & Sons. Also shown (at top) is a straight-handled dovetail saw known as a gent's saw, so named (we're told) because it was used by gentlemen hobbyist woodworkers in the 19th century.

Why Use Western Handsaws?

If you do the math, mass-produced high-quality Japanese saws are a bargain. You can buy a Japanese dovetail saw for $35 that works just as well as a $125 Western-style dovetail saw. Plus, the consensus among many craftsmen and woodworking magazines is that the Japanese saws are easier to start and cut smoother.

So why would anyone (with the exception of a historical re-enactor or pigheaded purist) buy an expensive Western saw? The differences between the two tools are more extensive than the fact that one cuts on the pull stroke and the other cuts on the push. The sawplate on Japanese saws is thinner. Japanese teeth are more complex and longer. And sharpening Japanese teeth yourself can be difficult or impossible, depending on the saw.

As a result of these differences, Japanese saws are easier to kink and ruin, especially in unskilled hands. The teeth can break off in some hard Western-hemisphere woods – I've had particular problems in ring-porous species such as white oak. The expensive Japanese saws need to be sent to a specialist for resharpening (sometimes this specialist is in Japan). The inexpensive saws have impulse-hardened teeth, which makes them last a long time but also makes them impossible to refile. The teeth are as hard as a file, so a saw-sharpening file cannot abrade them. This makes the saws somewhat disposable – though you can cut up the sawplates, discard the super-hard teeth and make some thin scrapers with the steel.

In contrast to Japanese saws, Western saws have robust teeth. When I tally the tooth-decay problems I've had with saws, I've probably lost 20 teeth in Japanese saws but have yet to chip a tooth on a Western saw. You can resharpen Western teeth yourself, or get the job done domestically. Any Western saw can last for generations.

For some woodworkers, the above reasons are a compelling reason to use Western saws. If you are one of those, read on. If you still prefer Japanese saws and want to learn more about using them for joinery, I recommend you get your hands on the immensely readable "Japanese Tools: Their Tradition, Spirit and Use" (Linden) by Toshio Odate.

Four Western Backsaws

The backsaws shown in this article are particular to the English-speaking world for the most part. Traditional European woodworkers still use frame saws, where a thin sawblade is held in tension in a wooden frame, though other saw forms are available and used on the Continent.

Western backsaws are typically separated into four forms, and their details (blade length, number of teeth etc.) are usually traced back to Edward H. Knight's 1876 opus "American Mechanical Dictionary." But some modern woodworkers are confused about which of these four saws they need in their shop, so here is a discussion of each saw, its details and the operations that it excels at.

The Dovetail Saw

The most familiar saw to modern eyes, the dovetail saw is the smallest backsaw and has a blade that is 6" to 10" long. The blade's width is between 1½" and 2". It can have a pistol-grip or a straight handle. Most beginners seem to prefer the pistol grip because it whispers to your body when the

"If not for the sea, we'd have to carry our boats".

— Norwegian saying

blade is straight up and down. However, using a straight-handled "gent's saw" isn't difficult. It just takes a little more getting used to.

The teeth of a dovetail saw are quite fine, between 14 and 18 points per inch (ppi) is typical. However I've seen dovetail saws with as many as 23 ppi.

Most woodworkers prefer the teeth filed for a rip cut – a rip tooth has its cutting face filed so it is 90° (or nearly so) to the sides of the tooth.

Recently, Lie-Nielsen Toolworks has begun making a dovetail saw with what is called "progressive pitch." At its toe, the saw has 16 ppi. Each tooth gets bigger and bigger until the saw has 9 ppi at the heel. The fine teeth make the tool easy to start and the coarse teeth at the heel make it cut fast. The resulting finish is remarkably smooth and after using this saw for a couple years, I have become quite fond of it.

The number of teeth on your dovetail saw should relate to what kind of job you use that saw for. When you have fewer teeth, the saw will cut faster but coarser. The speed comes from the fact that fewer teeth equals deeper "gullets," which is the space between each tooth. When gullets fill up with waste, the saw stops cutting until the sawdust is removed as the tooth exits the work.

So a fine-tooth saw works well for small work in thin material, such as ½"-thick drawer sides. A coarse dovetail saw works better when sawing carcase dovetails in ¾" stock or thicker. You don't have to have two dovetail saws, however. I'd just pick a saw that reflects the work you do most of the time.

Speaking of pushing your tool into unfamiliar territory, many woodworkers end up using their dovetail saw for other chores, including some crosscutting. You can get away with this many times because the teeth of the saw are so fine.

woodworking-magazine.com ■ 21

A classic vintage carcase saw from Wheeler, Madden & Clemson. This saw is 14" long and has 12 ppi. The carcase saw is used for almost all joinery crosscuts when building furniture.

These two saws are so different in size that it's hard to believe that they both are called tenon saws. The big saw is a much older (and almost extinct) form.

However, your cut will be more ragged than if you used the correct tool: the carcase saw.

The Carcase Saw

By far, the most-used saw in my shop is my carcase saw. This saw is so named because it is useful for many operations in building a furniture carcase. A Western carcase saw always has a pistol grip, though ancient versions might have looked more like a chef's knife with a straight handle and no back.

The blade of a carcase saw is 10" to 14" long and 2" to 3" wide. It typically has 12 to 14 ppi, and the saw teeth are sharpened to make crosscuts. A crosscut tooth looks different than a rip tooth in that its cutting surface is at a 15° to 24° angle to the sides – 20° is typical. This angle is called "fleam" and it allows the tooth to sever the grain like a knife, reducing the raggedness that would be left behind by a rip tooth.

I haven't found the number of teeth in a carcase saw to be as critical as it is with the other forms of saws. A 12-point saw and a 14-point saw cut plenty fast enough for most operations, and they both leave an acceptable surface behind.

The difference I think you should pay attention to is the length of the blade. In general, longer saws tend to saw straighter, so I avoid saws that are 10" long. Getting an 11" saw makes a difference. A 14"-long saw even more so.

Keep in mind that a saw doesn't have to be labeled a carcase saw to be a carcase saw. There is some overlap in the saw forms. Pay attention to the specs of a saw in a catalog or in the store. A saw that is 14" long and filed crosscut with 12-14 ppi is a carcase saw, no matter what the tool seller might label it.

Carcase saws are the jack plane of the backsaw family. They get used for everything, from cutting tenon shoulders to trimming through-tenons to notching out corners to cutting miters. I use them for cutting door rails and stiles to length when working by hand – pretty much any precision crosscut that is on a board that is less than 6" wide. Plus, almost every time I reach for my carcase saw I'm also reaching for my bench hook.

Tenon Saws

When you start wading into tenon saws, it can get confusing. Knight's dictionary says a tenon saw should be 16" to 20" long (that's huge) and $3\frac{1}{2}$" to $4\frac{1}{2}$" wide (also huge). Tenon saws should have about 10 ppi.

Modern tenon saws are not nearly this big.

These ancient giant tenon saws have nearly disappeared, except in vintage tool collections and from one lone maker, Wenzloff & Sons. I purchased one of these old-school tenon saws and was surprised (strike that, amazed) at how easy it is to use, even when cutting tenons that were dwarfed by the saw's blade.

The long blade definitely helps the saw track a line straighter and work quickly – a $1\frac{1}{4}$" tenon cheek can be sawn down one side in six to seven long strokes. And the extra weight of the saw allowed the tool to supply all the downward force necessary when sawing.

The saw's size does intimidate some woodworkers and they worry that they will tip the tool too much as they begin the cut. However, if you use a second-class sawcut (see "How to Saw" on page 14 in this issue) then starting the saw isn't much of a challenge.

"In 20 years on this mountain, I've never been cheated by a hoe."
— Stonehouse (Shan shi)
poet

Some fellow woodworkers have also fronted the theory that this big saw was intended more for cutting the tenons to entryway and passage doors – not for furniture. Perhaps. But I have a couple great old photos that show some real old-timers sawing out huge tenon cheeks. They're using a big 26" rip saw. Wow.

I do have one caution if you choose to get a large tenon saw: The sawplate is more fragile than on other Western backsaws. Historically, the sawplate on a tenon saw is quite thin, and because of this vast acreage of thin metal and the fact that the brass back is so far away from the toothline, there is the danger of the saw bending if it is misused. I'm not saying you need to use your tool gingerly. I just don't know if lending it to your neighbor or teenager is a good idea.

No matter what size tenon saw you choose, the teeth should be filed for a rip cut. Tenon saws

Supplies

Adria Woodworking Tools
604-710-5748 or adriatools.com

Gramercy Tools
From Tools for Working Wood
800-426-4613 or
toolsforworkingwood.com

Lie-Nielsen Toolworks
800-327-2520 or lie-nielsen.com

Wenzloff & Sons Saw Makers
503-359-4191 or wenzloffandsons.com

Nice saws, but what are they good for? Sash saws are a bit of a mystery to modern woodworkers. Were they undersized tenon saws or oversized carcase saws? Or both?

are used to cut the cheeks of tenons, which is a rip cut. The carcase saw handles the shoulder cut, which is a crosscut. I also use my tenon saw for other sizable rip cuts, such as when defining the top of a cabriole leg – the square part that attaches to the table's apron. I also use it for laying a kerf down a tenon to accept wedges (a dovetail saw is slow and makes too small a kerf in most cases).

But if you don't think the ancient tenon saw is for you, then you should do what most woodworkers do and buy a true sash saw.

Sash Saws

If you think tenon saws are confusing, you haven't gotten into a discussion on sash saws. Their name suggests that they were used for cutting the joinery for window sashes, yet they show up in tool catalogs and inventories of people who built fine furniture. And there is no consensus among tool scholars as to whether they were filed rip or crosscut or both.

So what is a sash saw? Knight's dictionary says that a sash saw has a blade that's 14" to 16" long and $2\frac{1}{2}$" to $3\frac{1}{2}$" wide. The sash saw has 11 ppi. Those specifications look a lot like what we moderns would call a tenon saw.

To see if I could learn anything about the sash saw by using it, I bought two sash saws that were made to Knight's general specifications, one filed crosscut and the other rip. After a couple years of use I found that the crosscut sash saw was effortlessly doing all the jobs of my carcase saw, and the rip-tooth sash saw had somehow become my daily tenon saw.

This makes sense because the sash saw's spec-

Halfback Saws: A Jack of All Trades or a Half-baked Idea?

Recently some woodworkers (myself included) have become interested in halfback saws, a rare form of saw that was made by several sawmakers, including Disston, which made the saw between 1860 until the 1920s, according to Pete Taran.

The halfback was supposed to be a hybrid saw between a full-size handsaw and a backsaw. The small back wouldn't get in the way of many large crosscutting chores, but it would stiffen up the blade enough for joinery.

The saws are fairly rare, so it's safe to assume the idea didn't catch on with consumers. While that would doom the saw in the mind of a pragmatist, I reasoned that the halfback might be a tool whose time had not yet come. Perhaps it's like the low-angle jack plane – that tool was a commercial flop last century when it was invented but is an extremely popular plane in this one.

So I've been using a few versions of halfback saws in my shop for the last three years. And here's my conclusion: I think the halfback is a good tool for a woodworker who doesn't want to own both a carcase saw and a full-size handsaw that's filed for crosscuts. You can use this one tool for both. It's not perfect for both operations, but it does a yeoman's job.

When crosscutting stock on a sawbench, the halfback is fairly useful until you start trying to crosscut boards wider than 6". Then the little brass back tends to strike the work during the downstroke. When used at the workbench, the halfback is indeed stiff enough for most cuts that a carcase saw would be used for, but it's not as assured a tool as the carcase saw on small bits of work (it is, for example, overkill when crosscutting dowel pins).

This custom halfback saw is beautiful, but is it just wall jewelry?

So I don't think every shop needs a halfback saw. But mine does. I enjoy using it a great deal and it keeps me from shuffling as many saws around on my workbench when it's out.

— CS

ifications overlap with both the carcase and tenon saws, according to Knight's dictionary. What became clear to me in the end is that you might not need a sash saw if you already have a tenon saw and a carcase saw.

Your Basic Saw Kit

I think that most woodworkers who want to use Western handsaws can do all the common operations with three backsaws: A dovetail saw, a large backsaw that's filed crosscut (either a sash or a carcase saw), and a large backsaw that's filed rip (either a sash or a tenon saw). Exactly which saw you need depends on the size of your work and the characteristics of your body. Do you have large hands? Then you should try a tenon saw. Do you build jewelry boxes? Then you should select a fine-tooth dovetail saw.

Once you pick your three saws, I recommend that you stick with that set for a couple years before you get disgruntled and start test-driving other saws. Sawing (like sharpening) is a skill that develops over months and months. And one of the critical parts of learning to saw is getting comfortable with your saws. You need to understand – by instinct – how wide each saw's kerf is, and how fast each saw cuts.

Many woodworkers find that certain forms of saws speak to them when they use them. I've let more than 100 students use my saws and find that to be true. Certain people gravitate to certain forms of saws. A few people end up purchasing all the forms. But one thing is certain: After using a sharp well-made Western saw, almost none of them go back to their Japanese saws. WM

— *Christopher Schwarz*

Cutting Circles

Circles are perfect geometric shapes, but perfection in cutting circles is elusive.

This trammel jig makes use of the router's fence attachment to allow you to make fine adjustments to the cutting radius of the jig.

Circles are deceptively simple. Their simple perfection is appealing as a shape, but making a perfect circle from solid wood is not a simple task. The eye will easily detect the slightest variation in the finished work, and cutting and smoothing the shape involves dealing with every possible variation of grain direction.

Many methods and jigs promise foolproof results, but in reality, every method has its risks. And no jig will take you from start to finish without additional work somewhere along the line. In preparing this article, the editors compared our experiences with common techniques. In many areas of woodworking, we don't agree on methods, but for once we were unanimous.

None of us ever had any luck setting up a device to cut a perfect circle at the band saw, but we all begin by cutting as close as we can to a circular line using this machine. It takes too much time to build a fixture to spin a blank into a blade. Starting the cut is also a problem and all but the smallest circles need substantial outboard support. And, the surface still requires a lot of work to transform saw-blade marks into a finished surface.

Plan B is to cut the circle entirely with a router. All of us have tried this, but we found it too risky to remove material the full diameter of the bit. We had all experienced a disastrous failure of wood, bit, router or setup using this technique. But we all use a router and a trammel jig to trim the band-sawn blank to finished size. And we do additional work after routing to get the edge ready for finishing.

Other obvious methods are setting up a trammel for any saw other than a band saw, or cutting close to the line and cleaning up the saw marks with abrasives. We've heard of people cutting circles on the table saw, but none of us has had success with that. In theory, a jigsaw and trammel setup should work, but cleaning up the sawn surface and starting the cut are problems. Stationary disc and belt sanders can be fitted with a trammel, but as with other trammel methods, starting the work and locking in the finished radius at the same time are easier said than done.

Smoothing sawn edges with a handheld belt sander or a random-orbit sander is possible, as is using a rasp or sanding block. The power-assisted methods are fast but risky – tilt the sander as you move around the curve and you're in trouble. The manual efforts are safer, but not without risk, and will likely take considerably longer.

We don't have a quick and easy solution. Our method is a combination of techniques. We cut close to the line with a band saw, use a router with a trammel jig to remove the saw marks and create a perfect circle. Then we smooth the edge with a fine rasp and cabinet scraper, or a random-orbit sander. How much cleanup there is left to do depends a lot on the particular wood used.

Testing the Theory

I made several round pieces of solid maple to test our assumptions, and to look for ways to make each step easier. For layout, a compass works up to the tool's limits, which is usually less than 12" in diameter. Beyond that length, trammel points are easier to set and manipulate.

The first choice for making the cut is the band saw. A jigsaw can be used, but it gets awkward keeping most of the blank on the bench, and the cutting action off the bench. Starting and stopping the cut to reposition the workpiece will likely leave a bump or a dip on the edge.

Making the cut in a smooth, continuous motion gives the best results. Start by ripping, aiming for the left-hand quadrant of the circle. When I reach the edge of the circle I keep a smooth motion by spinning the blank into the blade, alternating hands to keep the motion continuous. It's easier to stay outside the line by watching the cut happen rather than trying to make the cut happen.

If a router and trammel will be used later, the cut doesn't need to be that close. If the cut is within $\frac{1}{8}$" of the outside of the line, the router will make it nice without straining. If cleanup is done

---

"A physician can bury his mistakes but an architect can only advise his clients to plant vines."

— Frank Lloyd Wright (1867 - 1959)
architect

any other way, the closer the cut to the line the better. Long, smooth arcs can easily be reduced in size. Bumps and dips are hard to remove while maintaining a fair curve on the edge.

With Rasp in Hand
The first method I used to remove the saw marks was a series of three rasps, beginning with a coarse one to bring the high spots down to the pencil line. If at all possible, it's best to work on an edge that is positioned horizontally. I clamped one side of the circle in the bench vise, and used a clamp to secure the other side.

This allows the rasp to be held in both hands. In this horizontal position, the edge can be seen and it's easy to tell when the rasp is flat. When working a curve, as opposed to a straight line, the changing grain direction requires a constant adjustment of pressure on the tool. End grain and transitional grain require more effort to cut than long grain. Make the longest possible strokes, and check the pencil line every few strokes.

Knowing when to stop is important. If the pencil line disappears then there is no reference to work to. It's a funny thing that we can visually see something out-of-round when the work is done, but it is extremely hard to judge a curve while working on it without a reference line.

An exact diameter is rarely as important as having a smooth curve. If the saw cuts are far outside the initial pencil line, you only need to work to the point where there is an even space between the line and the edge. If the line is crossed, either by the saw or the rasp, drawing a new circle just inside the first will give a reference, even if the finished circle ends up being slightly smaller.

After the work with the coarse rasp is complete, removing the marks with a medium rasp will be much faster than the initial shaping, and the final round with a fine rasp will be even quicker. Each grain of rasp will leave a distinctive scratch pattern, and when the old scratches are replaced with finer ones, it is time to move on. The remaining scratches from the finest rasp are removed with a cabinet scraper.

A Powerful Method
A stationary sander is faster than working by hand, but with increased speed comes increased risks. Two things can go wrong: You can burn the wood or you can go too far too fast. Good technique can avoid these problems, but it takes practice. Disc sanders work better than belt sanders because they are less likely to burn end grain.

Most disc sanders have a small table, so it is important to apply downward pressure against the table to keep the edge vertical. Work on the downward-moving side of the disc, and move the work gently into the abrasive. The proper hand motion is similar to that used at the band saw to make the cut. The work needs to be rotated as it is pushed in. Unlike a flat surface, there is only a small point of a circle's edge in contact at any time. Lingering on a point will either burn the work, or take the edge beyond the line.

Cleaning the disc with a rubber cleaning stick will help to prevent burning, as will keeping the work in motion. It is hard to make a long continuous motion without repositioning the hands, so try to make a comfortable sweep into the disc, then back off any forward pressure as you switch hands to complete the curve.

During initial smoothing, it is important to use a grit coarse enough to remove material without burning, #80 grit or #100 grit are good starting points. Changing discs involves diminishing returns as finer grits have a greater tendency to burn and will still leave marks on the edge. I don't think it's worth it to change to a finer-grit disc, so after getting the circle down to size, I use another method to remove the scratches left from sanding – usually a cabinet scraper followed by a random-orbit sander or I hand sand with a rigid sanding block.

The band saw is the ideal machine for cutting a large circle, but the time spent to make a trammel cutting jig for it isn't worth it. Cut by eye to just outside the line, then use a router trammel jig to trim off the excess and form a perfect circle.

A rasp is the fastest hand-tool method for removing the saw marks. Make long strokes with the tool held flat and keep your eye on the pencil line around the perimeter.

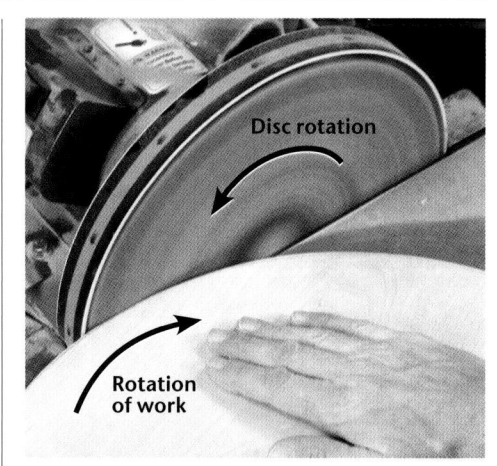

A stationary disc sander is effective, but it needs a delicate touch. Rotate the workpiece into the downhill side of the disc and keep it flat on the machine's table. Otherwise it will jump up on you.

Adjustable Circle-cutting Router Jig

I believe in keeping jigs as simple as possible, but sometimes an extra feature can improve a device by leaps and bounds. Such is the case with this jig. For years I used a simple extended baseplate for routing circles and arcs. A scrap of plywood the width of the router's base and a couple feet long, and a few holes for mounting and a measurement for setting the radius, and I was ready to go.

The problem with this was that there wasn't any room for making a fine adjustment to the radius. I could set the distance to any dimension I wanted, but if something went wrong with the first cut, the option of fixing it by making the circle a little smaller was troublesome. A new hole meant making a fine measurement and drilling again.

The answer, or at least part of it was on the router. The fine adjustment I needed was the same as that of the router's fence. All I needed was a way to attach a simple trammel jig to the router the same way the fence attached. One trip to the hardware store and less than $5 later, and I was ready to go.

A router trammel jig becomes more useful with the addition of a simple method for fine-tuning.

Steel Rods and Scraps

I used a piece of 1/4"-thick plywood, 6" wide x 22" long. I marked a centerline along the length and cut a piece of 3/4" x 1" poplar, 6" long. At the hardware store I picked up a piece of 5/16"-diameter steel rod to slide in the fence-mounting holes of my router. This size will vary with different routers – check the size with a drill bit. It doesn't need to be a piston fit. As long as the rod slides in the fence-mounting holes, and locks down with machine screws, close is good enough.

I used a hacksaw to cut two 8 1/2" lengths of the rod. This length can be varied; I wanted the rod to lock into the router securely and still allow for 3" or 4" of adjustment. At the measurements shown in the drawing, I can make circles ranging in size from 8" to 48". I ground off the rough-cut ends of the rods and mounted them in the router.

With the router base flat on my bench, I put the 1/4"-thick plywood next to the router, with the poplar across one end. I marked where the ends of the rod met the wood with a pencil, and drilled two holes through the block at the drill press. Then I glued the block of wood across the end of the piece of plywood, using yellow glue and a couple spring clamps.

When the glue had dried, I coated one end of each steel rod with Gorilla Glue (reactive polyurethane) and tapped the rods into the holes until the ends of the rods were flush with the wood on the exit side of the block. I let the glue dry overnight before using the jig.

Swinging Into Action

I purchased two machine screws that fit the threaded holes in the router base to lock the rods in place. I mounted a 1/2"-diameter spiral-upcut bit, and measured from the edge of the bit along the centerline of the jig and drilled a hole at the desired radius.

What to use for a center pin depends on what type of trail you're willing to leave behind on the bottom of your work. A piece of 1/4" metal rod, press-fit into a hole in the base of the jig and in a 1/4"-deep hole in the bottom of the work, is least likely to shift during use but leaves a noticeable hole.

A small brad or finishing nail tapped into the work won't leave much evidence, but can bend, shift or pop out of the hole during use. A short screw driven in a few turns is an effective, middle-of-the-road compromise between the two extremes.

The reason for creating the adjustable trammel jig is that even in the best of circumstances, with a steady hand and good technique, there is still a chance for the wood to tear or the cutter to inadvertantly dig in. Be prepared to make the circle a little smaller. Smaller with a clean edge won't be noticed. The intended size with an ugly spot on the edge will be noticed. When you've made a good cut with the router, a few minutes with a card scraper, sanding block or random-orbit sander will finish the work. — *RL*

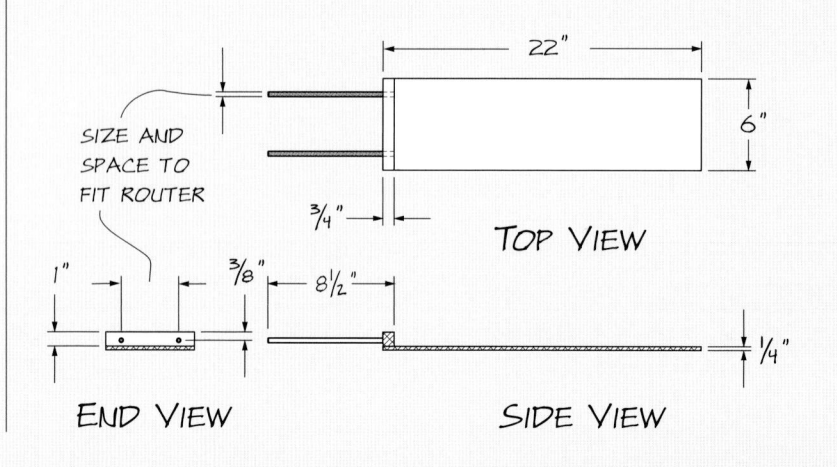

Easier Said Than Done

While it's possible to use a handheld belt sander to remove saw marks and shape the edge down to the pencil line, I wouldn't recommend it. Clamping the work with the edge up means balancing the sander on a narrow edge. It's almost impossible to see what is happening in this position. The alternative, clamping the blank flat on the bench and holding the sander sideways, lets you see what is going on, but it takes finesse to hold the belt sander with the platen vertical.

Random-orbit sanders are effective for removing saw marks and coarse scratches – if the sander can be held with the pad vertical and not tipped. Trying to grind down areas where the saw has strayed from the line with this tool is awkward.

The dedicated hand-tool user might decide that a low-angle block plane or a flat-bottomed spokeshave would be effective at removing the saw marks. While there is some merit to this in theory, in practice it is a slow method with mixed results, especially while working a hard wood. To prevent tearing out the end grain on the perimeter, the blade must be set for a very fine cut, slowing down the work on the long-grain portions.

The changing grain direction will also mean a different direction of attack as you go around the circle. There will be places where tearing out the grain is almost inevitable. In the interest of experimentation, I tried both a block plane and spokeshave, but abandoned the effort in favor of the rasp for shaping the curve by hand.

If you should tear out a chunk somewhere, there isn't any easy fix. On a straight surface you might be able to plane a gentle dip along the length to remove some tear-out, but on a circle the only good solution is to reduce the diameter of the entire circle. That will take time.

Router to the Rescue

A plunge router on a trammel jig is the best solution to cutting a nice clean circle. You don't need to worry about sawing close to a line because the distance between the center and the edge is fixed by the jig. You can control the depth of cut and remove material in manageable steps. But again, theory and reality don't always agree.

In our experience, something will go wrong when trying to make a complete circular cut with the router only. Taking shallow passes in solid hardwood means going around the circle five or six times. Each additional pass increases the chance of something bad happening.

There are several little things that can go wrong; any one of them can mean starting over. The cord to the router can snag, pulling the bit toward the center and creating a divot. Using a small-diameter bit can lead to the bit flexing or chattering. A large-diameter bit can cause a big chunk of wood to tear out where the grain reverses. Leaning in one direction or another as the depth changes or as you shift hands can tilt the router enough to leave a noticeable ridge around the edge of what should be a nice circle.

Cutting the circle to shape before routing, while leaving 1/8" or less for the router bit to remove, reduces the risk because you only need to run the router around once or twice. Place the rough-cut blank on scraps of wood attached to the bench, so one pass can be made without needing to stop and restart to avoid clamps. The blank can be held to the scrap and the scrap can be held to the bench with double-sided tape or hot-melt glue.

An upcut-spiral bit makes a cleaner cut and is less likely to tear out the grain than a straight bit. When the blank is secure, raise the router motor so that the bit is clear of the work, and attach the jig to the center point of the circle. Drape the cord of the router over your shoulder. Turn the router on, plunge to your cutting depth and move the router around the pivot as smoothly as you can. When the cut is complete, turn the router off and hold the jig steady until the bit stops turning.

This is the best method we've found, but it isn't without risk. As the router starts, it can jerk or jump so keep a firm grip on the tool. When turning the router off, or when plunging the bit, don't relax your grip and let the cutter move toward the center. And lastly, the direction the router is moved around the circle can cause tear-out in some parts of the circle.

The accepted direction when routing is to go against the direction of the cutter, or counterclockwise around the perimeter. The exception to this rule is when routing across end grain, or into grain that is running downhill toward the cutter. With a circle of solid wood you will be routing across the grain on opposite sides, and going downhill at two other locations. Even though it is difficult to control, the cut will be cleaner if you go clockwise for the entire cut. And you will need some luck and a firm grip on the tool and jig to get it right on the first attempt. **WM**

— *Robert W. Lang*

A random-orbit sander is good for removing coarser rasp or sanding marks, but difficult to use for removing band-saw marks and truing the circle. Keep the sanding pad vertical against the edge of the work and keep the sander moving around the perimeter as you work to the pencil line.

Routing the circle presents uphill and downhill grain to the router bit. Climb-cutting the entire perimeter will give the best results, but there aren't any guarantees. Starting and stopping the cut to change direction is more likely to cause a problem. Be prepared to make your circle smaller if you need to.

Circular Cutting Board

Bring your woodworking into the kitchen with this simple, circular project. It will make you look like a big wheel as you practice circles.

A well-equipped kitchen deserves to have a nice maple cutting board, especially if the kitchen is in a woodworking household. The cutting board may be an animal-shaped survivor from 8th grade shop class, or a more sophisticated design. For many woodworkers it is an introduction to working with shapes that aren't straight.

Maple has been used as a food preparation surface for hundreds of years and there are good reasons to follow tradition. While getting a perfectly smooth, tear-out free surface may be vexing, the finished product is both practical and attractive, despite unsuccessful attempts in recent years to label it as unsanitary.

This design began as a way to practice making circles. The three feet raise the cutting board above the counter, allowing it to be easily picked up and put down. The size and contrasting color of the feet add some visual interest, and if you have an adjustable trammel jig, like the one shown on page 24, it's easy to add them, bringing a simple project to a slightly higher level.

The cutting board shown here is about 18" in diameter. The basic design can be scaled down if you prefer. To obtain a piece wide enough, I glued together two pieces a little larger than 9"-wide. A simple butt joint is more than strong enough in this application. I selected the pieces, and when I had them arranged the way I wanted them, I marked the faces with a carpenter's triangle.

If you plan on surfacing the finished board with a handplane, arrange the boards so that the grain on the edges runs the same way. Maple is notorious for tearing out, and if one piece runs downhill while the other runs uphill, you may find it impossible to get a good surface after gluing.

I ran the edges to be glued over the jointer just before assembly, with the face of one board against the fence and the face of the other away from the fence. This cancels out any minute deviation of the jointer's fence from square. Even if the angles are slightly off from 90°, they will be complementary, ensuring a flat surface.

Straight matching edges and a level surface to lay the pieces on when gluing are important when gluing solid wood edge-to-edge. I ripped a few strips of scrap to a consistent width and placed them across my bench to support the pieces. After lining the triangle sides back up, I rotated one board up on edge and applied a bead of glue to one edge only.

Because this will be used in the kitchen and washed frequently, I used a waterproof polyurethane glue (Gorilla Glue). This glue tends to foam

Solid maple makes an ideal surface for a cutting board, and feet in a wood of a contrasting color help it sit solidly, and make it easy to lift. A canola-oil finish contributes to an elegant look and is easy to maintain.

"... when you make something that says 'sleep,' by God you've made a bed."
— Art Espenet Carpenter (1920 - 2006)
cabinetmaker

after assembly, so after laying on a bead from the glue bottle, I spread the bead with a palette knife to cover the edge with a thin, consistent film. I wiped the other, unglued edge with a damp rag because this glue cures only in the presence of moisture.

There are some other glues that also could be used; the key element is water resistance combined with some flexibility in the cured glue line. A waterproof PVA (such as Titebond III) would likely work as well as polyurethane. I have had epoxies fail after three or four years in cutting boards. I think this is due to the epoxy drying to a hard, brittle line. Wooden cutting boards are the objects of some inevitable abuse; soaked and dried repeatably as they are used, cleaned then put away.

Clamping Considerations

Despite the tendency of some of us to use as many clamps as is possible to fit for an "optimal" glue joint, practical experience demonstrates that two or three clamps across the joint will produce a good joint. The goal is a glue line that is barely visible, and this can be achieved with firm even pressure. I scraped off any wet glue that squeezed out to observe the glue line. This also allows the glue to cure in less time and with a better bond than letting it dry on the surface.

After letting the glue cure for 24 hours, I cut the circle on the band saw and trimmed it with the router and trammel jig as described on page 24. The particular piece of maple I used tore out a few times when trimming the edge. I think it would have preferred to serve humanity by staying in the woods and being tapped for syrup rather than being cut into lumber. For this project, it didn't make a difference that the circle was a fraction smaller than originally planned.

Best Foot Forward

After I had a good clean edge on the entire maple circle, I reset the trammel jig so that the outside edge of the cutter was lined up with the outer edge of the maple. This set the distance for the rabbets in the top of the feet. I screwed a scrap of the same material used for the feet (walnut) to my bench to serve as a center point.

I drew the outline of the board on the bench so that I could screw down the blanks for the feet securely, while avoiding the path of the router bit. I set the depth of cut to $1/4$" and routed an arc in the blank. I used a compass to scribe the inner and outer profiles of the foot on the top surface. At the band saw, I cut to the pencil lines, and cleaned up the saw marks.

I came close to a perfect surface with my smoothing plane and card scraper, but there were a couple torn spots that resisted my efforts. Following the dictum of, "If at first you don't succeed, try something else," I resorted to a random-orbit sander, and Abranet abrasives. Abranet is a new product from Mirka, with a mesh instead of a paper backing. It works very well, and stepping through the grits of #150, #240 and #320 left a very nice surface.

I use a 30°-60° drafting triangle to lay out the locations of the feet, one on the center line and the other two 120° apart. I again used Gorilla glue to attach the feet to the board, with a pair of small spring clamps to hold them in place. I left the clamps on overnight, and after rounding all the corners slightly with a piece of Abranet, the cutting board was ready for finishing.

For the finish, I saturated the wood with canola oil from the grocery store, let it sit for about 15 minutes then wiped it dry. Two coats a day apart are the initial finish, and I'll apply another coat of oil every month or so as the board is used. When it starts to look a bit dry, it's time to refresh the finish. To keep the board from warping, I will make sure to wash both flat surfaces with soap and water every time I use the board. **WM**

— *Robert W. Lang*

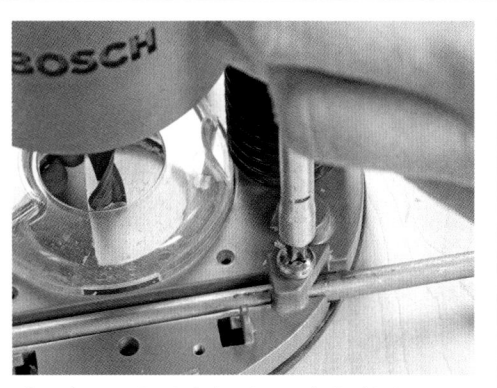

After the maple circle is trimmed, the bit is adjusted so that it is flush with the outer edge of the large circle.

This setting is used to rout a $1/4$"-deep rabbet in the blanks for the feet.

A compass is used to scribe an offset line from the edge of the rabbet. The feet are then band sawn to shape.

Cooking oil makes a good finish for a cutting board. It's cheap, easy to apply and can be renewed on a regular basis.

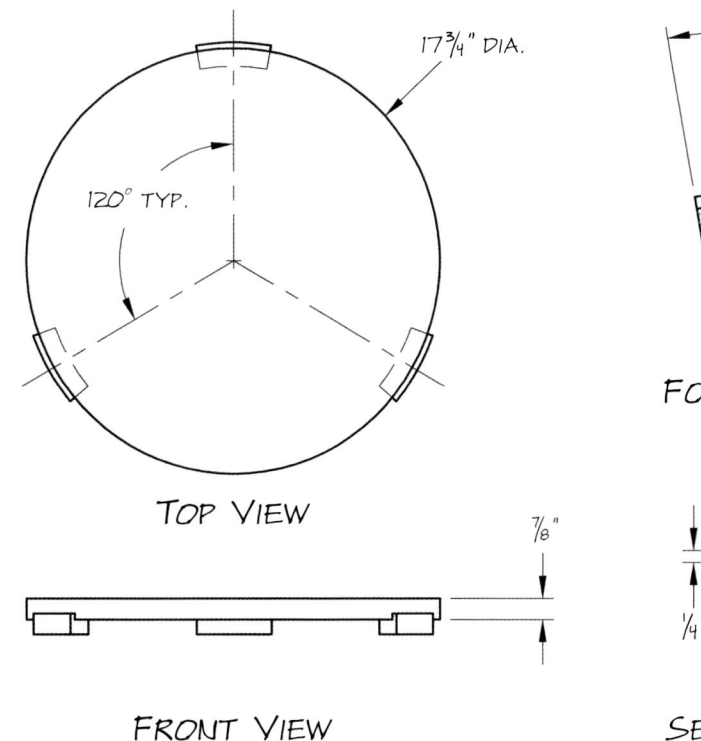

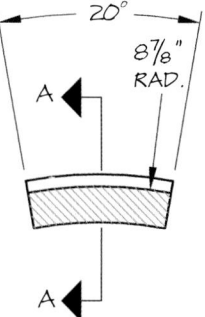

TOP VIEW

FRONT VIEW

FOOT DETAIL

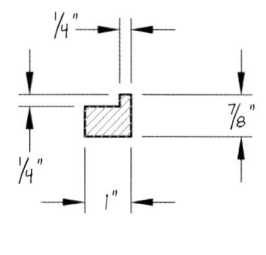

SECTION A-A

Glazing for the Ages

Sandwich stain between two layers of finish and you've found the best way to add age, blend tones and highlight carvings on your project.

Glaze is a layer of color sandwiched between two layers of finish. While finishing already takes nearly the same amount of time as building the project, why would you want to add another step to your finishing process? The answer is simple. The extra effort makes your work look its best. Glaze is to finish as chocolate chips are to ice cream. The base component is great by itself, but another layer, be it taste or color, is a great enhancement.

Glaze is forgiving, so why not try it? If you're not pleased with the results, simply wipe it away with mineral spirits and a clean cloth.

Why is it Called Glaze?
In furniture glazing, stain is generally used as a glaze. So why is this called glazing and not simply staining? The distinction is this: A stain is a glaze as long as it's applied between two layers of finish. Put the stain on bare wood, it's a stain. Trap the stain between two layers of finish and it becomes a glaze.

Many times you'll hear of products, such as wax, referred to as glaze. But it's only a glaze if layered properly. Applying a wax topcoat is not a glaze.

If you look at wood stain, gel stain and specifically designed glazing stains (the primary products for glazing), they're available in both oil-base or water-base. All are used as glazes.

Good Choices and Some Not so Good
Choosing between oil-base and water-base stain is an easy decision. Water-base stains dry very quickly, whereas oil-base stains afford enough time to manipulate the glaze layer for the desired effect. So, select an oil-base stain instead of a water-base product for glazing.

Brush, rag or spray the glaze onto a project, then wipe away the excess. The addition of glaze adds age and highlights to your furniture. Also, uneven tones are blended, which results in a more uniform look.

In many circumstances, glaze has to be applied to vertical surfaces such as case sides. Therefore, it's important to use a thick-viscosity stain as glaze, one that won't easily run or sag on the surface. To use "off the shelf" oil-base wood stains becomes a bit difficult due to the thin viscosity of the product. Most often I would pass on these, unless you allow the product to settle at the bottom of the can then pour off some of the thinning medium. This process would thicken the product to a workable consistency. The easier solution is to use a gel stain or a stain specifically designed for glazing.

Oil-base gel stains, as the name implies, are thick, mayonnaise-like stains that hold in place when applied on a vertical surface. Sometimes it's possible for oil-base gel stains to dry too quickly, similar to water-base products. To extend the "open time" (the time you have to manipulate the glaze before it dries completely), add a small amount of mineral spirits or boiled linseed oil.

Boiled linseed oil not only extends the open time, it also lengthens the overall drying time before you're able to add a topcoat. Mineral spirits increases the open time without affecting the dry time.

Heavy-bodied Glaze
I particularly like the heavy-bodied glazing stains, such as those from Mohawk (mohawkfinishing.com). These glazes are made from boiled linseed oil and fine pigments, therefore, as with all oil-base stains, if the product begins to set up too quickly, use mineral spirits to soften the glaze and continue to work. The glaze has the right viscosity to use one of several different application methods.

To keep the process simple and unless you're trying to specifically add color in addition to affecting the age and tone, brown hues are the trick to effective furniture glazing. Choose Van Dyke brown to impose a darker layer and burnt umber for a more neutral layer. I find either of these two glazes fills all my needs.

Doing the Glaze Dance

Applying glaze is a snap. You don't need to "dry brush" the glaze (where you apply glaze a little at a time to specific areas with an almost-dry brush). That's more artistic than necessary; just coat the piece.

Use a brush, rag or spray setup to load the project with glaze. Make sure that you get it into all corners, cracks and crevices.

If you're using gel stain as glaze, work on a small portion of the project, then once it's complete move to another section. You'll be able to apply the material then immediately wipe away the excess and still achieve a glaze. Gel stains do not need time to seep into the finish.

To use heavy-bodied glaze, apply a coat over the entire surface. You should cover the whole project because most finish coats (shellac in this case) have miniature pores throughout the surface. Those pores retain glaze after you wipe away the excess. The residual amount evens the tone on the project and softens the overall finish.

A visual indication helps you know when to start wiping away the excess. That is a change in the appearance of the glaze. It converts from a shiny surface to one that's considered dull and whitish. That shifting process is called "flashing." After it flashes, start wiping.

The idea is to manipulate the glaze as you remove residual amounts. No matter how hard you try, you're not going to remove the glaze entirely. Leave excess in the corners and crevices to simulate age and an accumulation of wax, grease and grime. But, you also should remember that areas around knobs and catches (if you're going for the antique reproduction look) are usually lighter, so wipe away as much as possible in those places.

On to the Finish

Once the glaze is in place, it's time to make a decision about the look. If you feel there are heavy spots that need attention, dampen a clean rag with mineral spirts and continue to manipulate the glaze – I seldom find that necessary.

In addition, if you're just not happy with the overall look, take the time to wipe the glaze off the piece. Depending on the project this could be a big job, so, as with all finishing processes, try the glaze on a scrap or in an inconspicuous location before committing to the step.

Allow the glaze to dry sufficiently, then it's on to the top layer of the glaze sandwich. And remember, these products are oil-based, so take proper care in disposing of rags and other material used in the process. **WM**

— *Glen D. Huey*

Apply the glaze to the project with a brush (as in this case), a rag or with spray equipment. Start with glaze the consistency of mayonnaise so it stays in place on vertical surfaces.

Manipulate the glaze as you remove the excess. Try as you may, the glaze remains on the surface causing the tones to even out. And if you desire, distress small areas then fill them with glaze to make them stand out.

You can see how these chatter marks that remain on the pine door stile after staining blend to a more even tone where the glaze is applied.

End Grain

ILLUSTRATION BY BRUCE BOLINGER

The Tools I Never Use

Idle tools mock us, while others teach us lessons.

I've always considered myself an average-Joe kind of woodworker. But this time, for your sake, I hope I'm different.

For me, each trip into my workshop causes pain. Pain from walking into a space that's too little used (yes, we all have that in common) and from the fact that I have a new band saw (sitting idle just inside the overhead door) that mocks me each and every day. The machine has never been turned on. Why, it hasn't even been plugged into an outlet.

I know I'm not alone in this problem. I have woodworking friends who have tools that sit idle in their shops as well, not being used as intended. If you regularly visit most of the woodworking forums, you'll find a thread or two on tool purchases that didn't turn out to be worthwhile. Why do we woodworkers repeat these same mistakes over and over?

Here are the three reasons I purchased that band saw. My main motivation was to use the saw to slice shop-cut veneer using a ¾" blade while maintaining my current band saw and blade for everyday use. Although I didn't run into this need many times in the past, I thought that the time would come. Unfortunately, so far I haven't built a project where I needed that capability. But I still have hope.

The second reason for purchase was insurance. If my current band saw (nearly 20 years old) would ever call it quits, I wouldn't be left trying to improvise band saw deeds with a handsaw – heaven forbid – or be running out to my local tool dealer to purchase a replacement saw that either wouldn't live up to expectations or would be beyond my current financial means. Happily, I have not yet needed to collect on that policy.

Besides these two more-than-valid reasons, the price I paid made it a great deal.

However aggravating the non-use of my new tool is, it's not nearly as aggravating as other tools in my arsenal that don't earn their keep. I have more than one tool resting quietly in my shop. The question then becomes: Are these tools under-utilized (as is the case with my band saw)? Or are they not worth the materials from which they're made? Sorry to say, I have examples of both.

Where did these other inactive tools in my shop come from? I sat down one day to revisit when and where I made these less-than-useful purchases, hoping to discover a pattern that I might correct. Most of the slacker tools had been around a long time. These were the tools I bought as I began woodworking as a hobby – before I had gathered much knowledge or experience.

Why were these tools in my shop in the first place? Believe or not, I was persuaded to buy most them. I was coaxed by salespeople at the woodworking shows telling all newcomers to the craft how his or her tool would change the way we did woodworking.

That's not an excuse. It's an acknowledgement. I'm saying I was green to woodworking – and not in an environmental sense.

I'm sure I was anxious to buy these tools at the time. I was still overjoyed with them as I got back to the shop and put the tools to use. It was then the remorse set in – when I discovered they didn't change the way I worked wood at all. These tools didn't live up to the hype and they didn't meet my expectations. So, I set them aside and allowed them to ridicule me for a short time. Then I pushed each one into a cupboard and closed the door. Out of sight, out of mind.

If you don't have unused tools in your shop, congratulations on your purchasing habits. And, consider this a warning or a strong suggestion to find your way in woodworking before being persuaded to buy the next "best" or "latest and greatest" tool that's guaranteed to change or enhance your woodworking.

Read, study and gain knowledge before purchasing. Even that doesn't guarantee you won't some day make a purchase that sits idle in your shop, one that mocks you each time you arrive. But when it does happen, just remember you're not alone. It happens to most of us. **WM**

— *Glen D. Huey*

Extras

"I'm a great believer in luck, and I find the harder I work, the more I have of it."

— Thomas Jefferson (1743 - 1826)

PDF Downloads Available For All Issues of *Woodworking Magazine*

If you're missing an issue of *Woodworking Magazine*, we now have an inexpensive and quick solution. Downloads of single issues of *Woodworking Magazine* are now available at our bookstore for just $6 each.

All you need to view and print these fully searchable electronic versions is Adobe Acrobat's free reader (and if you don't have it already, you can download it at adobe.com).

To download, visit woodworking-magazine.com/backissues.

Woodworking Magazine – the Book

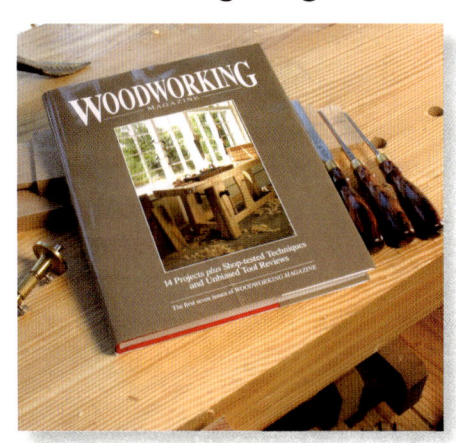

Though we now offer digital versions of all issues of *Woodworking Magazine*, we have an affection for the printed word. So, at the request of readers, we've also collected the first seven issues of the magazine and bound them into a book.

This hardcover book features a sturdy, red cover with a foil-stamped title, heavyweight interior matte-finish pages, colored end papers and a full-color glossy book jacket. This book belongs in your permanent collection.

Woodworking Magazine – The Book is available on our web site (woodworking-magazine.com/books) for $34.95 (includes s&h in the U.S.). It's a perfect way to ensure your collection will last for years to come. Order yours today – quantities are limited!

SUBSCRIBE NOW To *Woodworking Magazine!*

Now, you can subscribe to *Woodworking Magazine* and receive four issues for $19.96 – mailed to your door. No more will you have to haunt your local magazine vendor for the latest issue, miss an issue by mistake or even have to bid on a back issue on eBay.

To subscribe right away, visit woodworking-magazine.com and click on the "Subscribe" link. You can pay online with a credit card (which saves us some postage) or we can bill you if you prefer. Or, call 800-283-3542 and subscribe over the phone.

Other than the fact that you can now subscribe to *Woodworking Magazine*, nothing else about the publication will change. We will not accept advertising in our pages. We are still focused on unearthing the simplest and best techniques for both power tools and hand tools. And the projects we build will always be classics – designs that have remained fresh and alive for a century or more. Our mission – simply put – is to help you find a better way to build.

Also, we thank you for your support of *Woodworking Magazine*. Without your many kind letters and e-mails, we wouldn't now be able to offer subscriptions.

You see, we started *Woodworking Magazine* in 2004 without the blessing of our parent corporation. The market, they thought, was too crowded for another woodworking magazine. But we knew in our gut that this wasn't just another magazine. So we kept putting it out on the newsstands twice a year as an experiment to see if readers would embrace a magazine with black-and-white photos, techniques that frequently defied conventional wisdom and no advertising.

And because you did embrace the magazine, we are now able to publish *Woodworking Magazine* four times a year and offer subscriptions by mail. So again, thank you. We couldn't have done it without you.

IMPORTANT SAFETY NOTE

Safety is your responsibility. Manufacturers place safety devices on their equipment for a reason. In many photos you see in *Woodworking Magazine*, these have been removed to provide clarity. In some cases we'll use an awkward body position so you can better see what's being demonstrated. Don't copy us. Think about each procedure you're going to perform beforehand. Safety First!

CONTACT US

We welcome letters from readers with comments about this magazine, or about woodworking in general. We try to respond to all correspondence. To send us a letter:

- E-mail: letters@fwpubs.com
- Fax: 513-891-7196
- Mail carrier:
  Letters • Woodworking Magazine
  4700 E. Galbraith Road
  Cincinnati, OH 45236

Number 9, Spring 2008. *Woodworking Magazine* is published 4 times a year in March, May, August and December by F+W Publications, Inc. Editorial offices are located at 4700 E. Galbraith Road, Cincinnati, Ohio 45236; tel.: 513-531-2222. Unsolicited manuscripts are not accepted. Subscription rates: A year's subscription (4 issues) is $19.96 in the U.S., $24.96 in Canada, and $29.96 elsewhere. Produced and printed in the U.S.A.

Woodworking Magazine | Butt Hinges | Spring 2008

Anatomy of a Butt Hinge

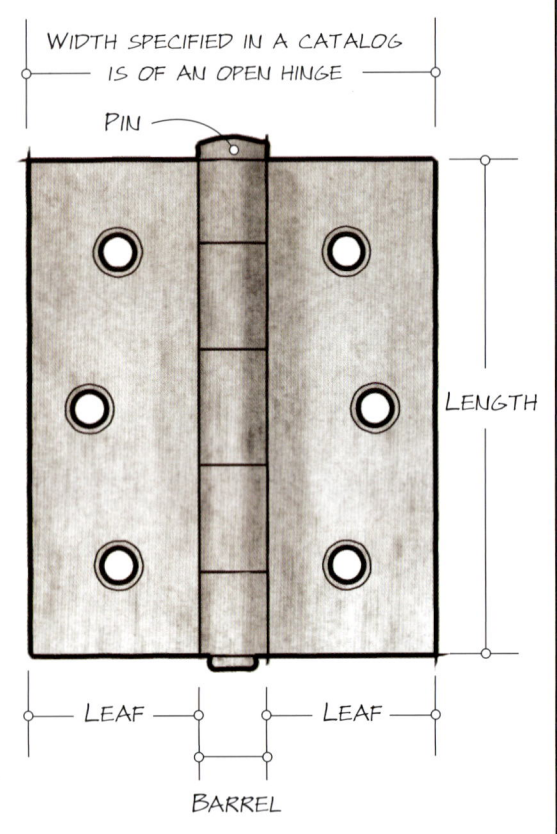

Width specified in a catalog is of an open hinge

Pin

Length

Leaf — Leaf

Barrel

Barrel width typ. 7/32", 1/4" or 5/16". To determine leaf width, subtract barrel width from overall width, and divide by 2.

Stamped vs. Extruded vs. Cast Hinges

- Inexpensive hinges are usually stamped out of thin steel or brass plates.

- Extruded hinges are molten metal forced into a die under high pressure. They are thicker, sturdier and more expensive.

- Cast bronze hinges are among the most expensive — bronze is melted and poured into a mold, resulting in a perfectly smooth surface and perfectly aligned pins.

How Many Hinges?

- Doors up to 24" high – two hinges. Each hinge is 2" in length or smaller.

- Doors up to 36" high – two hinges. Each hinge up to 3" long.

- Doors 36" and higher – usually three hinges, 3" long or bigger.

Countersink Angles

82° screw in a 90° countersink

90° screw in an 82° countersink

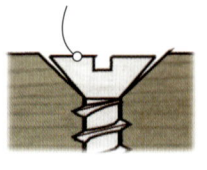

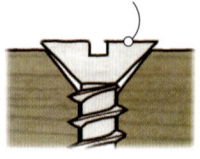

This refers to the angle of the edge of the screw holes in the hinge leaves. Good hinges come with screws that match that angle (standard is 82° in the U.S., 90° in the U.K.) But, countersink bits can be used to modify the holes to accept any number of angles on screws. It's important that the screw match the hole — if the angle on the screw is more than that of the hole, the screw won't seat. Thus the hinge won't close flush. If the angle on the screw head is less than in the leaf hole, the screw won't have the strongest possible holding power because the head will have room to wiggle around.

Placement of Hinges

For Strength

The farther apart the hinges, the stronger.

For Looks, Option A

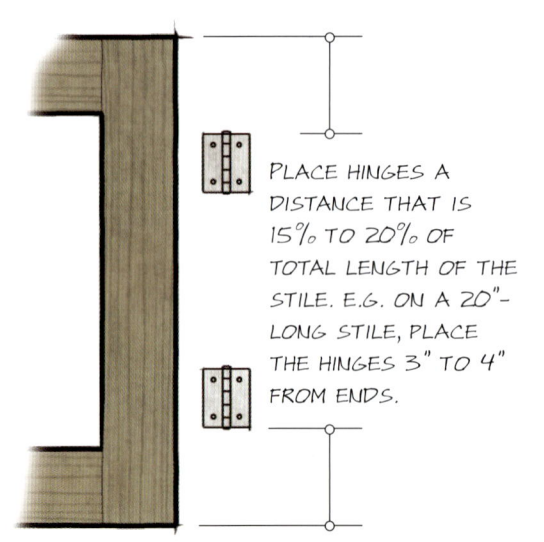

Place hinges a distance that is 15% to 20% of total length of the stile. E.g. on a 20"-long stile, place the hinges 3" to 4" from ends.

For Looks, Option B

Line up edge of hinge with door's rails.

Special thanks to Whitechapel Ltd and Robin Lee of Lee Valley Tools for technical assistance
Illustrations by Matt Bantly

A Magazine Committed to Finding the Better Way to Build
Filled With Good Craftsmanship, the Best Techniques and No Ads

WOODWORKING
MAGAZINE

Better Ways To Build Any Chest

The Cheapest Screws Are the Best Screws

Master the Fussy Finger Joint With a Quick and Simple Jig

Glue is the Secret To a Stunning Crackle Finish

Authentic Sea Chest Is a Cinch to Build

2 Outstanding Ways To Trim End Grain

POPULAR WOODWORKING PRESENTS

fw F+W PUBLICATIONS, INC.
US $5.99

Display until August 4, 2008

woodworking-magazine.com ■ SUMMER 2008

Contents

"Even a mistake may turn out to be the one thing necessary to a worthwhile achievement."
— Henry Ford (1863 - 1947)
founder of the Ford Motor Co.

1 On the Level
Competently made tools of good industrial design used to be available at a solid middle-class price. Those days are fast disappearing.

2 Letters
Questions, comments and wisdom from readers, experts and our staff.

4 Shortcuts
Tricks and tips that will make your woodworking simpler and more accurate.

A SIMPLE SEA CHEST: PAGE 26

6 Better Finger Joints
A joint that was once strictly utilitarian has become a centerpiece of modern design. Discover several methods to make this distinctive joint – including an easy-to-make jig.

12 Trim Proud End Grain
Whether you use hand or power methods to flush up proud joints, the trick to efficient and neat work has little to do with the tools.

15 Glossary
Woodworking's terminology can be overwhelming. Learn the terms used in this issue.

16 A Better Design For a Blanket Chest
Many common designs for blanket chests make the construction far more complicated than is necessary. We share this simple method that yields complex-looking results.

23 Screws are Screws – Aren't They?
Our comparison of big-box-bought screws versus premium screws reveals some surprising conclusions about cheap ones.

26 A Simple Sea Chest
The canted sides of this traditional chest for sailors were designed to cut down on barked shins. Now, they add visual interest and are easier to construct than you might think.

30 The Best Crackle Finish
We tested several methods for adding age and depth to a painted finish, and found the best way is cheap and easy. The key is the glue.

32 End Grain
A maker's stamp is always the last tool to touch Editor Christopher Schwarz's work – if it touches it at all.

BETTER FINGER JOINTS: PAGE 6

TRIM PROUD END GRAIN: PAGE 12

THE BEST CRACKLE FINISH: PAGE 30

WOODWORKING MAGAZINE

Summer 2008, Issue 10
woodworking-magazine.com
Editorial Offices 513-531-2690

PUBLISHER & GROUP EDITORIAL DIRECTOR
■ **Steve Shanesy**
ext. 1238, steve.shanesy@fwpubs.com

EDITOR ■ **Christopher Schwarz**
ext. 1407, chris.schwarz@fwpubs.com

ART DIRECTOR ■ **Linda Watts**
ext. 1396, linda.watts@fwpubs.com

SENIOR EDITOR ■ **Robert W. Lang**
ext. 1327, robert.lang@fwpubs.com

SENIOR EDITOR ■ **Glen D. Huey**
ext. 1293, glen.huey@fwpubs.com

MANAGING EDITOR ■ **Megan Fitzpatrick**
ext. 1348, megan.fitzpatrick@fwpubs.com

ILLUSTRATOR ■ **Matt Bantly**
PHOTOGRAPHER ■ **Al Parrish**
COVER PHOTOGRAPHER ■ **Ric Deliantoni**

F+W PUBLICATIONS, INC.
David Nussbaum ■ CHAIRMAN & CEO
John Speridakos ■ CFO
Phil Graham ■ SENIOR VP, MANUFACTURING & PRODUCTION
Barbara Schmitz ■ VP, MANUFACTURING
John Lerner ■ EXECUTIVE VP, INTERACTIVE MEDIA
Mike Kuehn ■ DIRECTOR, IT

F+W PUBLICATIONS, INC.
MAGAZINE GROUP
David Blansfield ■ PRESIDENT
Sara DeCarlo ■ VP, CONSUMER MARKETING
Tom Wiandt ■ DIRECTOR, BUSINESS PLANNING
Sara Dumford ■ CONFERENCE DIRECTOR
Linda Engel ■ CIRCULATION DIRECTOR
Susan Rose ■ NEWSSTAND DIRECTOR
Michael Kushner ■ DIRECTOR, DIGITAL MEDIA SOLUTIONS
Debbie Thomas ■ PRODUCTION COORDINATOR

SUBSCRIPTION RATES: A year's subscription (4 issues) is $19.96. In Canada: Add $5 for postage & handling (includes GST/HST). Outside the U.S. and Canada: Add $10 for postage & handling and remit payment in U.S. funds with order.
NEWSSTAND DISTRIBUTION: Curtis Circulation Co., 730 River Road, New Milford, NJ 07646
POSTMASTER: Send all address changes to Woodworking Magazine, P.O. Box 420235, Palm Coast, FL 32142-0235. Canada GST Reg # R122594716.
SUBSCRIPTION SERVICES: Subscription inquiries, orders and address changes can be made at woodworking-magazine.com (click on "Customer Service"). Or by mail: Woodworking Magazine, P.O. Box 420235, Palm Coast, FL 32142-0235. Or call toll-free 1-800-283-3542 or 386-597-4322. Include your address with all inquiries. Allow 4 to 6 weeks for delivery.
BACK ISSUES: Back issues are available. For pricing information or to order, call 800-258-0929, visit our web site at woodworking-magazine.com or send check or money order to: Woodworking Magazine Back Issues, F+W Publications Products, 700 E. State St., Iola, WI 54990. Please specify Woodworking Magazine and issue date.

fw ©2008

Highly Recommended

Anyone who has worked in our shop knows my deep affection for the Veritas Chamfer Guide ($21.50 from LeeValleyTools.com). This aluminum accessory replaces the sliding mouth plate on the Veritas block plane and allows you to cut crisp, ready-to-finish chamfers up to ½" wide. Once you reach the chamfer you want, the tool automatically stops cutting. Very cool.
— Christopher Schwarz

On the Level

No More Middleman

I've held and used handplanes that are worth more than my truck, but the most amazing tool I've seen lately is a bevel-edge chisel with a clear plastic handle, navy blue plastic accents and a JCPenney label.

One of my students pulled that chisel out of his tool bag in March to chop out some waste in the sawbench he was building, and placed it on his workbench. I snatched the chisel up as I walked past and gave it a long and longing look.

Judging from the industrial design and graphics, the tool looked fresh from the golden age of disco. At first I was impressed that the blade was rust-free, but then I noticed that the side bevels of the chisel were fairly fine. The bevels weren't as exquisitely tiny as those on an old Swan chisel or a new Lie-Nielsen, but they were small enough that it could chop dovetails without bruising the joint. Despite the tool's plastic handle, it was well-balanced, lightweight and comfortable in the hand.

Now don't fool yourself; it's unlikely that JCPenney actually made that tool. Chances are that the midmarket retailer had a large tool manufacturer such as Stanley Works make the tool and stamp the JCPenney name on it. But what was really amazing about this chisel was that it was a competently made tool, a good industrial design and was sold for a solid middle-class price.

And that's rare among tools these days.

Almost every day, I see the world of toolmaking moving into two camps: well-made tools with substantial price tags, and poorly made tools that aren't worth the bottlecaps they're made from. The middle-class tool is harder and harder to find in stores and in catalogs.

Why? Some of it is technology. Modern manufacturing has allowed companies such as Festool, Veritas and Lie-Nielsen to make tools with precision that puts the best vintage tools to shame. And that same technology has allowed companies to make tools that are quite inexpensive and good for just a couple jobs before they break.

This phenomenon isn't exclusive to woodworking tools. It's also common in another sector that is dear to our hearts: the furniture industry. The American consumer who wants to buy furniture thinks he or she is faced with two choices: High-dollar bespoke or manufactured furniture, or the railroad-salvage, pressed-wood, soul-choking stuff in department stores everywhere.

Of course, you and I know that there are two other oft-forgotten choices: Buy antique furniture (and fix it up) or learn to build your own. And the same choices are available to woodworkers: You can buy vintage tools (and learn to fix them up) or make your own – a decision that I think is becoming more common.

In my shop, I have made all four of these tool-acquisition choices. I have premium planes and chisels that I use every day. I have vintage tools that I've resurrected – a sometimes-grueling process that results in me owning a great tool and understanding completely how it works. These vintage tools are usually examples that no one makes anymore, like my Stanley No. 46 plane.

> *"The things we make show to the world what we are. The furniture of a period is a sure index to the ideals and aspirations of that period – or to the lack of them."*
> — Elbert Hubbard (1856 - 1915)
> author and teacher

I have made my own tools: drawbore pins, split-nut screwdrivers, marking knives, several planes and a handsaw. These I make because I cannot find vintage ones or – surprisingly – for the enjoyment of it.

And then there is my toolbox of shame. The broken drill bits, countersinks, flush-cut saws and band saw blades that I bought against my better judgment. I've kept them – some for 10 years – as a reminder not to buy cheap junk again.

Plus there's one other tool. It's a 72" folding rule that's bright yellow with brass fittings and fine graduations. It's labeled "Penncraft." Yup, that was JCPenney's line of tools. This tool I keep to remember the middle ground that is fast disappearing under our feet. **WM**

Christopher Schwarz
Editor

Letters

ILLUSTRATIONS BY HAYES SHANESY

Does Exposure to Sunlight Harm Wooden Hand Tools?

First and foremost, I want to thank you. As a self-taught amateur woodworker I appreciate and enjoy your sharing of traditional woodworking in *Woodworking Magazine*. I eagerly look forward to reading and rereading your articles.

Also, I've a question regarding having a window in the woodshop: Does the sunlight have any adverse effect on your wooden hand tools if they are constantly stored on the ledge?

Johnny Medina
Bakersfield, California

Johnny,
I've had my tools on racks like that for many years, both in my home shop and my shop at work. The light doesn't hurt the wood. However, what does imperil them while being out in the open on the tool rack is the dust on the steel.

Dust can contain salts, and dust can attract and absorb moisture from the air. And as I'm sure you know, moisture and salt are not kind to carbon steels in saws and chisels. As a result, I need to regularly wipe down my tools. I do this right before I put each tool back in its place, and I use a rag soaked with a little oil. Any oil will do, including good old WD-40.

Christopher Schwarz, editor

Protecting Workpieces in a Vise

I've almost finished building a workbench and this is the first time I've built a bench, much less mounted a vise. I have a Groz 9" quick-release vise on order and am now second guessing my choice. I'd really like a piece of wood mounted in my "yet to be determined" vise to butt directly against the front of the bench. My thought is to someday have dog holes on the front for a holdfast.

From what I've read on the subject, it seems I should put wood faces on my vise jaws. If I do that, the wood in my vise will stick out about an inch unless I mortise deeply enough to to accommodate that as well.

So, do I stick with the Groz vise, which I like, and not put a wood face on the back (and would I then risk marring my work)? Or, do I switch to a more traditional vise that is meant to have wood faces?

Corey Crooks
Erie, Colorado

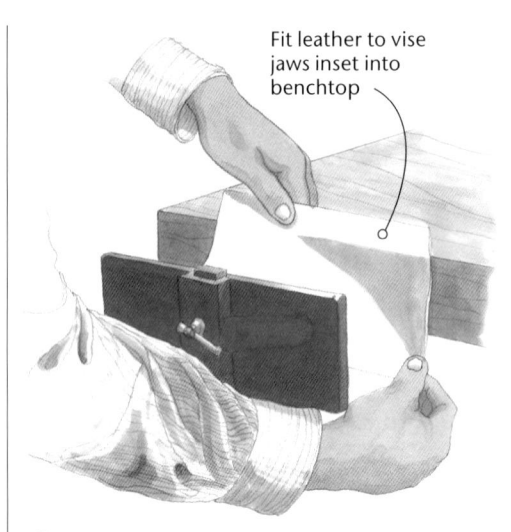

Fit leather to vise jaws inset into benchtop

Corey,
I use my bench as a power-tool woodworker does. I have yet to put any wood face on my two metal vises. I have worked for years without any wood attached to the vise. If I am working on a finished piece I simply add a piece of wood to the mix to eliminate marring. If I'm working on a piece that has yet to be sanded, I use the vise as-is.

If I worried about such matters, I would add a piece of leather to the vise faces (which I may do later), which would require that you set the vise a $^1/_8$" or so deeper into the top.

I would not give up my quick-release vise. I think that style vise is the perfect setup for woodworking at a bench.

Glen D. Huey, senior editor

I like to add a layer of leather to the jaws (you can use epoxy or polyurethane glue to do it), because it makes the jaws grippier and prevents any damage. Really, the major concern is the grip strength; damage to the workpiece is fairly rare.

I'd recommend you inset the rear jaw of your vise a little into the benchtop to fit the leather flush to the front edge. That will prevent some workpieces from vibrating as you work them.

Christopher Schwarz, editor

Doesn't Wood Harbor Harmful Bacteria in Cutting Boards?

From the editor: The topic of using wood in the kitchen is now a controversial one. While wooden spoons, bowls, plates, utensils, goblets and cutting boards were once common, now plastic, metal and ceramic are instead used in most kitchens. While the primary reason for this is surely the cost of manufacturing, there also is the now-popular opinion that these new materials are more hygienic. Robert W. Lang's "Circular Cutting Board" from Woodworking Magazine *Spring 2008, Issue 9*, has prompted several readers to question if building a wooden cutting board is wise. So I asked Robert to respond.

Christopher Schwarz, editor

Whether a plastic or a wood surface is safer for food preparation is one of the great debates of our times. I wasn't able to pinpoint a date when it started, but sometime in the 1970s the United States Department of Agriculture began recommending plastic for cutting boards, based on the reasoning that it was easier to clean and sanitize a nonporous plastic surface compared to a porous wooden one.

Like a whispered rumor in a classroom, as time went on people assigned good qualities to plastic and bad qualities to wood, the most common objection being that wood harbored bacteria.

As well-meaning as the USDA's advice was, there wasn't a shred of scientific testing done to back it up until 1994 when Dean Oliver, Ph.D., was told by them there was no scientific evidence to back their recommendations. Oliver, then at the University of Wisconsin, performed experiments on new and used plastic and wood cutting boards.

His main conclusion was that bacteria are not able to multiply in an environment of wood, yet they breed like tribbles on plastic. Additionally, as cutting-board surfaces are used, grooves from knife marks in plastic boards tend to be deeper and more hospitable homes for bacteria. In wood surfaces, particularly in hard maple, knives leave very shallow scratches that tend to close as the board is washed.

"Man is a shrewd inventor, and is ever taking the hint of a new machine from his own structure, adapting some secret of his own anatomy in iron, wood and leather, to some required function in the work of the world."

— Ralph Waldo Emerson (1803-1882)
essayist, philosopher and poet

With either material, the key to not poisoning your family is to keep the cutting board clean, especially after cutting raw meat. If you wash the surface with soap and water after each use, most of the harmful bugs will meet their doom.

One other point I'd like to emphasize was an experiment done by Bob Flexner several years ago about cutting-board warping. Bob found that boards tended to warp when only the working surface was washed. This can be eliminated by always washing both sides, keeping the exchange of moisture equal on the entire cutting board.
— Robert W. Lang, senior editor

Holtzapffel Bench Questions

I am a novice woodworker/carpenter (I do stress novice here) with a goal of building the Holtzapffel bench from *Woodworking Magazine* Issue 8, Autumn 2007. The challenge I face is not only my lack of experience but also my lack of a fully stocked shop. I don't own a power planer or jointer and don't have the room or budget to buy those.

I do own a small table saw, a benchtop drill press, assorted hand power tools and a growing and nice set of premium hand tools, which include a full set of bevel-edge chisels, a low-angle jack plane, a low-angle jointer plane, one mortise chisel and a couple backsaws. I have learned to sharpen decently and can at least "wield" my planes.

My question for you is this: Can I build the bench out of rough-sawn lumber (as you did in your magazine) with the tools I have, or is it just too big of a job until I get a power planer and jointer?

In addition, I did not understand in the article how you rounded the end of the vise chops. You mentioned routing them to give them the "traditional" look. Did you mean you actually rounded them with the router? If so, how?
— *Kipper Odom*
Fayetteville, Georgia

Kipper,
You can indeed build anything out of rough lumber with the tools you list. And though it will take more time than if you had a power planer and jointer, it will be a tremendous learning experience.

My only recommendation would be to use a species of wood that is easy to work with hand tools, such as yellow pine, poplar, Douglas fir or even white pine – or perhaps oak. I'd stay away from the really tough woods, such as hickory, as you develop your hand skills as tough woods will only frustrate you.

The other option would be to seek out a woodworking club in your area and join it. I've found the members of clubs to be very willing to open their shops to help along new woodworkers. I'll bet you could find someone who will help you mill the rough lumber so you can get started on the joinery for your bench.

As far as the vise chops, you can shape them with a large beading bit in a router table. However, the far less expensive way to do it would be to rough out the shape with a saw and chisel, then refine the curve with a rasp and sandpaper.
— *Christopher Schwarz, editor*

Perforated Diamond Stone Performs Better for Us

I just read your article "Sharpen a Chisel" in *Woodworking Magazine* Autumn 2004, Issue 2. You suggest to first use a coarse diamond stone. The DMT diamond stone is perforated; is there any advantage to using a solid-surface diamond stone instead of the perforated one?
— *John Gray*
via e-mail

Perforated stone

Solid-surface stone

John,
Personally, I like DMT's perforated pattern because it seems to clear the swarf (a fancy word for the metal filings created by sharpening) better. The solid ones seem (and that's an important word here) to clog faster to me, so you are cleaning them more frequently.

Lots of people have success with both types.
— *Christopher Schwarz, editor*

How Long Will Glue Joints Last? And are Nails Better than Screws?

Your magazine advocates the use of nails and drawboring to overcome flaws in the glue. And there are a couple things I'm wondering about.

One is glue longevity. If I glue together a tabletop with hide glue, will it fall apart in 100 years? Or 200? Or do glue joints fail only if they are stressed? (Presumably the side-grain-to-side-grain joint of a tabletop creates very little stress on the joint.) I haven't heard of people, say, putting together tabletops using sliding dovetails to ensure strength.

Also, why are nails better than screws? I haven't tried to use nails in cabinetry, but I've tried to use them in carpentry. My experience has led me to hate nails and to use screws instead whenever possible. Nails bend over, they split the work (sometimes even with a pilot hole), and hammering them in can be very loud and subjects the work to stresses, possibly causing parts to move or shift. Maybe a screw head is harder to hide than a nail head. But is there some other reason to prefer nails?
— *Adrian Mariano*
via e-mail

Adrian,
Any good glue joint can last centuries, as evidenced by the fine furniture from the 1600s that is in museums. Its life will be shortened by moisture, heat and stress. Moisture on a tabletop is a common factor. Heat can be. And tabletop joints are stressed at the ends by the seasonal migration of moisture through the end grain – that's why antique tops split on the ends typically.

Breadboard ends and cross-battens are typical and historically correct methods of helping to keep a top together.

To answer your second question, I don't consider nails to be better than screws for all occasions. The advantages of screws that you list are all statements that I would agree with.

But there are some advantages to using nails at times. Nails will bend to accommodate wood movement. Screws won't bend. They'll split the work instead. Nails are smaller and can be used in places that screws would be ugly (for example, nailing on face frames and moulding). Nails are inserted faster than screws (however removing nails sure can be slower!). And nails can be historically correct in pieces, which can be important to some woodworkers.
— *Christopher Schwarz, editor*

Issue 9 is a Cover-to-cover Read

I just received my first issue of *Woodworking Magazine* (Spring 2008, Issue 9) and I am pleasantly surprised. I subscribed to this magazine without ever reading one, which I never do, and I read the magazine cover to cover – every article, letter and tip. This is a first for me also. I honestly do not remember when I have ever read everything written cover to cover in a magazine before. Please keep up the good work. If *Woodworking Magazine* maintains this level of interest to me you will have a loyal subscriber for years to come. **WM**
— *Mark Hoard*
via e-mail

HOW TO CONTACT US

Send your comments and questions via e-mail to letters@fwpubs.com, or by regular mail to *Woodworking Magazine*, Letters, 4700 E. Galbraith Road, Cincinnati, OH 45236. Please include your complete mailing address and daytime phone number. All letters become property of *Woodworking Magazine*.

Shortcuts

ILLUSTRATIONS BY HAYES SHANESY

Plane Precise Chamfers with An Edge-trimming Plane

I own an edge-trimming block plane that is great for the purpose explained in its name. However, I figured there must be other ways to use this handy tool. I recently completed a cutting board on which I wanted chamfered edges on both corners, and I was hoping for something that would be a little more precise and symmetrical than freehand chamfering. My solution came in the form of my edge plane. I realized that if I scribed a line down the middle of the edge I wanted to chamfer, and kept the tool's corner where the fence meets the sole directly over that line, I would get a chamfer that was very close to 45°. I did several passes on one side, and when I switched to the other side, the plane's fence rode nicely on the chamfer I had just cut. The skewed blade helps in preventing tear-out.

It's not difficult to eyeball the chamfer sizes and stop when they're the same, or you can scribe lines on both edges and stop planing when you hit the line.

Andy Newhouse
Syracuse, New York

Editor's note: Another good option for planing precise chamfers with that plane is to affix a 45° fence to the tool – either with double-stick table or the screw holes provided in the tool's fence.

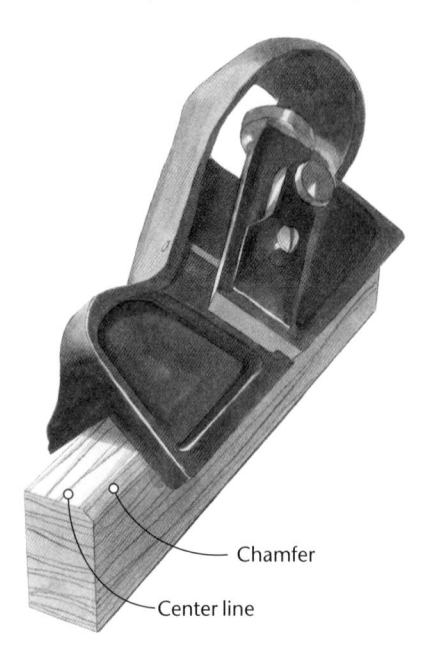

Chamfer
Center line

Add a Deadman to Your Bench Without Major Surgery

Dog holes
Deadman
Face vise

A deadman is a great addition to any workbench with a face vise because you can easily deal with long boards. You pinch one end in your face vise and the deadman supports the other end of the board from below.

However, not every bench can be easily retrofitted with a deadman. Here's how I did it to my bench with some dimensional pine boards.

As with many woodworkers, the rear jaw of my quick-release face vise is proud of the front edge of my benchtop (this makes the vise a snap to install). So my retrofitted deadman takes advantage of that fact.

My deadman hangs down the front of the workbench and is made of two parts and some dowels. The top plate rests on top of the workbench. Two dowels in the top plate fit into holes in my workbench top. When I want to move the deadman, I just shift it into a different pair of holes.

The part that hangs down the front of the bench is attached to the top plate with glue and screws. It's bored with nine holes (you might need more or fewer). A dowel serves as the movable peg for supporting the work from below.

Phil Baker
Ogdensburg, New Jersey

A Finish That is Difficult to Ruin and Inexpensive to Make

Until we can sneak a spray booth into our offices here at *Woodworking Magazine*, we will continue to use hand-applied finishes for projects.

We all have our favorite hand-applied film finishes, but they are all a variation of a simple and inexpensive all-purpose finish that we mix ourselves and apply with a rag.

The finish is one-third boiled linseed oil, one-third spar varnish and one third low-odor mineral spirits (some of us use turpentine, but its strong and lingering smell generates complaints from some of the employees in our building).

The linseed oil gives the wood a nice warm glow and brings out any unusual figure in the wood. The varnish gives you some scratch-protection. The mineral spirits makes the home-brew easy to rag on in even coats. Note: We use varnish instead of polyurethane because it is easier to sand it between coats if necessary.

Simply pour all three parts of the finish into a glass jar, mix them up and apply the finish in an even coat with a rag. Once the entire project is coated, use a second rag to remove the excess. Allow the project to dry overnight. After a couple coats, you can sand between the coats with lubricated #320-grit paper to remove dust nibs if necessary and prepare the surface for the next coat.

After three or four coats, the varnish will begin to build nicely and you can then stop when you get the look you want. If we want to make a surface feel really smooth, we'll let the finish cure for a couple days then rub it out with a 3M gray pad and a mixture of Murphy Oil Soap and warm water.

Woodworking Magazine staff

Use Your Burnisher for a Quick Fix for a Chipbreaker

Chipbreakers are one of the weakest links when it comes to tuning up a handplane. If a plane chokes with shavings or simply fails to cut correctly, the first place to look is the chipbreaker.

One common chipbreaker malady is that you have a gap between the breaker and the iron. Even a small gap is a trap for shavings. And once a shaving gets pushed into that gap, it usually clogs up the entire works and you are going to have to disassemble the iron and breaker to fix things.

To eliminate the gap between the chipbreaker and the iron, most woodworkers abrade the underside of the chipbreaker on a coarse sharpening stone. This flattens out the leading lip of your breaker and (usually) improves the fit.

Several years ago I stumbled on a 19th-century fix for gappy breakers. I rejected it at first as metal mangling. But recently I gave it a try on an old chipbreaker to see if it would work. It did. And it worked quite well. So here it is.

Tighten the breaker against the iron. Then take your burnisher and rub it firmly against the leading edge of the breaker (a burnisher with a point makes this easier). This action deforms the soft metal in the breaker and flows it into the gap. And (as an added bonus) the metal is highly burnished by the process, so shavings slide over the burnished areas.

Here are the catches: This won't work if the gap is large – it will eliminate only the small slivers of light you see between the breaker and iron. Second, the fix is not always permanent. The metal that you push into the gap isn't well-supported and can break off when you remove the breaker. But if you need to get back to work and you need a fast fix, this trick is a gem.

Christopher Schwarz, editor

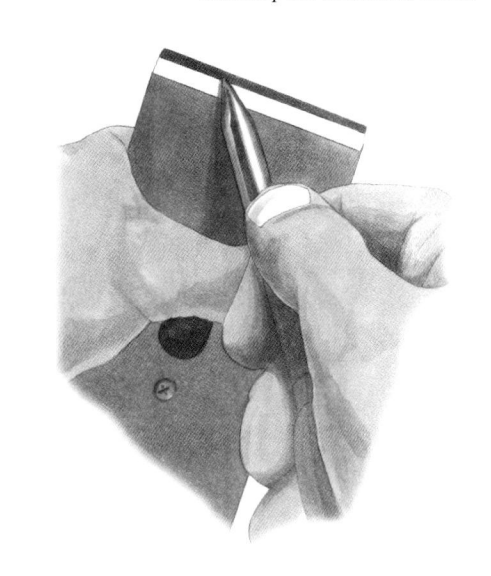

Old Trick Transfers Dovetails From One Board to Another

I was looking through William Fairham's "Woodwork Joints, How they are Set Out, How Made and Where Used" (I was doing some housed and mitered dovetails) and came across the reference below. I thought it novel. He had just explained how to use a knife and a saw for transferring the pin locations from the tail board on through-dovetails and then Fairham adds:

"Other workers prefer a pounce-bag instead of a saw. A pounce-bag consists of a piece of fairly open woven muslin filled with a mixture of French chalk and finely powdered whiting; the muslin is tied up with a piece of thin twine like the mouth of a flour sack. All that is necessary is to place the timber in position and bang the bag on the top of the saw-cuts, when sufficient powder will pass through the bag and down the saw kerf to mark the exact positions of the lines."

Mike Wenzloff
Forest Grove, Oregon

We decided to try this trick. The French chalk was fairly easy – it's essentially powered talc. You can find it at the fabric stores where it is used for marking cloth. Or you can go to the pharmacy and buy baby powder, which is talc and fragrance.

Whiting is calcium carbonate (ground chalk) and is used in preparing artist paints these days. You can find it at an artist supply store.

We didn't have muslin, so I tried some other fabrics. Surgical rags were too coarse and the powder went flying. Then I tried an athletic sock. Bingo. It deposited a fine dusting of powder when I whacked the sock on the dovetails.

As I was experimenting with the different whacking forces and whacking vectors, I cleaned off the pin board after each whack with a little water and a rag. And that water seemed to make the powder even easier to see. The powder also works to fill knife lines in dark woods.

Christopher Schwarz, editor

"Have no fear of perfection — you'll never reach it."

— Salvador Dali (1904 - 1989)
Surrealist painter

Stupid Tape Trick No. 312: How to Make Narrow Strips

With complex pieces of casework (especially ones assembled on-site), I often finish all my components before gluing them together. So I have to tape off my joints to avoid coating them with stain and finish, which can weaken my glue joints.

Usually, I use blue painter's tape for the job, but the most frustrating thing about it is that it is too wide when taping up mortises, biscuit slots or Domino recesses.

Wide tape has to be applied with precision so that you don't tape off something that should be finished. What I really want for this job is $3/8$"-wide painter's tape. I'm sure it exists but not in my town.

So I make my own. And it's shockingly fast and easy. I use a cutting gauge (shown is a Tite-Mark). Cutting gauges have a little knife on the end that is perfectly suited for cutting tape. So I simply set my cutting gauge for the thickness of tape I want ($3/8$" in this case) and run the gauge around the roll of $3/4$"-wide tape. After a few seconds, I have two perfect strips of $3/8$"-wide tape ready to apply over my joints. **WM**

Christopher Schwarz, editor

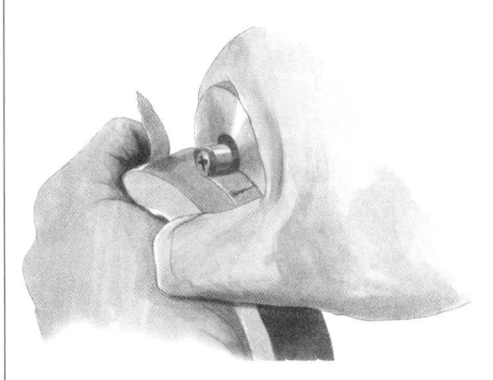

SEND US YOUR SHORTCUT

We will provide a complimentary one-year subscription (or extend your current subscription) for each Shortcut we print. Send your Shortcut via e-mail to shortcuts@fwpubs.com, or by post to *Woodworking Magazine*, Shortcuts, 4700 E. Galbraith Road, Cincinnati, OH 45236. Please include your complete mailing address and daytime phone number. All Shortcuts become property of *Woodworking Magazine*.

Better Finger Joints

The dovetail's machine-age cousin is fussy to cut and assemble. We've fixed both those faults.

Most woodworking joints can be traced back in time for centuries. Ancient Egyptians excelled at dovetails and the Romans relied on mortises and tenons. Joinery was all handwork until the Industrial Revolution mechanized most processes in the middle of the 19th century. Mortisers, table saws, tenoners and dovetailing machines were all in common use in furniture factories well before 1900.

In addition to new ways to make old joints, machinery and tooling were developed to create joints that weren't common at the time, but became popular because they could be made quickly. The finger joint, also called a box joint, is an example of this development.

Before the machine era, this joint was used only to form a wooden hinge. When first developed, and until recently, it was strictly utilitarian, used mainly to make strong shipping boxes and crates. With our current infatuation for visible and decorative joinery, the finger joint has moved from utility to visibility.

The effort to cut a finger joint entirely with hand tools is at least equal to the effort to hand cut dovetails. In many ways it takes more effort, and the return for the effort is dubious. It is a more demanding joint to make, and it lacks the inherent mechanical advantage and aesthetic appeal of the dovetail. But it is significantly easier and faster to make finger joints by machine, if one is willing to work precisely to set up the tools.

For example, the jig used to build the Blanket Chest on page 16 in this issue was intended to have slots and fingers ⅝" wide. When completed, the overall width of the jig was ¹⁄₁₆" bigger than planned. That translates to an error in each component of .0025", about half the thickness of the average human hair. Because the parts are all the same size, the joints produced fit together nicely, and if I hadn't told you about the variation, you wouldn't notice it in the finished piece.

If you're trying to cut finger joints with a fixed-width cutter such as a dado stack or router bit, that half-a-hair is about the outer limit of tolerance. If you can't set up, measure and adjust in those teeny increments, you'll be dependent on luck alone to make a nice finger joint. But working to that degree isn't as hard as you might think.

A shop-built router jig can make large, accurate finger joints. The solution for making a better jig proved to be finding a better duct tape.

A good fit on a finger joint can be assembled with hand pressure only. If you need to beat on it or clamp it to get it to close, it is too tight.

An attachment to the miter gauge shows the exact location of the cut, allowing you to make irregularly spaced joints.

Clamp the work securely to the miter gauge and make certain the cut is within the waste area.

Confidence in cutting is the key to a successful joint, whether it is cut by eye or by jig.

A Rout of Passage

Making finger joints is a good opportunity to develop skills. Even if you abandon finger joints after one or two tries, the exercise will expand your woodworking vocabulary. You may decide to move on to more attractive joinery, or you may decide that this is a worthy method for much of your work. In either case, the effort will make you a better woodworker. The lessons learned in finger joints will serve well in other areas.

Finger joints are very strong. The amount of interlocking surface area makes a corner with a large area of long-grain to long-grain glue surface and good mechanical strength. The only weak area is the way the joint resembles a hinge. A sharp impact directly on the corner can cause the joint to unfold or come apart. Except for that disastrous scenario it's as strong as a joint can be, and a good choice for small boxes and drawers.

The type of wood used will make a difference in how forgiving the joint is to put together. Softer woods, such as pine or poplar, will compress when assembled. White oak or maple aren't as cooperative, and may require more force to assemble, and more finesse to make the joint. This is a place where the science of the machinist and the art of the woodworker converge. The tolerances are close, but the joint should be made so that it can be assembled without resorting to clamps or hammer persuasion.

The location of the sweet spot for fitting will also vary with the width of the joint or the number of fingers. It's a matter of compounding errors, and like compounding interest, a number that seems insignificant can grow large enough to defeat you. A handful of finger joints for a drawer is fairly easy. A finger joint the size of those used on the blanket chest (especially in a hard, unforgiving wood) is pushing the limits, but not beyond possibility for the careful craftsman.

Consistency and repeatability is the key to finger joints. If you can cut accurately (and stay on the right side of the line) you can line up each cut individually. Attaching an L-shaped backer to the table saw's miter gauge shows the exact location of the cut, and this can be used quite effectively to make precise cuts on the table saw.

If the spacing of the fingers varies as shown, and you're only making a few joints, this is a faster method than making a dedicated jig.

Regularly sized and spaced fingers shout for a jig. It's fussy work, but repetitious. The secret is to use a method that builds consistency into the process. If the work is small enough to safely travel vertically over the saw blade, the jig pictured on page 8 is an old standby that works well.

woodworking-magazine.com ■ 7

Time-tested Method

This is the classic method of producing a finger joint with a jig that attaches to the table saw miter gauge, and it works very well for small pieces. It's reasonable to run a drawer side vertically over the table saw, but longer or wider work becomes unwieldy. If you're uneasy about holding the work on the table saw, try the router jig on page 10.

Because the table saw jig requires the saw to be set up with a dado head, cut all the parts you need before changing over to the stack dado set. You should prepare the parts for the jig, the parts you intend to join, and several extra pieces of stock for making test cuts.

You'll need a piece of plywood, at least $\frac{1}{2}$" thick and about 6" x 12". In addition, you'll need a piece of hardwood the exact thickness of the width of the cut and about 12" long. I rip the hardwood a little thicker than necessary, then use a handplane to sneak up on a good fit in the slot. It doesn't hurt to have an extra piece on hand in case you go too far with the plane.

Simple Concept – Precise Execution

After installing the stack dado head (we used $\frac{1}{4}$", but the fingers can be any width) make certain the head of the miter gauge is square to the blade and adjust the height of the blade to the thickness of the parts to be joined. Hold the plywood vertically against the miter gauge and make a cut near the end. The exact location isn't critical, but leave at least $\frac{3}{4}$" to 1" beyond the cut. From here on, you need to be as precise as you can be.

Reduce the thickness of the hardwood guide block until you can press it into the slot in the plywood. You need only worry about the thickness, not the width, as long as the width is less than the height of the slot. A set of calipers will help in letting you know how close you are. If you measure your plane shaving, you will be able to predict the size as you work, and you should check the fit of the actual piece in the slot frequently.

When the piece fits, cut a couple inches off one end and glue it in the slot. I use cyanoacrylate (Super Glue) so I don't have to wait too long for the glue to dry, but any wood glue will work.

After letting the glue dry, place the longer piece of hardwood against the edge of the dado stack. Slide the miter gauge into position, then move the plywood laterally until the two hardwood sticks are touching along their lengths.

Don't throw the longer piece away; you'll need it again in a few minutes. Clamp the plywood to the miter gauge and secure it with a couple pan head screws. If all went well, you'll be in the right position. If not, the flat areas under the screw heads will let you move the plywood side to side for a fine adjustment.

First Cut – Testing, Testing

Both halves of a joint are cut at the same time. One piece is held against the hardwood protruding from the plywood, and the other piece is offset by the width of the slot. The extra piece of hardwood is used as a spacer to align the parts for the first cut.

Table Saw Finger Joints

Jig construction for the table saw method starts with cutting a notch in the plywood backer that attaches to the miter gauge.

The hardwood guide block must match the width of the slot exactly. It's right when you can feel some resistance as you press it into the slot by hand.

An extra piece of hardwood is used to set the distance between the blade and the other block. Make it long enough to be held against the blade front and back.

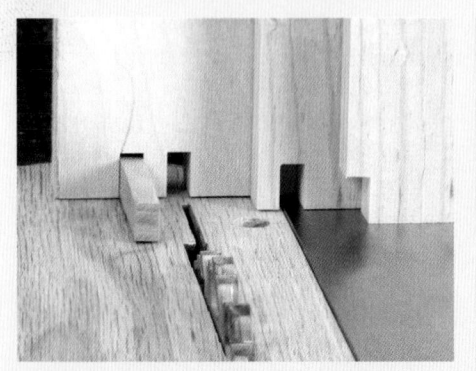

One half of the joint is cut against the guide block, forming a notch. The other half is held away by the spacer, cutting out the corner.

Both pieces are cut at the same time. After the first cut, the pieces are placed with the notches over the guide block.

As the cuts continue, each cut registers the next cut, and if the setup is correct, the work proceeds quickly.

Clamping the two pieces together, and to the plywood attached to the miter gauge, allows you to make the first cut safely. You won't have to worry about the pieces slipping, and you can concentrate on moving the miter gauge smoothly forward with your hands away from the dado stack.

After making the first cut, set the spacer aside. Each succeeding cut is made by placing the notch just made over the hardwood, as seen in the photos on the facing page. The spacer will keep the work from slipping sideways, so you don't need to use a clamp after the first cut. You can pause after the first few passes to see if the fingers and slots fit together, but it goes fast enough that I prefer to cut the entire width of the joint before making a test fit.

There are three possible outcomes. In the best case, the two parts of the joint will come together with hand pressure only and have no visible gaps. If the joint won't go together at all, the fingers are wider than the slots. To correct this, loosen the screws holding the plywood to the miter gauge, and move the plywood so that the hardwood guide is closer to the blade.

If the fit is sloppy, the fingers are too small, and the plywood needs to be moved in the opposite direction. When adjusting either way, use the extra hardwood spacer as an aid. It's easy for something to slip a little as you hold things in position and tighten the screws. When you're happy with the fit, making the joints goes quickly, and as long as the parts are the same width, there aren't many things that can go wrong. A similar jig can also be used on a router table.

Better Way for Bigger Boxes

On larger work, a better approach is to build a jig for moving the tool across the work. The first choice for this is the router instead of the table saw. Our solution is the shop-made jig on page 10. Equal-width material for the fingers and spacers is the key element to this jig. It is quick to assemble, adaptable to any practical width, and with a bit of tweaking is incredibly accurate.

Although finger joints look complex, the whole idea is that the cuts be made efficiently. With many joints, the bulk of your investment in time will be in tweaking the fit after machining. The opposite is true of finger joints; take your time getting set up to make the cuts so they will fit nicely directly from the machine.

Make extra pieces to test your jig, your setup and your technique. I start with two pieces of stock, and if the first test isn't quite where I want it, I trim a couple inches or so off the ends and try again. This leaves enough to have assembled joints to see if I'm really making progress, but doesn't waste material unnecessarily.

A Crazy (Glue) Solution

The downside to the finger joint is that it takes some time to apply glue during assembly. Water-based glues will swell the fingers and that can keep the joint from going together. Or the glue can begin to dry on one end before you have finished spreading the glue.

One solution is to partially assemble the joint, and apply the glue with a brush. If it's a large assembly, use a slow-setting glue such as liquid hide glue or polyurethane glue, and clamp the corners one at a time.

An alternative we found is to assemble and clamp the joint without glue. Thin cyanoacrylate is then applied along the outer intersections of the joint and allowed to wick into the joints. Set one side of the joint horizontally, apply the glue and wait about five minutes before turning the work and gluing the opposite side.

With this technique the glue won't dry instantly, but if left for a few hours it will become as strong as a conventionally glued joint.

We tried this method with some other glues, including thin PVAs intended for fixing loose joints in chairs. The "Chair Doctor" produced a strong joint, but sealed the end grain enough that it showed when the joint was finished. The cyanoacrylate left no visible traces after the completed joint was trimmed with a block plane. **WM**

— *Robert W. Lang*

This may look crazy, but it works. Thin cyanoacrylate glue will wick into the joint after it is clamped together and hold as well as any other method of gluing.

"We have not the reverent feeling for the rainbow that the savage has, because we know how it is made. We have lost as much as we gained by prying into that matter."

— Mark Twain (1835 - 1910)
author and riverboat pilot

The final step is to trim the surfaces of the joint flush. Close cutting will mean little trimming.

A New Way to Rout Finger Joints on Large Pieces

When we began to plan this issue, the emphasis on finger joints was a given, but the specific techniques weren't. We knew we would feature the table saw and dado method for small parts, but we weren't comfortable milling larger pieces that way. Our first thought for large case pieces was to use a commercially made router jig. That is indeed a workable solution, and many well-made jigs are on the market.

But it didn't seem right to offer no other alternative than sending readers out to make an expensive purchase for a joint they will likely make only on an occasional basis.

Being of frugal stock, I decided there must be another way. The key to finger joints is equal sizes, and I realized that by making fingers and spacers from stock ripped at the same time, I should be able to put together a jig that would perform as well as anything available on the market. In less than an hour I had a working prototype of the jig we used.

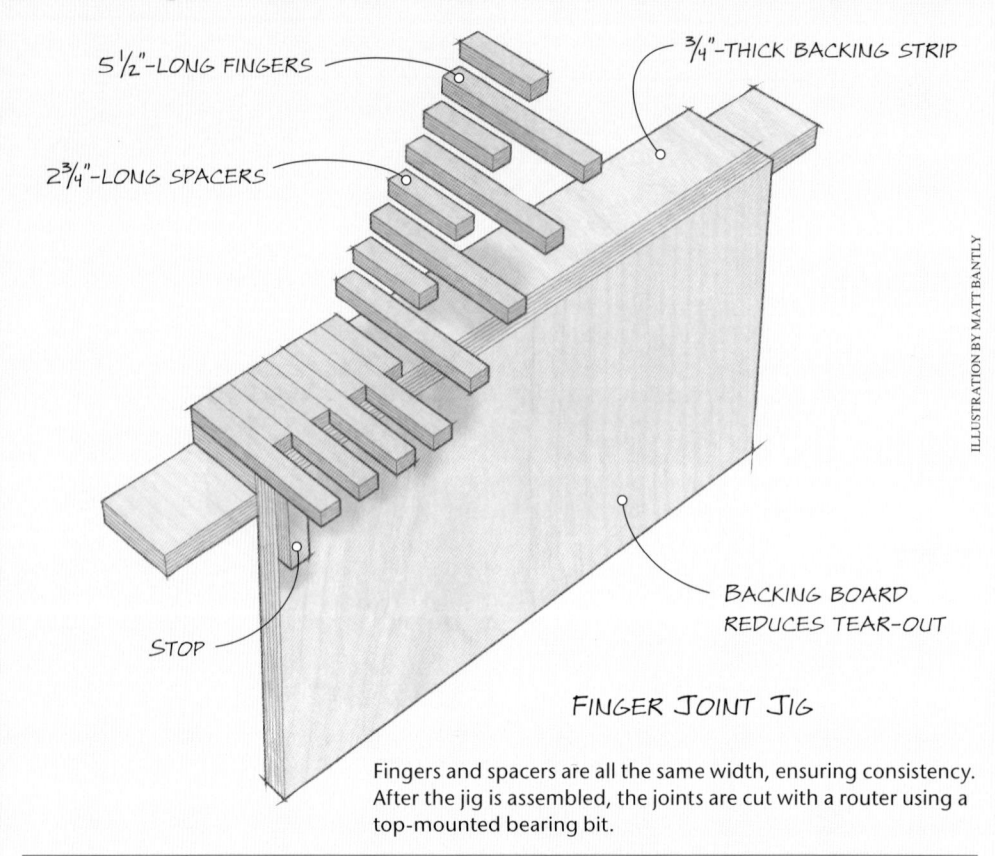

Rip the Strips

We were after joints with $5/8$"-wide fingers and slots, so I began by ripping $1/2$"-thick Baltic-birch plywood to that dimension. The reason for using the plywood was to eliminate wood movement from the equation. I made a couple test cuts and measured the results with calipers to get as close as possible to the proper size.

Ripping carefully from a wide piece of plywood stock yielded enough material to cut the $5 1/2$"-long fingers and the $2 3/4$"-long spacers. After cutting these parts to length, I attached the parts to a $2 3/4$"-wide, $3/4$"-thick plywood backing strip with yellow glue and 23-gauge pins. I laid a few beads of glue on the strip, started with a long piece, and made sure the first piece was squarely placed then butted the parts against one another one at a time and nailed them down. A longer $2 3/4$"-wide piece was added below to stiffen the jig and provide a place for clamping the jig to the bench.

A larger piece of plywood was glued and screwed at a right angle to the backing strip. I placed the screws below the fingers so that I wouldn't cut into them with the router later on. This piece prevents the wood from tearing out on the back of the cuts, and provides a way to attach the work to the jig. One edge of the

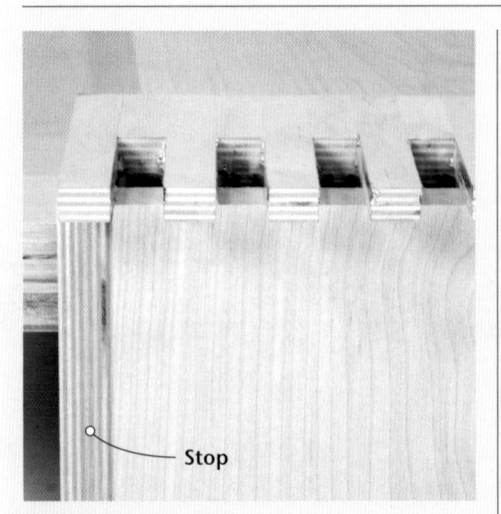

FINGER JOINT JIG

Fingers and spacers are all the same width, ensuring consistency. After the jig is assembled, the joints are cut with a router using a top-mounted bearing bit.

- $5 1/2$"-LONG FINGERS
- $2 3/4$"-LONG SPACERS
- $3/4$"-THICK BACKING STRIP
- STOP
- BACKING BOARD REDUCES TEAR-OUT

The first workpiece is placed with the end tight against the bottom of the fingers, and the left end against the stop.

The second piece is placed over the first, with the left side flush against the outer edge of the first finger on the jig.

Dial calipers will help you zero in on the exact measurement you need.

backer piece is aligned with the edge of the first finger, and a small piece of scrap is attached to the edge to act as a stop.

Both panels of the joint are cut at once. The edge of one piece is placed against the stop with the show side out. The edge of the other is aligned with the opposite side of the first finger, offsetting the joint one finger's width.

Making the fingers of the jig the same size as the finished parts simplified construction and reduced the chances of making an error in calculating the difference between the diameter of a router bit and a template guide. A $\frac{1}{2}$"-diameter flush-trimming bit with a bearing mounted above the cutter would trim the work exactly to the edges of the jig.

Or so I thought. The pieces from my first test cut went together too easily, leaving visible gaps at each joint. My quest for perfection was almost foiled by router and router-bit behavior. My measurements showed the bit and bearing to be the same diameter, and the width of the fingers and spacers to be equal. But the act of making the cuts produced slots a few thousandths of an inch wider than the fingers.

This wasn't entirely unexpected. To get a bit with a $\frac{1}{2}$"-diameter cutter and bearing, I had to use one with a $\frac{1}{4}$"-diameter shank. Even with a pretty good router and a quality bit, enough runout existed to increase the width of the slots by a few thousandths of an inch. This error was consistent, and rather than seek perfection where it didn't exist, I looked for an easy way to make an adjustment to the jig.

The fingers of the joints were undersized, so either the long fingers of the jig needed to be wider, or the spacers in between narrower. Either solution would mean taking the jig apart and starting over. The first step was to see how much change was needed, and answering that question led to a fast and simple solution.

I put blue masking tape on the sides of each finger. My guess was the thickness of the tape would move the router bit enough to obtain a good fit. My instincts were good, but the bearing on the router bit destroyed the tape while cutting the first test joint.

I headed down the street to the local hardware store in search of something thin, sticky and durable. The solution proved to be aluminum duct-sealing tape. This is not to be confused with common duct tape. Duct-sealing tape is much better.

This tape is a thin metal foil with a very sticky back. I cut small pieces off the roll with an X-Acto knife, peeled off the backing paper and placed a piece on the side of each finger. I pressed the handle of the knife over the tape to press it firmly in place. It held up well during routing, and the $9 roll of tape is likely a lifetime supply of an excellent shim material.

Using a router bit with a smaller diameter than the fingers is an advantage. As we experimented with different techniques, we found we achieved the best results by pushing the spinning bit straight in between the fingers to start each cut. This removed most of the waste without putting pressure on the fingers of the jig.

We then made two more passes, holding the bearing against each finger to make a light, clean cut. Both sides were cut by pushing the router into the jig instead of coming in on the left side and out on the right. This reduces tear-out that otherwise might occur as the router bit exits the work on the right-hand side of the slot. This may seem like extra work, but the final two cleanup passes take little time and produce cleaner edges.

With the large pieces of the blanket chest, it was easier to place the backing piece of the jig flat on the bench, clamp the work to the jig, then turn the jig and the work together to a vertical position before clamping the jig to the bench and routing the joints.

This was far easier than trying to hold the workpieces upright while aligning and clamping them to the jig. Fitting the end of the workpieces tight against the bottom of the fingers is critical to obtaining a good joint.

Ideally, the width of the work should be some multiple of the finger width. This leaves the joint with a whole finger or whole space at either side. The stop can be positioned to leave a partial finger at each end, as long as the second piece is offset by the width of a finger.

I considered buying some aluminum bar stock to make a permanent version of this jig – one that would last forever and be incredibly adjustable for any size of box or finger configuration. Luckily, I was talked out of that notion by a co-worker who pointed out that it was so fast and simple to put together this jig that it made more sense just to build a new iteration whenever the need occurred. **WM** — RL

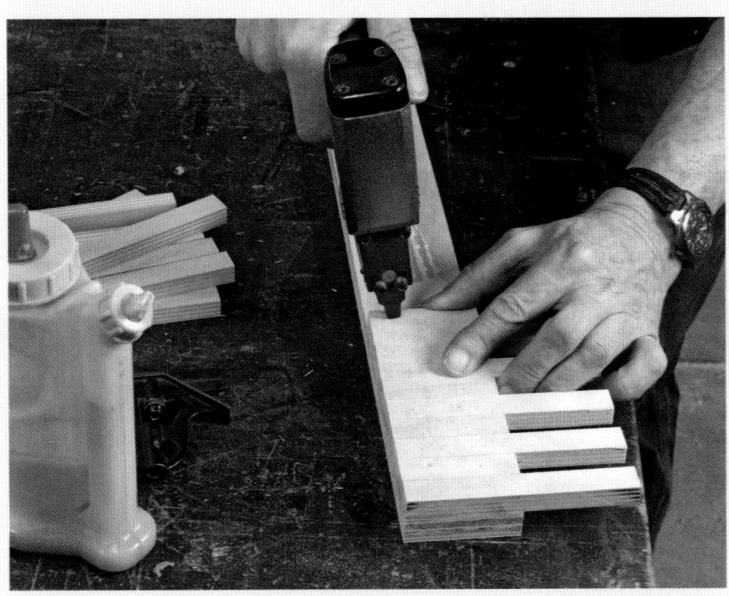

Assembly is simply a matter of gluing and nailing the fingers and spacers to a plywood strip. After making sure the first finger is square, butt one piece against another and nail in place.

Aluminum duct-sealing tape closes the gap caused by router and bit runout, and holds up well in use.

Trim Proud End Grain

Whether you use hand or power methods, the trick to efficient and neat work has little to do with the tools.

The best way to trim end grain is to do as little of it as possible.

Many woodworkers tend to design joints and assemblies with a good deal of proud end grain that has to be trimmed back after the carcase is assembled. Through-dovetails, through-tenons and even rabbeted corner joints are all common places for the woodworker to encounter end grain that needs to be cut flush to the surrounding surface.

With few guidelines as to how much end grain is the correct amount, many woodworkers overcompensate. I've seen through-dovetails that were almost $1/4$" proud after assembly. The problem with this generous allowance is that end grain is tough and can easily split loose when you trim it, whereas the surrounding face grain is easy to work. So when you open up a can of "belt sander" on the end grain, you end up dishing out the surrounding face grain as well. Sometimes this problem doesn't come to light until you apply a film finish to your project.

So the most important tool when trimming end grain is your pencil's eraser. Adjust your projects' cutting lists so that the end grain will end up about $1/64$" proud of the mating surface. That means, for example, that if you are building a 24"-long box with through-dovetails at the four corners, then the sides should be cut to $24^{1}/_{32}$" long.

Not only will this result in less work to trim the end grain, but you will be less likely to damage the surrounding face grain as you work. That's because you are more likely to make a mistake if you have to sand a joint for 10 minutes than if you are sanding it for less than a minute.

After much discussion in our shop about trimming end grain, the following story covers how we prefer to cut back proud end grain, a task that happens quite a lot in a shop where expressed joinery is commonplace.

End grain is the most difficult part of a board to cut accurately. With planning and the correct tools, you can make the process quick and predictable.

Two Tools for the Task

After many years of trimming end grain, we've settled on two primary tools for trimming it: a random-orbit sander loaded with #120-grit sandpaper, or a low-angle block plane used in conjunction with alcohol or mineral spirits.

Belt sanders are too aggressive for most furniture-making pursuits, except for those who are very familiar with this tool. In the wrong hands, belt sanders will wreak havoc on furniture.

Rasps and files are generally slower compared to a block plane, and the surface they leave in their wake will need to be touched up with a plane or sander in the end, so these tools generally stay on the rack when end grain is involved.

Likewise, routers can be set up with an accessory base and a straight bit to trim back end grain. This can be an effective technique for trimming proud plugs (see page 35 of *Woodworking Magazine* Autumn 2007, Issue 8, for an explanation), but it's not as effective when dealing with joints at corners.

Planing End Grain

If you are going to plane end grain, you can use almost any plane with a sharp iron, but we prefer a low-angle block plane for a few reasons. The tool's low angle of attack (typically 37° when you add the bevel and bedding angle) makes the tool easy to push through end grain. Plus, the tool's small size gives you more control to work a localized area, and its low center of gravity makes it easy to press the tool down firmly against the work without it tipping.

The plane's iron should be sharp for end-grain work. The cutting edge can be sharpened straight across or with a shallow curve, like a smoothing plane. Either shape is fine, but I like a gentle curve because I can then frequently plane an area without leaving behind "plane tracks," the little shelves left in the work when the corners of the iron dig in. These plane tracks have to be removed, and that's another step.

The other companion to the block plane is a rag moistened with alcohol or mineral spirits. The liquid softens the end grain, making it easier to slice.

With the tools in hand, the first task is to secure the work so it's firmly supported during planing. A typical setup involves a platform that is cantilevered off the workbench. I sleeve the workpiece over the platform and pinch a corner in a vise if possible.

Before planing the end grain, I recommend you plane a small chamfer on the corner of your assembled piece. When you plane end grain and it is not supported by surrounding face grain, the end grain will split loose and can ruin the appearance of your work. A chamfer helps support the end-grain fibers when planing them.

I plane this chamfer freehand with the block plane and stop when the chamfer appears on both the proud end grain and mating face grain, as shown in the photos.

When you plane end grain, you still need to follow the grain direction of the surrounding face grain because chances are you'll end up planing a little bit of that during the process. So you will end up sometimes planing in a direction that shoots you off the corner of your work or sometimes into the assembly. If you planed the chamfer as noted above, you should be able to do both with little difficulty or splitting.

Sanding End Grain

Using a random-orbit sander to cut back proud end grain is quick and effective with the right paper and the right touch. As to paper, use an

Almost any stout slab of wood can be used to support your work. Here I use a riser for our shop's sawhorses for the job so I can avoid cutting off a chunk of a 2x12 to use as a platform.

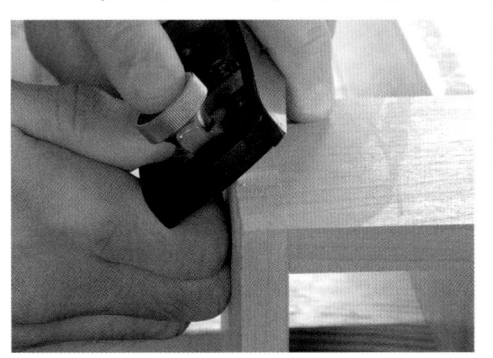

Trim the corner of the assembly freehand with a block plane. You're going to break this edge with some sandpaper before finishing your piece anyway, so the chamfer will disappear.

The chamfer is a tiny thing. Your work is done when you can see the chamfer on both the end grain and the face grain of the assembly.

Here you can see the end grain of the side should be planed so that the plane runs off the corner. With the chamfer in place, this approach is unlikely to split off the end grain.

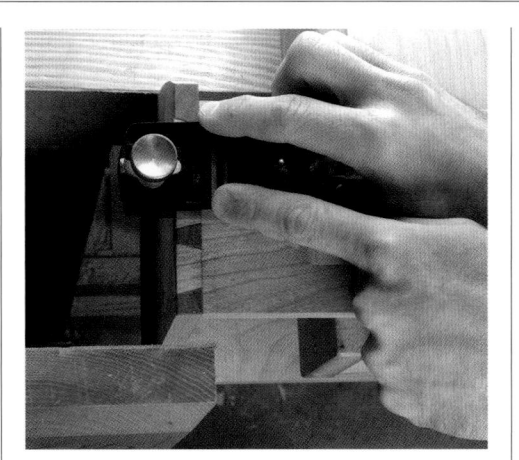

One of the biggest virtues of using a block plane to trim end grain is that you can cradle the entire tool in your hands, which gives you immense control over the downward pressure required to make clean cuts.

At the other corner, the grain direction dictates I plane into the corner as shown. This approach won't split your end grain, but you do have to be careful about pressing firmly on the front of the tool so it doesn't tip.

abrasive that is as coarse as what you typically start with when sanding an assembled case. For most woodworkers, this is #100- or #120-grit paper. Coarser grits will scratch the work more than necessary. Finer grit are slower, and the effort will be wasted when you sand the entire case with your #100- or #120-grit paper.

Another consideration is how you apply the sander's pad to the joint. Highly skilled woodworkers tip the tool slightly so that a small section of the pad touches the end grain. This approach isn't recommended by tool manufacturers or the woodworking intelligentsia. But you know what? We know it works; it just takes practice. If you want to go this route, practice on a few pieces of non-essential work first. You'll get the hang of it.

For the rest of us, we recommend sanding with the center of the pad directly over the end grain. This requires you to keep the tool balanced. Do not press the sander down firmly against the work to try to speed you along. You will lose your balance and likely gouge the face grain at the far limits of the sander's pad.

Work the end grain with the sander, but also move it entirely onto the face grain every four or five seconds so you can gauge your progress. This happens quickly and you don't want to sand too much. Plus, moving the tool off the end grain and onto the face grain starts the sanding process on the rest of your carcase.

If You are Too Proud

Sometimes, despite the best intentions, you will end up with end grain that is 1/4" proud and it has to be trimmed back. If that happens, then your choice of tools should change. We recommend you first trim the end grain with a flush-cutting saw. If you are worried about gouging the work with your saw, then lay the saw on a thin piece of cardboard on the work. That will trim the end grain so it's about 1/64" proud. Then you can plane or sand it.

One More Alternative

This article would be incomplete unless we mentioned one other historical way to trim end grain: Don't trim it at all.

Some early woodworking texts discuss how you should lay out your dovetails so that the pins and tails will actually be slightly recessed after assembly. This approach has risks and rewards.

The rewards: The joint can be clamped easily without cauls because end grain isn't there to interfere with your clamps' heads. Second: You have to sand or plane the assembled carcase anyway. So if you trim away the face grain until it is level to the end grain and stop, it can be quite an efficient way to work.

The risks: This approach requires more discipline. You have to be careful not to bruise the end grain during joinery. A nick or dent in the end grain is more likely to show with this approach. Second, your layout has to be spot-on. If your end grain is too recessed, you will end up spending far too long trimming back the face grain.

We've used both approaches and they are both valid. But at the outset, we'd recommend you make your end grain a wee bit proud. And once you master that, then you can move on to the techniques that require more skills: belt-sanding, tipping your random-orbit sander or laying out your carcase with veteran precision. **WM**

— *Christopher Schwarz*

When there is a lot of end grain to trim, such as with this tail board, first plane across the joint with the tool angled as shown to remove the bulk of the end grain. Then trim the last bit using other planing techniques.

Sanding grain flush is effective and easy if you don't have much material to remove. Shoot for 1/64", which is the amount shown here, and the work will be over quickly.

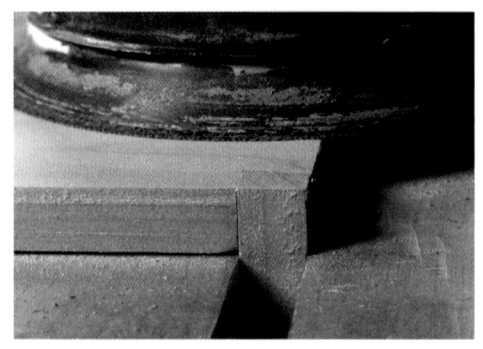

Here I'm moving the sander into position over the end grain. Use a light touch on the tool and don't move the tool too rapidly until you get a feel for how the tool is balancing on the work.

Use your fingers (not your eyes) to determine if your joint has been flushed up. As soon as the end grain is flush to the face grain, start work on the rest of the carcase.

Sanding 1/64" off a board is faster than you might think. This row of poplar tails required only 50 seconds of sanding to flush them up; the surrounding surface remained flat.

Glossary

"Speak properly, and in as few words as you can, but always plainly; for the end of speech is not ostentation, but to be understood."
— William Penn (1644 - 1718), founder of Pennsylvania

Woodworking's lexicon can be overwhelming for beginners. The following is a list of terms used in this issue that may be unfamiliar to you. Check woodworking-magazine.com for an expanded and searchable glossary.

aliphatic resin glue (n)
Technical name for basic yellow woodworking glue, which is really a polyvinyl acetate (PVA) glue with an aliphatic resin added to extend open time and increase the range of temperatures in which it will work.

becket (n)
Any type of loop or handle or more specifically, a fancy knotwork rope handle.

cam out (v)
When a rotating piece (such as a screwdriver bit) slips out of the recess of a screw and mars or destroys that recess.

countersink (v, n)
To cut a cone-shaped recess that allows a screw head to seat flush or below the surface; also, the hole itself.

cyanoacrylate (n)
The technical generic name for Super Glue; a type of adhesive that bonds because of polymerization rather than the evaporation of a carrier agent, such as water or a solvent, as with wood glue (aliphatic resin).

dado stack (n)
An adjustable set of blades for the table saw that cuts a dado (a three-sided trench cut across the grain of the board) or groove.

groove (n)
A three-sided trench cut with the grain of a board.

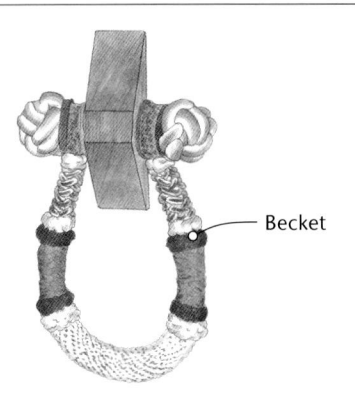

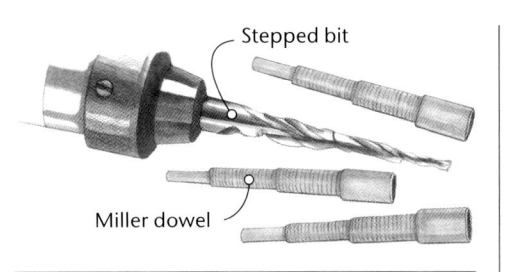

hide glue (n)
Traditional glue made by decomposing the collagen from animal hides. Available in different grades, the most common used in woodworking is 192-gram strength. Hide glue is more easily reversible than PVA and cyanoacrylate.

kerf (n)
The wood removed by a saw blade between the piece you keep and your offcut.

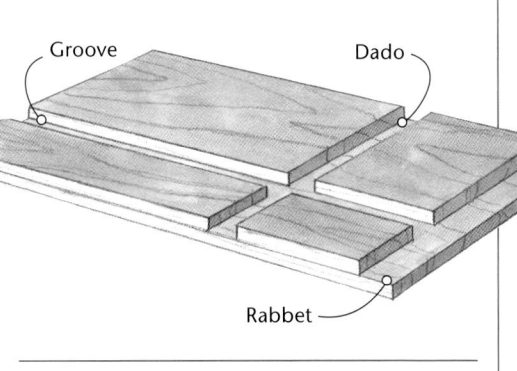

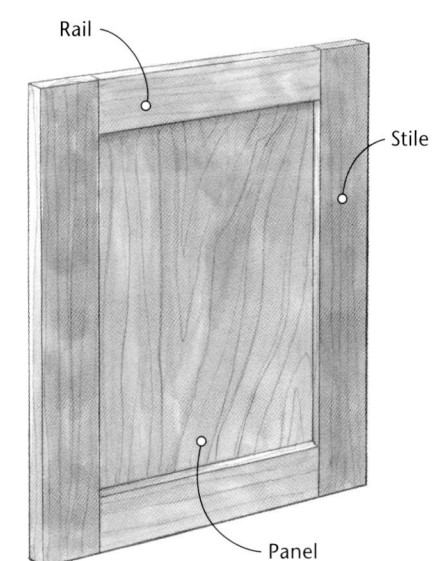

Miller dowel (n)
A stepped and grooved wooden dowel for which a special stepped bit is used to make the corresponding stepped hole. The stepped shoulders make it faster and easier to install than a regular dowel.

panel (n)
A large wood surface, sometimes made out of several boards glued edge-to-edge.

plinth (n)
The base upon which a piece of casework stands.

polyvinyl acetate glue (PVA) (n)
Technical name for white glue (such as the Elmer's Glue children use) and many yellow wood glues.

proud (adj)
In a joint where the two mating surfaces aren't flush, the surface that protrudes is the "proud" surface.

rabbet (n)
A two-sided trench cut on the edge or end of a board.

rail (n)
The horizontal member of any frame, such as a door, window or face frame.

riven board (n)
A board that is split or cleaved from a log or other larger piece of wood.

shiplapped joint (n)
Adjoining boards rabbeted along the edge so as to make an overlapping flush joint.

stile (n)
The vertical member of any frame, such as a door, window or face frame. **WM**

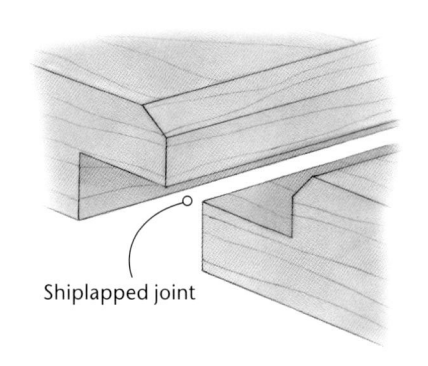

A Better Blanket Chest Design

Many common designs for chests make construction far more difficult than necessary.

Though the chest is one of the oldest forms of furniture, that doesn't mean that the human race has settled on the best way to build it.

There are, in fact, many ways to build chests that make the process fussy, challenging and time-consuming – and the results look identical to a simpler chest.

To find the best way to build a chest, we surveyed plans and historical photographs of hundreds of examples from 1600 to the present. And then we boiled all that down to find the simplest way to build the complex chest shown here, which is an adaptation of a blanket box from the Shaker's Union Village community.

This may not actually look like a complex chest. But compared to historical examples, this chest was fancy in many ways. To understand why, let's look at the development of the form.

Community Chests

The first chests had all the joinery you'd find in a dugout canoe (that is, none at all). Early chests were made from one block of wood hollowed out with tools, fire or other forms of gumption.

Later, when riven boards became common, chests were built with two ends that also served as feet (the grain of these ends ran vertical). Then the front and back were fastened to the ends. This grain ran horizontal.

There were some other common variations as well, including assemblies where the ends, front and back became frame-and-panel constructions – and the stiles ran to the floor. Another type of chest was a simple box propped up on feet that were turned or were slabs of wood (such as with the Sea Chest on page 26 of this issue).

Three common forms of chests that show different strategies for the base.

On all forms of chests, moulding typically appears as a transition point between the box and the base or the box and the lid.

From there it was a short hop to make the chests out of two separate assemblies: the box itself and the base, which we call the plinth.

How to join the box and the plinth is the focus of this story. It doesn't have to be difficult for the chest's maker, but it sure can be.

Two Trying Designs
Traveling down the more difficult design path when building a chest begins with one assumption: That the plinth is merely moulding and should be applied to the box as such.

Once you make this assumption, here's one difficult (and common) way to make a chest: You cut a moulding profile into the top edge of the plinth pieces, join the plinth pieces at the corners and wrap them around the box. If you use a miter joint at the corner, it's fussy to fit the plinth exactly to the box – errors are easy to make and hard to hide. If you use dovetails, it is even fussier to wrap the plinth pieces because you'll have to cope the moulded edges at the corners.

Oh, one more thing – the plinth is like Atlas. It supports the whole chest, so you should use some fairly thick stock when making it, at least $3/4$" for a sizable chest. Or you need to add some glue blocks at the corners to support the box.

But what if you don't want that big $3/4$" step between the plinth and box? Well, you can cut a rabbet into the top edges of the plinth pieces, but then you are rabbeting, dovetailing and coping all your plinth pieces, and any error is going to result in a noticeable gap.

A variation of this particular design is supposed to make some of this easier. You wrap the plinth pieces around the box, and then you apply mitered moulding to the top edge of the plinth pieces. This hides any errors and makes the moulding easy to join at the corners.

And this does improve things. But it's still more work than necessary.

A second common way of building a plinth is to use bracket feet below a mitered frame that

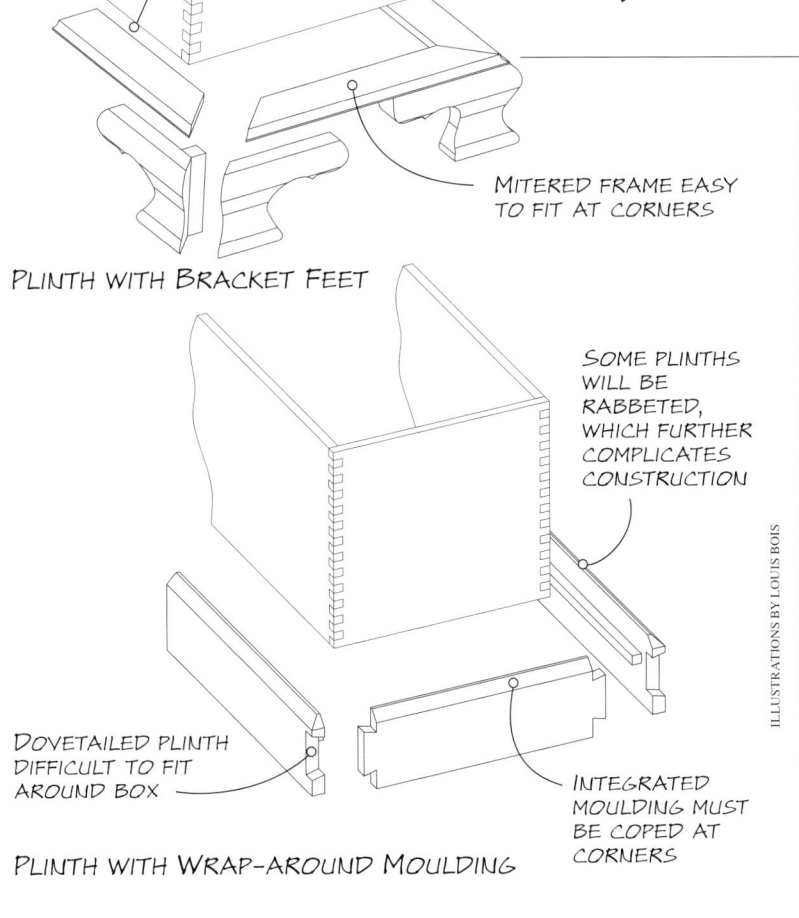

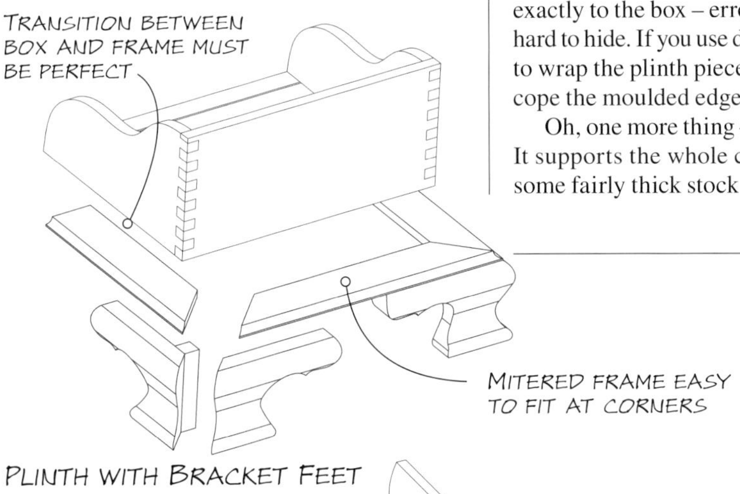

TRANSITION BETWEEN BOX AND FRAME MUST BE PERFECT

MITERED FRAME EASY TO FIT AT CORNERS

PLINTH WITH BRACKET FEET

SOME PLINTHS WILL BE RABBETED, WHICH FURTHER COMPLICATES CONSTRUCTION

DOVETAILED PLINTH DIFFICULT TO FIT AROUND BOX

INTEGRATED MOULDING MUST BE COPED AT CORNERS

PLINTH WITH WRAP-AROUND MOULDING

When setting out all your joinery for the plinth (and the box above it), it's critical to mark your parts. I use a cabinetmaker's triangle to orient my front, back and end pieces.

has its edge moulded. The mitered and moulded frame supports the box above. The bracket feet below support the frame. What's the downside? You need to get the fit between the box and the frame dead-on – or add another layer of moulding to hide any gap between the box and frame.

The above method is easier than wrapping your moulding around the box, but we think there's an even better way to build this chest.

Detach Your Plinth

Though it seems counter-intuitive, it's easier to get a more accurate result with a chest like this if you build the plinth separate from the box so it acts as a platform for the box. Then you set the box on the plinth, drive a few fasteners and run moulding around the transition point to hide errors or irregularities.

Why is this better? For starters, you don't have to be as fussy with your joinery to make the outside dimension of your box match the inside dimension of your plinth. If your box or plinth end up a little bigger or smaller than intended, then you can size your moulding to accommodate the difference. It's a lot easier to trim $1/16$" off a skinny piece of moulding than it is to remove that off the front and ends of a 16"-tall chest.

The other distinct advantage is that you don't have to jump through hoops if you want to use a delicate transition moulding. It's just as easy to make the transition large as it is small.

Plus, making the plinth separate doesn't require much more wood (it can be as little as two sticks). And the extra material is hidden so it can be an inexpensive or ugly species.

Finally, making a separate plinth allows for easier repairs, should that ever be necessary. You can easily detach the plinth or even replace it.

About the Union Village Chest

The Union Village Shaker community is near our offices in Cincinnati, Ohio, but it doesn't figure large in the world of Shaker furniture like the eastern Shaker communities do. Union Village was the first and largest Shaker community west of the Allegheny Mountains, and it was the parent community for the western Shaker communities in Ohio, Kentucky, Indiana and Georgia.

Founded in 1805, more than 4,000 Shakers lived at Union Village during its peak, selling herbal medicines, seeds and brooms. The community declined until it was sold in 1912, and the structures are now a retirement community.

One of the artifacts from the village is a walnut blanket box with fine lines and tight dovetails. The box is similar to many Shaker chests that are extant, but this one has always been a favorite.

We chose to adapt this design because it highlights the advantages of our preferred chest-building method. The fine bit of transition moulding around the plinth is easy to accomplish with this construction technique.

While we retained the proportions and lines of the Union Village original, we used finger joints instead of dovetails. And we used figured maple instead of walnut. These alterations give the box a contemporary feel without looking like a pack of cigarettes with cabriole legs, or some such post-modern nonsense.

Begin the Building

Unless you possess wide boards (as the Union Village Shakers did), you need to glue up narrow boards into wider panels for the lid, front, back and ends of the box. The plinth and bottom are made from narrow stock. So while the glue in my panels was curing, I worked on the plinth.

The plinth has a front, back and ends that are joined with finger joints. Plus there are two "carcase supports" sunk into the plinth pieces. The carcase supports are housed in $3/8$" x $1/2$" rabbets that run the full length of the front and back, plus $3/8$" x $1/2$" stopped rabbets in the ends.

Cut the finger joints on the corners of the

Don't try to clamp your work in our finger-joint jig vertically. Gravity will fight you the entire time. Lay the jig flat and let gravity lend a hand as you position your pieces for routing.

When routing between the fingers, try to stay clear of the jig as you plow through the workpiece, as shown above. Then clean up the walls of the joint. This makes tighter joints.

Be sure to plan your plinth's finger joints so that the top of the front and back pieces can take a through-rabbet as shown.

The two keys to a successful glue-up: A slow-setting glue and small plywood blocks that press the fingers together.

plinth pieces. After much experimentation, we found the best results came from plowing down the middle of the joint with a straight bit and then routing the sides. This eliminated the risk of our router shifting the parts around.

Once you get the corner joinery cut, plow the $\frac{3}{8}$" x $\frac{1}{2}$" rabbet on the top edge of the plinth's front and back pieces. Note that if you lay out your finger joints correctly, this rabbet runs through the entire length of the front and back pieces.

To cut this rabbet, I used a dado stack that was buried in an accessory wooden fence on our table saw. This method allows you to cut the joint with the work flat on the table, not on its edge.

Before you cut the curves on the plinth, assemble it. The corner joints will strengthen the feet as you cut the dramatic curve. To glue the joints, you can choose cyanoacrylate, as explained in this issue, or use a slow-setting polyurethane or liquid hide glue. Yellow glue sets up too fast.

To clamp the finger joints, I made a bunch of small blocks of wood that I taped to the fingers. These little blocks allowed my clamps to put pressure right where it was needed.

After the glue has cured, remove the clamps, trim the end grain bits flush and make the $\frac{3}{8}$" x $\frac{1}{2}$" stopped rabbet in the ends of the assembled plinth. First cut a bunch of kerfs with a handsaw, then chisel the waste.

Then fit those carcase supports into the rabbets in the plinth. Glue and nail the carcase supports into the plinth's rabbets. Then get ready to cut the curves on the assembled plinth.

To cut the curves, first remove the bulk of the waste with a jigsaw, then clean up the curves with a plywood pattern and a router equipped with a pattern-cutting straight bit.

The curves on the ends, front and back are identical, so one short plywood pattern handles all the curves. To rout the straight run between all the curves, I clamped a straight piece of stock to the plinth and used that as a pattern.

Build the Box

The box above the plinth is fairly simple. Here's how it goes together: The corners are joined with finger joints. The bottom boards are shiplapped and nailed into rabbets in the front and back of the box. The till wall slides into a dado in the front and back. The till's bottom is nailed to cleats below.

The hinges are let into notches cut into both the back and the two hinge blocks, which are glued to the outside of the box's back. The hinge blocks support the hinge out to its barrel. And finally, the chest's lid is screwed to the hinges.

A little alcohol and a block plane make light work of the proud end grain from the completed finger joints. The alcohol softens the tough end grain.

After you saw out the extents of the notch for the carcase supports, chisel the waste with some light chopping.

This is what you paid your money for when you bought this magazine: The two carcase supports hold the carcase in place and give you a place for your transition moulding.

Saw the curved shape of the plinth after assembly. If you do it before, the corners will be too fragile to clamp up without fussy cauls.

Normally, I would shape these curves with a rasp, but at the encouragement of our power-tool expert, I used a pattern-cutting bit and our trim router. I still like my rasps, but this is a very close second.

Union Village Blanket Chest

NO.	PART	T	W	L	MATERIAL	NOTES
Carcase						
❏ 1	Top	3/4	18	39	Maple	Edges radiused by hand
❏ 2	Front & back	3/4	15⅝	37½*	Maple	3/8" x 1/2" rabbet, bottom edge
❏ 2	Ends	3/4	15⅝	17¼*	Maple	
❏ 2	Hinge blocks	3/4	3	6	Maple	1/2" x 1/2" chamfer, one end
❏	Case bottom	1/2	36	16½	Poplar	Several shiplapped boards
❏ 1	Till wall	1/2	6½	16¼	Poplar	In 1/4" x 1/2" x 6½" dados
❏ 1	Till bottom	1/2	8	15¾	Poplar	Nailed to till cleats below
❏ 2	Till cleats	3/4	3/4	7	Poplar	Nailed to front & back
Plinth						
❏ 2	Front & back	3/4	5	38½*	Maple	3/8" x 1/2" rabbet, top edge
❏ 2	Ends	3/4	5	18¼*	Maple	3/8" x 1/2" notches, top edge
❏ 2	Carcase supports	1/2	3	37¾	Poplar	Fit in rabbets & notches
❏	Cove moulding	1/2	1/2	130	Maple	1/2" r. cove, nailed to plinth

*Cut these parts slightly longer and trim to final length after assembly

Begin by ensuring the front, back and ends of the carcase are indeed square. If they are out, you need to correct them before you rout the finger joints. Otherwise your carcase will go together all cockeyed. I prefer to shoot the ends of panels with a shooting board and a heavy plane. This is slower than making one mighty cut on the table saw, but it is unlikely to make things worse.

Cut your finger joints for the box. Then mill the 3/8" x 1/2" rabbet in the front and back pieces. Don't cut stopped rabbets in the ends – that's more trouble than it's worth. The dado stack set-up you used for the plinth's rabbets will do the same yeoman's job in the carcase.

Before you assemble the carcase, rout the 1/4" x 1/2" x 6" dados for the till wall. This job is handled by a right-angle jig we developed for the router, shown in the photo below right.

Preparing for Assembly; Pulling the Trigger
Assembling finger-jointed carcases used to be one of the most stressful glue-ups in our shop. It usually involved every clamp in the shop, a helper and a bottle of Mylanta. That was back when we used yellow glue for the job. No more.

Yellow glue is probably the last glue you should use for this job. It sets up entirely too fast, leaving you with open joints and a sinking feeling in your stomach. Either use the cyanoacrylate glue method we explain on page 9, or use polyurethane or liquid hide glue. The last two solutions will give you an hour of assembly time. If you are still unsure of your skills, use liquid hide glue, which is reversible with a little heat and water.

The easiest way to glue the corners together is to get them semi-assembled, then wipe glue on the long-grain surfaces inside the joint with a flat little scrap. Then apply the little blocks like you did with the plinth and turn on the clamping pressure. After the glue has cured, level all your joints and get ready to fit the interior parts.

Thinking Inside the Box
The bottom boards are shiplapped on their long edges, then nailed into the rabbets on the bottom of the carcase. Cut the shiplap rabbets on the table saw like you cut all the rabbets for the plinth and carcase. Cut the bottom boards to fit snugly, then space them out by inserting a couple quarters between each board. The 25-cent space allows the boards to swell during the wet months. Then nail the boards into the carcase's rabbets. No glue.

My shooting board and jack plane ensure that all my panels are dead square. These needed tweaking even after a ride on the sliding table on our table saw.

The router dado jig from *Woodworking Magazine* Spring 2005, Issue 3, is a favorite in our shop. (Any jig that lasts more than a few weeks in our shop is to be admired.)

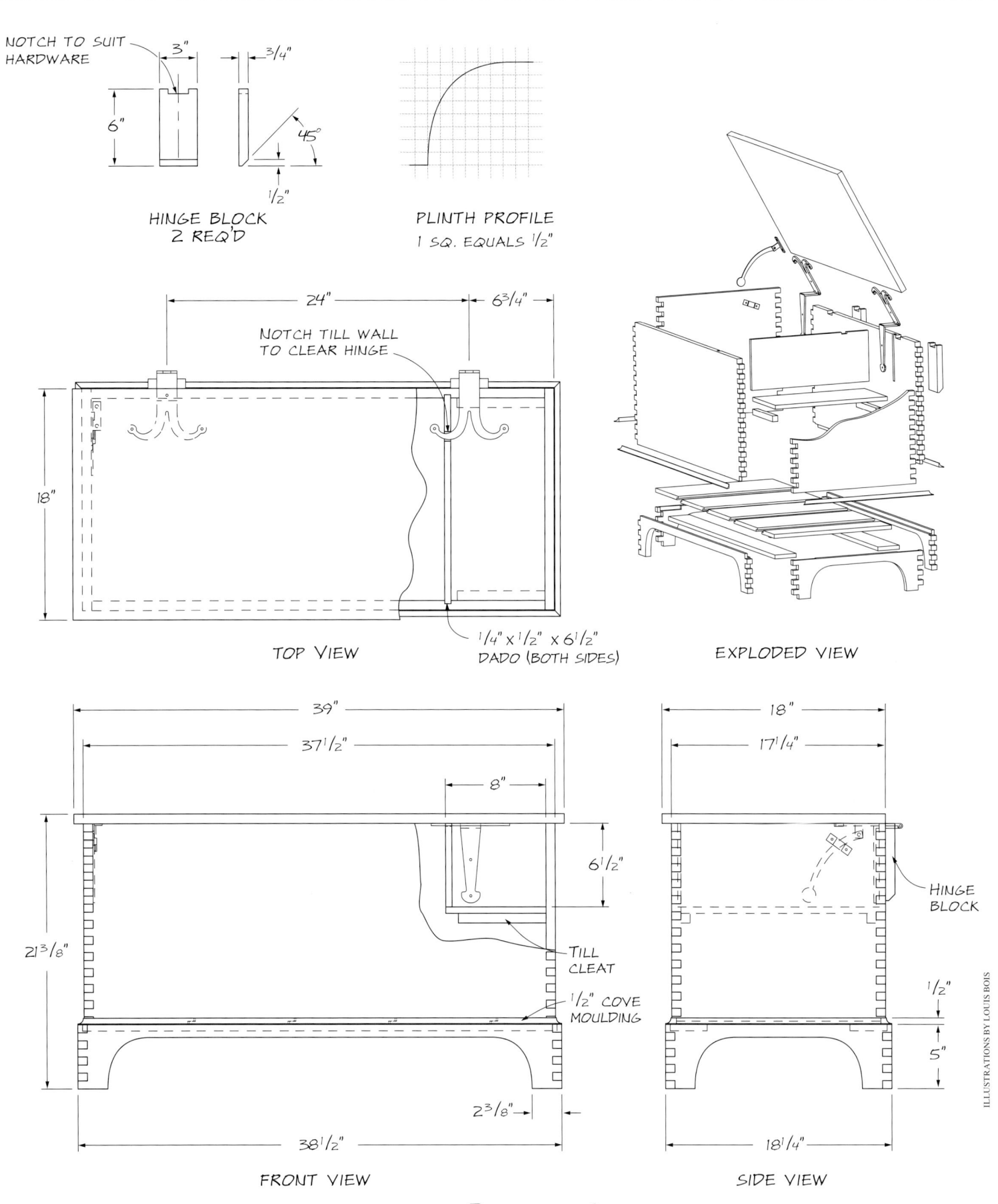

BLANKET CHEST

Here the corners are nearly fitted and I'm smearing an oh-so-thin layer of polyurethane glue into each joint.

The till is simple. Fit the till wall into the dados in the front and back. Glue it in place. Then trim the till bottom to size. Glue and nail two till cleats below the bottom. Then nail the till bottom to its cleats. Again, rely on gravity and nails – not glue.

Carcase, Meet Plinth

Now you can join the plinth and carcase. Put the carcase upside down on the benchtop and center the plinth on the carcase. Screw the plinth to the carcase by driving through the carcase supports and into the bottom boards. About four screws in each carcase support will do the job.

Now you can figure out exactly how big your transitional moulding should be. Make your moulding (I used a ½"-radius cove bit and left a 1/16" fillet at each edge). Then miter it, tweak it, glue it and nail it.

Shape the hinge blocks, attach them to the back of the carcase and then cut the recesses for the iron hinges. Screw the hinges to the carcase and then clean up your top piece for the last important detail.

Shaping the edges of a lid is something I always enjoy doing by hand with a plane. First shape the ends (which will blow out the long edges). Then shape the long edges to clean up the previous step's mess.

To shape the edges, I first mark the curve using a quarter, then I worked to that line with a traditional hollow moulding plane. A block plane will do the job, but it will leave a faceted surface that you should fair with hand sanding.

Then it's just a simple matter of screwing the lid to the hinges and adding some sort of stay to keep the lid propped open.

The Finish is Simple and Easy

This blanket chest was built during the winter months, so I had to use a hand-applied finish instead of spraying it in my driveway. We prefer an inexpensive and forgiving home brew that is detailed in the Shortcuts section on page 4.

I've built a fair number of chests during the last 15 years, from tool chests to toy chests to other blanket chests similar to this Union Village version. Each had its charms, but each also had its rough spots, especially when massaging the transition between the base and carcase.

Not so with this chest. The only real challenge will be to decide which room of the house it belongs in. WM

— *Christopher Schwarz*

Supplies

Van Dyke's Restorers
800-558-1234 or vandykes.com

2 ■ black iron chest hinges
   #02018071, $9.99 each

Lee Valley Tools
800-871-8158 or leevalley.com

1 ■ pair 8⅝" steel stays
   # 01A62.20, $22.40/pair

2 ■ pkgs. #7 x ¾" pyramid screws
   pkg. of 10, #01X38.76, $1.85/pkg.

Prices correct at time of publication.

Clamp the corners and then across the corners to pull the carcase into square. One clamp squared the entire carcase. You might need a clamp on the bottom as well.

With just eight screws, you'll keep the bottom rigid, the carcase in place and have a delicate step for the transition moulding.

Screws are Screws – Aren't They?

Just as with building any woodworking project, eliminate one step from the manufacturing process and the results can be fatal.

It usually happens as you hang a door or install a shelf. You've got a balancing act going as you hold one piece, steady a second piece and attempt to drive a screw all at the same time. Then, as you snug the screw those final few threads, the connection pulls tight and the screw snaps.

I was curious to find out why some screws break and others don't. I know what I discovered will amaze you as much as it did me.

I bought four different boxes of screws to test – a common drywall screw (because most woodworkers use this screw as they start woodworking), a zinc-plated screw off the shelf from a home center, as well as a premium square-drive screw from McFeely's (mcfeelys.com) and a box of Spax screws (also considered premium) purchased online (highlandwoodworking.com).

My first surprise – rest assured there are more to come – was that premium screws were actually cheaper by the piece ($.041) than screws purchased from the home center ($.0447).

Twisting, bending and breaking are just three of many results you sometimes experience when working with screws. Choose better – not necessarily more expensive – screws to reduce those occurrences.

Drywall screws are included in the test due to the ease of acquisition, however I would not consider using these screws when building fine furniture.

Screw Fabrication

How a screw is created is interesting and influences a screw's strength. Some manufacturers bring in steel stock that is ready to be made into screws while others bring in stock that needs to be pulled and thinned to the appropriate size; bulky material is passed through a series of shaping stations that stretch the stock to arrive at a needed diameter.

Once the material is sized it's fed into a machine that pounds the stock one time to form the head and a second time (or possibly a third time) to form the recess – the area in the head of a screw for the screwdriver. I've been told this process shakes the entire facility floor with each pound.

Head Designs

There are many screwhead designs of which the most common used for woodworking is a flat head, where the top of the head is flush with the surface when the screw is properly seated. Other head styles include:

■ **Trim head:** These are like the flat head but with a smaller diameter flat surface.
■ **Oval head:** These screws also have a countersink design, but the surface is slightly elliptical in shape.
■ **Pan head:** A dome-shaped head that stays above the wood's surface while the flat surface under the head is the bearing surface.
■ **Truss head:** Similar to a pan head screw, but with a lower head profile and a slightly larger bearing surface.
■ **Washer head:** This screw has an even larger bearing surface, used in cabinetry for mounting wall cabinets.

There are also a few other designs that are found from time to time.

The beveled area just below the head is the countersink. The countersink on wood screws is generally an 80° to 82° angle on American screws. That angle matches most commerically available countersink bits. Again, you occasionally find screws being fabricated with other angles.

Recess Design

The number of recess types available in screws is vast, but I've found that woodworkers primarily use three different designs.

The slot head was the first recess used in screws. I choose slot-head screws for most, if not all, of my projects. That's a decision I make in an attempt to keep true to building reproduction furniture. This oldest of recesses has declined in use over the years because it's difficult to keep the screwdriver engaged with the screw recess as significant torque is applied to drive the screws.

It wasn't until 1936 that Henry Phillips patented the Phillips recess. This recess, sometimes referred to as "cross-drive," is still popular in the U.S. woodworking industry. The ability to maintain contact between the screwdriver and the Phillips screw recess is greatly enhanced versus the slot screw. People exert approximately 12 foot-pounds of pressure to keep the driver engaged into a Phillips recess. This is the recess design most woodworkers use if they are not concerned with achieving an authentic, antique look.

While the slot head allowed the driver to slip causing damage to the screw's head, the Phillips recess created a new problem – "cam-out." Cam-out occurs when the recess is damaged by the screwdriver due to an excessive amount of torque applied while driving a screw.

The third screw recess used in many woodworking shops is the square drive. This design helps to eliminate or substantially reduce cam-out. A square-drive screw requires only about 4 foot-pounds of pressure to keep the driver in contact with the recess as you drive the screw. Therefore, you're less apt to have the driver slip.

I use square-drive screws for assembling jigs and shop fixtures. Why? I was having trouble with screws breaking and decided to try a deck screw to see if there was a difference. The screws I selected were a square-drive design. There was a difference, but I later found out it wasn't due to the recess. It was a difference in screws. Read on.

Thread Styles

After the head and recess is formed, screws are cut to length, then threads are added. Historically, threads were cut into the shank of the screws – this left the outer diameter of the threads equal to the diameter of the shank (a great method for dating screws pulled from older furniture). Today, threads are pressed into the shanks. As a result, the thread profile extends beyond the diameter of the shank.

To illustrate how threads are added to screws, place your hands in a prayer position then slide your right hand back so the tips of your fingers are at the palm of your left hand. In this example your right hand is the thread-cutting tool while the left hand is the screw. Now, apply pressure with your right hand and slide it forward across your left hand.

Thread patterns for woodscrews have traditionally been a "single lead," or one parallel thread, wrapped around the length of the screw. This design is still the most-used thread style in woodworking screws.

Due to the use of particleboard in the furniture industry (isn't that a lovely thought), deep-thread screws were introduced. This thread design has a thinner shank and deeper threads set at a sharper angle. Deep-thread screws are said to hold better in composite woods and drive with less splitting, bursting or displacement of material.

Another thread design is "double lead" where two parallel threads circle the shank, originating at the point of the screw. The double-lead thread design produces more threads per inch. As a result, screws drive faster. However, double-lead threads are primarily used on screws longer than 3½" in length. The double lead provides stability to the screw in the heat-treating process, reducing the screw's tendency to bend.

Heat Treatment: The Next Step

With the threads created, screws travel through a heat-treating process. Heat-treating is the most important step in making screws that are strong or weak. (Another element that increases strength is the ingredients of the raw materials from which the screws are made.)

Heat-treating is accomplished using a variety of methods. The best method is to separate the screws into smaller portions, as in hoppers, and run the screws through the process. This method allows the screws to travel more evenly, ensuring each screw is heat-treated properly. To increase that efficiency even more, some manufacturers shake the conveyor belt as the screws ride along. Shaking allows the screws to mix and heat more evenly.

The temperature in heat-treating varies somewhat by the length of screw being made, but as a general rule the furnace temperature is near 1,600° Fahrenheit. A temperature far in excess of 1,600°F causes the screws to be more brittle. If they're too brittle, they tend to snap when driven.

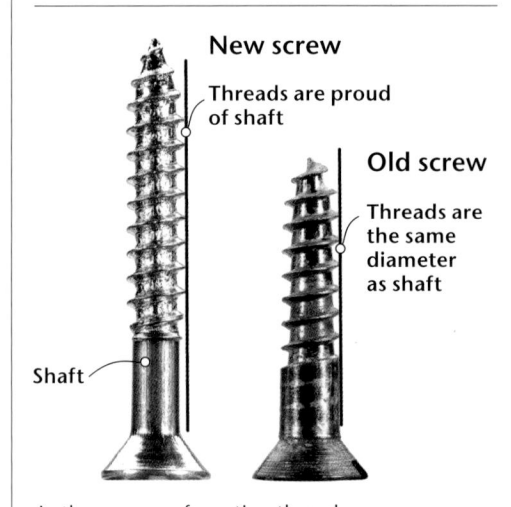

The invention of Phillips and square-drive recesses improved the ease of driving screws. Each reduced the amount of foot-pounds needed to keep the bit engaged with the screw head.

Counterbores and pilot holes help to reduce the tiny amount of shredded steel collected on the tip of the driver, which is a clear indication of "cam-out."

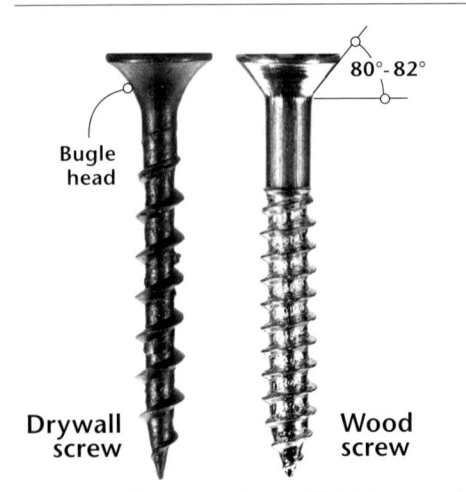

A countersink on a wood screw (right) is tapered at 80°-82° in the U.S. (90° in the U.K.), while the countersink on a typical drywall screw (left) is slightly concave or of a "bugle" design.

As the process of creating threads on screws evolved, the relationship of thread size to screw shaft changed. The threads on the right screw were cut into the shaft leaving, the thread diameter equal with the shaft. Threads on new screws (the screw on the left) are pressed into the shaft causing the thread diameter to be larger that that of the shaft.

Here's the Shocker!
Heat-treating is not done on all screws. One of the single-most important steps used to build strength in screws is left out of the process by some manufacturers. This is the main reason some screws break and others do not.

Drywall Screws
The properties we've discussed so far relate to wood screws. Contrary to what you read or hear, drywall screws are not wood screws and should not be used in woodworking projects for a number of reasons.

Besides being heat-treated at a higher temperature and being brittle, drywall screws have a smooth "bugle head" – a curved transition between the shank and head. This design is to keep the screw head from breaking the paper of drywall wallboard (the only true use for drywall screws.) In addition, the countersink of the drywall screw does not match the recess made when using a typical countersink bit.

Antiquing Screws

If you're building reproduction furniture or any project that you want to look as though it was not completed yesterday, nothing looks worse than a shiny screw peeking out for everyone to see, boasting its youthful appearance.

A quick trip to or an online visit with an outfitters store such as Bass Pro Shops (basspro.com) or Cabela's (cabelas.com) and you can change screws and most unplated hardware (including brass, but not stainless or aluminum) from "recently made" to "from the past" in a short amount of time. Simply pick up a product known as gun bluing.

Gun bluing is used in the sports world to refurbish and recondition gun barrels – to touch up scratches and worn spots and bring the surface to a blue-black, streakless finish.

For steel screws and hardware aging, gun bluing removes the shiny surface and replaces it with a blackish patina. Submerge the piece into the solution then swirl until blackened. I leave hardware as-is once removed from the solution.

On brass hardware, I use a pad of #0000 steel wool to adjust the patina after darkening in the solution. Rub the hardware with light strokes until the desired level of patination is achieved.

A word of caution: Take care when using gun bluing. It's a caustic solution and should be treated as such. Wear appropriate protection, especially eye protection.   — GH

Also, drywall screws generally have thin shanks equal to the size of a #6 wood screw and oversized heads that are the size of a #8 wood screw. The oversized head helps to minimize tearing through the drywall's paper face as well.

It's easy to understand that if you tighten a screw with those characteristics, it's more likely to break when driven into wood. The bugle-head design doesn't fit the countersink and the thin shank reaches a point of stress prior to the larger head being properly seated.

About Our Testing
The test was to drive a number of each screw, keeping track of the screws that break or cam-out when being driven. When you install screws in your work, you should always drill a countersink. For the test however, I simply drove the screws into maple. No countersink. No starter hole of any kind. This keeps the test on a level playing field.

Surprise, Surprise
Because I have years of experience working with screws and because I'm a bit of a skeptic, I had a notion as to what to expect. Let me say, I wasn't surprised with the results of the test. But I was aghast at the severity of difference.

I began the test by driving five home-center screws. All five screws broke. They didn't just break as the countersink made contact with the maple; the screws broke near the mid-point in length. Not one screw seated properly. Wow.

Not wanting to reach a quick conclusion (albeit difficult given the results), I continued to drive home-center screw after home-center screw. In the end, all 20 screws fell victim to the same type of destruction.

The next contenders were the drywall screws. I expected the same results. Again, I was surprised. Drywall screws held up better than the home-center wood screws, but not by much. I drove 20 drywall screws to find that only four screws were equal to the challenge. Interestingly, most of the drywall screws reached the countersink portion of the screw, then broke. Clearly, this reinforces earlier statements.

Better Screws Beget Better Results
Down to the final two contenders. I wondered if these screws could withstand the test. After all, maple is a hard wood. Maybe I would experience all screws failing and need to start at the beginning and rethink the test.

Upon driving the first Spax screw, I knew the test would not need to be repeated. This premium screw drove easily. As the countersink portion of the screw reached the maple, the screw properly seated – as a screw should. The head was flush with the hardwood. Of the 20 screws tested, all 20 screws seated without any evidence of breakage or recess damage.

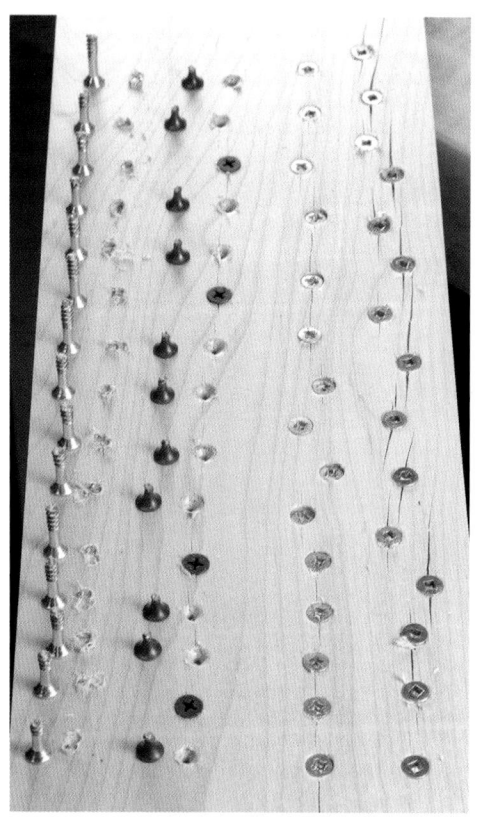

Proper heat-treating is extremely important in wood screws. The results of the test clearly demonstrate the effect of this manufacturing step. Premium screws, the right-most two rows, not only seated fully into the maple, they seated with enough force to start splits in the wood.

Did the less-costly McFeely's premium screws, the most inexpensive screws in the test, compare well to the Spax? You bet they did. Again, I drove 20 screws; all seated perfectly and held firm. The McFeely's screws, like the Spax, showed no signs of breakage or recess damage.

I expected the premium screws to test better than the others, but I expected at least a few to break during the test. Neither screw, the Spax nor the McFeely's, flinched at the job. That surprised me.

From now on I'll make sure to have so-called premium screws from Spax or McFeely's on hand. Not only can you save money with the purchase, you save time and headaches in the shop while building your project. And that's a savings of which I'm happy to take advantage. WM

— *Glen D. Huey*

"Be studious in your profession, and you will be learned. Be industrious and frugal, and you'll be rich."

— Benjamin Franklin (1706 - 1790)
inventor, statesman

A Simple Sea Chest

Whether you're a polished skipper or a certified landlubber, you'll find many reasons to build this canted-side sea chest.

If you were a sailor who sailed deep waters prior to 1870, you packed your belongings into a sea chest. (Coastal sailors, those who returned to port often, used a sea bag.) Sea chests – banned by the United States Navy in 1870 due to the lack of space for each sailor to have his own chest – are simply six-board chests.

Designs range from straight-sided chests, to those that are canted or angled on the front, to examples with both the front and back canted.

Why are the sides angled? That was to help protect sailor's shins from knocking the lid as the ship rocked with the swells of the water.

While most sea chests feature dovetailed corners, we've simplified the construction of this example and maintained the design to build a chest with basic joinery.

Set Sail on the Project

To begin construction, mill the four case panels – both ends, the front and back – to size and thickness. With the two ends front and center, establish the chest's shin-saving angle. Mark a point along the top edge of the panel that's 2" in from each end. Next, use a straightedge to draw a line connecting those points with the nearest bottom-edge corner. Bingo: the angle is set.

Because this type of cut doesn't work well at the table saw, I think it's best to use an alternative

"We must free ourselves of the hope that the sea will ever rest. We must learn to sail in high winds."

— Aristotle Onassis (1906 - 1975)
shipping magnate

While the angled panels make this chest look difficult to build, the construction is actually quite simple. It's a great introduction to angled work for the beginning woodworker.

method. Cut close to the line at your band saw then finish the cut with a router and a pattern bit. Use the bottom edge of the opposite end panel for a simple straightedge.

The most important measurement you'll use in building this chest is that angle created on the end panels. Use a bevel gauge to find the angle.

Take the gauge to your table saw and tilt the blade to match the setting of the bevel gauge and remember that degree setting.

With the blade tilted, cut one edge of the previously squared front and back panels with the face side up. You just want to remove material to create the bevel, not much more. Next, move the fence closer to the blade, flip the face side down and cut the opposite edge of the panels. If you cut both panels at the same setting, you ensure the front and back panels match in width.

Both ends of the front and back panels receive rabbets on the interior face. Install a dado stack at its widest setting in the table saw, attach an auxiliary fence and bury some of the stack into the fence, but leave ¾" exposed. Set the blade height to ½" then run the panels against the auxiliary fence to cut the four rabbets.

Fit, Trim and Nail

When the angle is cut on the edges of the front and back panels, the widths of the pieces diminish slightly. As a result, the ends need to be trimmed. Position one end to either the front or back panel then mark the amount needed to restore the match. Trim the ends at the table saw.

Assemble the box one end at a time. With the pieces aligned and in position, remove one end panel then add glue along the entire rabbet – the grain on all panels runs the same direction so there are no concerns with cross-grain construction. Replace the end panel on the box then add clamps as shown in the photo at right.

Tap the ends to make sure they seat into the glue and are tight to the other panels, then you're ready to nail the joint together. That's right, nail. Building a chest couldn't get much easier.

There is a secret to nailing this chest without incident. If you're using reproduction cut nails,

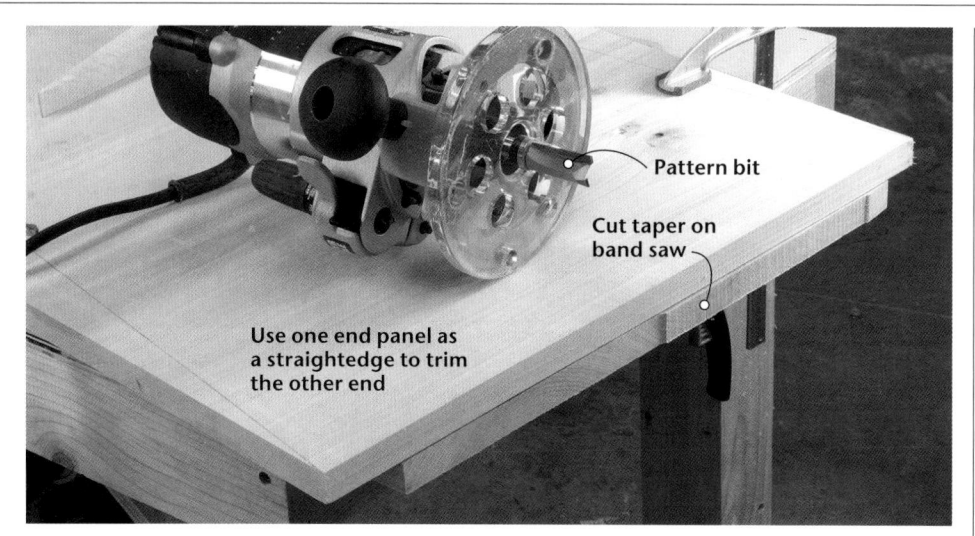

A router with a pattern bit is a perfect method of obtaining a square, straight edge – given you start with a straightedge as your pattern.

Transfer the angle of the canted front and back from the chest to the table saw with a bevel gauge. Set the angle dead-on to make the cuts accurate.

Drawing pencil lines along the board's edge allows you to sneak up on the cut without removing too much material. Due to the angle of the saw blade, you'll nibble the bottom of the edge and work your way to the top. When the pencil lines are gone, you're at the top edge.

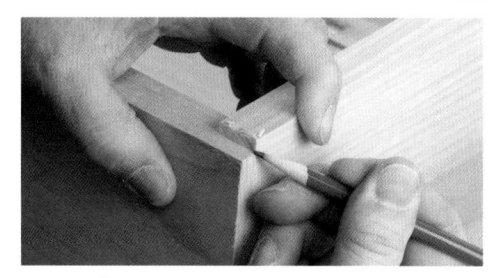

Look for 1/8" shrinkage once the front and back are trimmed to match the angle of the end pieces. The ends need to be trimmed to an exact match.

Thanks to the rabbeted corners, clamps positioned at the top and bottom hold the case square and are away from the corners to make nailing the corners a simple task.

it's necessary to align the widest part of the nail with the grain direction of the wood. That, along with drilling a proper-sized pilot hole, keeps the grain from splitting. Nail both corners of the first end, then repeat the steps for the second end.

Board Number Five
The fifth board of this six-board chest is the bottom. The bottom of the chest is actually a series of three boards affixed onto a rim that encompasses the entire box. Begin by milling the long rim pieces to size, then angle-cut their edges just as you did on the front and back panels – again the angle measurements are important.

The long rim pieces are fit to the front and back on the interior of the chest, flush with the bottom edge. The end cuts are square and made with a miter saw. I used a thin bead of glue and nails to attach the rim.

Because the width of the long rim pieces change when cut, as did the panels, you also have to adjust the width of the short rim pieces. The short rim pieces run from side to side, between the installed long rims. Make the end cuts at a miter saw with the blade angled to the correct setting. The cut is across the end, not along the edge. Add glue, then nail the short rims to the chest.

Mill the three pieces for the bottom to thick-

A guaranteed way to split the grain of the front and back panels is to attempt to install a reproduction fine finish nail into your chest with the head of the nail positioned across the grain.

ness. Then, at the table saw, create one angled edge with the blade once again set to match the bevel gauge.

The opposite edges of the two outside bottom boards receive rabbets. It's important to cut the rabbets on the top edge of the boards, or on the narrow face. The angled edge has to fit against the chest sides with the rabbeted edge showing as you peer into the chest.

Cut the outside bottom boards to length then position them inside the case. Push the pieces against the front and back of the chest then measure the distance between the two rabbeted edges. The distance measured is the width of the third board that completes the bottom.

Once that piece is sized at the table saw, create rabbets that match those on the outside boards. Cut the middle board to length then slip it into the chest. A couple screws at each end of the middle board keep the bottom in place – but it wouldn't hurt to add a fastener to the outside boards too.

Add a Little Lift
This chest is raised off the floor with four feet. One edge of the feet, the 4" edge, is cut at an angle to match the chest, while the edges facing the ends are square cut.

Mill the stock to size, then cut the matching angle at the table saw. Next, move to the miter saw and cut four pieces to the final size (3¼").

With the chest upside down on its top, position the feet so both show edges are flush with the chest. Drill countersinks into the feet, two into the front/back panels and one into the end panels.

To add a nice touch to an area of the chest that's seldom seen, clip the interior corner of the feet. Position the foot to the chest, mark the foot at the inside edge of the rim pieces then use a miter saw to cut between those two points.

Add a thin bead of glue to the foot, orient the foot to the chest and attach the two using #8 x 1¼" wood screws.

Last But Not Least
The base of the chest is finished in paint, but I chose to stain the lid, battens and cleats. Mill the

---

Supplies

Lee Valley Tools
800-871-8158 or leevalley.com

2 ■ unequal strap hinges,
     #01H20.12, $6.10 each

Prices correct at time of publication.

Horton Brasses, Inc.
800-754-9127 or horton-brasses.com

1 ■ pkg. fine furniture nails, #N-20

Call for pricing.

The outer bottom pieces cannot lift up due to the angle of the chest. To keep the opposite edge in position make sure the rabbets are cut into the face of the bottom pieces and get the center board rabbeted to fit.

material necessary for the stained parts, then size the lid according to the cut sheet.

Work begins at a router table. The edge profile is not a true roundover, but it is made with a ½" roundover router bit. Adjust the bit height so only the upper portion is being used (see photo at right.) Shape the ends first then the front edge. Flip the panel and repeat on the opposite face to finish the complete profile. The rear edge of the top panels is left square.

Battens, found on most sea chests, are a snap to create. Cut the stock to size then lay out the cut lines. Mark the halfway point on both ends of each batten (¾"), move in along the bottom edge and place a mark at 2½". Connect those points. Cut close to the lines with a band saw then smooth to the lines with a sander.

The battens are screwed to the lid. Make sure your screws hold firm, but be careful – if you drive the screw too far, the face of the lid is damaged.

Use a drill press to countersink three ⅝" holes (one centered along the length and one 1¼" in from each end). Set your depth stop at ¾" off the drill press table – leaving the material that thickness works perfectly for #12 x 1¼" pan head screws. Once the countersink is drilled, continue through the batten with a ¼" drill bit.

Position the battens just inside the moulded edge, ¼" from the outside edge of the chest. Add a bead of glue along the front 4" and use clamps to hold the pieces firm. Drill a small pilot hole prior to installing the screws, cinching them tight.

The ¼" hole is a larger diameter than the screw, which affords a small amount of compensation for wood movement while the glue at the front forces movement toward the rear of the top.

Strap hinges used for chests are most often crooked to fit inside the chest back and under the lid. The hinges selected for this chest require some simple bends to fit that profile. These bends

Add feet to the base of the chest to raise the bottom off a floor (or a ship's deck). These feet are cut to the appropriate angle to match the slope of the front and rear faces.

Nowhere is it written you have to use the entire router bit. Use only a portion of the roundover router bit to create the edge profile for the chest.

can be easily accomplished with a vise and hammer. Install the hinges but remove them prior to finishing the chest. (For step-by-step instructions of the bending process, visit woodworkingmagazine.com/blog/.)

Get a Handle on It
Handles on many antique sea chests are considered works of art. The cleat is only part of the story for top-quality chests. A second important aspect is the rope pulls or "beckets." Many beckets are extremely fancy. This chest is basic and the beckets are grommet style – rope tied through holes in the cleat.

The cleats, one on each side of the chest, begin as pieces that are as thick as can be garnered from rough 4/4 stock, or ⅞" at minimum. Arcs cut at the ends of each cleat are decorative. To match the look on this chest, remove ¾" of the width and 1½" along the length at each end. Make the cut at a band saw then smooth the area with a spindle sander.

The beckets are attached through two holes drilled into each cleat. Draw a line across each

28 ■ WOODWORKING MAGAZINE Summer 2008

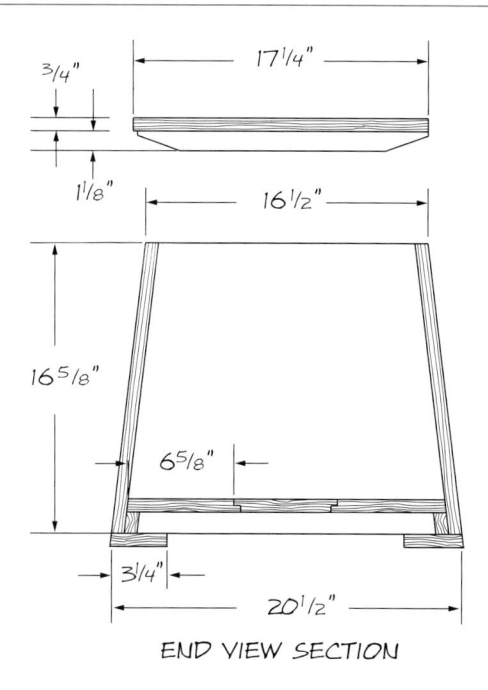

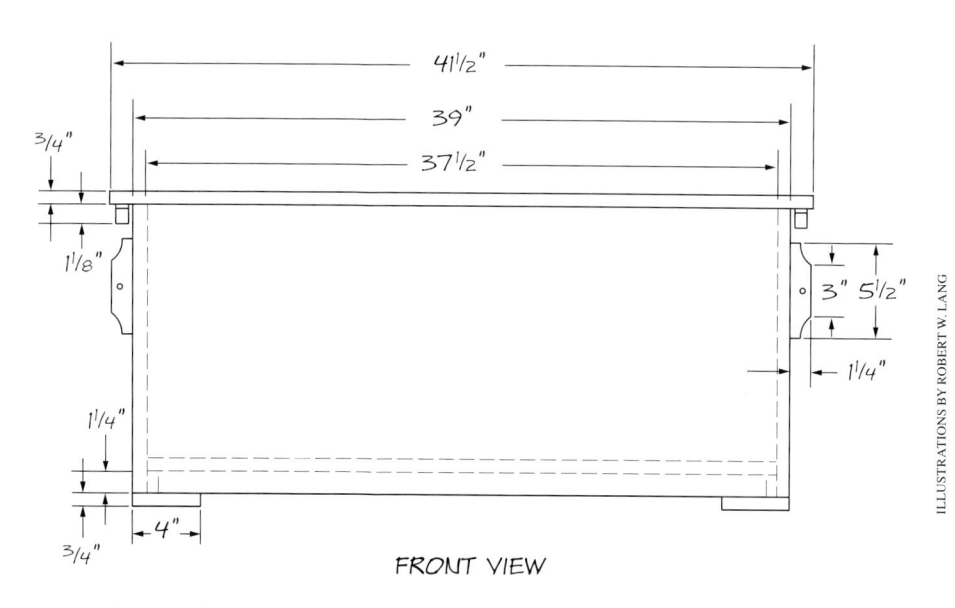

END VIEW SECTION

FRONT VIEW

SEA CHEST

cleat that's centered from top to bottom, then equally space and drill two $^5/_{16}$" holes along that line. Slightly oversized holes allow easy installation of the $^1/_4$" rope.

The cleats are attached with two screws through the interior of the chest. Position the cleats prior to any finishing steps, then drill and countersink holes for the screws. Install the cleats, but remove them prior to finishing the chest. Note which side of the chest each cleat fits so installation after finishing is less frustrating.

When the chest is completely finished and the cleats are once again installed, on goes the rope or beckets. Start with a 27" piece of rope, tie one end in a figure-eight knot then slide the opposite end into the rear hole of the cleat. Loop the piece through the front hole to form a handle, and tie a second knot to secure the handle near the end. Each pull of the beckets squeezes the knots tighter.

About the Finish

Sand the entire project with #150-grit sandpaper and prepare to paint and stain. The finish on this sea chest base is a painted crackle finish. (Learn how to "Crackle Finish" on page 30 in this issue.) The crackle effect adds age to any project as well as an interesting look. A few products available at most home-center stores are all you'll need.

The stain finish is a coat of Olympic Interior "Special Walnut" oil-based stain with a layer of Watco "Dark Walnut" Danish oil, topped with a layer of shellac. For further explanation of this finish, see "Authentic Arts & Crafts Finish," *Woodworking Magazine* Spring 2007, Issue 7 or visit woodworking-magazine.com/blog/. **WM**

— *Glen D. Huey*

Seasonal-adjustment stress is relieved by mounting the battens with pan head screws through slightly oversized holes. Drill a pilot hole then add wax to the screw to reduce chances of splitting the lid.

Position the cleat to the case sides, mark for screws then drill small pilot holes from the outside in. This establishes a precise interior location for countersink holes.

The softer metal of the strap hinges affords an opportunity to bend the hinge to a "proper" design for trunks and chest. Matching screws to the hardware improves the aesthetics of the project.

Sea Chest

NO.	PART	T	W	L	MATERIAL
❏ 2	Front/back panels	3/4	16 3/4†	39	Poplar
❏ 2	End panels	3/4	16 3/4†	20	Poplar
❏ 1	Lid	3/4	17 1/4	41 1/2	QSWO*
❏ 2	Battens	3/4	1 1/8	17	QSWO*
❏ 2	Long rims	3/4	1 1/4†	38†	Poplar
❏ 2	Short rims	3/4	1 1/4†	18†	Poplar
❏ 4	Feet	3/4	3 1/4	4	Poplar
❏ 2	Outer bottom	3/4	7	37 1/2	Poplar
❏ 1	Center bottom	3/4	5 1/4†	37 1/2	Poplar
❏ 2	Cleats	7/8	1 1/2	5 1/2	QSWO*

*Quartersawn white oak; †Trim to fit

Best Crackle Finish

Create an authentic crackle finish with a product that's straight from a home center. It's fast, cheap and easy.

Crackle finish on antique or nearly antique pieces is not something that happens overnight. It takes years to evolve. But, being part of an "instant gratification" age, we're asked to replicate a crackle finish in short time. But how?

In the past when adding a crackle finish to my work, I turned to an HVLP (high volume, low pressure) system and lacquer, but I also have a method of producing a crackle effect that involves hide glue. And, it's been suggested that other glue types will work as well. In addition, I found a crackle-finish product at a home center. Which products work and which don't?

I purchased a fresh bottle of liquid hide glue (hide glue ages, so look closely at the date on the bottle) and classic white glue. I almost always have yellow glue (aliphatic resin) in my shop and we had a small jug of American Traditions "Faux Weathered Crackle Glaze" already in the shop.

I had been told the crackle glaze did not work when previously called upon, but I decided to try it for myself. So one afternoon, prior to actually beginning with test pieces, I loaded the glaze onto a slab of poplar and waited for the layer to reach a stage that was dry enough to add paint, but not too dry.

When that stage was reached, I added a layer of flat, water-based paint. A crackling effect was not instant, but developed nonetheless. My outcome was obviously different from the earlier attempt. I figured that I must have the touch for producing a crackle finish.

With at least two viable products to produce a crackle finish not involving a sprayer, I ducked back into the shop to begin testing.

Why This Process Works

Because the glues and the glaze are water-based products, the crackling process works only when water-based paints are used. The glue is dry or nearly dry when the paint is added on top. Due to the water in the paint, the glue surface is reactivated and stretched. The paint dries more rapidly than the glue or glaze, then as the glue and glaze dry, the paint layer is separated to form small, and sometimes not so small, cracks.

On to the Test

I began the testing by milling several pieces of poplar for painting. The plan of attack was to coat the #150-grit sanded surfaces with a layer of crackle medium, be it glue or crackle glaze, then apply a coat of paint on top to watch the crackle come to life.

First up was the crackle glaze. I knew this would work and I anticipated a good start. With the glaze in place and tacky, but not dry to the touch, I spread on a layer of paint. I waited. And waited. Nothing happened.

Achieving a crackle effect for your painted furniture can be complicated if you make it that way. But in this case, simple is best. Hide glue, a paintbrush and water-based paint is all that's needed for a finish that appears aged – but is completed in less than a day.

How strange to have great results with the first try and less-than-adequate results the next day. What changed?

I went back to look at the paint that was used in my coworker's unsuccessful effort. That paint was a semi-gloss. My perfect-result paint was dead flat, and the paint I selected for testing had a slight sheen. I had found the reason for the inconsistencies with the crackle glaze. This product works, but you need to keep a keen eye on your choice of paint. A flat sheen works best.

Glue Would Work

With one product shot down due to its specific sheen requirements, I moved on to glue – knowing that hide glue was sure to work. But how would the other more common types of glue perform? That's something to discover.

In order to brush out any of the glue products, I

found it necessary to thin the adhesive; otherwise I had to smash the brush into the wood's surface. I added enough water to the glues to be able to spread them with a paintbrush. Look for a small amount of brush drag, but keep the thinning to a minimum. Too thin equates to no crackle.

I went to ordinary white glue straight away. If this grade-school favorite worked, then the effect would be a snap for just about any woodworker. White glue might be found in a closet or junk drawer somewhere in your home or workshop.

After the white glue was spread on the wood and allowed to reach a tacky state, I added a layer of flat paint, the one with a low sheen, then waited. This time there was a small amount of movement in the paint layer. Slowly, the crackle appeared. But it was nothing like what I wanted to achieve. I decided to move on.

The Last Two Glues

Aliphatic resin glue is a product most woodworking shops have at hand. I again thinned the glue with a small amount of water, brushed it onto the poplar board and allowed the adhesive to become tacky.

Next, I loaded my flat paint onto the glue and watched with anticipation for the cracks to come forward. This time the crackle was non-existent. I had a much better result using white glue. It's best to leave the yellow glue for woodshop uses – assembling panels and furniture joints.

I felt confident that liquid hide glue would give me the crackle finish results I wanted. I mixed water into the glue so I could brush it easily, then layered the mixture onto another board. When the coat became tacky, I slathered on the paint to await the results.

The action kicked in so quickly I barely had time to paint the entire board. The finished crackled surface was everything I was looking for – a clear-cut winner. And, hide glue produces a crackle finish with any water-based paint I've tried. That's easy to work with.

Fine-tuning the Crack

Here are a couple pointers I discovered along the way. To make crackle paint using hide glue an easy task, don't panic after you apply a glue layer to the project; the layer looks terrible, then levels as it becomes tacky. Also, for the best results, work on horizontal surfaces if possible. And, if you apply the paint to a glue layer that is especially wet, the crackle that comes about is extremely wide and not so pleasing to the eye.

Occasionally, it looks better to crackle small areas as opposed to an entire façade. If the majority of your painted area is at eye level, too much crackle can be overpowering. But the lower to the ground the painted area is, the less intense the crackled finish appears.

In addition, make sure to apply the paint layer with variations in film thickness to provide variations in the crackle lines. And while you're able to apply a glue layer with brush strokes going in all directions, you need to apply the paint in an orderly fashion. Brush only in one direction, horizontally or vertically.

However, the most important tip I can convey is to try the process on scrap pieces before loading it onto your project. **WM**

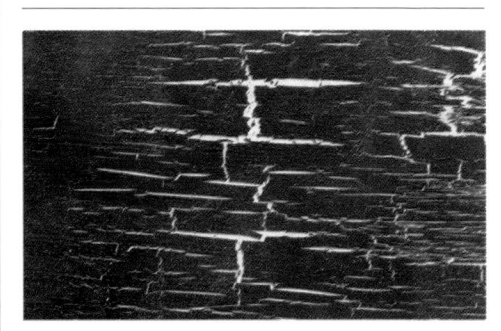

— *Glen D. Huey*

It's important to watch the type of paint used with store-purchased glazes. Flat paint worked with the glaze, but the crackle finish was a "no show" when the paint was glossier.

You'll find that thinning the glue products helps greatly when you brush on a layer. Look for a bit of drag on the brush as you work.

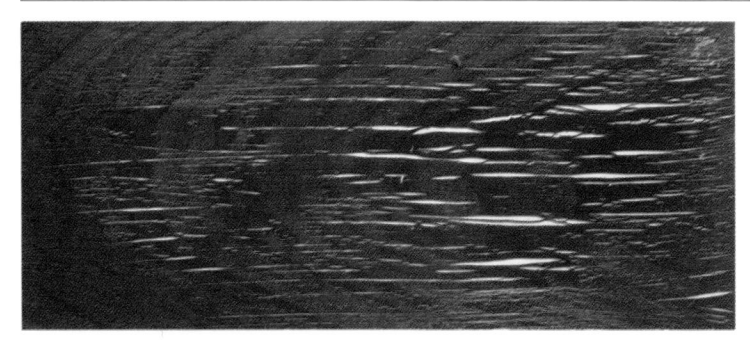

Ordinary white glue did show cracked lines, but if you compare this finish to that of the hide glue process, you'll notice a big difference in the design of the crackle.

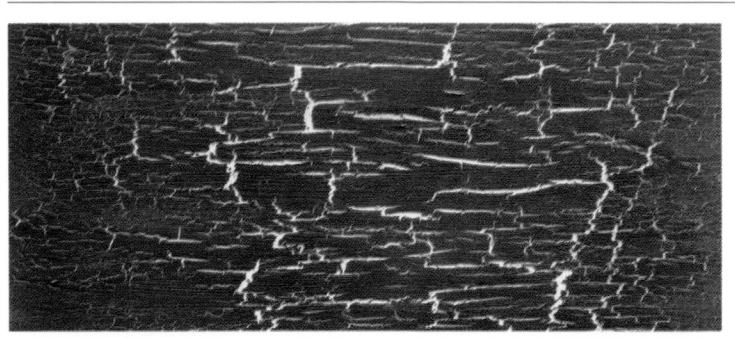

Hide glue is "tried and true." Crackling a painted finish using hide glue is easy and the look is authentic.

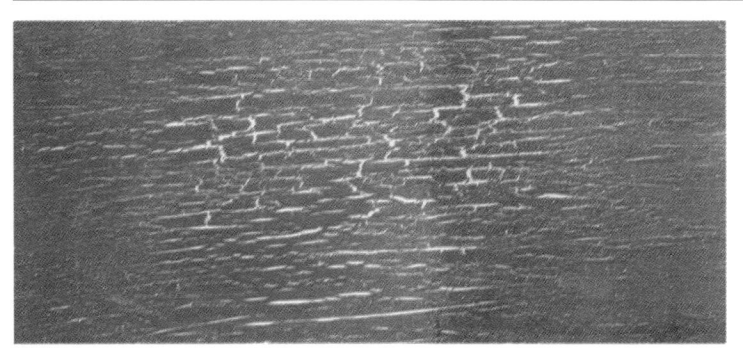

Variations in the thickness of the paint layer helps vary the design of the crackle finish. In the middle of this sample, the paint was on the thick side; around the perimeter of the block, you'll notice a finer, lighter effect.

End Grain

PHOTO BY CHRISTOPHER SCHWARZ

Als Ik Kan: As Best I Can

The last thing I do to a project is hit it with a hammer. Here's why.

No matter how long you have been working at the craft, you sometimes flirt with the idea that you can buy your way to better craftsmanship.

I first picked up a crosscut saw at age 8, so I should know better than to fall for this false promise. But occasionally as I page through a tool catalog or look over someone's tool collection I think:

"If I only had that Felder/Lie-Nielsen/Ultimatum thingy. Then it would be easy for me to be fast/skilled/way sexy to other British bit brace collectors."

And so now I bet you're thinking that I'm going to lecture you on how, "It's not the arrows; it's the Indian," or that skill is something independent of our personal pile of brass, rosewood and high-carbon steel.

Actually, I'm not.

I'd like to share with you the one tool that has improved my craftsmanship every day I've owned it for the last nine years. And I expect it to continue performing this astounding feat for another 30 years.

The tool is a maker's stamp that my wife purchased for me for my 30th birthday from Mazzaglia Tools in Salem, N.H. It's a simple piece of steel that's $3/16$" thick, $1 1/4$" wide and $2 1/2$" long. And cut into reverse on one end is "C. SCHWARZ."

This is always the last tool to touch my work – if it touches it at all. You see, this stamp is the tool that determines if my work is up to snuff. If I won't sign the piece with this permanent stamp, then I probably need to throw the project on the burn pile (which I've done – right after a satisfying hatchet session). Or perhaps I need to go back and remake some assembly or part of the project, try to bring the finish up to a higher level or find some better hardware.

As an added bonus, the completed project has to be sturdy enough to receive the beating necessary to leave my name in crisp letters. That beating is necessary because the name stamp has the letters incised into the steel block. (Stamps that have the letters raised off the block leave a mark with a much lighter tap.) As a result, you have to hit the stamp very hard with a hammer into the end grain of your project to make it work.

When done correctly, the letters stand proud of a recessed background that is surrounded by a decorative border. Very nice.

I usually pick someplace inconspicuous to apply the stamp, such as the lower edge of a door stile or the bottom of a leg. Then I place the project on the concrete floor of my shop and pinch the stamp between the thumb and forefinger of my left hand. I rest my hammer's head on the end of the stamp (which is now mushroomed over from the beatings from my 16 oz. hammer).

I pause for a few moments to make sure I am ready to bring the hammer down in one fell stroke. You get only one chance to do it right. It's just like building a piece of furniture for someone else; there are no do-overs.

As I write this, I'm just about ready to sign the blanket chest I finished for this issue of *Woodworking Magazine*. But there's just one little bit of roughness on the chest's lid. Perhaps it needs a little wetsanding first before I fetch the stamp.

If you'd like more information about the name stamps from Mazzaglia Tools, write for a brochure: 12 Palmer St., Salem, N.H. 03079. There are several other companies out there that make fancier stamps as well, such as Engraving Arts (brandingirons.net) and Microstamp (microstampusa.com). Plus there are the branding irons that burn your name or logo into your project that are available in many woodworking catalogs.

And if you don't have the coin for a stamp, you can always use a Sharpie marker to do the same job. **WM**

— *Christopher Schwarz*

Extras

"That is what learning is. You suddenly understand something you've understood all your life, but in a new way."
— Doris Lessing (1919 -), Nobel Prize-winning author

SUBSCRIBE NOW To *Woodworking Magazine*

Now, you can subscribe to *Woodworking Magazine* and receive four issues for $19.96 – mailed to your door. No more will you have to haunt your local magazine vendor for the latest issue, miss an issue by mistake or even have to bid on a back issue on eBay.

To subscribe right away, visit woodworking-magazine.com and click on the "Subscribe" link. You can pay online with a credit card (which saves us some postage) or we can bill you if you prefer. Or, call 800-283-3542 and subscribe over the phone.

Other than the fact that you can now subscribe to *Woodworking Magazine*, nothing else about the publication will change. We will not accept advertising in our pages. We are still focused on unearthing the simplest and best techniques for both power tools and hand tools. And the projects we build will always be classics – designs that have remained fresh and alive for a century or more. Our mission – simply put – is to help you find a better way to build.

Also, we thank you for your support of *Woodworking Magazine*. Without your many kind letters and e-mails, we wouldn't now be able to offer subscriptions.

You see, we started *Woodworking Magazine* in 2004 without the blessing of our parent corporation. The market, they thought, was too crowded for another woodworking magazine. But we knew in our gut that this wasn't just another magazine. So we kept putting it out on the newsstands twice a year as an experiment to see if readers would embrace a magazine with black-and-white photos, techniques that frequently defied conventional wisdom and no advertising.

And because you did embrace the magazine, we are now able to publish *Woodworking Magazine* four times a year and offer subscriptions by mail. So again, thank you. We couldn't have done it without you.

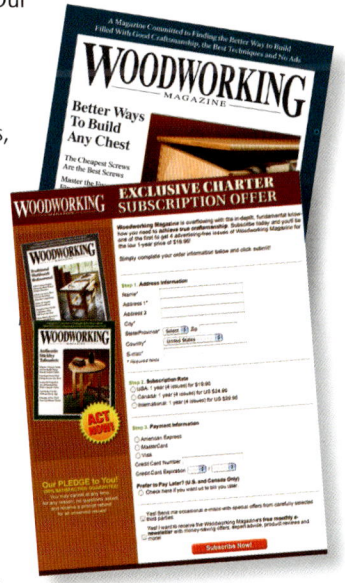

IMPORTANT SAFETY NOTE

Safety is your responsibility. Manufacturers place safety devices on their equipment for a reason. In many photos you see in *Woodworking Magazine*, these have been removed to provide clarity. In some cases we'll use an awkward body position so you can better see what's being demonstrated. Don't copy us. Think about each procedure you're going to perform beforehand. Safety First!

CONTACT US

We welcome letters from readers with comments about this magazine, or about woodworking in general. We try to respond to all correspondence. To send us a letter:
- E-mail: letters@fwpubs.com
- Fax: 513-891-7196
- Mail carrier:
  Letters • *Woodworking Magazine*
  4700 E. Galbraith Road
  Cincinnati, OH 45236

Woodworking in America Hand Tools & Techniques Conference 2008

After many years of teaching people how to set up and use hand tools, I've come to realize that it's best to handle a wide variety of sizes and brands of any tool before making a buying decision and that techniques are best learned with a skilled practitioner to show you how to go about it.

That's why we've spent many months planning a special weekend conference in Berea, Ky., for Nov. 14-16, 2008, that is designed to expose you to a rich and wide variety of expert craftsmen, tools and hand woodworking skills.

The conference, which we're calling "Woodworking in America," is going to help hundreds of woodworkers jump-start their hand-tool skills, expose them to tools they've seen only in catalogs and offer them face-to-face instruction with some of today's best hand-tool woodworkers.

As I write this, we're still working out the details, but here is the conference in broad strokes (and more information and conference newsletter signup is available on the soon-to-be-launched conference web site at WoodworkingInAmerica.com):

- We're lining up many of the country's large and small manufacturers of well-made hand tools. As a result, you'll be able to try a wide variety of tools – and get to know the maker – before you make that once-in-a-lifetime purchase.

- Many of the country's leading hand-tool craftsmen will be teaching seminars and hands-on classes on a wide variety of topics, from basic sharpening, planing and sawing to workbench design and advanced joinery.

So I hope you'll mark your calendar for Nov. 14-16 and visit the conference's web site at WoodworkingInAmerica.com for full details. One more thing: Space is extremely limited at the conference. We want to keep things personal and intimate so that you will have the richest and most rewarding hand-tool experience possible.

— Christopher Schwarz

Number 10, Summer 2008. *Woodworking Magazine* is published 4 times a year in March, May, August and December by F+W Publications, Inc. Editorial offices are located at 4700 E. Galbraith Road, Cincinnati, Ohio 45236; tel.: 513-531-2222. Unsolicited manuscripts are not accepted. Subscription rates: A year's subscription (4 issues) is $19.96 in the U.S., $24.96 in Canada, and $29.96 elsewhere. Produced and printed in the U.S.A.

BLOCK PLANES

WOODWORKING MAGAZINE | SUMMER 2008

Anatomy of a Block Plane

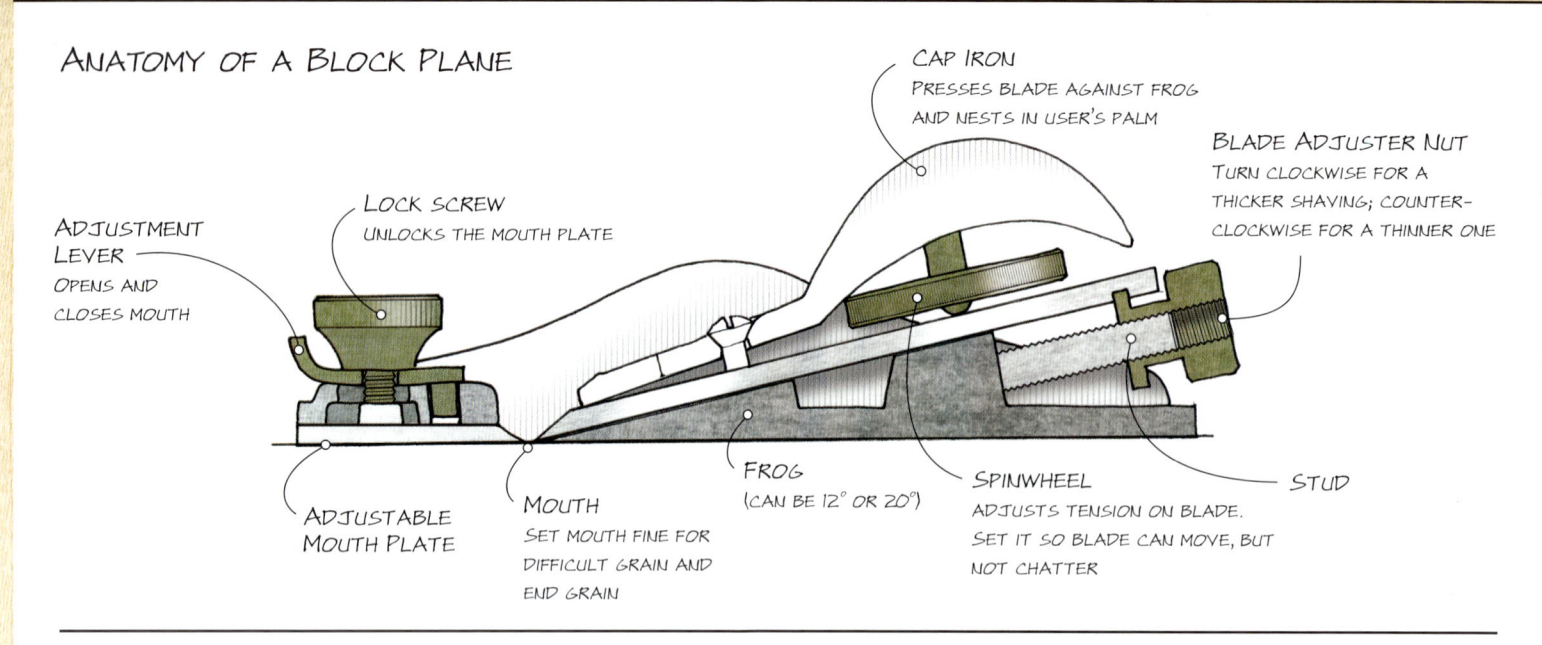

- **Adjustment Lever** – Opens and closes mouth
- **Lock Screw** – Unlocks the mouth plate
- **Cap Iron** – Presses blade against frog and nests in user's palm
- **Blade Adjuster Nut** – Turn clockwise for a thicker shaving; counter-clockwise for a thinner one
- **Adjustable Mouth Plate**
- **Mouth** – Set mouth fine for difficult grain and end grain
- **Frog** (can be 12° or 20°)
- **Spinwheel** – Adjusts tension on blade. Set it so blade can move, but not chatter
- **Stud**

Why an Adjustable Mouth Helps

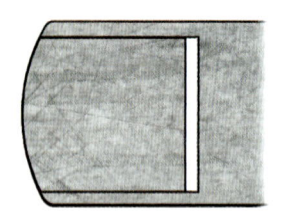

An adjustable mouth allows you to quickly tighten the mouth to work difficult grain. Also, tightening the mouth for end grain prevents the iron from gouging the corner as you begin planing.

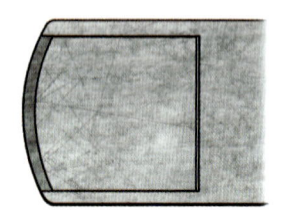

Different Angles for Different Woods

The angle of attack of a block plane is calculated by adding the bed angle (either 12° or 20°) to the angle sharpened on the plane's cutter (typically anywhere from 25° to 35°).

Use lower angles of attack (such as 37°) for end grain. Use higher angles of attack (such as 55°) for difficult grain.

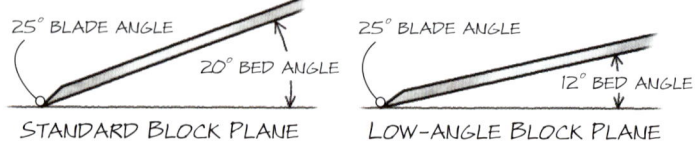

- 25° blade angle / 20° bed angle — **Standard Block Plane**
- 25° blade angle / 12° bed angle — **Low-angle Block Plane**

The Cutting Edge: Curved or Straight?

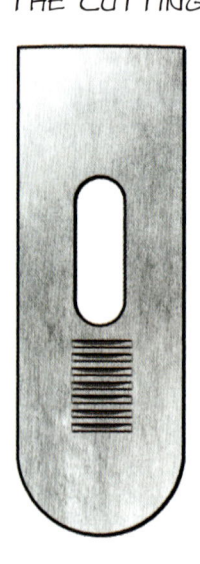

Conventional wisdom is that you should sharpen the edge of a block plane straight across, like you would a chisel.

While a straight edge is the simplest to sharpen, some craftsmen prefer a slight curve – just a few thousandths of curvature over the entire edge. Or they will simply relieve the corners with a file.

A curve allows you to plane finished work without the risk of the corners of the iron digging into the wood.

Different Lengths for Different Work

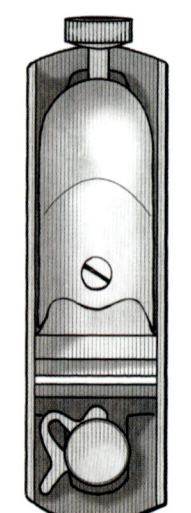

Typical block planes range in length from 3½" up to 7".

Longer block planes are easier to hold and help maintain the flatness of your work.

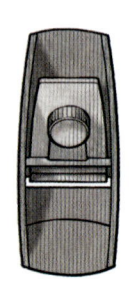

Shorter block planes allow you to plane in restricted areas or to remove several shavings from a very localized area where large block planes may be able to take only one shaving.

Illustrations by Matt Bantly

A Magazine Committed to Finding the Better Way to Build
Filled with Good Craftsmanship, the Best Techniques and No Ads

WOODWORKING
MAGAZINE

American Hanging Cupboard

Make the Face Frame First to Make Everything Easier

The Must-Have Tools To Set Up Your Shop

2 Bevel Gauges Lock Up the Competition

Warm Up Your Walnut With Dye and Shellac

No-fail Dovetails: Traditional Tool Tote is Great for Beginners

POPULAR WOODWORKING PRESENTS

fw F+W PUBLICATIONS, INC.
US $5.99
CAN $7.99

Display until November 2, 2008

woodworking-magazine.com ■ AUTUMN 2008

Contents

"It is better to turn over a question without deciding it than to decide it without turning it over."
— Joseph Joubert (1754-1824), French moralist and essayist

1 On the Level
Beauty (or lack thereof) in your dovetails is for the birds. We think there are bigger fish to fry.

2 Letters
Questions, comments and wisdom from readers, experts and our staff.

4 Shortcuts
Tricks and tips that will make your woodworking simpler and more accurate.

6 Build a Better Cabinet
Many methods for building cabinets are filled with opportunities for error. We blend several systems to eliminate measuring and mistakes.

10 Fitting Inset Doors
The key to achieving an even reveal is preparation. Make good parts, and the gaps will fall perfectly in place (with just a little handwork).

14 American Wall Cupboard
Picture books and good planning help to make this classic walnut cupboard look equally at home in the 18th and 21st centuries.

FITTING INSET DOORS: PAGE 10

21 Glossary
Woodworking's terminology can be overwhelming. Learn the terms used in this issue.

22 The Best Sliding Bevel Gauges
Out of the eight bevel gauges we tested, two are "recommended." Three others are "acceptable" in a pinch.

THE BEST SLIDING BEVEL GAUGES: PAGE 22

TOOL TOTE: PAGE 26

26 Tool Tote
Don't let the angled ends scare you away; this traditional tote is excellent practice ground for cutting serviceable dovetails (and the heck with making them pretty).

28 Tools for Woodwork
Here's our best list (borrowed in large part from Charles Hayward) of all the tools a serious beginner needs to equip an excellent shop.

30 Tinted Shellac Warms Walnut
A few drops of aniline dye added to amber shellac imparts a pleasing warmth to walnut – without muddying the grain.

32 Really, It's OK to Make Mistakes
Mistakes may cost you (in both time and money) the first time, but they'll pay off down the line.

BUILD A BETTER CABINET: PAGE 6

TINTED SHELLAC WARMS WALNUT: PAGE 30

On the Level

True Dovetales

Most people have the wrong idea about dovetails. They look at the interlocking pins and tails of this fundamental joint and look for gaps as a way to measure the maker's craftsmanship.

This is akin to liking the steel in a chisel because it can be polished to such a nice mirror sheen. It misses the point entirely. Dovetails were developed because they were the strongest way to join two pieces of wood without reliable adhesives at hand.

Their beauty (or ugliness) is incidental.

And so I worry about beginning woodworkers who fret they will never cut a dovetail worth using in a piece of casework. So here's the truth: The first set of dovetails you cut will be great. They might look like the teeth of an 18th-century British deckhand, but they will hold two boards together better than any other joint you can cut by hand.

When you are done, cover them with moulding. That's what our ancestors did. Until the Arts & Crafts movement kicked into high gear, most woodworkers went to great lengths to conceal their joinery. They concocted joints – such as the secret mitered dovetail – to conceal the fact that these two boards were dovetailed together. The connection was supposed to be seamless. The joinery invisible.

But about 100 years ago, as machinery pushed out the hand-cut joinery of the 19th century, we became fascinated by expressed joinery. Perhaps this was a reaction to the shoddily made furniture of the Victorian era. Seeing the joinery was your guarantee it wasn't made from dowels. Or perhaps it was because our machines allowed us to join with perfection every time, even if we didn't have the hand skills.

In any case, this was the beginning of a national obsession with tidy rows of perfectly cut dovetails. And once we invented dovetail jigs for the router, we raised the bar even higher. Now we had to imitate a machine that could make them 100-percent airtight.

And so the hand-cutters emphasized the fact that they could space their dovetails irregularly. Then the machines developed the capacity to space the dovetails irregularly. So now the hand-cutters say they can make dovetails so closely spaced that the distance between them is only a saw kerf (about .042"). And I'm sure the dovetail jig manufacturers are hard at work on a way to counter the hand-dovetailers.

As a result of this tension, we have scads of dovetail jigs and too many magazine articles that show you how to cut the joint by hand (or fool your friends into thinking you did). We here at *Woodworking Magazine* have resolved to focus our efforts elsewhere and skip this conflict entirely. We think there are bigger fish to fry.

However, I'm sure that you need a recommendation for where to begin learning to cut dovetails. My personal favorite is Rob Cosman's book and DVD on the topic, which he sells for about $55 on his web site at robcosman.com. We cannot do any better.

Rob's DVD shows what the body positioning, sawing and chiseling looks like. The accompanying spiral-bound book is a great companion for the shop because it shows you exactly what each step should look like in close-up detail, from layout to the final glue-up.

Rob has taught thousands of people to cut dovetails (heck, I took his advanced class about eight years ago), and he really knows how to teach the process.

I guarantee that dovetailing is something that comes with regular practice. Start to dovetail all your carcases together and within a short period of time, your dovetails will become tidy and tight. And eventually you will reach the point where you think: Boy, it sure will be a shame to cover those joints with moulding.

And that's exactly what I was thinking as I nailed on the cove moulding on the cover project. WM

Christopher Schwarz
Editor

> "We need 18th-century woodworking tools and techniques about as much as we need 18th-century dentistry."
> — Dr. Andrew Friede
> woodworker

Letters

ILLUSTRATIONS BY MARY JANE FAVORITE

'Scoop' the Middle to Overcome Handplaning Challenges

I love handplanes, but no matter what I do I seem to always come out with a "thick to thin" board. I've read several tips on changing the pressure I exert from the toe to the heel of the plane, but I still seem to come out with the same result. What am I doing wrong?

Doug Calvert
Sacramento, California

Doug,
It sounds like a pressure issue to me as well. At the start of the stroke, put all your downward pressure on the toe of the plane. The other hand should only push forward.

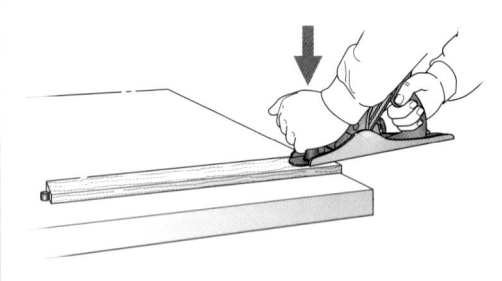

In the middle of the stroke, put equal downward pressure fore and aft on the plane.

And at the end of the stroke, put all the downward pressure on the heel.

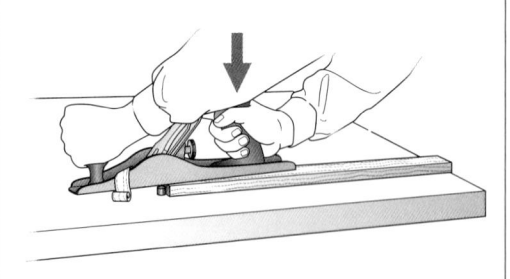

You use these same techniques whether you are planing the broad faces or narrow edges of a board.

When I'm working in my own shop (or teaching others to plane) I like to think that when I apply a plane to a board, I'm trying to scoop out its middle section. That's actually impossible (except with really short planes), but it does tell the right muscles to do the right things at the right time. Hope this helps to straighten you out.

Christopher Schwarz, editor

A Correction on How Torque is Really Measured

The article on screws in the Summer 2008 issue (#10) had a minor error and an omission.

First, the article talked about how many "foot-pounds of pressure" it took to keep the driver engaged. This is incorrect. Pressure is measured in "pounds per square inch," while "foot-pounds" is a unit of torque. In any case, it's probably more accurate to say that a certain amount of force (as opposed to pressure) is required to keep the driver engaged in the screw head. In that case, units of "pounds" would be correct.

Second, the article made it sound like cam-out in the Phillips head was accidental. From everything I've read, the original Phillips head was intentionally designed to cam out, as it was intended for power driving where the machines didn't have torque control.

Chris Friesen
Saskatoon, Saskatchewan

Chris,
Point taken! I should have used the phrase "foot-pounds of torque," not "pressure."

And you're right about Phillips screws. They were designed to cam out. However, in today's woodworking, cam-out is not a benefit – it's a problem. With most battery-powered drill/drivers having torque settings, cam-out should be eliminated.

Glen D. Huey, senior editor

A Knotty Workbench Question

I searched through your magazine articles and *Woodworking Magazine* book, but can't find an answer to this: If I'm gluing up a workbench top from Southern yellow pine, does it matter if there are knots embedded in the top or exposed on the bottom? Or am I correct in assuming it is fine as long as the knots aren't where I'm trying to drill dog holes?

Mark Wells
Austin, Texas

Mark,
Knots are no problem. My top has them embedded in the thickness and on the underside. They are on the back of the legs and on and on. Tight knots, but knots nonetheless.

Christopher Schwarz, editor

What Blade Radii are Appropriate For Various Handplanes?

What do you consider a useful range of plane-blade radii in these planes: jack, fore, smoother and jointer?

Mike Darrah
Naugatuck, Connecticut

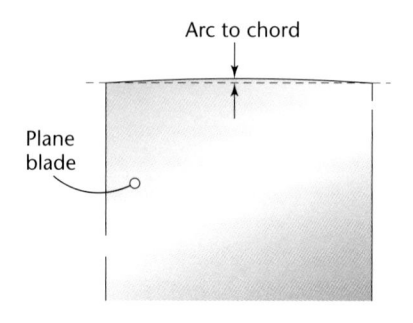

Mike,
The jack plane can be at any radius – from the tight 8" radius of a fore plane to a dead-straight iron. That's because you can set up the jack plane to almost any job. It can be for shooting (with a straight iron), a fore plane, a shortish jointer plane or a longish smoothing plane.

The fore plane's iron should be heavily curved – in a thumbnail shape. I like somewhere between an 8"- and 12"-radius arc.

The jointer plane can be straight or curved. I like curved. The "arc to chord" distance (which is the height of the curve measured from the corners to the apogee of the curve) should be about .005" to .008".

The smoothing plane can be straight (with the corners rounded) or curved (again, I like curved). The arc to chord there is about .002" to .003".

Christopher Schwarz, editor

Do Vintage Saws Require Frequent Sharpening?

Thanks for all the great information on saws (*Woodworking Magazine* Spring 2008, Issue 9). I do have a question though. I'll soon start sawing some 3" x 10" x 10' rough-cut white ash for a workbench top that will be 30" x 4"-5" x 10'. That's about 200 linear feet of sawing. (Yes, I know; if I were half-smart I'd mortgage the farm and buy a band saw, a jointer and a planer.)

But, because the wait on a big Wenzloff & Sons ripsaw is at least 21 weeks, I'm thinking of buying a circa 1900 Disston D-8 5.5ppi-28" ripsaw from vintagesaws.com. I may also buy a big crosscut saw as well.

My question is: Do vintage saws have to be sharpened more often than new current-day handsaws?

Obviously, I mean when cutting woods of comparable hardness. I guess that this is the same as asking "to what hardness is the steel in the teeth tempered," but there may be other factors that I'm not aware of, and it's easier to compare sharpening frequency.

Don Haines
Bremerton, Washington

Don,
My answer is based on conversations with Tom Law, who has probably sharpened more handsaws than anyone else alive.

Law says that the steel in vintage saws is less consistent than in the saws made during the last 50 years. Sometimes a vintage saw will be too soft and have to be sharpened quite a lot. Sometimes it will be perfect and hold its edge as long as that of a modern saw. Sometimes it will be too hard, and the teeth will be brittle and can snap when they are set during the sharpening process.

It all depends on how the saw was heat-treated, Law says. The saw plates were heat-treated in piles. Saws on the outside of the pile would sometimes get too hard. Saws at the core of the pile would end up too soft. Saws in the middle might turn out just right. Steel manufacturing then was still a "black art," Law says.

So what do you do? You can buy a saw from Law himself, who can pick one out that will hold its edge (301-824-5223). Or, if you want to do this thing yourself, Law recommends a Disston D-23. These saws aren't collectible or as pretty as older saws, but the steel is excellent, the handles are robust and they are generally in better shape because they are newer (Disston stopped making them in the 1950s).

You can read more about D-23s here: http://disstonianinstitute.com/d23page.html

Christopher Schwarz, editor

"Equating time spent and quality may in fact be empirically false. Painting teachers encourage students not to overpaint a picture, continuing to put paint on the canvas until an initially good idea is buried in a muddy mess."

Howie Becker (1928 -)
sociologist and author

The Correct Angle on Screws

First, thanks for a wonderful magazine. *Woodworking Magazine* has inspired me to take up the plane again! It really is a treasure.

However, in reading the article on screws in the last issue, Summer 2008, I notice that on page 24 the angle for the screw head is measured from the wrong points.

David Owen
Calgary, Alberta

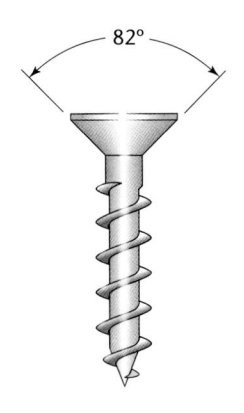

David,
You are correct. The 82° arc is across the top of the screw head, not where the head meets the shaft, as we indicated in the photo. In the illustration above, we've corrected the problem.

Megan Fitzpatrick, managing editor

Won't That Ruin a File?

On the back page of the Summer 2008 issue, it states that you can relieve the corners of a plane iron with a file. Doing that will ruin a file; use a stone.

Michael E. Siemsen
via e-mail

Mike,
Perhaps filing the corners of plane irons will ruin the file, but it has taken me more than 12 years to ruin the Nicholson file I've been using for that task (and scrapers etc.). I've never had a problem with it.

Christopher Schwarz, editor

Spar Varnish – Really?

I read with interest your recipe for an "all purpose finish" in the Summer 2008 "Shortcuts" (Issue 10). I was surprised to see spar varnish as one of the ingredients. I was taught that spar varnish never really dries. Do you in fact use spar varnish – or was it a misprint?

Ed Grant
Burlington Township, Pennsylvania

Ed,
We do, in fact, use spar varnish in our "all-purpose finish." The term "spar" is another name for "long-oil" varnish, which is created with a higher percentage of oil to resin than regular or "short-oil" varnish. And according to finishing guru Bob Flexner, "the more oil, the softer and more flexible the resulting cured-varnish film." The increased flexibility is great for wood due to wood's tendency to expand and contract.

The mixture of tung oils and polyurethanes in spar varnish, specifically McCloskey's Spar Varnish, combine to form long chain molecules, called polymers. Polymers are more flexible than regular polyurethanes, so they resist cracking during temperature fluctuations (day to night, etc.). As a result, the finish lasts longer.

The difference between spar varnish and marine varnish (another long-oil varnish) is the addition of UV absorbers – not so important with interior furniture finishes, but the products work the same if used.

Glen D. Huey, senior editor

Your Unique Outlook Is a Welcome Find

I wish to take a moment to express my thanks for you and your most excellent staff of creative artisans. I picked up a copy of *Woodworking Magazine* on somewhat of a whim last week and was totally blown away!

I work as a laser engineer, and certain characteristics are needed in order to look at problems in a certain manner: a blend of art, meticulous attention to detail, visualization, aesthetics, creativity and sensitivity to wholeness. Your magazine has these qualities in abundance, and along with the use of quotes, it's a stroke of genius!

Your people and your magazine are unique – which in a world of commonplace is a very needful thing indeed. **WM**

Don Lubin
via e-mail

HOW TO CONTACT US

Send your comments and questions via e-mail to letters@fwpubs.com, or by regular mail to *Woodworking Magazine*, Letters, 4700 E. Galbraith Road, Cincinnati, OH 45236. Please include your complete mailing address and daytime phone number. All letters become property of *Woodworking Magazine*.

Shortcuts

ILLUSTRATIONS BY MARY JANE FAVORITE

Pressure Where You Need It

This Shortcut allows easier control of holding a plane blade while flattening its unbeveled face. Secure a "Mag-Jig" rare earth magnet as a handle to hold on to as you flatten the face. It gives you more control and is easier on the fingers. The Mag-Jig is available from Lee Valley Tools (leevalley.com or 800-871-8158).

Robert Davison
Georgetown, Ontario

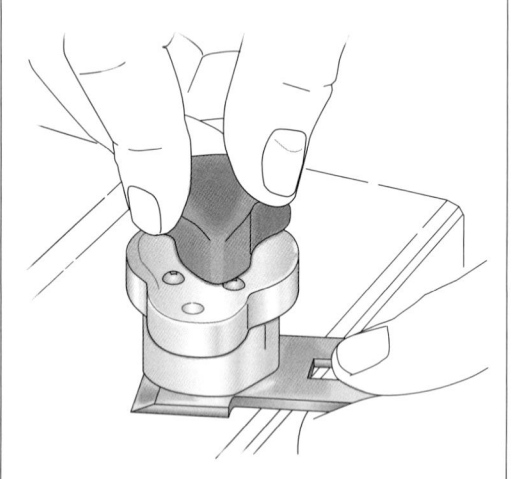

Knob rotates to activate or deactivate magnet.

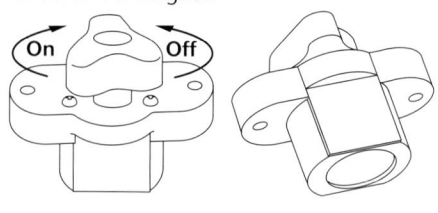

"If the crafts survive, their work will be done for love more than for money.... People are beginning to believe that you cannot make even toothpicks without ten thousand pounds of capital. We forget the prodigies one man and a kit of tools can do if he likes the work enough."

— David Pye (1914 - 1993)
Master craftsman and author

Easier Square Holes

When pegging mortise-and-tenon joints, many woodworkers like the look of a square peg. A square peg can be a stylistic statement, or simply a detail correct to the period of the furniture reproduction.

In either case, some woodworkers struggle with getting a square peg to fit neatly into a round hole. Sometimes the square peg will compress the circumference of a round hole into a perfect square; but often there are gaps left behind. Or worse, the work splits.

To combat this problem, I hacksawed off the tapered ends of some old square-shanked auger bits (rusty ones can be had for a song at any flea market). They come in two sizes typically. The smaller square shank tapers up to $1/4$". The larger ones taper up to $3/8$".

Hacksaw off the tapered shank, plus about 2" of the round section of the shank. Dress the round area of the shank with a file to remove any sharp edges left from the hacksawing.

Now you can use these two tools to transform round holes into ones with square lips. Here's how: Drill your round hole for your peg. Then drop your new tool into the round hole and tap it with a hammer until it cuts the right square lip. Now drive your peg home. It helps to whittle one end of the square peg round and to stop tapping the peg as soon as the square section of the peg seats in the square section of the hole. Use a flush-cut saw to flush the peg to your workpiece surface then sand to finish.

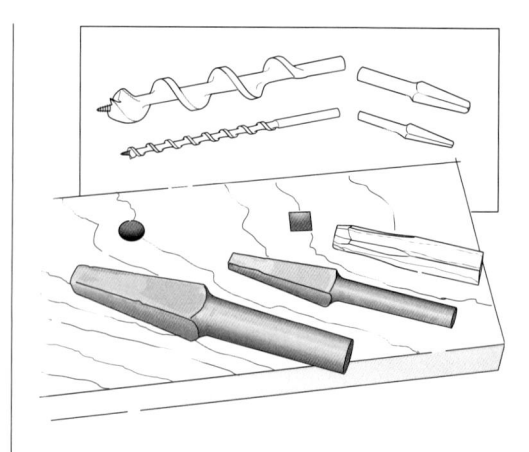

Marc Adams
Franklin, Indiana

Accurate, Inexpensive Woodworking Squares

Inexpensive drafting triangles can be "drafted" into service as a highly accurate square for marking out perpendicular lines and directly confirming the fact that assemblies are square (or not). I've never trusted measuring assemblies on the diagonal because that can be an inaccurate measurement at times.

So here's what you do: Take a plastic 12" 45° drafting triangle (you can buy one at any store for architects, artists or students). Then carefully joint and rip a narrow strip of $1/2$" x $1/2$" hardwood so it is slightly shorter in length than one of the legs of the right triangle. Plow a shallow groove in the hardwood. Our square was .010" thick, so a single saw blade kerf from a thin-kerf blade was perfect. In any case, the groove should be the same width as the thickness of the drafting square and the hardwood should fit tightly on the plastic square. Finally, epoxy the hardwood strip onto the square, using tape as a clamp.

Now you have a versatile square ideal for casework layout. It rests easily in place on your work without tipping off (like a framing square will do), and the transparency is a plus for seeing your work. And you have a much longer reach than a typical 6" combination square. Make several squares in several sizes, and you'll be set.

Robert W. Lang, senior editor

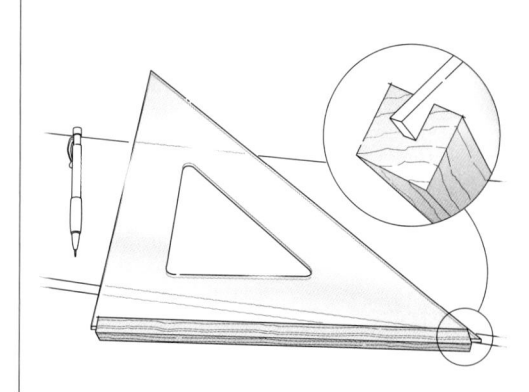

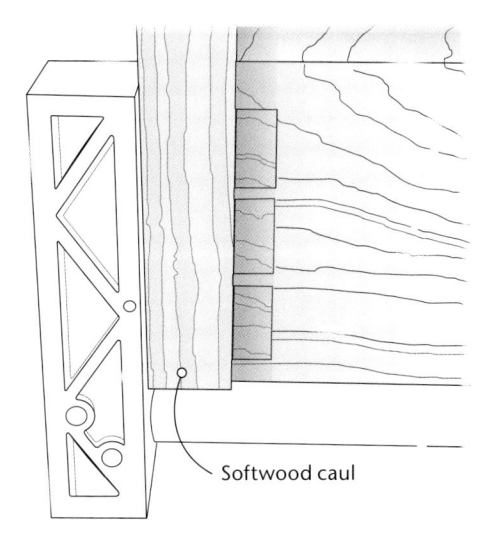

Softwood caul

A Simple Way to Clamp Dovetails and Finger Joints

I noticed your description of setting up little cauls under your clamps to pull the finger joints of the blanket chest together during glue-up ("Union Village Blanket Chest," *Woodworking Magazine* Summer 2008, Issue 10). Given the magazine's philosophy of eschewing "fussy" operations, I have an alternative that takes a lot less futzing with tape and little scraps of wood.

This works only when the project is a hard wood such as maple, walnut or cherry, and the excess end grain of the fingers when the joint is closed is less than about $\frac{1}{16}$".

First obtain a scrap piece of white pine (fir, hemlock or other very soft, cheap wood works as well) that's the length of your joint (use one scrap for each side of the joint). Cover one side of it with wax or clear packing tape to avoid gluing it to the project, and use it as a caul under the clamp heads.

The force of the clamp will deform the cauls' wood around the end-grain fingers so that the wood on the long-grain fingers makes a nice, perfectly fitting distributor of the clamping force. And it's a heck of a lot easier to put one board under the clamp head during glue-up than lots of little scraps, even with the shortcut of taping them to the joint.

I've used this trick for a number of years with dovetails, and it should work even better with finger joints.

David Keller
Raleigh, North Carolina

Editor's note: This trick works best using the absolute softest pine from the home center. Also good to know: Many people (myself included) don't actually clamp dovetail joints. After gluing and knocking them together, I just let the assembly sit until the glue has cured.

Making 'Forged' Forged Nails

When I first became interested in period furniture, I had this romanticized view of it, so it came as quite a shock to find my perception and reality weren't in sync. One of the things that surprised me the most was the extensive use of nails. Where I would have expected a glue joint, or at the very least a screw, I found that nails were more common.

So as I began in the craft, I purchased reproduction cut nails. These had the period look, but each one was exactly the same, so I ended up doing a little "hand forging" on them to give them some individuality. I will admit I dislike cut nails. Despite the fact that they crush the fibers ahead of the point, they still have a tendency to split the wood, and their tapered shape makes a pilot hole a compromise. Of course they do offer tremendous holding power, but in furniture they are used where they are loaded mostly in shear, so this is of lesser importance.

At some point I read about a restorer who used common upholstery tacks that were handworked and used to conceal modern nails. And the idea hit me to take common wire nails and "forge" my own from the modern nails.

I use only uncoated common wire nails and have used nails from *4d* to *10d*. I look for nails that have fairly thick heads; some of the box and sinker nails have heads that are too thin to forge.

Start by heating the head with a gas torch until it glows yellow. Then hammer it on its side, drawing out the head. Then rotate it 90° and strike it a few times to square up the "ends." You don't want a square head, but you also don't want a long narrow head.

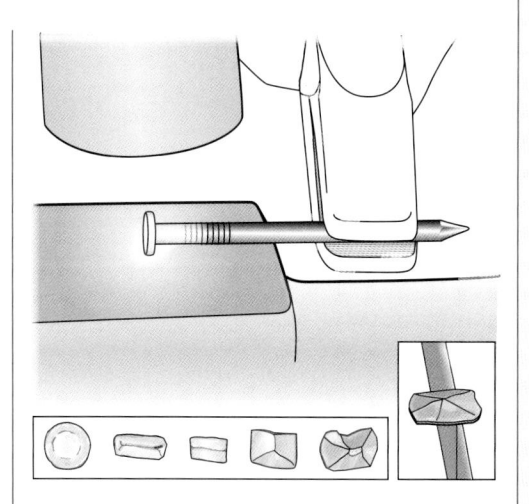

The rest of the process can be done with the steel in a cold state. I have used two different methods to further form the head. The first is simply holding the nail in a vise and hammering the head to shape. The other involves a stout block of steel with a hole the approximate size of the nail's shank.

In looking at period nails, the most common head shapes had three or five facets, although not every blacksmith got that memo. I like the look of five facets.

One of my favorite memories of the first furniture show I went to is of an older gentleman who examined the back of a desk I'd built. He said, "Nice work sonny, right down to the nails." I said: "Yep, they are 'forged.'"

Rob Millard
Dayton, Ohio

How to Taper Pegs Like a Professional Writer

I've pegged thousands of joints, and one of the most important tools I own for that job is a pencil sharpener. Instead of whittling the end of every peg I merely sharpen it in a pencil sharpener. A typical pencil sharpener will work for pegs up to $\frac{1}{4}$" x $\frac{1}{4}$", though some sharpeners will accept larger "pencils." I know of no better or faster way to prepare pegs for any size project. **WM**

Glen D. Huey, senior editor

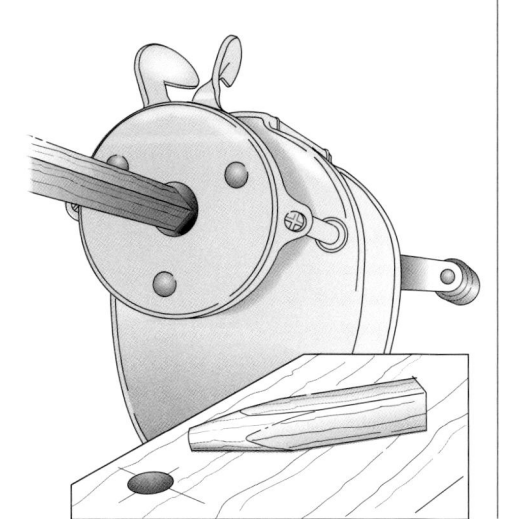

SEND US YOUR SHORTCUT

We will provide a complimentary one-year subscription (or extend your current subscription) for each Shortcut we print. Send your Shortcut via e-mail to shortcuts@fwpubs.com, or by post to *Woodworking Magazine*, Shortcuts, 4700 E. Galbraith Road, Cincinnati, OH 45236. Please include your complete mailing address and daytime phone number. All Shortcuts become property of *Woodworking Magazine*.

Build a Better Cabinet

Many methods to build cabinets invite error. We distill several systems into a process that eliminates measuring and mistakes.

Woodworking magazines and books are cluttered with explanations of how to do the small stuff: cut an accurate joint, prepare a surface for finishing or build a door or drawer. What is mostly absent is a discussion of how to put those small steps together into a system of building that makes sense.

I've been in shops all over the world, and each has a different way of gluing boards together to make cabinets, doors and tables. All of the systems work. But some waste time. Some require precise measuring. And some curry simple, obvious and disastrous errors – such as making a door that is 1" too small.

About 10 years ago, I started spending time with Troy Sexton, a cabinetmaker in Sunbury, Ohio, who builds early American pieces in his one-person shop. Troy is unusual in that he has spent lots of time compressing the procedures to make a cabinet so that he reduces error at every turn, and he arranges each step in building a cabinet so the process flows smoothly.

Many people would say that Troy builds cabinets backward. He starts with the face frame, then he builds the doors and hangs them in the face frame. Then he builds the carcase and fits the drawers. In other shops, they typically start with building the carcase of the project, then they build the face frame and attach it to the carcase. Then they hang the doors in the openings and finally build the drawers to suit.

After adopting Troy's "face frame first" method years ago, I found other professional woodworkers who also work that way, and I started tweaking this method to incorporate handplanes into the system (Troy uses power equipment almost exclusively). What follows is the result of lots of trials, errors and cabinets.

If you build the face frame of a cabinet first, you can save construction time and reduce mistakes caused by measuring. Plus, this technique works well in a shop that uses both hand and power tools.

The 'Face Frame First' Approach to Cabinets

STEP 1

The face frame uses the least amount of material and determines the ultimate sizes of all the subsequent assemblies, such as the carcase, doors and drawers. So begin by assembling the face frame.

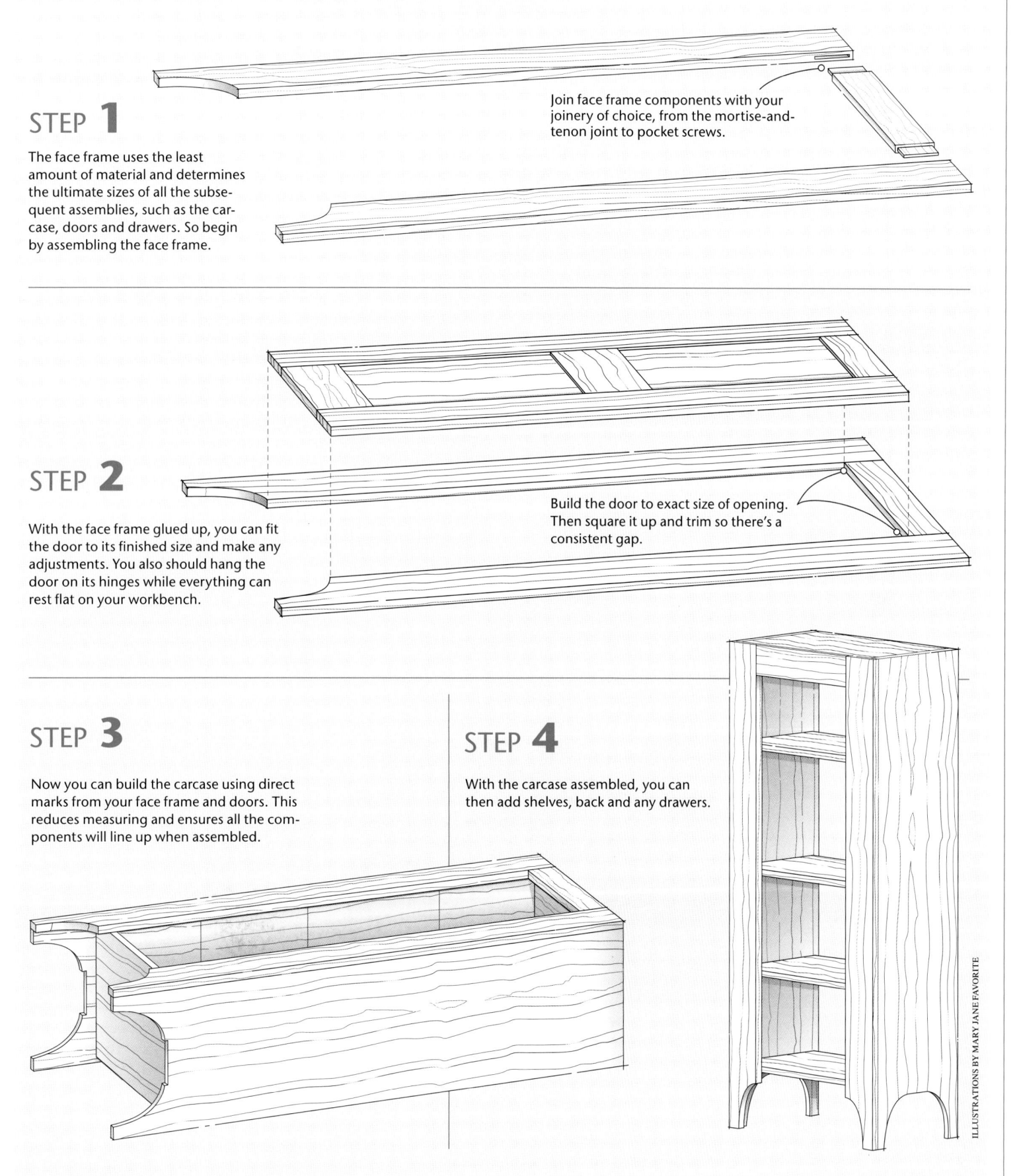

Join face frame components with your joinery of choice, from the mortise-and-tenon joint to pocket screws.

STEP 2

With the face frame glued up, you can fit the door to its finished size and make any adjustments. You also should hang the door on its hinges while everything can rest flat on your workbench.

Build the door to exact size of opening. Then square it up and trim so there's a consistent gap.

STEP 3

Now you can build the carcase using direct marks from your face frame and doors. This reduces measuring and ensures all the components will line up when assembled.

STEP 4

With the carcase assembled, you can then add shelves, back and any drawers.

ILLUSTRATIONS BY MARY JANE FAVORITE

Why Build the Face Frame First?

Not every cabinet uses a face frame. If you live on the West Coast or prefer modern furniture, chances are you aren't going to attach a face frame to your cabinet. If you build these so-called "frameless" cabinets, move on to the next section.

But if you build American furniture in historical styles from the 17th to mid-20th centuries, chances are that your cabinets will have a face frame – a framework of ¾"-thick wood that defines the openings of your doors and drawers and strengthens the carcase behind it.

Building the face frame first has several advantages. First, it uses less material than any other step in the process. So if you make a serious goof, you're not out a lot of material.

Second: The face frame determines the size of your doors and drawers. So once those are fixed by the construction of the frame, you can then build your doors with confidence.

Third, you can hang the doors in the face frame more easily with the face frame detached from the carcase. Most woodworkers hang their doors after the face frame is on the carcase. So they are fighting gravity all the way home. Either the cabinet is upright and they are balancing the door on its skinny bottom edge, or the cabinet is on its back and the door is prone to droop into the carcase. This is a problem particularly if the doors are inset into the frame instead of doors with edges that lip over the face frame.

It's far easier to fit a door when everything is flat on your workbench or assembly table. Plus you have easy access to both the inside and outside of the face frame – something you give up when you attach the face frame to the carcase.

Also, you do less measuring. You can use your assembled face frame and door to directly lay out the dados in your carcase sides. So there's less opportunity for a measurement error.

And finally, building the face frame first allows you to make mistakes from which you can easily recover. Say you place a rail at the wrong position when you build your face frame. No problem. You simply adjust the size of your doors and change the position of your shelves and dividers to suit. If you build the carcase first, a mistake on the face frame usually means that the face frame is headed for the scrap pile.

The Frameless Variant

If your cabinet is a frameless one, you should begin with building the doors. The doors will then determine where the dividers will go in the carcase. Once you build your doors, you can lay them directly on your case sides to mark out where the dados should go for shelves and dividers – this also reduces errors.

Incorporating Handplanes

The face-frame first system works great with power tools, but many beginning hand-tool users might be confused about how to incorporate planes into the system. Here's how:

Most woodworkers know that the jointer plane is for flattening stock and the smoothing plane is for preparing it for finishing, but some get confused as to when these planes should be used in construction. Is the jointer plane used before or after assembly? Do you smooth plane the finished assemblies or the individual pieces?

Part of the answer is contained in the names of the planes. The jointer plane flattens the stock before the joinery. The smoothing plane is used when assembly is complete and you get to a point where the next step won't allow you to use a plane. For example, you should smooth plane the side of a carcase right before you attach the moulding. After you attach the moulding the smoothing plane can't access that entire area.

So let's walk through the three types of assemblies in furniture construction: frames, slab boxes

Here I'm thinning down the rails a bit more than the stiles with a jointer plane that is set up like a smoothing plane. Then I'll assemble this frame and smooth plane the long stiles to finished thickness.

If you look closely at this photo you can see the stiles are slightly proud of the rails. Thinning the stiles is easier than thinning the rails with a handplane because most face frames are vertical and so they fit on your benchtop better that way.

With the face frame and door flat on my work surface, it's much easier to position the door so there is a uniform gap all around. Plus adding the hinges is a great deal easier.

The individual boards in these panels have been prepped with a jointer plane. Then I glued up the panels and will be able to go right to the smoothing plane because the seams are tidy and flush.

and tables/stools to see how planes can be incorporated into the "face frame first" approach.

Frames: Face Frames and Doors

After preparing all the stock with my power jointer and planer for my face frame, I'll flatten all the boards with a jointer plane before cutting the joinery on them. The jointer plane removes the milling marks, twists, cups and bows left over from the power equipment.

Then cut your joints and plane the rails only with either a smoothing plane or a jointer plane set up for a fine cut. This will make the horizontal rails a bit thinner than their adjoining vertical stiles. If there's a panel that goes into this frame, flatten it with a jointer plane, cut the joinery on it and smooth plane it before assembly.

Then assemble the frame. When the glue is dry you have a frame where the rails and panel are ready for finish, but the long stiles are slightly proud. So use a smoothing plane to reduce the stiles in thickness to the same thickness as the rails. This takes some practice to do well, but you'll be an expert after a couple attempts.

Then build the doors, fit them and hang the doors on their hinges.

Dealing with Panels and Boxes

Most solid-wood carcases involve some sort of slab sides or slab shelves. As a result, you need to glue up several boards into wider panels. Here's how you do that with handplanes: First arrange the individual boards for best appearance when you plan your panel, but try to get the grain running in all the same direction in the slab. This makes it easier to plane after assembly.

Then use the jointer plane on all your individual boards to flatten them. Now you can cut any joinery on the boards' long edges. Some woodworkers use splines, some use biscuits, many use nothing but the glue. When you glue things up, make every effort to keep the boards flush at the seams. If you struggle with this step, switch to a slow-setting glue, such as liquid hide glue.

When the glue has cured, remove the panel from the clamps and evaluate it. If you kept your seams flush, you should be able to clean up the panel with a smoothing plane to remove glue and dress the panel to go in a frame.

If you have misalignments at the seams (more than $1/32$"), you need to attack the panel with a jointer plane – first diagonally to the grain and then with it. This gets the panel back to a flat state in an efficient manner (a jointer plane takes a cut that is about three or four times thicker than that of a smoothing plane).

With the panel flat and the glue removed, you can cut the joinery on it. Cut your dados, grooves and rabbets. Then assemble the carcase with your flattened slabs. Or if you are making a raised panel for a frame, cut its moulded edge, and then prepare it for finishing with a smoothing plane.

With the carcase assembled, you can then attach the face frame (if you have one) and then smooth plane the entire carcase for finishing.

Tables, Stools, Post-and-rail

The other kind of assembly is similar to a stool or table. You have stretchers or aprons running between thick legs or posts. These are treated much like a frame construction with a minor variation. Use the jointer plane to dress all the surfaces, then cut your joinery. Then smooth plane everything before assembly.

The reason you do this is that the legs will likely be too fragile to smooth plane after assembly. After assembly, you might have to clean up some spots with a plane, scraper or sandpaper, but you want to minimize this because the assembly is awkward to secure to your workbench.

After assembly, you will need to level the top edges of the aprons so they're level to the top of the legs. Do this with a jointer plane. Then you can go on to build your table or stool's top using the procedures above for slab panels.

The techniques above don't account for every single situation in the shop, but the principles are sound. Use your jointer plane to get your stock flat at the first. Assemble your cabinets by first tackling the assembly that uses the least amount of wood and is the most critical. And keep your mind open for new ways to work. **WM**

— *Christopher Schwarz*

Fitting Inset Doors

Achieving a good fit with consistent gaps is a hallmark of craftsmanship. The hard part may be convincing yourself that you can do it.

When I worked as a professional cabinetmaker I was always surprised at the number of so-called professionals who would go to any length to avoid making inset doors. Most of them just won't do it. The excuse was usually along the lines that it is too difficult and takes too long.

Nice work isn't possible if you talk yourself out of it before you begin.

But if you simplify the problem, it comes down to making a square piece of wood fit inside a square opening, and that is a basic skill in woodworking. It shouldn't be a terrifying experience, and with a systematic approach and a bit of practice it will become second nature. Achieving a good fit on an inset door or drawer begins long before the assembled door goes into the completed frame.

It begins with making good parts. Learn to prepare stock with square corners, straight edges and flat faces. Throw out the notion of "close enough," and replace it with seeing how close you can get. The temptation to let something a little long or a little wide go, with the hope that it will all work out later, is strong. Little mistakes don't work themselves out as a project nears completion; they gang up and accumulate, most often in the most visible spot they can find.

I begin fitting doors to their opening by doing some surveying. I check the corners with a large square. At this point, someone is likely to chime in with the advice to measure the diagonals of the opening to see if it is square. It's OK to do that, but the only thing it usually proves is that you'd like to put off really fitting the door to its opening for a few more minutes.

It isn't easy to get an accurate measurement from corner to corner, and even if the numbers are the same, there are several other conditions that will yield equal numbers but crooked corners. A short rail will create a trapezoid instead of a rectangle and slightly bowed pieces can create any number of odd shapes that will pass the corner test but still fail to fit.

One of the cruel yet effective ways that woodworking teaches us is this: You don't know how well you have performed one step until you are halfway through the following step. If your opening isn't right, you may not realize it until it is too late to correct. Next time around, you'll be more careful, but this time you'll need to do extra work. If the frame is out of whack you can still fit the door, but it will take longer and won't look quite as nice as it could.

> "If you think small things don't make a difference, try spending a night in a room with a mosquito."
> — Tenzin Gyatso (1932-)
> the 14th Dalai Lama, exiled leader of Tibet

Fitting doors to their openings can be intimidating, but with a systematic approach it is nothing beyond cutting one piece of wood to an exact size and shape. The first thing to tackle is accurately determining the parameters of the opening.

The same thing holds true for doors: Check them to see if the edges are straight and the assembly is square. If something is amiss, it can usually be corrected, but you need to know exactly what is wrong in order to fix it. I'm relatively confident, so I build doors to the size of the opening and ideally trim an equal amount off all four edges in fitting.

Some people will make the doors larger than the opening, but I think this encourages sloppy work, and it complicates matters when you need to decide exactly how much to trim and where you need to trim it.

Nobody is Perfect

Systematic fitting has to start somewhere, and the first decision is how large to make the gaps. As seen in the picture above, a dime or a piece of plastic laminate is a good starting point. Smaller than that is possible, but it raises the chances of something binding or sticking.

The laminate and the dime are each less than $1/16"$ thick; standard-grade laminate is .048" thick, and a dime is about .049". This presents a challenge and a choice. The choice is to become comfortable working with fractions that small, or to set a lower limit of numbers you can work to.

With a set of fractional dial calipers you can easily measure small fractions. If creating nice work is your goal, it doesn't make sense to start guessing when you're trying to achieve a nice fit. Knowing how much to remove, and how to remove a predictable small amount, is critical.

Either machines or hand tools can be used. Measure a plane shaving with calipers, and with a little division and multiplication you will know how many plane swipes it will take to remove just enough. The jointer is the tool of choice for a powered approach, and the picture at far right shows how to set up the machine to remove a predictable amount of material with each pass.

The ruler on the infeed table is $1/32$" thick. With a long straightedge across the outfeed table, position the infeed table until the ruler meets the bottom of the straightedge, then lock the infeed table in place. You can double-check how much is removed in one pass by measuring the width of a piece of scrap with the calipers, making a pass across the jointer and measuring again.

One Edge at a Time

All of the fitting work is fussy, and this is an area where it's a real advantage to complete the face frame first, then fit the doors and drawers before assembling the frame and cabinet. If you put the door and drawer fitting off until after assembly, you won't be able to work on a nice flat surface. You'll be floating in space, trying to judge critical distances while balancing a door in mid-air.

The hinge stile is the best place to start for fitting a door. It's usually the longest edge, and for the hinges to function, the stiles on the cabinet and the door need to match. When fitting a drawer front, start with the longest edge. It's too late at this point to do much to the cabinet stile if it isn't straight. Corrections to the door are far easier to make than corrections to the opening.

If the cabinet stile is bowed into the opening in the middle, you may be able to get a block plane in the opening to remove it. If it is bowed in the other direction, material must be removed in the corner – not an easy task. Tool catalogs promise that a chisel plane will work for this, but this is a clumsy tool and the chances for success are slim.

If you can get away with it, taking a slight amount off the corners of the door to match the frame is a better choice. If conditions are really bad at this point, reworking or remaking the frame might be a less painful way to cut your losses. Once again, this is another good reason to leave the face frame and cabinet separate entities as long as possible.

It's also important to keep opposite components of the door as close to equal in width as possible. After running the hinge stile over the jointer, I compare its width to the other stile. When I trim to the finished width, I'll leave the hinge stile alone, and remove stock from the lock stile only to keep things equal.

An Opportunity to Ruin Everything

Getting the hinge stile straight, or at least a decent match to the frame stile, is only the starting point. The door is still too large for the opening. For the power-tool woodworker, the temptation is strong to head to the saw and cut the door to length. This is the next step, but it pays to make sure of two things: that a square cut is needed and that the saw setup is correct.

I think this one operation is a good reason to invest in a sliding table for the table saw. Lacking a sliding table, having a crosscut sled or panel-cutting jig are good alternatives. Unless the door

Good fitting begins with knowledge of what you are fitting to. A large drafting square is ideal for checking corners.

Set the jointer to remove a predictable amount of material. The steel rule on the infeed table under the straightedge is $1/32$" thick.

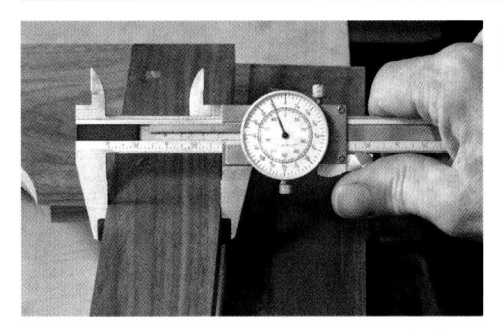

When trimming parts on opposite sides of a door, it's important to keep them as close as possible to the same size.

Dial calipers that read in fractions enable you to measure small distances precisely.

Squaring up a door is quick work with a table saw, but you must be able to make an accurate cut. There is no second chance.

woodworking-magazine.com ■ 11

is narrow and short, the standard miter gauge likely won't be up to the task.

I like to establish the bottom edge as the second step. This is a good time to recheck the corners of the frame and the door. If the opening is square, and the hinge stile straight, a crosscut will do. Some woodworkers will use the jointer, but care must be taken to avoid blowing out the end grain as the last stile passes over the knives.

Begin making the cut, but back the door out from the cutterhead after an inch or less. Reverse the position of the door, keeping the uncut portion flat on the infeed table until the previously cut area is on the outfeed table. Continue to feed the door, keeping it against the fence with downward pressure on the outfeed table. This tends to leave a rough cut on the end grain, so leave some extra material to be sanded or planed smooth.

If the opening isn't quite square, the bottom of the door must be trimmed to match. If you forged ahead and made a straight cut, the door won't fit – or if it does there will be a noticeable difference in the gaps at each side. To determine how much to remove, place the bottom end of the hinge stile in the corner of the frame and place the door across the opening. The opposite corner will either overlap the frame or show a gap.

If it overlaps, make note of the distance, and mark the edge of the lock stile. If there is a gap, that distance should be marked on the hinge stile. With one leg of a framing square, or some other straightedge, mark the bottom of the door. A pencil line will work, but clamping the straightedge and cutting in the line with the knife will give a better reference.

The knife line becomes essential if you're using hand tools to trim the bottom edge. The same issue that causes problems with the powered jointer will also make trouble if you're handplaning – the end grain will likely tear out as the plane exits the cut. The solution is also the same. Begin by cutting in on the widest part of the cut, working in from the end. Then work from the opposite direction until you reach the knife line.

Trimming the end with a plane allows you to make adjustments progressively. Mark the desired end result with a straightedge and a knife.

Begin the process by planing the end grain on one stile, working from the outside in to prevent tear-out.

Continue trimming by planing in the opposite direction until you reach the marked layout line.

Check frequently for square as you plane. It's easy to tilt the plane as you concentrate on reaching the line.

As an alternative to a plane, a shim behind one end will allow you to quickly make a slight adjustment to cut an angle slightly out of square using your table saw.

Some woodworkers put the door in a vise or otherwise clamp it so the edge to be trimmed is horizontal. I find it awkward to balance the plane on a narrow edge, especially if the edge is far above the benchtop. I work with the edge vertical, and the door clamped flat to the bench. Other planes will work, but I prefer a low-angle block plane because it works well at cutting end grain, and it is easy to reverse it in my hand if I want to cut on the pull stroke. With either method, check frequently that the edge is square.

The table saw is also a viable option for making these odd cuts. Instead of trying to make a tiny adjustment to the angle of the fence, or if you're using a sled with a fixed 90° fence, insert a thin shim between the corner of the door and the fence as seen in the photo on page 12, bottom right. Start with a shim that's thinner than the gap, and make the first cut removing as little material as possible. The angle can be changed in miniscule increments by moving the shim laterally.

On Top of the Situation

The procedure for trimming the top is the same as the bottom. A shim equal in thickness to the desired gap can be placed between the bottom of the door and the top of the lower cabinet rail to better gauge how much material ought to be removed from the top. The same cautions for matching the opening and methods for making the cuts apply.

The amount removed from the top will determine the sum of the gaps at both the top and bottom of the door. It pays to check the fit as you go. Even though the door will likely be too wide for the opening, the up-and-down fit can be checked directly by holding the door at a right angle to the frame and sliding it into place.

The big advantage of using a plane for this fitting is the ability to remove controlled amounts of material in smaller increments than can be reasonably achieved with power tools. The second-best reason to use a plane is that you can arrive at a ready-to-finish edge at the same time as you reach a good fit. When using power tools, sanding the edges to remove tool marks can easily widen the gaps, or knock them out of square.

With three of the four edges complete, the last long edge can be trimmed. If the opening and the door are both square, this is simply a matter of reducing the width of the last stile. If things are off slightly, I work to get the door to fit within the opening, shim the top and bottom gaps equally, then scribe the edge of the door to the edge of the frame. A pencil can be run along the edge, marking the high and low points.

It All Hinges on This

At this point, the hinges can be set. Because we used surface-mount hinges in this project, the door was placed in the frame opening with shims wedged in place to hold the door in position. If butt hinges are used, mark the locations on both the frame and the door. Go ahead and mount the hinges.

If all goes well, the even gaps at the top, bottom and hinge stile will remain as they were before placing the hinges. If not, you will need to choose between adjusting the hinge placement or readjusting the door gaps. Readjusting the door gaps will result in making them larger than originally planned and repeating steps already taken. This is where the lessons of carefully setting hinges are learned.

With butt hinges, make the initial setting using only one screw per hinge leaf. If the door needs to be relocated up or down, a second attempt can be made, fastening the hinge with a screw in an unused hole. When the fit is good, fill the first hole with a whittled scrap of wood; then fasten the hinge using all the screws.

If the gap between the door isn't even at the hinge stile, thin shims can be placed between the hinge leaf and the wood. Only a small adjustment can be made with this technique, as any but the thinnest shim will begin to show as a curious gap between the hinge and the wood it attaches to.

After the hinges are set, the final gap between the lock stile and the cabinet can be finished. If the gap is small, a square edge on the back stile will prevent the door from closing. Make a pencil mark on the door where the back edge of the lock stile hits the opening at both the door top and bottom. Connect these two marks with a line.

If the marks are the same distance from the edge, an adjustable square or a marking gauge can be used to place a line along the back face of the lock stile. If there is a variation, use a straightedge to connect the two marks. In an ideal world, the long edge should be square to the top and bottom edges, and the gap should be consistent. If both can't be achieved at this point, an even gap is the better option.

If the gap was even before setting the hinges and didn't change, a slight bevel can be planed on the back of the door. With the door flat and the back facing up, begin planing by knocking off the corner. Hold the plane away from vertical a few degrees to establish the angle.

The angle can be established by eye, comparing the gap between the lower edge of the door stile and the sole of the plane with the distance marked on the upper face of the door. As the plane strokes become wider, stop and look at the end of the door to ensure that the angle is close. Stop planing just before the bevel reaches half the thickness of the door and reattach the hinges.

The last few light strokes can be made with the door on the hinges. The edge should not come to a sharp point, as this will be likely to chip or tear at some point in the life of the door. On a $3/4$"-thick door, the flat area from the front of the door coming back should be between $1/8$" and $1/4$" wide. WM

— *Robert W. Lang*

> *"Anyone who starts to make a piece of furniture with a decorative form in mind starts at the wrong end."*
> — Gustav Stickley (1858 - 1942) furniture maker, spokesman of the American Arts & Crafts Movement

After the door has been hinged, the other stile will need a bevel to allow it to open and close. Mark directly from the cabinet opening.

Work from the back side, planing a bevel until the line is reached.

Correct the angle to take wider shavings, leaving $1/8$" to $1/4$" of flat area at the edge.

American Wall Cupboard

We set out to design a piece that would be at home in the 18th or 21st century. The work with a pencil proved to be as important as the work with a plane.

When you design a piece of furniture to build, there are three well-worn paths (some might call them ruts) to follow.

The first path is to design a piece in a wholly original style. This actually happens about once or twice a century, and its rarity is why we don't have furniture styles such as "Early Bill," "Middle Chuck" or the "Late Butch Period." Few people alive can claim they have successfully launched a style, but don't let that stop you from trying.

The second approach is to build replicas, either spot-on or with mild alterations, such as an additional drawer, or substituting a square ovolo moulding for a bead. This is a good way to learn the vocabulary of different styles, though it is time-consuming to learn everything by the doing. Some woodworkers (even professionals) might build only six pieces in a year.

The third approach is to design a new piece with vintage parts, like rebuilding an old car. With this approach, you expose yourself to hundreds of images of the form. You could look at tables, cabriole legs or Arts & Crafts desks, for example. Then you select your piece's dominant element from the library – say a leg, a door or a bonnet – and design your piece around that. (However, you can't easily mix parts from different genres. It might seem like a good idea to put a Honda push rod in a Chevy, until you hit that metric barrier.)

When asked the secret to good design, Steve Hamilton, a builder at Mack S. Headley & Sons (headleyandsons.com), boiled it down to two words: "Picture books," he said. "Get a bunch. Look them over."

What I like about this cabinet is that it doesn't hide all the contents when you close the door. You can set one precious object in the right spot (a plow plane, perhaps), that will be the center of attention when you lock the door.

Design on the Run

Designing a suitable early American wall cupboard for *Woodworking Magazine* began with a day in our collection of books and images. You don't need to spend a lot of money to build a book collection, most of the resources you need are at the public library and on the Internet.

My first stop was Wallace Nutting's "A Furniture Treasury." This book is available in many different forms, and it's common to find copies for about $25. The book is as-advertised. It's hundreds of pages of images of early American stuff that has been organized into categories such as "chests" and "Windsor chairs."

The second source was auction catalogs from Christie's (christies.com) and Sotheby's (sothebys.com) auction houses. The catalogs these houses publish for their Americana auctions are outstanding. Good images. Good overall dimensions. And good history lessons as well. These catalogs can be pricey at $50 or more, but you can usually browse the catalogs on the Internet for free, though sometimes you have to register with the auction house (registration is free).

The third source was an old favorite of mine from my grandparents' library: "Fine Points of Furniture: Early American" (Crown) by Albert Sack. This common book can be had for about $10 – the new revised edition is much more expensive and rare. Sack's book compares different kinds of pieces and ranks them as "good," "better" or "best." This book helps hone your tastes in mouldings, proportion and turnings.

After a day of reading, I chose a fetching tombstone door from Nutting's book and found many tall and skinny shapes for wall cupboards that looked like pieces I had seen at Winterthur, the DuPont's Delaware estate and museum.

My design firmed up when my doctor got too busy for me one Wednesday. After showing up for my appointment, I was told there would be an hour delay. So I sat in my car and sketched about 10 wall cabinets. I didn't worry about dimensions or joinery, just the overall look and feel of the piece. Each sketch took about five minutes and tried out variations on the door (one or two?), the drawer (one, two or none?) and the width of the stiles and rails (chunky or light?).

After those sketches, I chose the best two designs, sketched them again and showed them around to woodworkers and friends. It sounds like a lot of work, but I have found that good design is like making stir fry: You first chop vegetables and mix sauces for a long time. The active cooking time is real short – if you've done your prep work.

From Face to Back

This cabinet is built using the techniques outlined in "Build a Better Cabinet" on page 6 of this issue. So if you want to know why I began with the face frame, read that story first and decide how you are going to proceed.

This wall cabinet begins with a face frame that's joined with mortise-and-tenon joints. Then you build and fit the door. Then you build the carcase around those established dimensions. The rest – mouldings, the back and the drawer – are the final details.

After you dimension your stock, the face frame and the door begins with cutting $1/4$"-thick tenons on the ends of all the rails. Test the results in a sample mortise, though you can tune up the tight-fitting miscreants before assembly.

With all the tenons cut, you can use them to lay out the locations of your mortises on the stiles of your face frame (don't lay them out on the door's stiles yet). Then cut your mortises. A hollow-chisel mortiser is the typical choice in our shop, though a mortise chisel would be a good choice if you were building only one of these cabinets.

Then assemble your face frame and confirm (twice) that the openings for the drawer and door are as you planned them. If you make a mistake, you can adjust your drawing to accommodate your door and drawer. This sort of mistake is why I usually mill my door stiles an inch longer than the cutting list states – sometimes you need a slightly bigger door.

Go for a Tight Fit

When you make your door, the temptation is to build it so it drops right into the face frame with a perfect $1/16$" gap all around. As that is unlikely to happen in such a complex assembly, the better bet is to shoot to build the door to the same size as the opening in the face frame and shave the door down when you hang it.

Lay out the mortises on your stiles and cut those. Then lay out the 5"-radius arc in the top rail (the centerpoint of the 5"-radius arc is $1 1/2$" below the bottom edge of the rail). Remove the waste using a band saw, bowsaw or jigsaw and smooth the arc's saw-blade marks.

The lower rails require a groove that is $1/4$" wide and $1/4$" deep to house the door's panel. These grooves can run the entire length of the rails.

Using a dado stack to make tenons allows you to use one setup for the face cheeks and a second assembly for edge cheeks. Other approaches use four setups or more. Test each tenon in a sample mortise (below) for best results.

The leading cause of errors is measuring. Use your tenons to lay out your mortises, and you will make fewer mistakes where a rail ends up too high or low. Even if you goof, you still can recover by adjusting the door and carcase.

To keep all my door rails oriented I draw a large triangle across the face of all three parts using a grease pencil. That way I'll be able to determine where each piece goes with just a glance.

"We construct and construct, yet intuition is still a good thing."
— Paul Klee (1879 - 1940)
Swiss painter

Lay out the arc with a board butted against the top rail to give the compass' point a place to bite into. Then you can clean up the curve with a spindle sander (below left) or rasps and scrapers (below right).

However, you need to cut these same grooves in the lower section of the stiles only. The section of the door that holds the glass doesn't need a groove – it needs a rabbet instead. (You'll cut this rabbet after assembly.)

The stopped groove in the stiles is troublesome. You can make it on power equipment, but only with some risk – you'll have to drop the piece onto a spinning router bit or saw blade.

So I made my grooves by hand. It's safer and not a burden on time when it's just one door. First I plowed out as much as I could with the aptly named plow plane. This left a ramped area where the groove stopped. So I broke that up with a mortising chisel and cleared out the waste with a router plane. It takes longer to write the sentences above than to do the act, so give it a whirl.

The tenons on the bottom rail will have to be haunched to fill the groove you just cut. Yes, you could rig this on the table saw, but two short cuts with a fine-tooth saw also will fill the bill (and the groove).

Perilous Panel; Pounding Pegs

Then comes the part of any casework project that I dislike: The raised panel. I don't own the router bit for this profile, and I don't own the right kind of panel-raising plane. So I have to do it on the

A plow plane can be used to make a stopped groove. Begin making short strokes where the groove stops, and then make longer and longer strokes until you are plowing the whole length of the groove.

A ¼" mortise chisel breaks up the waste in the ramp left behind by the plow. This is why metric and Imperial tools don't play nice together.

A small router plane zips out the waste with little effort – leaving a perfect stopped groove behind. It takes more tools to do than with a plunge router, though not much more effort.

16 ■ woodworking magazine Autumn 2008

Tilt the sawblade to 12° and sneak up on the cut until the panel fits your groove. Then remove the inevitable tool marks with a rabbeting plane (right) followed by sandpaper.

Here's what a peg looks like before being knocked in. The sharp corners of the peg will cut the round hole into a square and create a tight fit and neat appearance.

table saw. Use a zero-clearance insert for maximum support of the thin edge of your workpiece and a high accessory fence to keep your hands away from the blade.

Now you can assemble the door and peg all the joints in the door and face frame. I used 1/4" x 1/4" white oak stock for the square pegs. First drill a 1/4"-diameter hole through the tenon (its centerpoint is 3/8" from the shoulder of your tenon). Then whittle one end of your peg round, drip in a little glue and pound the peg home.

Now you can cut the rabbet for the glass. I used a 1/4"-wide rabbeting bit in a router table and took small bites until I reached the final 1/2" depth. Chisel the rounded corners square; and round over the square corner up by the tombstone shape – that will make the glass easier to fit.

Fitting the Door

Now you can trim the door square and decide how thick the cockbead moulding needs to be to fill the gap between the face frame and door. This is another place you have some built-in forgiveness for errors. If you made your door correctly, it should be 3/8" smaller than the hole in the face frame, which means you need 3/16"-thick cockbeading for the face frame.

Make the cockbeading with a beading plane or router on a wide board, then rip the resulting bead free of the mother piece. Miter, glue and nail it in place all around the door and drawer opening. Then fit and hang the door in its opening.

And Now the Carcase

With the face frame and door complete, you use those as a guide for building the carcase behind. Lay the face frame directly onto the sides and lay out the locations of the divider and shelf. You cannot miss now.

With your joints laid out, you can cut the 1/4"-deep x 3/4"-wide dados for the shelf and dividers – plus the 1/2" x 1/2" rabbet for the backboards. Then dovetail the carcase. Mark out the tails on the side pieces; the pins are on the top and bottom. This allows the case to better resist gravity.

Traditional cabinets have this moulding incorporated directly into the stiles and rails. Applying it after assembly allows you to adjust the door and drawer opening to suit your situation (if an adjustment is necessary). Don't forget to glue the miters.

Here the sides of the case are on edge on my bench and I'm marking the location of the divider directly on the front edge of the sides. When I cut the dado for the divider I'm going to shoot for the middle of this mediary rail, which will make fitting everything even easier.

woodworking-magazine.com ■ 17

Remember: These dovetails are for structure only. You will cover them all with moulding. So you can practice your speed rather than go for a joint you can flaunt. Save that compulsion for when you are building the drawer.

Clean up your dovetails and the exterior of your carcase and glue the divider and shelf in place. Then attach the face frame with glue (and cut nails, if you please). Let the glue dry overnight, then trim the face frame flush to the carcase with a plane or a flush-cutting bit in a router.

I cut a shallow 1/8"-deep x 5/8"-wide rabbet on the ends of the sides to assist with the dovetailing (top photo). It makes it easier to transfer the tails to the pin board and it helps when chopping the waste (above).

When I have a lot of material to hog off, a router is the right tool. Here I'm trimming the face frame close to the carcase. Then I follow up with a scraping plane to level the joints without worrying about grain direction.

American Wall Cupboard

NO.	PART	T	W	L	MATERIAL	NOTES
Face Frame						
2	Stiles	3/4	2 5/16	36 7/8	Walnut	Each is 1/16" over-wide for trimming
2	Rails	3/4	2 5/16	18 7/8	Walnut	1 1/4" TBE, and over-wide
1	Mediary rail	3/4	1	18 7/8	Walnut	1 1/4" TBE
	Cockbeading	3/16	3/4		Walnut	3/16" d. bead
Door						
2	Stiles	3/4	2	27	Walnut	Add 1" to length at rough milling
1	Top rail	3/4	5 1/2	14 1/2	Walnut	1 1/4" TBE
1	Mediary rail	3/4	1 1/2	14 1/2	Walnut	1 1/4" TBE
1	Bottom rail	3/4	2	14 1/2	Walnut	1 1/4" TBE
1	Panel	5/8	12 1/2	8 1/2	Walnut	In 1/4" x 1/4" groove
Carcase						
2	Sides	3/4	8	36 7/8	Walnut	
2	Top and bottom	5/8	7 1/2	20 7/8	Walnut	
2	Shelf and divider	3/4	7 1/2	19 7/8	Poplar	In 1/4"-deep dados
2	Drawer runners	3/4	2	7 1/2	Poplar	Rabbeted to fit drawer
	Backboards	1/2	20 3/8	36 7/8	Poplar	In 1/2" x 1/2" rabbet in sides
	Top moulding	7/8	3	50	Walnut	1" r. roundover
	Top cove	5/8	5/8	50	Walnut	1/2" r. cove
	Base moulding	1	3	50	Walnut	Square, no profile
	Base cove	1	1	50	Walnut	1" r. cove
Drawer						
1	Drawer front	3/4	3 5/8	16	Walnut	
2	Drawer sides	1/2	3 5/8	8	Poplar	
1	Back	1/2	3 1/8	16	Poplar	
1	Bottom	1/2	15 1/2	7 3/4	Poplar	In 1/4" x 1/4" groove

TBE = Tenon both ends

Rat-tail Hinges: Easy to Install

Traditional rat-tail hinges are a nice touch to an early American piece, and we're fond of the handmade ones from Horton Brasses. These look like the real deal, hammer marks and all. But the great thing about them is they are easy to install.

Begin by positioning the hinge where you want it on the face frame – we think it looks best to line up one of the flags on the leaf so it is in line with a door's rail. Then you bore a 1/8"-diameter hole for the hinge's through-bolt. This hole pierces the face frame. Place the center of this hole 1/2" in from the edge of your door opening.

Now bolt the hinge in place and screw the tail piece to the face frame. The rest is simple. Thread the leaf over the hinge's post and screw it to the door. You're done.

What's nice about rat-tails is that you can easily lift the whole door off its hinges, which is handy for fitting the door to its opening.

— CS

Rat-tail hinges are my favorite surface-mounted hinges. With a little care and planning, they are also a snap to install.

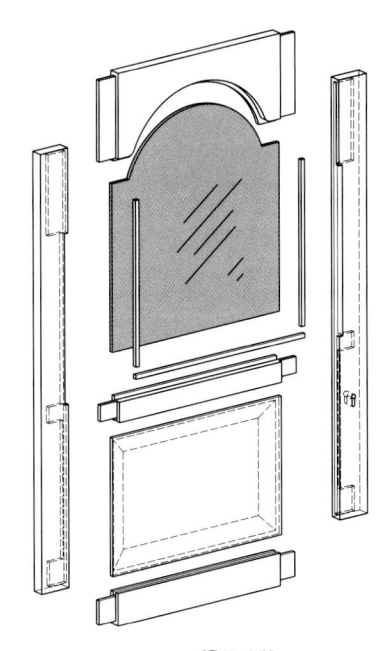

DOOR
EXPLODED VIEW (SHOWN FROM BACK)

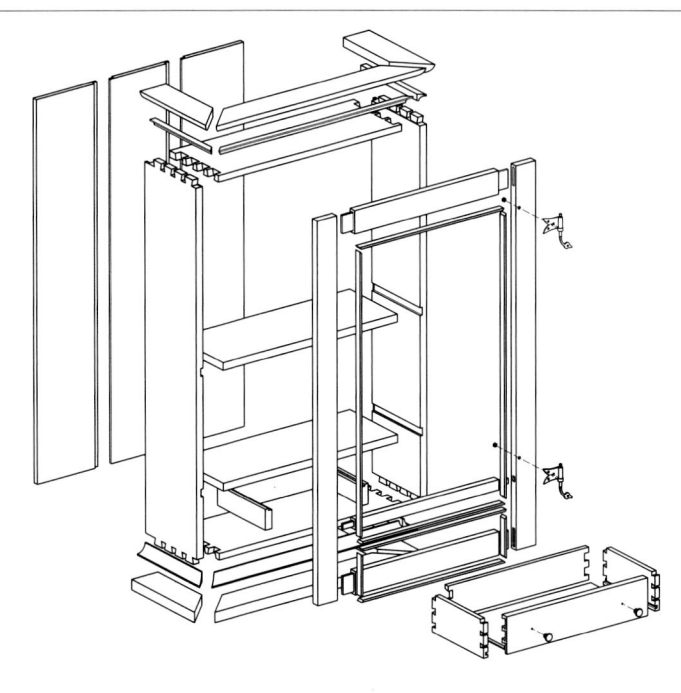

FACE FRAME, CARCASE AND DRAWER
EXPLODED VIEW

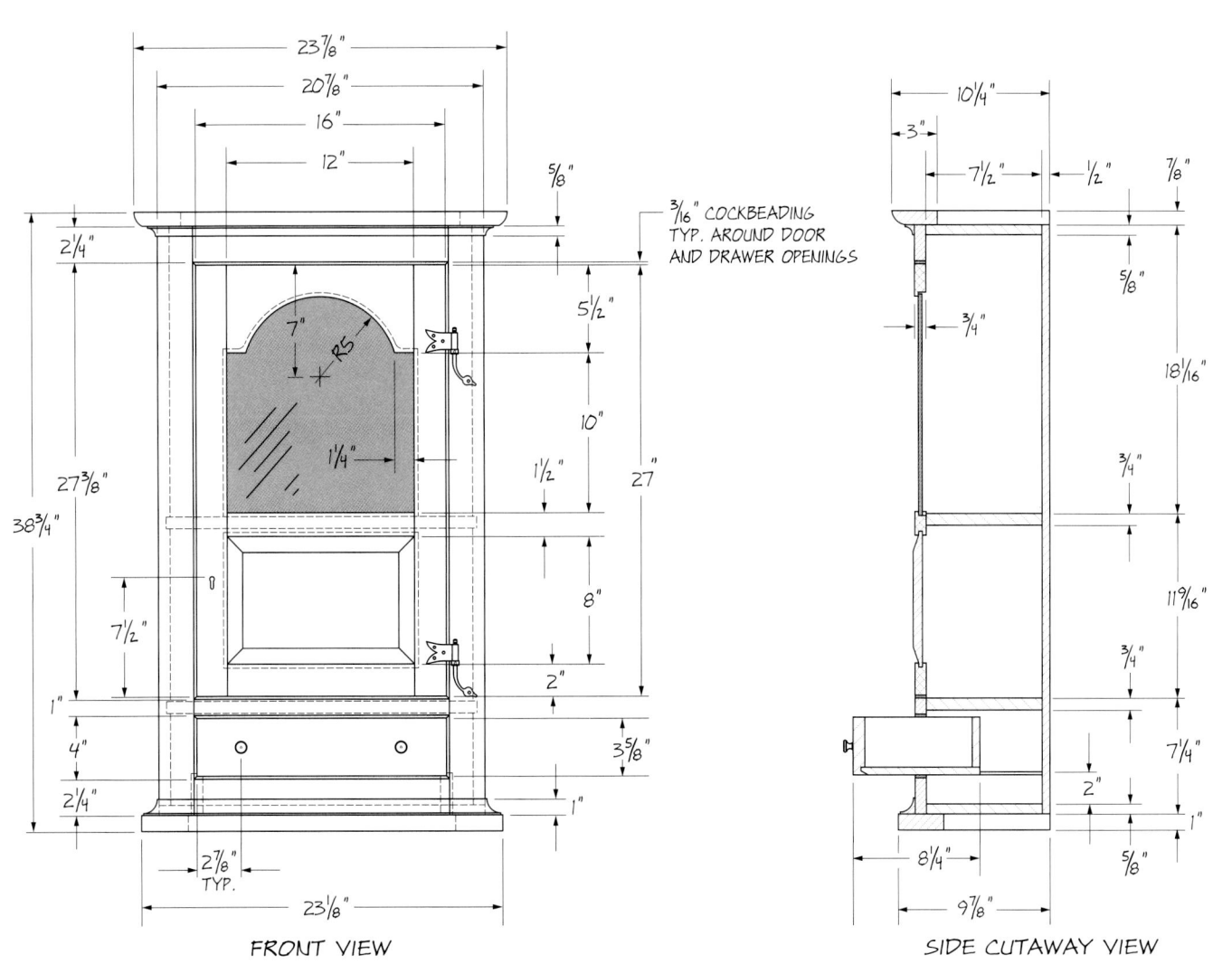

FRONT VIEW

SIDE CUTAWAY VIEW

AMERICAN WALL CUPBOARD

ILLUSTRATIONS BY LOUIS BOIS

woodworking-magazine.com ■ 19

The Drawer and Back

The drawer runners are simply leftover pieces of poplar that I scooped off the floor and rabbeted. The "L" shape at the top captures the drawer. I glued these in place to the bottom of the carcase. When the glue was dry, I drove in some nails from below to further secure these essential cabinet guts.

You can build the drawer in any manner you please. I went full-on traditional. That meant that the sides join the back with through-dovetails. The sides join the front with lapped dovetails (sometimes called half-blinds). And the bottom sits in a ¼" x ¼" groove in the sides and drawer front. The underside of the drawer bottom is like a raised panel.

With the drawer complete, you can add the moulding. Each profile consists of three pieces: the part that crosses the front of the case and the two that run back along the sides, commonly called the "returns." All the moulding is attached in the same way. Glue and nail the front pieces firmly to the case. When you attach the returns, add glue at the miter and the front 3" of the case. Then nail the moulding in place. This will allow the case sides to move with the seasons.

The back is merely shiplapped pieces of poplar that are nailed into the ½" x ½" rabbet in the side pieces. Nail them in place after finishing. The finishing process is covered in detail on page 30 of this issue. Using a clear finish alone on walnut is not advisable – it gives the wood a cold cast. We're proud of the simple process and warm color that results from our dye-tinted shellac.

After finishing, secure the glass with water putty or by nailing in strips of ¼" x ¼" walnut around the sides and bottom of the glass's opening. Putty is the more traditional touch.

Supplies

Horton Brasses
800-754-9127 or horton-brasses.com

- 1 pair ▪ right-hand rattail hinges
  #RT-R, call for pricing
- 2 ▪ ¾" black iron knobs
  #BK-1, call for pricing

Lee Valley Tools
800-871-8158 or leevalley.com

- 1 ▪ 25mm surface-mount lock
  #00N2925, $4.40
- 1 ▪ plain key
  #00N2990, $3
- 1 ▪ old brass 1¹³⁄₁₆" vertical escutcheon
  #01A5003, $1.80

Prices correct at time of publication.

Design vs. Construction

I keep a log of my shop time for every project, and for this wall cupboard I logged only about 23 hours of active construction time (I don't log the time I'm waiting for glue to dry). What might come as a surprise is that I spent at least 12 additional hours in the design phase of this project. Though that seems excessive, it pays off.

I'd rather have a great-looking piece with a few cosmetic issues than a technically perfect piece with awkward proportions.

As a result, the most important tools for completing this wall cupboard were an eraser, a chewed-up ink pen and a small notebook that I carry everywhere I go. WM

— *Christopher Schwarz*

Apply glue to only the front 3" of each drawer runner. Then use a combination square to position the drawer runner while the glue is still wet. Clamp the runners in place, let the glue dry, then nail them in from beneath. The nails will hold the runners and bend as the case expands and contracts with the seasons.

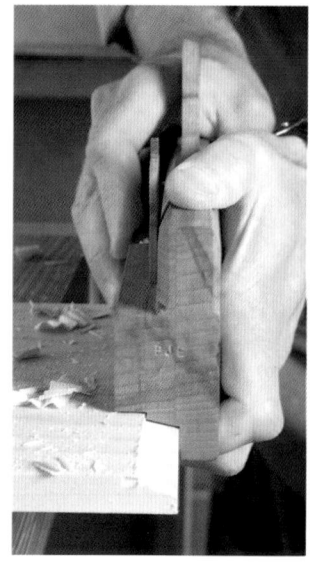

I've borrowed this small drawer-bottom plane from Philly Planes (phillyplanes.co.uk). As they say in England: "It works a treat."

The moulding is in three pieces and is attached with glue and nails – I used 23-gauge headless pins. It's easier to attach the smaller cove mouldings with gravity assisting you, as shown here.

Glossary

"Do not be afraid of enthusiasm. You need it. You can do nothing effectually without it."
— Francois Guizot (1787 - 1874), French statesman and historian

Woodworking's lexicon can be overwhelming for beginners. The following is a list of terms used in this issue that may be unfamiliar to you. Check woodworking-magazine.com for an expanded and searchable glossary.

applied hinge (n)
A hinge that is attached to the face of both a door and frame. Also known as a surface-mounted hinge.

butt hinge (n)
A hinge that is mortised into a door's stile and the face frame on the carcase.

compass plane (n)
A plane with a curved bottom used for trimming circular work to final shape.

cockbead (n)
A small and rounded projecting profile, often used around doors and drawers.

cove moulding (a.k.a. cavetto) (n)
A concave arched moulding.

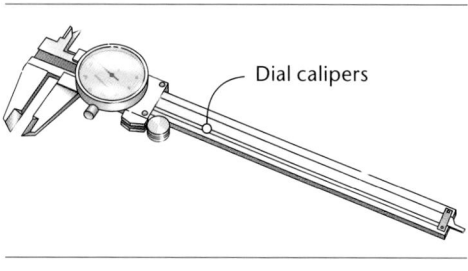

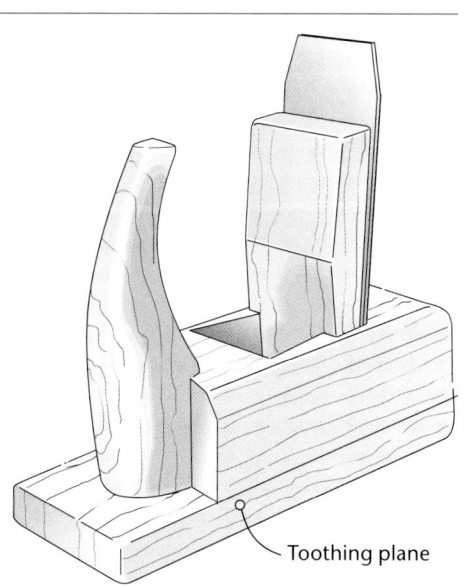

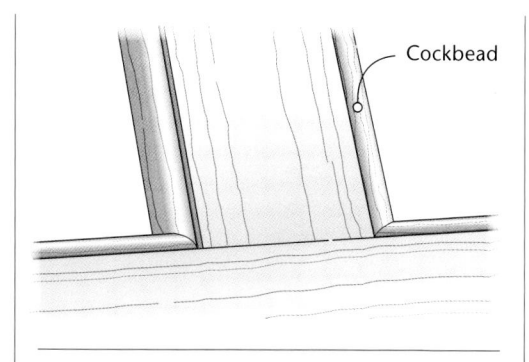

expressed joinery (n)
Joinery meant to be seen on the exterior of a piece, such as through-tenons, made popular during the Arts & Crafts movement.

dial calipers (n)
A device used to measure the distance between two symmetrically opposing surfaces, adjusted with a dial. Can take both inside and outside measurements. Scales are available in both metric and imperial measures.

lapped dovetail (n)
A joint in which one part (usually the pins) has a covering piece so that the ends of the dovetails are concealed on one face (often a drawer front or carcase front). Also known as half-blind dovetails.

ovolo moulding (a.k.a. bead) (n)
Moulding consisting of a quarter-circle or quarter-ellipse with quirks at each side.

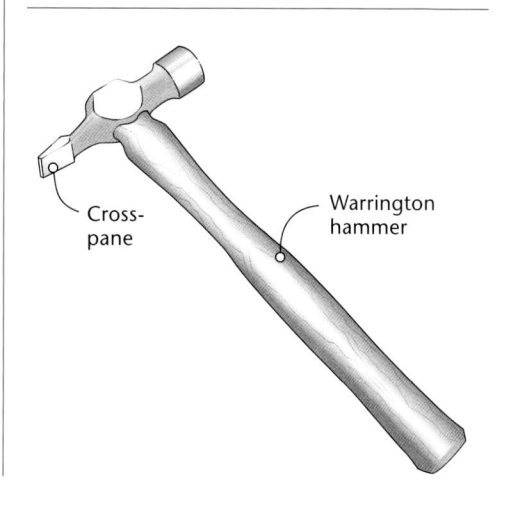

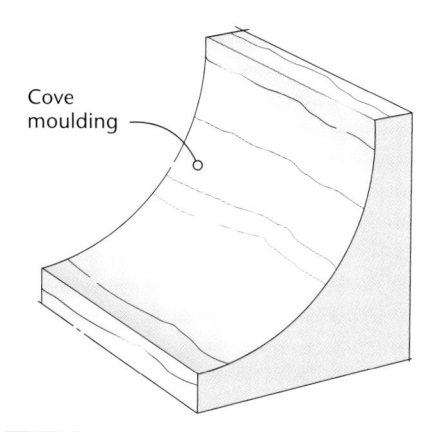

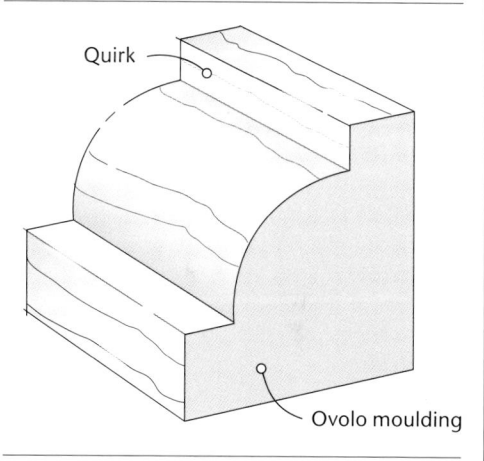

returns (n)
The common name for pieces of moulding applied to the sides of a case, running front to back.

shim (n)
A thin strip of material, often wedge-shaped, that is sometimes used to align parts.

standard-grade laminate (n)
Plastic laminate normally used for countertops. Standard grade is for flat surfaces, and is .048" thick. It makes a reliably sized shim.

toothing plane (n)
Used after a jack or try plane to rough up a surface in preparation for veneer or laminate. A toothing plane blade consists of a series of ridges (teeth) that scratch the surface. The 90° angle minimizes tear-out.

Warrington hammer (n)
The narrow cross-pane end on this hammer makes it easy to start small brads and nails, while the round end is used to drive and seat them.

The Best Sliding Bevel Gauges

A good new tool can be hard to find. With sliding bevels, the best place to look is in the attic – or across the Pacific.

The sliding bevel gauge is similar to a backup quarterback on a football team. Most of its time is spent doing nothing, but when it's needed, top performance is expected. To carry the sports analogy one step further, most sliding bevels made today are not first-class performers. They may look nice while they wait to get into the game, but when put into action, they likely will drop the ball or throw an interception.

Many woodworkers can go for years without needing a bevel gauge, so the first question to ask should be "do I need one at all?" instead of "which one should I get?" If you are only doing work that involves 90° and 45° angles, the answer is "no." But when you have a project involving any other angle, you should have a bevel gauge.

The beauty of this tool is its simplicity. You line it up on a drawing or an existing piece, lock the two parts together, and you have a handy reference available for marking odd-angled lines or setting up your tools. This is a wonderful way to work – free from numbers, marks on a protractor, or the mental gymnastics of trigonometry.

The key to working with angles is consistency. The margin of error in angled work is miniscule. A fraction of a degree of error results in a sizable gap, and angles are extremely difficult to measure and mark precisely. But if you have an example of the correct angle, then it is an easy task involving nothing more than lining one surface up with another.

"It is not doing the things we like to do, but liking the thing we have to do, that makes life blessed."
— Johann Wolfgang von Goethe (1749 - 1832)
German poet and philosopher

Bevel gauges are not often used, but when you need one, it should be accurate and reliable.

Much of our experience with sliding bevels is shaded with frustration. This is a bench-warmer tool that often turns into a prima donna when needed most. There are two problems inherent to most sliding bevels: setting the gauge firmly and accurately; and the tendency of the tool to easily shift out of alignment.

In an effort to separate the satisfying from the frustrating, we brought in eight different bevel gauges for testing. This is such a simple tool that we didn't run them through a battery of tests to obtain measurable, objective data. This tool's job is to make measuring and transferring of angles easier, and what makes a difference between one and another is subjective.

With a tool this simple, can there really be significant differences from one to another? After looking at the eight specimens, our answer is an emphatic yes. In fact, we can only recommend one old tool and one currently manufactured tool. There are also a few we are calling "acceptable" because they are well-made and good values. They have some shortcomings, however, that will require vigilance on the part of the user.

What Makes a Good Bevel?
In a project involving angles, the sliding bevel takes the place of a square as a reliable, repeatable reference. We set the bevel at the beginning of a project and will put it down and pick it back up countless times before we are through. Once set, it should stay in place. It isn't a timesaver if it has to be rechecked and reset every time it is used.

Reliably keeping a setting was our number-one criteria in judging the bevels, mainly because we have all experienced a blade moving out of adjustment when put down on the bench or in an apron pocket, when inadvertently bumped

Squeezing with a screw may make the blade snug, but can't make it tight. This is a good design for a hinge, not a sliding bevel.

The old-school method of setting angles is by ratio, not degrees. Using increments on a framing square to set an angle (in this case 1:6) is simple.

The ability to keep a setting is a major issue in choosing a bevel gauge. If it slips under finger pressure, it can't be trusted.

Reaching into an acute angle leaves little space to tighten a wing nut or thumbscrew.

Locking devices that keep your hand out of the angle are much easier to use.

against something in the shop, and even when used to adjust the position of a blade or fence on a machine.

Next on our list was the initial ease of setting the gauge. A bevel gauge is often used inside a tight corner so a locking mechanism that may be easy to use flat on a bench may be too cumbersome or ineffective in actual use. Ideally we want an easy-to-use mechanism that holds solidly. Our recommended tools weren't the easiest to set, but they allowed working in tight places and held steady under pressure.

The design of the tool is essentially the same as a hinge; the adjustable blade swivels within the slot in the handle. In most designs, a threaded fastener squeezes the blade against the handle, supposedly securing it in place. But it's almost impossible to get the fastener tight enough to prevent the blade from moving.

This issue is compounded by the type of fastener used to tighten the blade, especially if you're trying to use the tool in a tight inside corner. It can be a challenge to even get your fingers on a knob or wing nut, let alone exert firm pressure. Bevel gauges that use wing nuts introduce a second problem in attempting to solve the first: The wings protrude from the edges of the tool, rendering it incapable of performing its primary task.

Some tools replace the wing nut or knurled knob with a lever, as in the design of the old-style Stanley No. 25. The lever allows the user to tighten the blade setting with one hand in a tight corner, and it generates more force than the wing nut or knob.

Some modern versions of this style are not as well-made as the originals, and occasionally they will be shipped with the lever oriented so that it sticks out when tightened. The tool can be disassembled, and the bolt rotated 90° before reassembly. This will locate the lever where it belongs when you tighten it.

The better method for securing the blade is found in the Stanley No. 18 and in the Shinwa No. 780. In these designs, a threaded rod extends the length of the handle. Tightening the thumbscrew on the end of the rod tilts a cylinder at the other end that holds the blade firmly by wedging it in place. You need to use one hand to hold the bevel in place and the other to tighten, but it is nearly impossible to make the blade slip.

Reasonable Expectations

The reader might conclude that we are expecting too much from our tools and perhaps aren't as careful as we should be. The biggest difference between bevel gauges is the type of locking mechanism, and if we had never seen a Stanley No. 18 or a Shinwa No. 780, we might agree that a bevel gauge needs to be treated gingerly and checked before each use. Most gauges on the market today are simply different takes on an inherently poor design.

So we have strayed from our usual two categories of "recommended" and "not recommended" and added a third category: "acceptable." The two tools in that group are nicely made, and we would use them if we couldn't obtain one from the "recommended" group. WM

— *Robert W. Lang*

Wing nuts protrude beyond the edges of the bevel and can get in the way when attempting to use them for setting machinery.

The mechanism on the Stanley No. 18 pushes down on one point, effectively wedging the blade in place.

Sliding Bevel Gauges

Recommended

STANLEY NO. 18

■ GOOD FEATURES

Made in both 6" and 8" sizes, this is likely the best mass-produced bevel gauge ever made. The locking mechanism is rock solid and the thumbscrew never gets in the way.

■ BAD FEATURES

No longer manufactured.

■ AVAILABLE FROM

Used tool dealers, flea markets, Internet auctions
Either size: $10 – $30

SHINWA NO. 780

■ GOOD FEATURES

A modern version of the Stanley No.18, this tool has an aluminum body and a steel blade. Functions nearly as well, but lighter in weight.

■ BAD FEATURES

Bent-wire thumbscrew lacks the solid feel of the Stanley thumbscrew.

■ AVAILABLE FROM

Tools for Working Wood: 800-426-4613 or toolsforworkingwood.com
8" blade: $20.34; 10" blade: $22.41

Acceptable

STANLEY NO. 25

■ GOOD FEATURES

While not as solid as the No. 18, older versions of this tool with the locking lever are superior to modern knock-offs. Look for straight edges on the wooden stock and a straight blade. Manufactured in several sizes, the 6" version is suitable for most work and fits easily in an apron pocket.

■ BAD FEATURES

No longer manufactured.

■ AVAILABLE FROM

Used tool dealers, flea markets, Internet auctions
Either size: $10 - $30

VERITAS SLIDING BEVELS

■ GOOD FEATURES

By far the best fit and finish of any currently manufactured sliding bevel. Blade locks by adjustable cam-action clamp on holding nut and can be operated with one hand in tight corners.

■ BAD FEATURES

Adjusting for maximum holding power leaves cam-clamp lever difficult to move.

■ AVAILABLE FROM

Lee Valley: 800-871-8158 or leevalley.com
10" bevel: $48; 4" bevel $42.50

Acceptable

SHINWA SMALL SLIDING BEVEL

■ GOOD FEATURES

This low-profile design is well-made from stainless steel at an attractive price. The large slot in the thumbscrew allows a screwdriver to be used to tighten the blade.

■ BAD FEATURES

The thumbscrew is hard to grip in tight spaces and, even when snugged down with a screwdriver, tends to slip.

■ AVAILABLE FROM

The Japan Woodworker: 800-537-7820 or japanwoodworker.com
6" blade: $9.60; 10" blade $15.70

Not Recommended

JOSEPH MARPLES SLIDING BEVEL

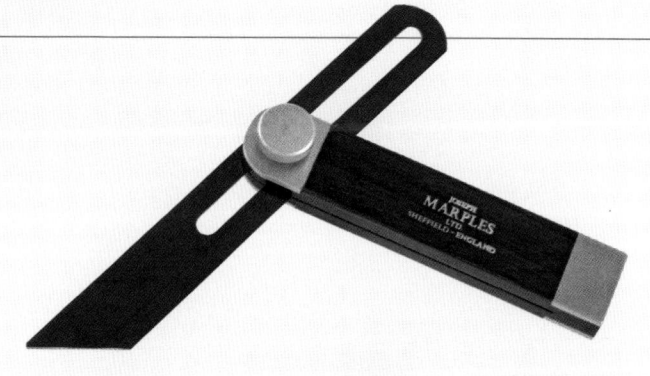

■ GOOD FEATURES

This version is not quite as bad as the two shown below. The blade is tightened with a knurled thumbscrew that doesn't protrude from the handle.

■ BAD FEATURES

Difficult to tighten in tight spaces and impossible to tighten enough to firmly hold its setting.

■ AVAILABLE FROM

Tools for Working Wood: 800-426-4613 or toolsforworkingwood.com
$7^1/2$": $18.95; 9": $19.95; $10^1/2$": $21.95; 12": $28.95

STANLEY 46-813 8" BEVEL

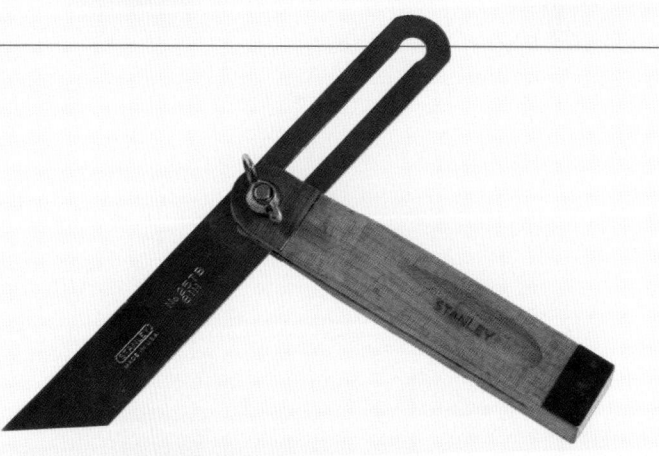

■ GOOD FEATURES

This and a similar plastic version are available in most hardware stores and will do the job if you must have one today (and can work around the shortcomings).

■ BAD FEATURES

The most aggravating thing about this tool is the wing nut. Eventually it will be in your way. You'll discover this while trying to set your saw after climbing down from a ladder. On the second trip to the saw, you'll bump something and it will lose its setting.

■ AVAILABLE FROM

Amazon: amazon.com
46-813 (wood): $11.28; 46-825 (plastic): $3.78

CROWN 8" BEVEL

■ GOOD FEATURES

If you prefer darker wood in a dysfunctional tool, this is a bit more attractive than the Stanley shown above.

■ BAD FEATURES

Construction is similar to the modern Stanley and it suffers from the same issues at more than twice the price.

■ AVAILABLE FROM

Rockler: 800-279-4441 or rockler.com
$26.99

Tool Tote

A good bevel gauge makes the angles in this simple piece easy to make (and perfect dovetails be darned – sloppy will hold just fine).

Don't let the angled ends put you off – this simple tool tote is a great beginner project. Even if your dovetails don't look perfect, they'll still impart the strength necessary to hold up under a heavy load.

Before the advent of plastic tool boxes, carpenters, joiners and the like would carry their tools from job to job in a wooden tote. (In fact, we have a family picture of my great grandfather carrying a similar tote, and he was a plumber). For this tote, we took the 24" interior bottom length (just long enough to hold a framing square) from an early 19th-century Canterbury, N.Y., Shaker example that sold for $400 at a recent Willis Henry auction. I decided on 12½" x 6½" for the interior width and height. The ends are about 22° off vertical.

This piece presents an excellent opportunity to practice your dovetails without having to worry about cutting them perfectly. Even if your pins and tails look like an illustration from an 18th-century dentistry tome, they'll still hold. And after all, this is a working piece, which means it's going to quickly get munged when you toss tools into it and lug it around the house or to a job site. (And paint is an excellent way to cover small gaps and wonky cuts.)

But first things first. I chose to use poplar not only because it's affordable and readily available, but because it's relatively lightweight. Once this sucker gets loaded down with hunks of metal, it's fairly heavy, so it's best to avoid adding to the tare weight, which can tear up your back.

Mill all your stock except the handle to ⅝", then joint the edges. The sides are 7¾" wide x 30¼" long, and the ends begin at 8½" wide x 13¼" long (however, the angle dictates the width, so rough-cut and tweak your final width later after the pieces are dry fit). Initially, I had milled the handle to ½" to gain a smidge more interior room, but concluded afterward that ½" cut into my palm too much. So, I milled another piece to ¾" and rough-cut it to 11" x 30".

Glue up a 14" x 25" panel for the bottom (a bit larger than finished size in width and length so you'll have enough extra stock to angle the ends and to fit it) then set it aside to dry.

Now, lay one of your side pieces flat on your workbench, and grab your sliding bevel gauge (see page 22 for tool recommendations). Set it to an angle that pleases your eye and lock the blade in place. You're going to leave your bevel gauge at that setting until you're done with construction. Mark that angle on one end of a side piece.

Because you're going to gang cut the sides on the miter saw, you need only mark the angle on one end of one piece. Line up your two side

As you can see, all my tails are a bit proud, and the fit at the baseline is gappier than I'd like. But they'll do for a workaday project like this one.

pieces at the top and bottom, then secure them together by sinking a 1" nail into the waste portions at both ends.

With the saw off, pull the blade down on your work and adjust the cut angle by eye. When you're close, press the handle of your bevel gauge against the miter saw fence, and tweak the saw blade angle until the gauge's blade is flat against the saw blade along its entire length. Lock in the angle. (As with your bevel gauge, once you lock the angle on the miter saw, leave it set until the project is complete.)

Now align the angled mark on the side piece with the blade and make the cut. Flip the pieces over carefully (you've cut away one of the nails securing them together), measure 24⅜" along the bottom edge, and make the second cut.

It's time to cut the angles on the top and bottom of the end pieces – maybe. You may prefer to cut your dovetails now using your preferred method, and plane the top and bottom edges to the correct angle once the box is assembled. These are not compound joints, but regular old dovetails, so if you haven't cut too many dovetails, it might be easier to leave the edges square while you do so – just be sure to leave enough overhang at the top and bottom so that you can plane the angles flush with the sides when you're done.

Or, you can set up your table saw for an angled cut (again using your bevel gauge to set the blade), and cut the proper angle at the bottom of each side, then line up the bottom edges of the side and ends before marking out and cutting the joints. I chose this option because I'm not a virtuoso with the plane; the table saw blade was far more likely to result in a matching profile to the sides, ensuring the tote would sit flat on a surface.

After I cut and dry-fit my dovetail joints, I pulled them apart, added yellow glue, then reassembled them. Check the bottom edges of the box for square (theoretically both the top and bottom edges should be square, but because you have to fit the tote bottom, if it's a choice between the two, go with the bottom).

Once the glue is dry, use a block plane to bring the top edges of the end pieces flush with the side pieces (and if you didn't cut the bottom angle before dovetailing, flush the bottom edges now as well).

Now align, glue and nail 1/2" x 1/2" cleats to the bottom edge of the side pieces. For added strength, you could also add angled cleats to the end pieces, then plane them to flush the angle with the ends. But that's fairly involved.

Measure 5/8" up from the cleats, and calculate your measurements for the size of the bottom panel from that point. Cut the ends to the proper angle at the table saw, or plane them to fit. The bottom panel should drop in and sit flat on the cleats. There's no need to secure it; the handle will keep it in place.

Now it's back to the miter saw to cut the angles on each end of the handle. As you did with the side pieces, simply mark one angle with the bevel gauge, make the cut, flip the board end for end then measure 24" at the bottom's length and make the second cut. (It's a good idea to confirm your length by measuring at the bottom of the tote, or make your initial cut a little long, and sneak up on the final dimension.)

What I found trickiest about this project was shaping the handle – or actually, deciding on what shape and handhold size looked and felt best. As I mentioned, I first milled wood to 1/2" thick for the handle, and after cutting out the handhold, found that was too narrow a width to be comfortable. So I went with 3/4" instead. To lay out the curve at the top, I first measured in 3" from where the handle ends would meet the box at the top edge, and sunk a nail just outside the line on the waste side on either end.

I then found the centerpoint at the top edge, grabbed a thin offcut from the trash can, and used the nails to hold it in place while I pushed up at the center to find the curve. Then I marked it with a pencil (see picture at right).

"It is not only fine feathers that make fine birds."

— Aesop (c. 550 B.C.)
fable writer

I cut to my line at the band saw, then measured 1 1/4" down from top center, and 1 1/4" to the right and left from that point. I chucked a 7/8" Forstner bit in the drill press, lined up the center of the bit with my two outside marks, and drilled holes (you may wish to make a larger handhold, depending on your hand size). I cut away the rest of the handhold with a jigsaw, curving the top edge slightly to match the handle profile, and to provide a more comfortable grip.

With a rasp, I rounded over all the edges in the handhold, then used #120-grit sandpaper to break all the edges and clean up the rasp marks.

I decided to paint my tote a smoky gray-blue … my default color. But, to make it a little more interesting (and to avoid constantly chipping the paint with the movement of tools), I masked off the inside top edges with tape, and painted only the outside surfaces of the box (filling in my dovetail gaps in the process) and the handle.

After the paint dried, I marked the centerpoint on each end piece, dropped the handle in place, drilled three pilot holes through each end into the handle, and secured the handle in place with 1 1/4" cut nails. **WM**

— *Megan Fitzpatrick*

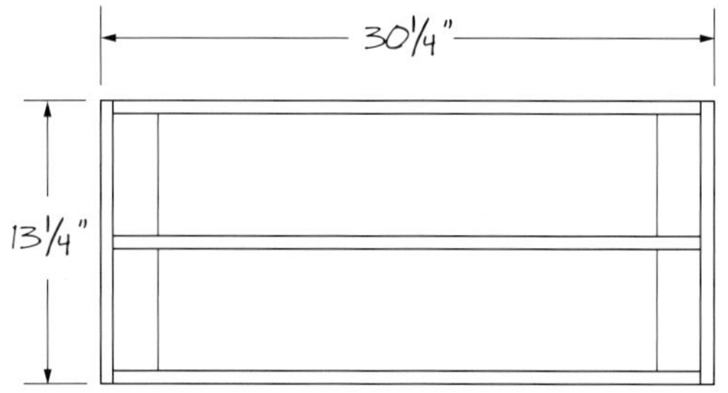

Two nails and a thin piece of offcut make a fine (and cheap) arc marker.

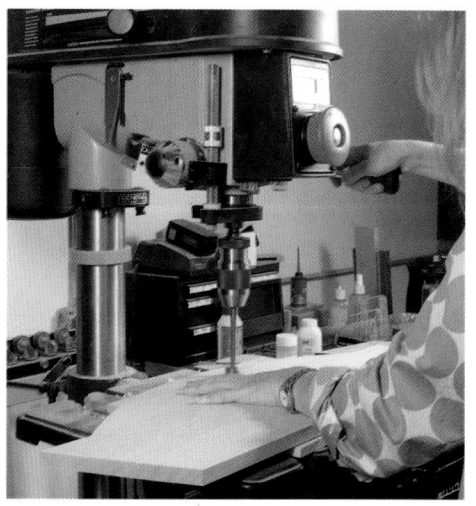

Use a drill press to cut the outside ends of your handhold, and a jigsaw to remove the remaining waste. You'll do the final shaping with a rasp and sandpaper.

TOP VIEW

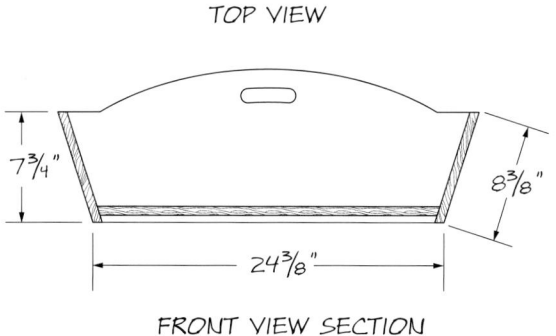

FRONT VIEW SECTION

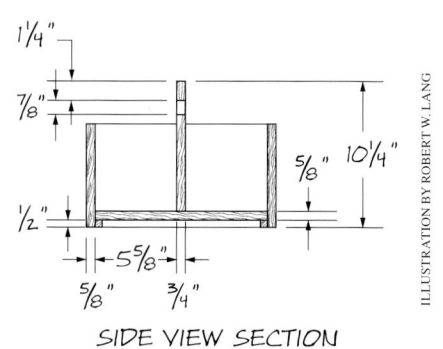

SIDE VIEW SECTION

ILLUSTRATION BY ROBERT W. LANG

Tool Tote

	NO.	PART	T	W	L	MATERIAL	NOTES
❏	2	Sides	5/8	7 3/4	30 1/4	Poplar	Dimension w/out angles
❏	2	Ends	5/8	8 1/2	13 1/4	Poplar	Dimension w/out angles
❏	1	Bottom	5/8	12	24	Poplar	Dimension w/out angles
❏	1	Handle	3/4	10 3/4	29 1/8	Poplar	Dimension w/out angles
❏	2	Cleats	1/2	1/2	23	Scrap	

Tools for Woodwork

What hand and power tools does the serious beginner need? Here's our best list.

When setting up shop, probably the last place you should search for the tools you need is in a tool catalog. The catalogs and supply stores are clogged with an array of tools, jigs and other equipment that all look absolutely essential.

Truth is, most of those tools are essential, but just not for every shop and every woodworker. The core list of tools you need to build furniture is actually pretty small.

We set out to develop our own list of "must-have" tools for a shop that blends hand and power tools, but we quickly discovered that someone had already done the job for us – and done it well.

The late Charles H. Hayward was a 20th-century woodworking writer who had been traditionally trained in professional English shops when both hand and power tools were common. Hayward wrote many classics, including "Woodwork Joints," "Cabinetmaking for Beginners" and "English Period Furniture." He also was the editor of England's *Woodworker Magazine*.

All of his books are out of print, though they are easy to find used on the Internet.

One of Hayward's best books, "Tools for Woodwork," explains how to use most basic hand tools and hand-held power tools. At the back of

The Necessary Power Equipment

In addition to that list of hand tools, we think the well-equipped shop should start with these pieces of power equipment.
- 10" table saw
- 8" jointer
- 12" benchtop planer
- ½" drill
- Random-orbit sander
- Drill press or hollow-chisel mortiser
- Jigsaw or band saw
- Two-base router kit (2hp)
- 10" miter saw

What's inside your tool cabinet? And what should be? Here's our list of what belongs in a beginning woodworker's tool kit.

that book is a "suggested kit for the man taking up woodwork seriously." We've decided to print his basic list and illustration (at right) with our commentary following each entry. Plus, we've included a list of what we consider to be the essential and recommended power tools.

The Preliminary Tool Kit

These are the hand tools Hayward says you should purchase before you cut your first stick of wood. The numbers before each entry correspond with the numbers in the illustration.

1. Crosscut handsaw, 22": This is technically a panel saw. It is useful for breaking down large planks you before flatten them.

2. Backsaw, 10": Presumably a carcase saw and filed crosscut, this tool will make your finishing cuts and is typically used with the bench hook.

3. Dovetail saw, 8": We prefer a 15-point saw that is filed for ripping cuts.

7. Jack plane: Hayward seems to prefer this plane for processing rough lumber. A 14"-long plane is typical.

8. Fore plane: Hayward seems to prefer this size plane (about 18") for shooting the edges of boards instead of a jointer plane.

9. Smoothing plane: The smoothing plane is the last plane to touch the work before scrapers or sandpaper. A 10"-long plane is a typical size.

15. Firmer chisels, ¼" and ¾": These were once common tools without the beveled edges that are common in catalogs today.

18. Warrington hammer: These small hammers have a cross-pane on one end for starting brad nails. Very handy and still available.

21. Mallet, 5" head. For driving chisels. Beech is the preferred wood.

20. Nail punch, fine: A small tool for setting nail heads below the wood's surface with a few short blows.

22. Pincers: A handy tool for pulling errant nails.

23. and **24.** Screwdrivers, 8" and 3": Traditionally, these would be straight drivers. You'll also need Phillips, square-drive and others.

25. Cutting gauge: A marking tool with a knife for making its mark (instead of a pin).

28. Ratcheting brace, 8": Still useful, even in a power-tool shop.

29. Auger bit, ⅜".

30. Twist or brad-point bit, ³⁄₁₆".

31. Countersink bit.

32. Center bit, ¾": A bit for making flat-bottomed holes. Now Forstners are the standard.

33. Brad awl: Designed to start holes for nails and small screws.

34. Try square, 6".

41. Card scraper: This tool cleans up tear-out left by the smoothing plane.

42. Oilstone: Buy one with coarse and fine grits. Waterstones are now common.

43. Folding rule: Or a tape measure.

Useful Additional Tools

The following tools should be added to your kit as you encounter a need for them when building individual projects.

4. Bow saw, 12": This saw is useful for deep and curved cuts.

53. Keyhole saw: Used for fine work, particularly keyholes. These days one with a Japanese tooth pattern are more common and useful.

54: Coping saw: Useful for clearing out waste between dovetails and shallow curved cuts.

11. Bullnose plane: A now-uncommon tool for cleaning up rabbets.

56. Shoulder plane: A useful tool for trimming the cheeks and shoulders of tenons.

55. Compass plane: If you do circular work, this plane is helpful. Others never need it.

12. Rabbet plane: For the woodworker who prefers to cut rabbets by hand.

13. Toothing plane: A useful plane for roughing up surfaces prior to veneering.

10. Plow plane: A useful hand tool for making grooves and small rabbets. Not found in a typical power-tool shop.

15. Firmer chisels, $1/8$" and $1/2$".

16. Paring chisel, $1 1/2$": Useful for a wide variety of fine cuts. Beveled edges are typical.

17. Mortise chisels, $5/16$": If you work with machine-processed stock, you'll probably want a $1/4$" tool instead.

19. Patternmaker's hammer: Like the Warrington next to it, but smaller.

26. Marking gauge: A gauge with a pin used for marking across and with the grain.

27. Mortise gauge: A marking gauge with two cutters to mark the two walls of a mortise simultaneously.

44. Spokeshave, wood body: Useful for curved shapes in easy-to-cut woods.

29. Auger bits, $1/4$" and $1/2$".

32. Center bits, 1" or as required: Again, substitute Forstners. Buy them as you need them.

47. Sash clamps, 36": Begin with one pair and purchase as needed.

49. C-clamps: A modern equivalent would also be F-style clamps.

48. Handscrews: Useful for all sorts of tapered and odd workholding needs.

35. Try square or combination square, 12".

37. Miter square: Useful for laying out and checking mitered work.

38. Sliding bevel, 8": For marking and measuring angles other than 90°.

45. Gouge: A large tool for removing large amounts of wood quickly – not a carving tool.

58. Surform tool: It looks like a cheese grater and is used for shaping curved and compound work, such as cabriole legs.

57. Router plane: Used to trim tenon cheeks, deepen grooves and to cut hinge mortises.

61. Dividers: Basic tools that step off dovetails or other joinery.

Homemade Tools and Jigs
Hayward also showed several homemade devices that make your hand tools work more accurately. He called them "appliances"; we call them "very useful."

5. Miter block: A sawing device used to help cut small miters.

6. Miter box: A more complex and accurate device for cutting miters in mouldings.

14. Shooting board, 36" long: An appliance used to plane the long edges of boards true.

39. Straightedge: Make as many as you need; they're wood.

36. Square, 24": Useful for laying out joinery full-scale on cabinet sides.

40. Winding sticks: Two identically sized, straight sticks used to check boards for twisting and cupping.

42. Oilstone case.

50. Veneering hammer: This tool presses veneer against its substrate.

46. Bench hook: An essential appliance for accurate crosscuts with a handsaw.

59. Scratch stock: A small tool with homemade cutters filed to cut small shapes, such as beads.

60. Miter template: An appliance clamped to your work that allows you to chisel accurate miters. **WM**

— *Christopher Schwarz*

Tinted Shellac Warms Walnut

Few woodworkers consider topcoat tinting, but adding a couple drops of aniline dye imparts a pleasing antique appearance to walnut.

Bell-bottoms, wide ties and leisure suits have something in common with walnut. No, I don't suspect you have walnut stashed in the far reaches of your closet next to the leisure suits. The commonality is that each item was in vogue at one time, then fell out of fashion. And while I'm not so sure leisure suits are going to make a comeback, I know walnut is once again gaining in popularity with woodworkers. So now might just be the time to stock the shelves in your shop.

If we're picking up the pace of creating projects with this favorite American hardwood (the choice lumber for furniture built in the William & Mary period (1690-1730) prior to increased importation of mahogany), we need to find a finish that is more than simply adding a coat or two of linseed or tung oil.

Same Old, Same Old

Oil finishes deepen the color of walnut. That's a nice look and the oil adds protection, but it does nothing to warm the cool characteristics of the hardwood, especially the look of steamed walnut, which is grayish brown when freshly milled.

If you study antique walnut furniture, you'll notice a reddish cast to the older pieces – a look that's much warmer and more pleasing. That's what happens as walnut ages and the gray shading begins to warm. It's a result of time. But, how can we manipulate time to achieve a warm, reddish finish in a relatively short period?

We wanted a finish that was easy to use, simple to repeat and quick to apply. A five- to seven-step process that required hours of work or drying time wasn't going to work. It had to be something that was achievable in just a couple simple steps.

A few samples using dye under shellac were tried. (Orange dyes were suggested by a number of woodworkers.) That was close to the color we were searching for, but the finish muddied the wood. We wanted the walnut grain to stand out, not be masked.

Next we turned to shellac. You may wonder how to get a reddish cast with shellac. While there are a few shellacs that are red in color (available as shellac flakes that are dissolved in alcohol before use), most over-the-counter shellac provides an orange or amber tint at most. The amber color undoubtedly warms the grayish brown hardwood. And to gain that slight reddish look found on antique furniture, we focused on aniline dye added directly into the shellac.

I've mixed dyes with my topcoat before and found TransTint liquid dyes (available at any woodworking store) work best. It's easy because the dye is a concentrated liquid. For our new finish, add a few drops of Reddish Brown (#6003) into shellac, mix and the finish is ready.

First, we mixed two drops of dye into 2 ounces of amber shellac, then applied three coats to a sample board with a rag dipped in the mixture, only to find the red cast was not as strong as desired. Then we repeated the mixture and application process using a four drops per 2-ounce mixture. That did it. After three coats, applied with the shop cloth, we had a red cast that mimicked antique walnut furniture.

After sampling a few different finishes to warm walnut, we discovered that aniline dye added to amber shellac was the ticket – a simple mixture that's easy to apply, with results that mimic antique furniture.

Varying a drop as you add the dye to the shellac is not going to create a significant difference in the final look of the finish, but try to keep each batch consistent.

Application is Key

When using tinted shellac or any shellac other than "clear," a run or sag in your finish will show in the completed piece. The defect shows due to the color in the shellac being thicker at the run or sag. So pay close attention as you apply the finish.

There are three methods of applying finish. You can spray, apply the finish with a brush or simply use a clean shop cloth. Let the project size determine which method to use.

If the project is large, use a spray setup. This method allows the smoothest layering of shellac – provided you are accurate with a spray gun. Spray three coats of shellac. (Each coat must dry completely before adding the next layer.) Thin the shellac to a 1½-pound cut. Store-bought, pre-mixed shellac is generally available in a 3-pound cut. To reduce the viscosity, mix the shellac in a 50/50 ratio with denatured alcohol. Thinner viscosity allows the shellac to atomize into finer particles, producing a smooth coat.

If spraying the mixture is not in the cards for you, by all means, resort to a brush. If you apply the shellac with a brush, it's not necessary to thin the mixture. Apply the first coat making sure that you keep a wet edge and brush as little as possible, always brushing with the grain. If you attack this as most would in painting a house (a back-and-forth action), you'll likely create more brush lines and a less-than-smooth finish.

No matter how you apply shellac, it might be necessary to sand between coats to remove nibs. And there is a caveat here. Sand lightly. Tinted shellac shows variations with differences in thickness and layers. If you cut through a layer of shellac to expose bare wood, you could change the look of the finish just as a run or sag does.

Because most of us brush on a thicker coat than we spray, apply a second brushed coat, then assess the color and film thickness. The color needs to be right and there should be a sufficient buildup of finish to achieve a smooth, even layer. If a third coat is needed, sand the second coat before adding another.

A better quality brush translates into smoother finish application because a good brush holds more finish. You'll have more continuous strokes because you don't have to stop to reload as often.

"The purest and most thoughtful minds are those which love color the most."
— John Ruskin (1819 - 1900)
English writer and critic

Apply shellac with a rag on small projects only. To keep the finish under control, thin the shellac mixture to a 2-pound cut. Adding one cup of alcohol into two cups of shellac does this. The thinner viscosity dries more quickly and reduces any gumming of the shellac. Keep the rag wet. If you experience "drag" (the cloth sticking to previously applied shellac), add shellac to the cloth. Use the same technique and precautions as suggested when brushing.

On large, flat surfaces, #0000 steel wool can knock the high sheen off a shellac finish. Adding a lubricant such as "wool lube" slows the scratching process and provides an even sheen.

Knock Down the Sheen

As shellac builds the sheen also builds – the more coats, the higher the gloss. Of course you can leave the higher sheen as your finish, but a high shine, or glossy finish, amplifies any imperfections. A dull or a medium sheen is better. Rubbing out the finish with #0000 steel wool or applying a different topcoat will dull the sheen.

To achieve a satin finish with steel wool, you're scratching the surface to no longer reflect light as much. This is a time-consuming step and the results are varied due to one's ability to get tight into corners, and it's possible to rub through the finish, again causing variations in the color.

Our choice for reducing the high shellac sheen to a satin or dull sheen is to add a layer of a different topcoat after one final sanding (this also helps level the finish). The resulting sheen is uniform over the entire piece. One caution: Confirm that your topcoat is compatible with the waxy properties of amber shellac. Some topcoats, polyurethane for example, don't bond to wax.

If you are spraying your finish, a dull-rubbed effect lacquer is great. In addition, a wipe-on varnish is perfect for this step as well. Yes, each adds a small amount of yellowing, but that color increases the warming of the finish.

If you want to add a topcoat such as waterborne polyurethane (because it dries quickly and has a clear, non-yellowing appearance), apply a single coat of Zinsser's Sealcoat, which is clear, de-waxed shellac. Then apply any dull-rubbed or satin topcoat.

This walnut finish met our requirements. Its two ingredients easily blended into one mixture, it can be sprayed, brushed or ragged on and the final color simulates the finish on antique walnut furniture. If you decide to rag-on the finish, I doubt that old leisure suit is an acceptable shop cloth – but that wide tie might just do the job. **WM**

— *Glen D. Huey*

Applying a waterborne satin finish is an easy way to reduce the sheen of shellac. But first, you need to add a layer of dewaxed shellac to ensure proper adhesion.

End Grain

Really, It's OK to Make Mistakes

Be it spilled coffee or sloppy joinery, mistakes cost time but increase knowledge.

I make mistakes and I'm OK with that. Take my coffee maker as an example. My Keurig machine produces one cup at a time. Of course I make a cup in the morning, but I also have a mug after dinner, on my way to the woodshop.

For traveling to the shop, I have an insulated cup that's too tall to fit the coffee maker. I make a cup in a regular mug, then make the transfer to the travel mug.

One evening, as I pushed the brew button, I forgot to put the coffee cup under the spout. Hot, steaming coffee spilled from the machine like Old Faithful working in reverse. Coming to my senses, I quickly shoved a cup under the spout. The coffee maker finished its cycle, and I had a mess to clean up due to the collection of liquid dispersed into the cup stand (not to mention I had a less-than-full cup of coffee).

As I pulled the stand from the coffee maker, much to my surprise I uncovered a second cup stand located directly below the normal stand I used on an everyday basis. It seemed my travel mug would, indeed, fit the machine. No more did I need to transfer between cups. If I hadn't made a mistake (forgetting to put the cup in position), I would not have discovered the lower stand.

Clearly, mistakes in life provide more information than doing something correctly. The same holds true for woodworking. I've always learned more from mistakes than from doing an operation right the first time.

Once the mistake is made, you assess the steps, find where you veered off course or when the problem first appeared, and know what not to do the next time. A lesson is learned, albeit a sometimes costly education. And the feedback from a mistake is immediate – the mortise and tenon is sloppy, the dovetail joint doesn't fit or the topcoat has an unsightly sag – and the lesson is appreciated because it cost you either money or time. And time is the most costly of the two.

In addition, you discover methods to fix the issues that do arise. I would not have known how to close small gaps in my early dovetails (place a saw kerf beside the "gappy" dovetail then drive a wood-matching wedge into that kerf) if I had tight-fitting joints. Or, if I hadn't sprayed the finish too heavily around the door frame on a cupboard, which creates a sag only visible with light directed from above, I wouldn't have unearthed how to use a single-edge razor blade as a small but efficient scraper. These events build our knowledge as woodworkers, as well as add to our experience. That experience makes us better craftsmen.

By making mistakes and dealing with the consequences, you begin to fully understand the processes. With a complete understanding of the processes, you know why a joint fits accurately or what a good finish looks like. The woodworking picture comes into focus. It becomes clear. You can then make small changes and anticipate the results. You can tweak a step here or there in the process and know you'll not have a problem from which to recover.

But if you do the task at hand without incident, do you stop and question why it happened the way it did? No. So what have you learned? You don't know why the joint fit or why the case assembly is square. It just happened.

If you can precisely duplicate the process again, you can complete the same task many times. Can you remember the exact steps? More than likely you cannot. And if you cannot, you're destined to make another attempt and hopefully the process runs successfully a second time.

So don't be afraid to make mistakes. Get going. Do something. Even if it doesn't work, you've gained as a woodworker. No, I don't particularly want to toss a half-carved cabriole leg into the trash or throw away an ill-fitting joint – but I've done just that. And it hurts.

They don't call it the "school of hard knocks" for nothing.

As I stated at the beginning, I make mistakes and I accept that fact. What I don't accept is making the same mistake twice. WM

— *Glen D. Huey*

Extras

"It is common sense to take a method and try it; if it fails, admit it frankly and try another. But above all, try something."
— Franklin D. Roosevelt (1882 - 1945), 32nd President of the United States

Register Now for Woodworking in America: Hand Tools & Techniques Conference 2008

Registration is now open for Woodworking in America: Hand Tools & Techniques Conference 2008.

This weekend hand-tool woodworking conference will be held Nov. 14-16, 2008, at Berea College in Berea, Ky.

Woodworking in America will help you jump-start your hand-tool skills by exposing you to tools you may have seen only in catalogs and magazines, along with face-to-face instruction with more than 20 of today's best hand-tool woodworkers and toolmakers including Roy Underhill, Frank Klausz and Mike Dunbar.

There will be more than 40 short classes on tools and techniques during the long weekend, plus a marketplace where toolmakers can display (and sell) their wares, social events with the demonstrators and toolmakers and more. For complete information and to register, visit the web site at WoodworkingInAmerica.com.

Woodworking Magazine – the Book

Although we offer digital versions of all issues of *Woodworking Magazine,* we have an affection for the printed word. So, at the request of readers, we've also collected the first seven issues of the magazine and bound them into a book. In fact, the book has been so popular that we're now on our second printing!

This hardcover book features a sturdy, red cover with a foil-stamped title, heavyweight interior matte-finish pages, colored end papers and a full-color glossy book jacket. This is a book that belongs in your permanent collection.

Woodworking Magazine – The Book is available on our web site (woodworking-magazine.com/books) for $34.95 (includes s&h in the U.S.). It's a perfect way to ensure your collection will last for years to come. Order your copy today!

IMPORTANT SAFETY NOTE

Safety is your responsibility. Manufacturers place safety devices on their equipment for a reason. In many photos you see in *Woodworking Magazine,* these have been removed to provide clarity. In some cases we'll use an awkward body position so you can better see what's being demonstrated. Don't copy us. Think about each procedure you're going to perform beforehand. Safety First!

CONTACT US

We welcome letters from readers with comments about this magazine, or about woodworking in general. We try to respond to all correspondence. To send us a letter:
- E-mail: letters@fwpubs.com
- Fax: 513-891-7196
- Mail carrier:
  Letters • *Woodworking Magazine*
  4700 E. Galbraith Road
  Cincinnati, OH 45236

Warming Up Walnut

While aged walnut has a lovely reddish cast, what comes out of kilns can look cold and lifeless. We wanted a finish that would be easy to make, easy to apply and would add a warm tone without muddying the grain. We tested various formulas before deciding on our favorite recipe (it's featured in the finishing story on page 30). Below are the less-than-perfect results. The winner is pictured on the cover; we used it for the American Wall Cupboard.

- $1/4$ teaspoon of reddish brown dye into 4 ounces of amber shellac, three coats
- $1/4$ teaspoon of reddish brown dye into 2 ounces of amber shellac, three coats 
- Three coats of amber shellac over reddish brown analine dye
- Three coats of amber shellac over orange analine dye 
- Three coats of amber shellac 
- $1/8$ teaspoon of reddish brown dye into 2 ounces of amber shellac, three coats 

Number 11, Autumn 2008. *Woodworking Magazine* (ISSN 1941-5834) is published 4 times a year in March, May, August and December by F+W Publications, Inc. Editorial offices are located at 4700 E. Galbraith Road, Cincinnati, Ohio 45236; tel.: 513-531-2222. Unsolicited manuscripts are not accepted. Subscription rates: A year's subscription (4 issues) is $19.96 in the U.S., $24.96 in Canada, and $29.96 elsewhere. Produced and printed in the U.S.A.

Screw Extraction

Autumn 2008

Tube Extractors are the Best Option

Sawtooth edges make these small tools very handy to have around the shop. Use a drill press, if possible, to bore a clean hole around the screw. Or, a hand-held drill with a guide block works fine for screws located outside of the reach of a drill press. Once the screw is out, patch the hole with a length of dowel or a matching plug.

For screw sizes #4 – #8, use a 1/4" tube

For screw sizes #4 – #10, use a 5/16" tube

For screw sizes #10 – #12, use a 3/8" tube

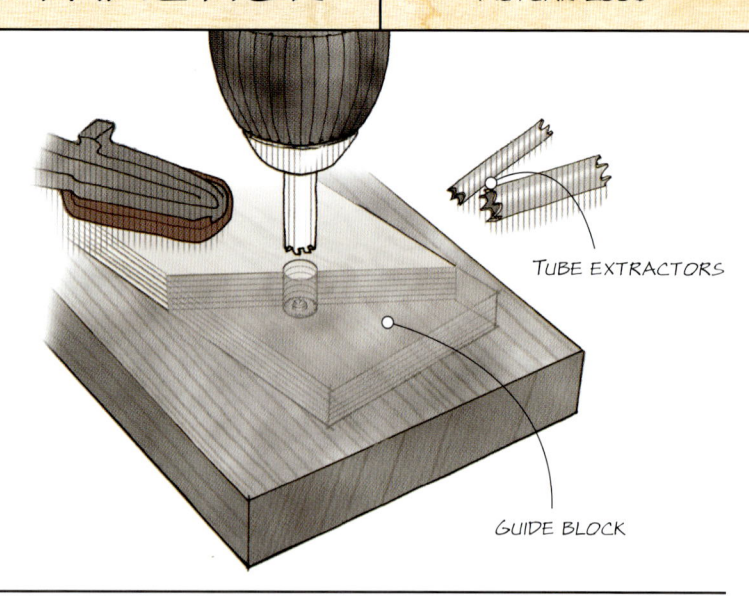

Removing Broken Screws with Pliers

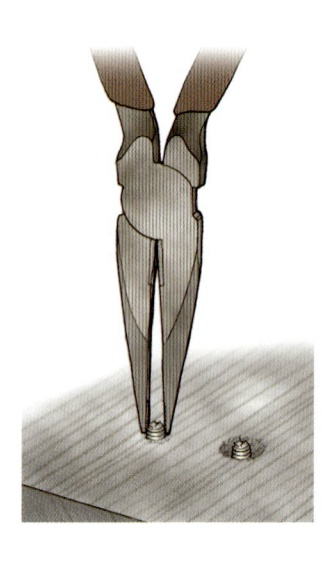

- If the screw shank is fully above the surface, simply grab the shank with needle-nose pliers and twist the broken screw out.
- If the area won't be visible when finished or the shank is flush with the surface, excavate around the shank, then use pliers to extract the screw.
- Stubborn screws may loosen with heat applied directly to the screw with a soldering iron.

Rotary Tool to the Rescue

Use a cut-off wheel on a rotary tool to cut a slot into the top of the broken screw. Then, use a slot-head screwdriver to reverse the screw's shaft out of the hole.

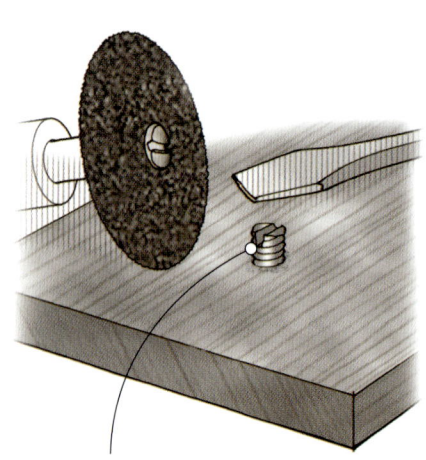

Tips to Avoid Breaking Screws

- Use a better quality screw. (See Premium Screws in Woodworking Magazine Summer 2008, issue 10.)
- Drill properly sized pilot holes, which are different for hardwood and softwood (see chart at right).
- Lubricate the screw with wax or paraffin. Grease or oil may leach into the wood causing finish problems.
- Always clamp the workpiece to your bench or in a vise to hold the piece securely.
- For brass screws, first install a steel screw of equal size to thread the hole, then replace that screw with the brass screw.

Proper Sizes for Pilot Holes

Screw Size	Shank Clearance Hole	Pilot Hole for Softwood	Pilot Hole for Hardwood
#4	7/64"	3/64"	1/16"
#5	1/8"	1/16"	5/64"
#6	9/64"	1/16"	5/64"
#7	5/32"	1/16"	3/32"
#8	11/64"	5/64"	3/32"
#9	3/16"	5/64"	7/64"
#10	3/16"	3/32"	7/64"
#11	13/64"	3/32"	1/8"
#12	7/32"	7/64"	1/8"

Illustrations by Matt Bantly

A Magazine Committed to Finding the Better Way to Build
Filled with Good Craftsmanship, the Best Techniques and No Ads

WOODWORKING
MAGAZINE

Stickley Tile-Topped Plant Stand

3 Methods to Make Through-Mortises

Better Ways to Cut Crisp Chamfers

The Right Way to Use Grain Fillers

Why You Should Sand Your Finish Without Sandpaper

Saddle Squares – Buy a Nice One (Or a Butt Hinge)

POPULAR WOODWORKING PRESENTS

fw F+W PUBLICATIONS, INC.
US $5.99
CAN $7.99

Display until March 15, 2009

woodworking-magazine.com ■ WINTER 2008

Contents

"Nequeo monstrare, et sentio tantum."
("I cannot describe it, I can only feel it.")
— Juvenal, late 1st-century Roman satirist

1 On the Level
Pretty is as pretty does when it comes to vintage tools and furniture – and pretty is oftentimes pretty useless.

2 Letters
Questions, comments and wisdom from readers, experts and our staff.

4 Shortcuts
Tricks and tips that will make your woodworking simpler and more accurate.

6 Make Clean Through-mortises
Woodworkers expect this joint to be tidy and tight, not ragged and gappy. We explore the best ways to make this sometimes-vexing hole.

10 Gustav Stickley Plant Stand
Building a piece that focuses on existing skills can help you refine your techniques while producing high-quality work.

26 Saddle Squares
This little-known layout tool may change the way you work immeasurably (and you might already have one in your hardware drawer).

28 A Super Smooth Surface
Grain fillers can level open-grained wood in a single step and save time when it comes to building up a beautiful finish.

30 Sanding Finishes
Improper sanding can ruin a carefully wrought finish. Here you'll find out how to avoid problems, and discover a few new products.

32 Reviving Techniques Forgotten (and Gross)
Our forebears wasted little when it came to woodworking – find new (old) uses for spittle, earwax and more.

HANGING SHELVES: PAGE 22

SADDLE SQUARES: PAGE 26

18 Improving Small Chamfers
We investigate several methods to make precise small chamfers on end grain, then share our results and favorite techniques.

21 Glossary
Woodworking's terminology can be overwhelming. Learn the terms used in this issue.

22 Hanging Shelves
On this simple project, practice perfecting authentic details as you produce a handsome and useful display.

A SUPER SMOOTH SURFACE: PAGE 28

MAKE CLEAN THROUGH-MORTISES: PAGE 6

SANDING FINISHES: PAGE 30

On the Level

Pretty, Stupid

I have a shiny bronze edge plane perched on my bookshelf that's nestled in an attractive red velvet bag. Wait, let me clarify that. It's actually a plane-shaped object. The thing couldn't cut its way out of a wet paper bag.

The plane's adjuster is hopelessly coarse, the iron is warped like a potato chip, and the tool's integral fence isn't 90°. But it is a pretty thing and visitors often pick it up to admire it.

Me, I hate the plane, but I keep it around to remind me not to be such a crow – a hoarder of bright and shiny objects. It's a lesson that I apparently needed to learn.

When I first started buying vintage hand tools I went for the ones that looked new. And if the tool was still in its original box, even better.

I soon discovered that often there are reasons a tool has survived for 100 years with nary a blemish or chipped handle. Sure, sometimes you get lucky and you stumble on a perfectly preserved tool that was put away new and forgotten.

But more times than not, vintage tools in pristine condition are usually the victims of poor design or faulty manufacturing.

I have a gorgeous jointer plane with a rear tote that is designed to come loose after 15 minutes of use – no matter how tightly you screw the tote to the body of the plane. I have a pristine bird-cage awl that hurts your hand every time you use it. I have a marking knife that slips from your fingers like a watermelon seed no matter how tightly you squeeze it.

In the category of tools that were made by a drunk monkey, I have a jack plane with a sole shaped like a banana. I have a gorgeous hammer with its original handle rotated about 5° off from its head. And I have a brace (it was still in the original wrapper!) with a pad that wobbles like a newborn's oversized noggin.

On the other hand, there is my Stanley Type 11 No. 5 handplane. I bought the thing at a flea market for just $12 – the hippie selling it normally dealt in books and was tired of toting the thing from show to show.

The tool had been repainted. The rear tote had been replaced with a somewhat-crude shop-made handle. The metalwork was a dull battleship gray. But if I ever enter a handplaning contest, that's the tool I'm going to bring along. I swear the thing is haunted. Despite its dowager appearance, the tool is unerringly precise and stable. It will be the last tool I sell when I am penniless and hungry.

These principles of buying tools also apply to furniture. Too often I encounter products that are dresser-shaped objects or table-shaped objects. Just like the tools, these things (I hate to call them furniture) are the victims of poor manufacturing, poor design or both.

In fact, when I look at old furniture, I am now drawn to pieces that are well-worn but still sturdy. Case-in-point: My wife and I used to haunt an antiques store stuffed with European imports. We always walked past the pristine and imposing bureaus to wander among the French farmhouse tables with worn edges and scarred tops. The fact that these tables had survived so much use and abuse was more impressive than any finial or carved knee block.

"Tools were made and born with hands, every farmer understands."
— William Blake (1757 - 1827)
English poet, artist, engraver and publisher

So no matter how much my daughters scratch the dining table, I refuse to refinish its top, though it would take only an afternoon to restore. I allow my tools to patinate (though not to rust). On one of my brass-walled planes you can clearly see the whorls of my fingerprints.

These are the marks that these objects were useful in life, as telling as the lines in our faces that show up from smiling or frowning a lot.

And when I pick up that bronze edge plane, I do my share of both smiling and frowning. I frown because I spent $85 on something that's as useful as a rock for building nice furniture. And I smile because the company that made this object in the 1990s is now out of business. So perhaps there is hope. **WM**

Christopher Schwarz
Editor

Letters

ILLUSTRATIONS BY MARY JANE FAVORITE

Does Powered-up, Traditional Woodworking Exist?

Christopher Schwarz's recent article on building a traditional blanket chest (Summer 2008, Issue 10) was excellent. I was surprised, however, that he used a router to create the curves on the feet of the plinth. If it's tradition you seek, why not reach for a spokeshave or rasps?

I hope you guys will craft an article that identifies traditional joints that you can and cannot do with power tools (not just routed vs. handsawn dovetails). What are the hard choices that today's "traditional" woodworker has to make in order to achieve the traditional look given all of the bit, blade and machine choices – including custom-order items – out there today? Is the business of antique reproduction still all handplanes and wood rasps? What if strict timelines and tight budgets are only secondary concerns? Is there such a thing as a powered-up, traditional woodworker?

Skye Cooley
Spokane, Washington

Skye,
These are all good questions and suggestions.
In the case of the blanket chest, the curve was too tight for any spokeshave except a cigar shave (which I do not own).
And because this piece has a contemporary look (with the box joints and clear maple finish), I decided that the feet needed to have the machine-like crispness and regularity offered by a routed pattern.
Of course, I made the pattern itself with rasps, so I guess there might just be such a thing as a powered-up hand-tool woodworker.
Christopher Schwarz, editor

Drill Press Screw Extraction

Tube screw extractors are valuable tools, but they can't be used in a drill press (as was printed in Autumn 2008, Issue 11).

The reason is that the teeth are designed to cut while the bit is turning counterclockwise. There is, of course, a logic to this design. The idea is that the bit will "hole saw" down around the broken screw until it gets enough of a grip on it to back the remaining engaged threads out. Your illustration, which I suspect was developed from a photograph, clearly shows the counterclockwise tooth design.

No single-spindle drill press that I've seen has the capability of running in reverse.

Mark Bouquet
Burlingame, California

Mark,
You're correct that the teeth on a tube extractor are created to cut while turning counterclockwise. But it is possible to use this tool in a drill press because the teeth also cut while rotating clockwise – much like handsaws that will do some cutting on the return stroke. Keep your press's speed slow and your extractor will work as described.
Glen D. Huey, senior editor

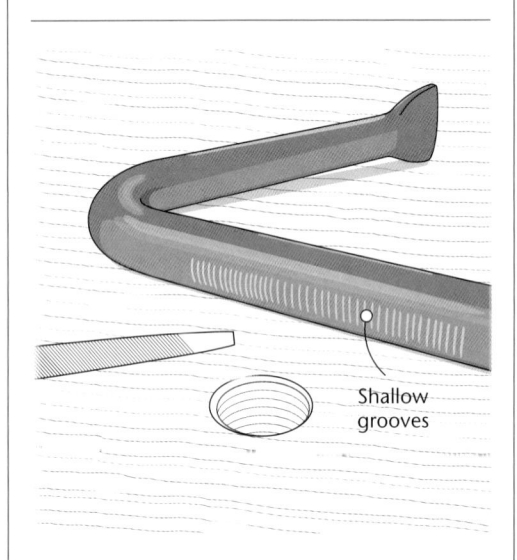

Shallow grooves

Shallow Grooves Make Holdfasts Hold Fast in 3/4" Holes

I thought I'd drop you a line concerning my eventual success using the Gramercy holdfasts in my new Holtzapffel bench (Autumn 2007, Issue 8). I built the bench using Southern yellow pine and used the 24" Veritas twin-screw vise for the face vise. I drilled the benchtop and leg holes all 3/4". I was very disappointed when the Gramercy holdfasts wouldn't "hold fast" in the top or leg holes. I tried roughing the holdfasts with #80-grit sandpaper, but they still held poorly. I then got out my mill file and filed a series of very shallow grooves along small parts of the circumference of the holdfast about 1/16" apart.

The grooves were filed in the rear of the holdfast near the top, and on the front near the bottom where they would be in contact with the benchtop when placed under stress. The holdfast now works perfectly; it holds very well and releases easily when whacked on the back. I had considered drilling some 11/16" holes because of the problems others had reported. With this simple modification I see no reason to drill anything but the 3/4" holes that are compatible with more bench accessories. My only regret concerning the bench is that I didn't order the wooden screws.

On an additional note, Lee Valley now has a product called "bench anchors" that are useful for securing bench accessories to benches with 3/4" holes. I made a modification to that device, too. The 1/2" screws that secure your accessories to the anchors work well. My modification, however, makes them even more versatile.

I drilled a hole down the center of the 1/2" screw to allow an Allen wrench to be placed through the screw to loosen the anchor without having to remove the anchor from the accessories. This allows me to make a planing stop that I can drop into its holes and then simply tighten both Allen screws to secure it – no loose parts, no two-step assembly. The 1/2" screw is plenty big to allow for the hole and still have adequate strength.

Michael Baker
Winston-Salem, North Carolina

When Rising Water Threatens, Magazines Must be Saved!

I watched nervously as tropical storm Fay filled up the lake in my backyard quicker than the drainage system could remove it. When the water reached within a foot of the berm, I told my wife to pack whatever was important to her in the event we had to evacuate. If the water crested the berm, our way out would be flooded! Like a good wife, she packed family photos, important papers and my daughter's most-loved stuffed animals. I, on the other hand, packed my handplanes, chisels and saws. What also made its way into the van was my hardbound copy of the first seven issues of *Woodworking Magazine* and the subsequent four issues.

Fortunately, the rain slowed, the lake receded and we didn't have to evacuate. I've lived in Florida most of my life, and this was the first time I was forced to make a grab-and-run decision. I'm lucky enough to have a wife who'll do the right thing. It gives me the freedom to choose the less-than-right thing.

When faced with it, the quality of *Woodworking Magazine* made it important enough for me to save. I assume my issues could have been replaced; however, their loss would have been a loss to me. Additionally, I have a new appreciation for the printed word as opposed to the digital word. When the power is out and the battery dies in your laptop, pdfs are really hard to read!

Bill Killingsworth
Jacksonville, Florida

A Green Alternative to WD-40

In one of the letters in the Summer 2008 issue of *Woodworking Magazine* you mention the use of WD-40. In these eco-friendlier times, I have an alternative for you. Last year while shopping for milk paint at the Homestead House Paint Company (homesteadhouse.ca) I came across BioD-42, a hemp-oil-based product from a company called Hempola (hempola.com). It performs well. It cleans metal, stops squeaks and displaces moisture – plus it's biodegradable!

Michael Wirth
Toronto, Ontario

Just Plane Sore (At Us)

I am very excited about being a new subscriber to *Woodworking Magazine*. I have been following your articles and blogs and have taken a liking to your way of woodworking.

But I have to let you know that I did call you bad names this morning.

I am building a small toolbox that has hand-cut dovetails. I had some nice 12"-wide walnut and I did not want to cut it and reglue the stock just to be able to run it through my 6" jointer. So I thought, "Well Chris used handplanes to flatten his workbench, so I will do that. Heck, my boards are only 30" long and 12" wide, so how bad can it be?"

I grabbed my No. 7½ jointer plane and went to work on flattening the front and back panels. Two hours later the boards were dead flat and smooth. I had shavings everywhere and I was sweating! I put my tools away and headed to the house. All was well – so far.

"He that gives good advice, builds with one hand; he that gives good counsel and example, builds with both; but he that gives good admonition and bad example, builds with one hand and pulls down with the other."

— Francis Bacon (1561 - 1626)
English lawyer and philosopher

I woke up this morning and I could not lift my arms. It hurt to raise them at all. My wife asked me what was wrong. I said I was trying to follow Chris Schwarz's methods and my arms are killing me from planing. She laughed! I told her: "If I get pulled over by the police today and they tell me to put my arms above my head, I'm going to tell them that I can't and to just go ahead and shoot me."

Jeff Jackson
Fort Wayne, Indiana

Jeff,
You'll toughen up. It happens fairly quickly. You start using your long leg muscles instead of your arms. Planing never wears out my arms now – just my legs.

Christopher Schwarz, editor

What's With That Story Title?

Just before returning to the Netherlands, I picked up a copy of *Woodworking Magazine*'s Summer 2008 issue. Thank you for a great magazine. I am about to add a subscription to my list!

Just a question: What's with the title of Christopher Schwarz's article on page 32: "Als Ik Kan"? I am all for keeping readers interested and on their toes, but will they get this one?

Sjoerd van Valkenburg
Netherlands

Sjoerd,
"Als Ik Kan" (which translates, as you know, to "as best I can" or "to the best of my ability") is a Flemish phrase that Gustav Stickley adopted from the writings of William Morris and incorporated into The Craftsman logo, along with the medieval joiner's compass. It's a fairly well-known saying in the U.S. woodworking community – especially among Arts & Crafts aficionados.

Megan Fitzpatrick, managing editor

Will a Vertical Position Work For a Twin-screw Vise?

I'm preparing to build my first serious workbench based on the Roubo (Autumn 2005, Issue 4), and after agonizing over the style of vise to put where the leg vise goes, a thought entered my brain. Would it be functionally feasible to mount a Veritas twin-screw vise vertically as the leg vise? And would it prevent racking? Or is the idea ludicrous and using the traditional leg vise a simpler device that provides the same result?

Rob Crowson
Saxtons River, Vermont

Rob,
You can indeed do that. You could even mount a quick-release vise on its side for much the same effect. The only real downside to these ideas is the expense. One of the great merits of the leg vise is its inexpensive design and robust nature. It's an amazingly good value.

I've been using my leg vise for more than three years now and would not trade it. The occasional stooping is a minor inconvenience for its remarkable holding power.

Christopher Schwarz, editor

Why No Drawer Kickers in The Hanging Cupboard Design?

In looking at the plans for the hanging cupboard (which I like a lot) in the Autumn 2008 issue of *Woodworking Magazine* I noticed that there are no kickers or stops for the drawer.

Were these typically not included in this type of cabinet, is it just to keep the project simple, or is that sort of thing so basic that we're supposed to infer their presence?

Chris Friesen
via e-mail

Chris,
The middle divider works fairly well as a kicker for the drawer – though it's not perfect.

Feel free to add both. I kept them out of the project for one of the reasons you mentioned – keeping it simple for a small drawer. **WM**

Christopher Schwarz, editor

HOW TO CONTACT US

Send your comments and questions via e-mail to letters@fwpubs.com, or by regular mail to *Woodworking Magazine*, Letters, 4700 E. Galbraith Road, Cincinnati, OH 45236. Please include your complete mailing address and daytime phone number. All letters become property of *Woodworking Magazine*.

Shortcuts

ILLUSTRATIONS BY MARY JANE FAVORITE

The Right-hand Thumb Trick

I learned this in engineering school and soon found out it worked for my router. It is called the "right-hand thumb rule."

When trying to remember which way your router bit is spinning so you can feed the wood in the correct direction, you can use the right-hand thumb rule.

Pretend your right hand is a router and your thumb is the router bit. If you are holding the machine with your hands and the bit is pointing down to the floor, then hold your hand in front of you with your thumb pointing to the floor. Then curl your fingers. That's the direction your router bit is spinning.

If you are using a router table, hold your hand with your thumb pointing to the sky. Curl your fingers, and that's the direction your router bit is spinning.

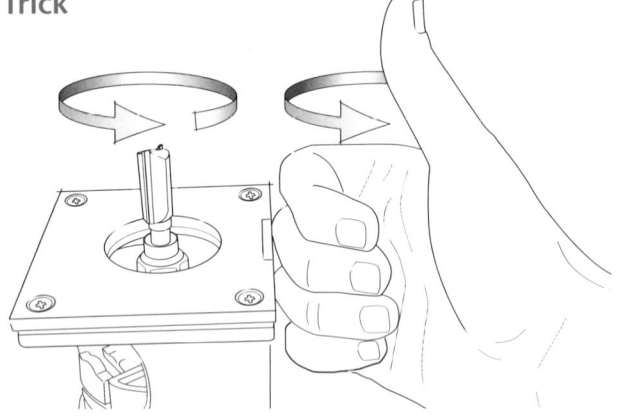

That way you will never get confused again and always know the correct feed direction.

And it works for almost anything that spins, such as faucets, regular-thread screws, changing a tire (if you want to know which way to tighten or loosen the nuts), etc.

Regis de Andrade
Tigard, Oregon

Band Saw Blades: Keeping Track

I know a few guys with more than one band saw in their shops, or band saws they use in a couple different configurations (i.e. with or without a riser block). So keeping blades sorted out for machines that require different blade lengths can be a pain. When looking through my pile of folded blades, I've become accustomed to using this easy method to find the right one.

1) Count the number of loops (usually three or five, never four – go ahead, try to fold a band saw blade an even number of times. I double-dog dare you);

2) Measure the diameter of the folded blade, I just ballpark it to the nearest half inch;

3) Multiply by three because it's really close to pi (3.1416 …)

This will give you the total length of the blade, or it will be close enough to differentiate between a 93" blade and a 111" blade (which is what I'm always looking for in my shop). This has also helped me when I'm buying blades – a couple of times, I've been sold the wrong length blade.

Frank Gibbons
Victoria, British Columbia

"Every great mistake has a halfway moment, a split second when it can be recalled and perhaps remedied."
— Pearl S. Buck (1892 - 1973)
author, won Pulitzer and Nobel prizes

Avoid Splinters With Strategically Placed Tape

Whenever I do a lot of ripping on the table saw, jointing on the jointer or running moulding on the router table I used to get cuts and slivers in the finger that I used to guide the wood through the machine (my left index finger). This also could happen when I used my fingers as edge guides with my hand tools. Then I would go and get some tape and tape up the wound. Now I have learned to put masking tape on the finger before I do the operation. I then remove the tape when I am finished. I also don't get blood on the wood this way. (I do not like to wear gloves while running equipment, I consider it unsafe.)

Michael E. Siemsen
Chisago City, Minnesota

Spark-plug Gauge is an All-purpose Screwdriver

Ever need to loosen the screw for your plane iron's chipbreaker, but can't find a screwdriver? Or worse yet, ever have your screwdriver slip and catch your hand on those "locked-up" screws?

A simple (and small) solution is to keep a couple of inexpensive spark plug gap gauges handy in your apron or on your bench. They are tiny, yet they will replace almost any flat-head screwdriver because of the graduated thickness of the rim of the gauge. They can even substitute as a feeler gauge in some instances. At only 99 cents each at most auto-supply stores, you can afford to keep a few on hand.

Benjamin Shaw
Long Beach, California

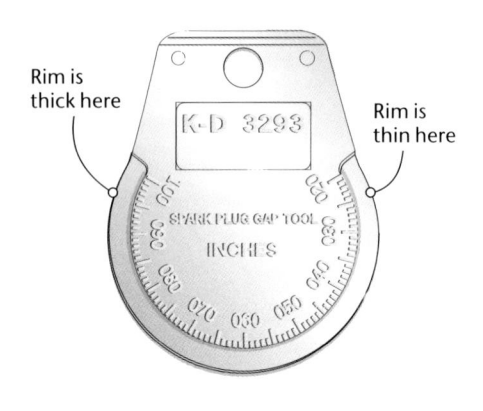

Rim is thick here

Rim is thin here

How to Add 200 Pounds (or so) To Your Workbench

We've all dealt with the problem of keeping our workbenches stationary and stable. We've ignored the most available solution – our body weight.

Turn your bench on its side and nail a scrap sheet of plywood to the bottom of the legs with the extra board out in front of the bench. Right the bench, stand on the plywood whilst planing or sawing and you will notice a marked increase in your bench's stability. Have a big dinner for a really big increase!

If you know which part of the bench you use most, orient the plywood to stick out where you would stand on it for best results.

Walter Lees
Phoenix, Arizona

Use the Table Saw for Handplaning

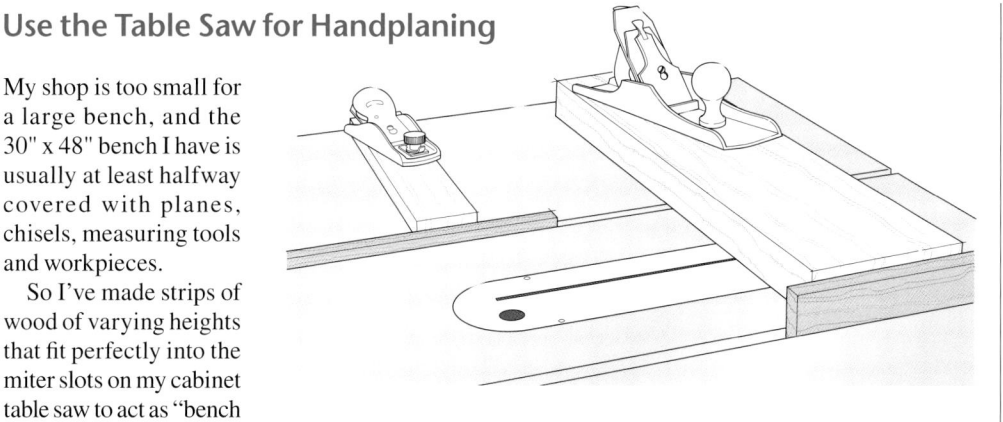

My shop is too small for a large bench, and the 30" x 48" bench I have is usually at least halfway covered with planes, chisels, measuring tools and workpieces.

So I've made strips of wood of varying heights that fit perfectly into the miter slots on my cabinet table saw to act as "bench hooks" or "bench dogs." The varying heights work with different thicknesses, while the choice of miter slot works with different lengths. The table saw itself is perfectly flat. And because it is (for me) the perfect height for handplaning, it works perfectly.

Jack Camillo
Sykesville, Maryland

Toothbrush Makes for Quick Corner Cleanups

When gluing up a carcase, some woodworkers clean up the glue when it's wet and some do it when it's semi-hard or dry. This is a trick for those of us who clean when the glue is wet. Use an old toothbrush to get into the tricky inside corners of a carcase. I perform this operation with a small bowl of water and a rag. I dip the toothbrush in the water, scrub away the offending glue and wipe the excess water away with a rag.

The scrubbing action of the toothbrush bristles ensures you won't leave any dried glue in the sharp corners, which would interfere with staining and finishing.

Kelly Mehler
Berea, Kentucky

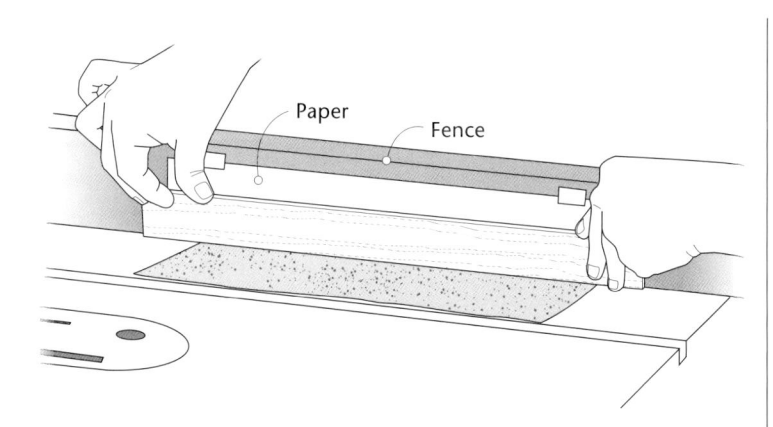

Perfectly Sanded Thin Edges

To sand thin edges perfectly square, slip a piece of sandpaper under the fence of your table saw then sand the edge while running the wood along the fence. Also, so that your wood doesn't get mucked up, affix a piece of paper to the fence.

John Short
St. John's, Newfoundland

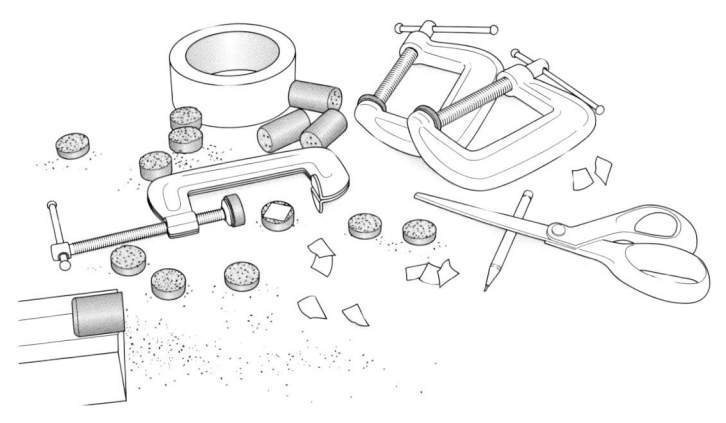

Bottoms-up for Better Clamping

I have saved a lot of time and aggravation by taking a handful of wine bottle corks, cutting them into $1/4$"-thick disks and sticking them to the faces of my C-clamps with double-sided tape. This is a big time saver because I don't have to look for scraps of $1/4$" stock, which is what I previously used to pad the faces of my clamps. Also, I save some aggravation by no longer having to hold the clamp, the project and two clamp pads while I tighten the clamp.

David Leard
Mobile, Alabama

More Tape Tricks: Use it to Make Accurate Crosscuts

If I'm cutting two boards to identical length, I tape them together first around all the edges to ensure they don't slide around. I also tape over the cutline, which minimizes splintering at the back of the cut (this is particularly helpful for cuts on a table saw). If I want to plane an edge, I plane them together. The broader edge is more stable, and there is less variation during the cut. Matching curves on a band saw? Good to go. Once the cut is made, the three taped sides hold everything stable while I sand or plane the curves fair. The tape can also help keep the wood from getting dinged up on the corners.

The nice thing about the tape is that it won't ever hurt your blades. After a cut, if the workpieces have any residue left on them, standard cleaner will take it off (it's much easier to deal with than pitch). The only problem I've ever had was if I left the tape on for a number of days on a softer- and shorter-grained wood, such as mahogany, which tends to lose a few fibers if you're not careful. But I'll trade that for mismatched cuts, different lengths or tear-out any day. WM

Mark Rasmussen
Princeton, New Jersey

SEND US YOUR SHORTCUT

We will provide a complimentary one-year subscription (or extend your current subscription) for each Shortcut we print. Send your Shortcut via e-mail to shortcuts@fwpubs.com, or by post to *Woodworking Magazine*, Shortcuts, 4700 E. Galbraith Road, Cincinnati, OH 45236. Please include your complete mailing address and daytime phone number. All Shortcuts become property of *Woodworking Magazine*.

Make Clean Through-mortises

Woodworkers expect this joint to be tidy and tight, not ragged and gappy. We explore the best ways to make this sometimes-vexing hole.

The history of the through-mortise begins with a joint that was necessary because of the tools and technology of the day, and it ends with a joint that flaunts the skills of the modern woodworker like a prize chicken at a county fair.

A through-mortise – which is where the joint passes entirely through a leg or stile – is rarely structurally necessary in modern furniture thanks to high-strength glues and machine-cut joinery surfaces that maximize the amount of wood-to-wood contact.

But they are sometimes necessary for other reasons: They are a hallmark of certain furniture styles, including some early American and European pieces, Arts & Crafts furniture and stick chairs, such as Windsors and Welsh chairs.

And in contemporary work, through-mortises are often used as the calling card for a handmade piece of furniture. Few furniture factories go to the trouble of making this joint, so individual makers use it to differentiate their work from the fiberboard garbage that clogs our stores, homes and landfills.

The reason the through-mortise is a poster child for handmade furniture is that it is a challenge to make well – much like the dovetail joint. People's eyes are drawn to expressed joints like this, and small gaps make big impressions.

I've spent years investigating various techniques for making this joint tidy and show-worthy. The following story is the result of my trials and occasional revelations.

Real-world Through-mortises

Through-mortises appear in the earliest extant furniture. Egyptian beds and stools typically used the through-mortise to join their legs and rails. Exactly why this joint was employed isn't known, but we can guess. With a lack of reliable glues, a through-mortise joint allows lots of wood-to-wood contact – friction if you will – that will keep the joint together. Sometimes these joints were even lashed together, and the tenon passing through the mortise allowed this.

As furniture evolved through the 18th and 19th centuries, it became much more the norm to obscure joinery rather than show it off. Furniture craftsmen avoided the problem of unreliable glues by cutting a blind mortise (which is open only on one end) and then driving a peg through the finished mortise and tenon to mechanically lock the pieces.

The torn grain, gaps and general loose fit around these through-mortises are unacceptable to the modern woodworker – though these defects were once common. This is an Arts & Crafts bookcase that once graced a church library in Lexington, Ky.

"Only the mediocre are always at their best."
— Jean Giraudoux (1882 – 1944)
French diplomat, dramatist and novelist

However, in the world of the workers who fitted out houses with doors and window sash, the through-mortise remained a staple of the trade. When joining the rails and stiles of windows and doors, through-mortises are typical even in houses built at the dawn of the 20th century.

The reason for that is two-fold. Doors and windows are made up of heavier pieces that need to take more abuse than a piece of fine furniture. Plus, a through-mortise has other advantages. It can be cut using fewer jobsite tools (a chisel and a mallet is all that is needed) and you don't have to take the time to clean the bottom of the mortise. It can be assembled and wedged with fewer clamps – you can put one clamp on the joint, wedge it from the outside and immediately remove the clamp. And things can be more easily dismantled for repair – dig out the wedges and pull the joint apart.

And because the result was usually hidden by paint or by its location on the edges of doors or in a window casing, the joint didn't have to look perfect. It just had to hold things together.

That's how things stood until the furniture factories came along. Some of the earliest factory machinery was designed to cut mortises and tenons. But in an effort to make less-expensive furniture for the masses, factories began using less-reliable joints – such as dowels – that could be made quickly and cheaply with precision machinery.

From the outside of the furniture, the results looked the same. A blind tenon and a doweled joint are indistinguishable from the exterior of a piece. And I've even seen doweled pieces that have a fake exterior peg, which implies there is a tenon in there instead of two skimpy bits of dowel.

Some furniture consumers were unhappy with this mass-produced flimsy furniture coming out of the factories. And from this discontent rose the Arts & Crafts movement. At its best, the Arts & Crafts movement celebrated stout joinery. High-quality pieces used through-mortises as a way to show the consumer how the joint was made. (Let's ignore, for a moment, the Arts & Crafts shysters that would nail on a fake through-tenon to fool the customer.)

These visible joints were put in visible places – on the tops of chair arms, on the fronts and ends of casework pieces, on legs. However, making these visible joints must have proved to be a challenge. They appear on only the best pieces. And they don't always look tidy (especially the ones that are close to the floor).

And then the through-mortise began to disappear again from furniture as the popular styles began to change to favor surface ornamentation to structural honesty.

Today the through-mortise joint is used when you are reproducing certain furniture styles or are attempting to display your craftsmanship. No matter why you make this joint, the standards for what is acceptable have changed. Gaps between a through-mortise and its tenon aren't acceptable in good work.

Two Kinds of Through-mortises

So the imperative is to make this joint look perfect, and the tolerances are tough to hit. Where do you begin? First, it's helpful to know there are two kinds of through-mortises, each of which requires a different strategy.

The first kind of through-mortise has an opening that is skinny and long – for example, $1/4$" wide x 3" long. This is the kind of through-mortise you would see when you join a side rail on a Morris chair with the chair's front leg. It also is common to see this mortise where a shelf intersects the side of the carcase.

The other kind of through-mortise is simply larger – it can be either rectangular or square. This is the kind of through-mortise you would see when you join a chair leg to an arm.

This through-mortise on the lower leg of a Gustav Stickley rocker would not pass modern muster. The ends of the mortise were left round and the tenon was square. On other joints in this chair you can see tearing left from the boring machine.

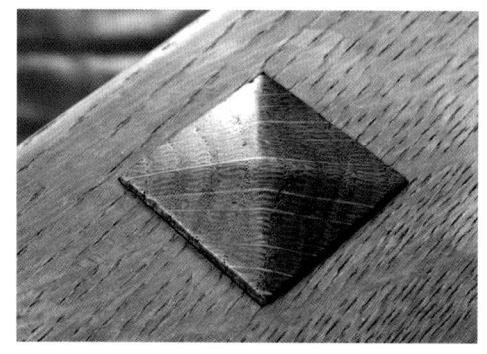

This through-tenon on an arm of a Charles Stickley side chair shows what good work looks like in a highly visible area. The joint isn't airtight, but it's quite good considering the 100 years that have passed since its making.

On the show side of a mortise, the edges must be crisp and not rounded over by the tool. Make lots of light cuts, then sweep the first bits of waste away using your chisel's edge flat on your work.

Let's walk through some of the techniques for cutting each of these.

Skinny and Long: Use Square Tooling

For any through-mortise, you can use a mortise chisel and a mallet. And if I have four or fewer to do, that is typically how I'll proceed. You lay out the mortise opening on both sides of the joint and then begin the banging. When I make my layout marks, I score them as deeply as possible on the face of the joint that will be visible. Deep score lines help you remove waste cleanly.

This is particularly important if the long axis of the mortise runs across the grain (like it does in the bookshelf in this issue). When you chisel out a mortise across the grain, it has a tendency to tear out around the joint, particularly in woods such as oak and ash.

Begin chopping out the side that will be obscured. Working from this side first allows you to get your chisel skills warmed up. If the chisel is cutting true, I'll drive down beyond the halfway point. Though removing waste is more difficult in deep cavities, it's more important to get the two ends of the mortise to meet. So don't stop if things are going well.

Then flip the work and make a light cut on the face that will be visible. Some people will chop up the surface of the mortise with tight cuts then sweep the waste off the top of the mortise using the shaft of the chisel.

Once the initial opening is cut, you can drive more deeply. Just be certain not to lever the chisel against the ends of the mortise when prying out the waste. This pry-bar action rounds over the rim of the exit wound.

If you are not going to cut the through-mortise by hand, two other common options are to use a hollow-chisel mortiser or a plunge router with a straight bit and an edge guide.

I almost always choose the hollow-chisel mortiser. Here's why: The router method is slow. Through-mortises that are shaped this way (long and skinny) are typically in thick material – 3" thick is not uncommon. That can be a lot to ask of a $1/4$"-diameter router bit. In fact, I've snapped off quite a few in deep cuts. If you go the router route, take little bites. It slows you down, but it's easier on the tooling.

You also have to square up the ends of these router cuts (unless you want to make an authentic and gappy Gustav Stickley-style joint). This is a lot to ask of a hand-held chisel in thick material.

You have to take care and take smaller bites so your tool doesn't go astray.

The hollow-chisel mortiser is fast and can make a clean cut if you set up the machine with care. Let's begin there. You need sharp tooling. File the cutter of the auger-bit part of the tooling and stone the inside and outside of the hollow chisel. For complete details on choosing the right bit and sharpening it, read our story on hollow-chisel tooling in the Spring 2007 issue.

You need to have your hollow chisel set dead parallel to the machine's fence. You can get there by trial-and-error. But here's how to make it there with less error. Lay out a sample mortise on some test scrap. Bring the hollow chisel close to your layout lines. Now press a 6"-long ruler against the hollow chisel and compare it to your layout line. The ruler will exaggerate any twist in the chisel and allow you to fine-tune it in the bushing of your hollow-chisel mortiser.

Now make a sample mortise to confirm that you are cutting where you want to cut and that the chisel is parallel to the fence. Now get ready to prepare your live stock. Normally, most instructions assume that your project parts are square. When making through-mortises, your parts have to be as square as possible. Double-check each part after you square it up and before you make your mortises. Small errors make joints that won't go together. I've found that it pays to have the part's jointed face against the mortiser's fence.

To bore the mortise, first work halfway through on one side. Then flip the work over and do the same thing on the other. If the machine is set up well, this work is extremely fast and clean.

In router-cut mortises like this, the corners are tough to square up without botching them. You can score your layout lines with deep knife cuts, which helps. Ultimately, if you take this path you are going to have to get good with a chisel.

Press and hold a ruler to a flat face of your hollow chisel. Compare the ruler to your layout lines to see if the chisel is twisted. This trick is remarkably accurate.

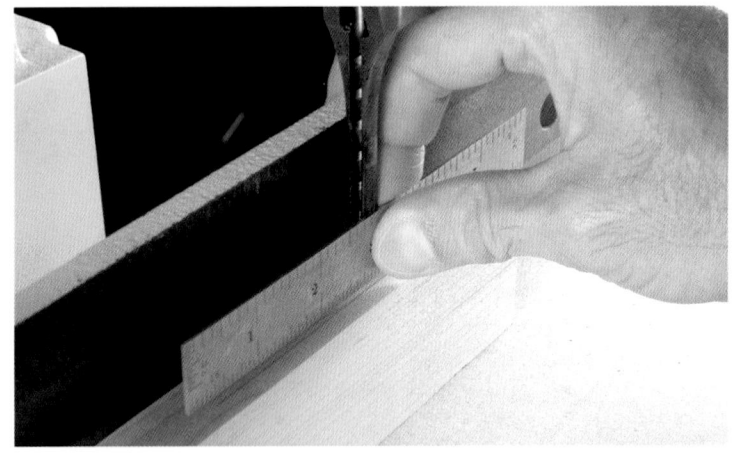

I'm in the habit of using the leap-frog method of mortising. Skip a space with every hole, then clean up between the holes. Other craftsmen I respect say the holes should overlap slightly to improve chisel cutting. Try both and decide.

Here you can see the result of accurate machine setup and careful layout. The mortise goes clear through, and the rim of the mortise is crisp enough for close inspection.

Bigger Joints Require Different Tools

The rules change when the through-mortises get bigger. Once your joints are wider than ½", then hollow-chisel mortisers become difficult to use. When your mortises are wider than ½", you have to shift your work both left-to-right and back-to-front to clean out the mortise. That's not always a simple thing to do with accuracy. And you really need an X-and-Y sliding table. (Side note: I'm aware there are bigger bits available for hollow-chisel mortisers, but they don't work on the common benchtop machines.)

Here's the other thing that changes: Usually with larger through-mortises, you are working on thinner stock, typically ¾"- to ⅞"-thick stuff.

So a new strategy is in order: router templates. Because your stock is thinner, the 1"-long straight bits have no problem cutting these joints with ease. Plus, as you'll soon see, the routing template can also be a chiseling template for squaring up the corners.

You can make these router templates to use either a pattern-guided straight bit or a bushing installed in your router's baseplate. The templates for pattern-guided bits are simpler to make (no math), but it's tricky to get your bit's bearing and the thickness of your pattern all playing nice together.

On the other hand, the templates for bushing-guided bits require a little math (addition – plus its tricky friend, subtraction). But you're fooling around a lot less trying to match your bit and the thickness of the material out of which you are making your pattern. So really it's a wash as to which method is faster.

No matter which path you choose, you need to make a pattern out of plywood (or solid wood) that has an opening with perfectly sharp corners. Making that pattern is fairly simple: I saw up bits of plywood (typically ½" in thickness) and reassemble them as a panel that has the right-sized hole for my routing pattern.

Remove as much of the waste as you can with a Forstner bit, then clamp the router template in place. Be sure to secure the template to the outside face of your work. Rout out the rest of the waste but don't remove the template because its job isn't over. You can use its sharp corners to guide your chisel to square up the rounded corners.

This technique yields nice crisp corners on the outside of your work and ragged, torn-out corners on the inside surface (because there was no template to guide your chisel). This isn't a problem as long as the tearing isn't too severe.

Once you get the mortise cut, the tenons are easy. I cut them close on my power equipment, then trim them to a snug fit with a shoulder plane, which also removes the marks left by the power tooling. **WM**

— *Christopher Schwarz*

The pattern-cutting bit (left) seems simpler (just make a pattern that is the correct size), but you have to set things so the bearing rides the pattern and there is enough cutter showing to do the job. Bushing-guided patterns simply require a slightly oversized pattern.

Here you can see how a pattern was assembled for a through-mortise. I use only glue on the edges to join the parts – no biscuits or dowels. With plywood, there's always enough long grain at the edges to make this panel plenty strong.

Take little bites with the chisel. If you try to remove the entire corner in one whack, bad things can happen. The template can shift. Or the chisel will steer itself outside the template – but below the surface of your work.

Gustav Stickley Plant Stand

Does good work have to be flashy? Building a piece that focuses on existing skills can please both you and other woodworkers.

The clock read 3 a.m., but my body was still on East Coast time, so I was wide awake and shuffling around Gary Rogowski's house in Portland, Ore., like an unshaven ghost.

Rogowski is a long-time furniture maker and the owner of the Northwest Woodworking Studio school. And like most woodworkers, his house is filled with his own work. As I fumbled in the dark looking for the stairs, my hands came to rest on a dresser in the hallway.

The oak piece had simple Arts & Crafts lines and pleasing proportions, but it was not the sort of object that shouts for attention from the other side of a room. With time to kill and a curiosity about his work, I scrutinized the dresser the way only a woodworker can.

I pulled out each drawer. I poked around the interior of the carcase. I looked for filler in the dovetails. I examined the surfaces for defects in planing, sanding or finishing. It takes a lot to impress me before my first cup of coffee, but Rogowski's piece did just that.

Though simple in form, the piece was perfect in execution. For me, that dresser served as a reminder of something that I tend to lose sight of as I strive to become a better woodworker. Simply put: Refining your existing skills is as important as acquiring new ones.

So when I returned to Cincinnati, I vowed to build a piece that used basic joints, but that would require complete mastery of them to produce a finished project that could withstand the scrutiny of a fellow woodworker poking around my house in the wee hours.

The Gustav Stickley Plant Stand

For many years I've wanted to build a replica of this Gustav Stickley plant stand. The form doesn't show up in the catalogs I have for Stickley's furniture company, but I have stumbled upon signed examples at auctions and have seen them in a number of books.

Composed of only 16 significant sticks of wood, this plant stand is not flashy like a Morris chair or sideboard. But it is a well-proportioned and thoughtfully engineered piece of furniture.

The goal was to get the details right. Though simple in form, this piece is a challenge to do well. Building it will improve your ability to execute precision joinery and crisp corners.

All of the joinery has to be spot-on for the piece to work.

The version shown here had to be redesigned a tad for a practical reason. The green tile top in the original was an odd size (10" x 10") that you are unlikely to find at a store. So if I'd slavishly followed Stickley, you would be stuck cutting down a larger tile or commissioning a ceramic artist to make you one.

With a little work on the computer, I resized the project to accept a common floor tile from a home center (price $1.46) and it changed the overall dimensions of the piece by only 1".

So the first step in building this plant stand is to shop for a tile. The so-called 12" x 12" floor tiles at the home center were slightly smaller than 11 3/4" x 11 3/4". So I scaled all my parts around those dimensions. My tile doesn't match the beguiling green of the Grueby-made tile in the original, but I came close. As you shop for tile, check out the natural slate tiles, which vary in color. I found a few slate tiles that were a better historical match. When I returned to the bin the next day to buy them, they were gone.

Perfection Begins With Selection

When you build a simple and small piece of furniture, the importance of wood selection is magnified. Every stick carries more visual weight. Plus, this project doesn't have a front or back. It has to look good from all angles.

The trickiest part of stock selection is in the legs. Making legs with quartersawn white oak is a challenge because each board has two faces that exhibit quartersawn grain and two faces that exhibit flat-sawn grain. And they look so radically different that it is distracting.

To duck this problem, you can veneer quartersawn oak on the flat-sawn faces (a trick employed by Gustav Stickley on some pieces). You can make each leg out of four pieces of quartersawn material mitered at the corners (a trick employed by Gustav's brothers Leopold and John). Or you can do what I did: Don't use quartersawn oak for the legs.

I used rift-sawn (sometimes called bastard-sawn) white oak for my legs. Technically, a board has been rift-sawn when its annular rings intersect the face of the board at an angle that's somewhere between 30° and 60°. With quartersawn boards the angle is higher than 60°. With plainsawn boards, that angle is lower than 30°.

The beauty of rift-sawn boards is that their faces and edges look similar, especially if you select boards that have the annular rings at 45° to the face. As a result, a rift-sawn leg will usually look the same no matter where you are in the room.

A Tangle of Tenons

Another challenge with this project is making all the mortise-and-tenon joints come together. While all the stretchers and aprons join their legs with a simple mortise-and-tenon joint, the first complication is that the tenons intersect one another at the corners inside the legs. Plus, the four wide aprons aren't centered on the legs. Instead, they're pushed to the inside a bit to nestle closer to the tile top.

As a result, the tenons on the top stretchers are 1" long and are mitered to meet at the corners. The stretchers on the aprons can only be 3/4" long and these are also mitered to meet at the corners. This means you have to lay out the locations of your tenon shoulders with great care. All the stretchers and aprons need to measure exactly 11 3/4" from shoulder to shoulder. And then you add a third tricky part to the project's joinery: A through-tenon that pierces the lower stretcher and is secured with a tusk.

We'll tend to that through-tenon later. First cut the 1/4"-thick tenons on all the aprons and stretchers – by hand or by power – then prepare to use those tenons to lay out the locations of your mortises in the legs.

With the tenons cut, you can use those joints to lay out the location of mortises on your legs as shown in the photo above. This method requires less measuring and therefore offers less opportunity for error.

Mismatched Mortises

The mortises for the top stretchers and the lower stretchers are centered on the legs. So set up your hollow-chisel mortiser (or your mortising gauge) to poke a 1/4"-wide x 1 1/8"-deep mortise in the legs. Then make all those mortises.

Note that getting mortises that are dead-center on a leg is a challenge for many machines and

---

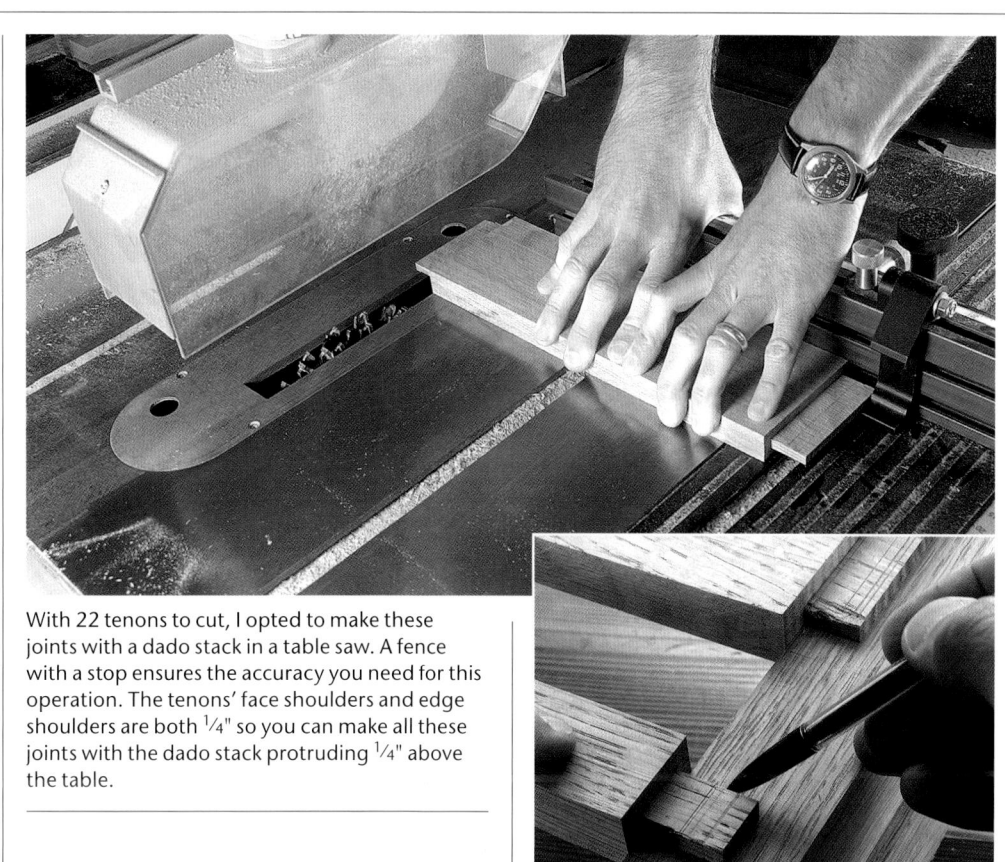

With 22 tenons to cut, I opted to make these joints with a dado stack in a table saw. A fence with a stop ensures the accuracy you need for this operation. The tenons' face shoulders and edge shoulders are both 1/4" so you can make all these joints with the dado stack protruding 1/4" above the table.

I mark out the location of my mortises by using my tenons like a ruler. Note that you can see here how the top stretcher has a longer tenon than the apron does.

Here are my four legs for the plant stand. Except for the leg at top right, they are rift-sawn. I got lucky with the leg at top right. Even though it is quartersawn on two faces and flat-sawn on the other two, its grain pattern is consistent all around. Trees are weird that way sometimes.

woodworking-magazine.com ■ 11

Here I'm making the mortises for the aprons, which are located ½" in from the inside edge of each leg. Each of the apron mortises measures ¼" wide, 3¾" long and ⅞" deep.

Gustav Stickley Plant Stand

	NO.	PART	T	W	L	MATERIAL	NOTES
☐	4	Legs	1⅝	1⅝	26	Oak	
☐	4	Top stretchers	¾	1¼	13¾	Oak	1" TBE
☐	4	Aprons	¾	4¼	13¼	Oak	¾" TBE
☐	2	Lower stretchers	¾	3½	13¾	Oak	1" TBE
☐	1	Cross stretcher	1¼	1⅝	17⅛	Oak	
☐	2	Tusks	⅝	⅞	2½	Oak	Start with 7" long
☐	4	Top strips	¼	¾	11¾	Oak	
☐	1	Panel	¾	12¼	12¼	Oak	Notched at corners
☐	2	Bottom cleats	¾	¾	11¾	Oak	

TBE = Tenon both ends

their operators. To side-step the problem, get the machine set as best you can. As you work, ensure that you always work with an inside face of the leg against the mortiser's fence. This ensures that even though the mortise might not be centered, all the mortises will match up on all four legs.

Then you'll need to adjust your machine (or layout tools) to cut the mortises for the four aprons. These aprons are set ¼" in from the inside corner of each leg, so the mortises for the aprons should be located ½" in from each inside corner. These mortises don't need to be as deep either – ⅞" deep will be enough to house the tenon and allow for a little gunk and glue at the bottom.

The mortises for the top stretchers and aprons intersect, which means you'll likely get some splintering on the inside corner where they meet. There's little you can do to prevent it (mortising is quite violent). If it's a minor split, you can pull the splinter out and ignore it. With oak, sometimes it splits badly and I'll glue the splinter back in and secure it with tape as the glue dries.

More Mortises Yet

The lower stretchers each get a highly visible through-mortise, which will house the through-tenons and tusks. I've experimented a lot with different methods to get clean through-mortises (see "Make Clean Through-mortises" on page 6 of this issue). For mortises that are nearly square, the best technique I have found is to first make a plywood pattern and rout them out. Then you come back and use the same pattern to chisel the corners square.

Yes, it seems like a lot of trouble. But this is a visible joint and worth the effort. I make my plywood patterns by sawing up scraps of plywood and assembling them into a panel that has a hole shaped like the mortise I want.

With your pattern assembled, use it to lay out the location of the ¾" x 1⅛" mortise and trace its shape onto the lower stretcher. Waste away as much of the mortise as you can using a Forstner bit (Forstner bits allow you to overlap your holes).

Then clamp the plywood pattern to your workpiece and install a pattern-cutting bit into your router. Cut around the mortise (go clockwise) until you have wasted away everything the pattern-cutting bit can get. Don't remove the pattern from your work.

Here are the four pieces of ½"-thick plywood that I have sawn up and will glue back together into a panel. Note that I don't use biscuits or dowels to join these pieces, just glue. The edge grain of the plywood is strong enough for this light-duty application.

When you glue up the pattern, wrangle the pieces as best you can so that they line up at the seams. Mismatched seams will end up as bumps that your router will have to travel over – spoiling your accuracy.

Apron Profile

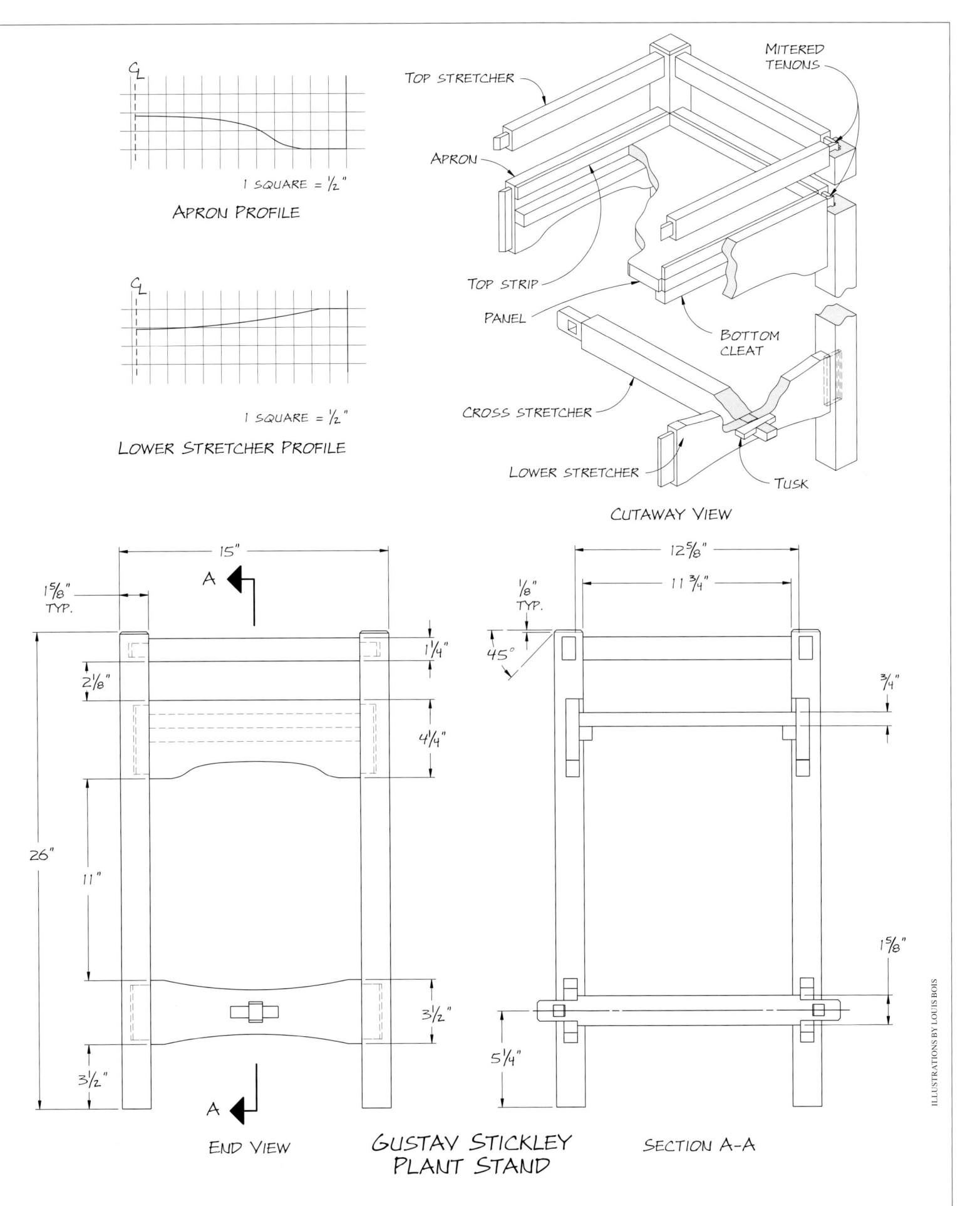

1 square = ½"

Lower Stretcher Profile

1 square = ½"

Cutaway View

- Mitered tenons
- Top stretcher
- Apron
- Top strip
- Panel
- Bottom cleat
- Cross stretcher
- Lower stretcher
- Tusk

End View

- 15"
- 1⅝" TYP.
- 1¼"
- 2⅛"
- 4¼"
- 26"
- 11"
- 3½"
- 3½"

Section A-A

- 12⅝"
- 11¾"
- ⅛" TYP.
- 45°
- ¾"
- 1⅝"
- 5¼"

Gustav Stickley Plant Stand

I used a ⅝" Forstner bit to waste away most of the mortise in the lower stretchers. You could use a smaller bit and a handheld drill as well. That just makes more work for the router.

Clamp the pattern on your work and cantilever things off your bench (you don't want to mortise your benchtop). Then use the pattern-cutting bit to hog out the waste that the Forstner bit couldn't get.

Use the plywood pattern as a chiseling guide to clean out the corners. Shown is a ⅜" corner chisel, though a garden-variety bench chisel will work just as well. It will just take twice the number of whacks.

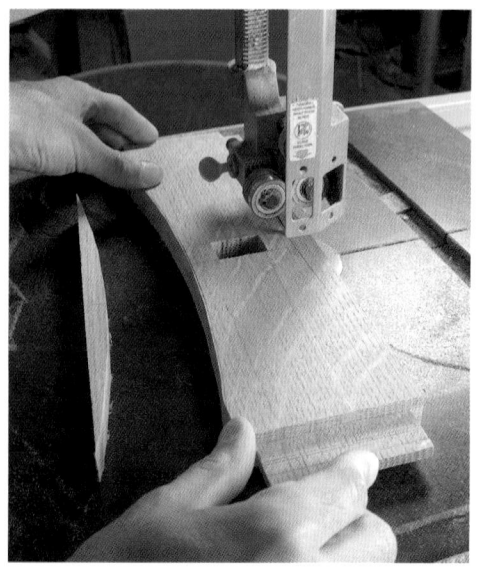

When you band saw a curve, the temptation is to leave a lot of waste behind so you don't accidentally cross the line. I try to saw right next to the line. I get smoother curves and have less waste to remove with a rasp or router in the end.

I actually do the bulk of my routing with a laminate trimmer. This small tool has more than enough power for most work-a-day tasks, plus the smaller footprint makes clamping setups such as this a breeze. A full-size router would run into my bench's hold-downs.

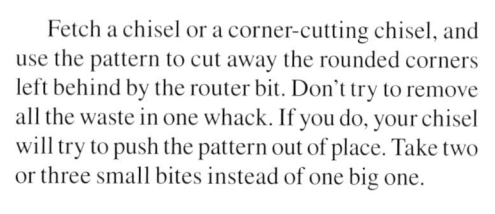

Fetch a chisel or a corner-cutting chisel, and use the pattern to cut away the rounded corners left behind by the router bit. Don't try to remove all the waste in one whack. If you do, your chisel will try to push the pattern out of place. Take two or three small bites instead of one big one.

Precision Curves

An Arts & Crafts piece with eight curved edges is a bit unusual, but it is these curves that really set apart this design from similar plant-stand designs that competitors built and sold during this era. The curves on the lower stretcher are simply a segment of a 24"-radius circle. The ogee-shaped edge on the aprons is a somewhat more complex piece of work.

When confronted with a curve or two, I'll band saw out the bulk of the waste and shape the curve with a rasp. But because each of these patterns is repeated four times on the piece, I thought it best to produce a plywood routing pattern then clean up the edges by hand.

I made one plywood pattern for both shapes: One edge had the simple curve; the other edge had the ogee shape. I scribed the 24"-radius curve with a set of trammel points. To make the ogee edge, I first scaled up photographs of original plant stands to full size and created the pattern from those – I wanted this unusual curve to be just right. You can use the scale drawings to make your plywood patterns. Then I used these patterns to lay out the curves on the aprons and lower stretchers.

Saw out the bulk of the waste, then use your plywood pattern to clean up the edge with the help of a router and a pattern-cutting router bit. Then clean up your edges with a scraper and sandpaper – the surface left behind by a router bit isn't good enough to finish.

After routing, I scuff each edge with #120-grit sandpaper. This makes it easy to see my progress with a card scraper. When all the fuzzy grain from the sandpaper is gone, the edge is clean and ready to finish.

When you miter the ends of tenons, it's unlikely you'll get them to mate at the center of the joint. That would be asking a lot (but if it happens, great). Instead, miter them so that they barely miss one another. That ensures your tenons will seat completely in their mortises.

Cleanup and Test Assembly

At long last it was time to break out the handplanes – the fun part. After cleaning up all the flat surfaces with a jointer plane and a smoothing plane,

With the plant stand clamped up, mark on the top edge of the lower stretchers where the cross stretcher will be located. Then lay the cross stretcher on those marks. Use a ruler to then measure the distance between the two lower stretchers.

If you cut the tenons on your cross stretcher with a router, you'll need to set up a fence with a stop. Honestly, I did this setup to see how much of a pain it was. By the time I started adding the fence to the miter gauge, I would have been done if I'd just cut these by hand.

The hole for the tusk is offset a bit so that part of the mortise will be inside the lower stretcher. This is a critical point for a snug-fitting tusk.

Take small bites when cleaning out the rounded corners of the mortise for your tusk. Begin with the corners that will be buried in the lower stretcher – if you botch these they will never show.

I hand-fit all the joints then mitered the corners of the aprons and top stretchers.

Now you can assemble the project without glue to determine the size of the cross stretcher that is wedged between the two lower stretchers. Clamp up the entire plant stand and determine the exact distance between the two lower stretchers – that will be the distance between the shoulders of your cross stretcher.

Now you can mark out the ¾" x 1⅛" tenons on the ends of the cross stretcher. The tenons should be 2¼" long, but you should confirm this with your dry-assembled piece. Now consider how you will cut these tenons. Using a dado stack will leave a surface that will require a lot of cleanup. I think you'll get cleaner results using a router or cutting them by hand.

That Touchy Tusk

If your tusks are designed properly, then installing them in the tenons is a simple operation. Most tusk troubles occur when the tenon is too short to handle the tusk. Then it's tap, tap, crack – and the end of your tenon pops off. That's why the tenons are so long on this project's cross stretcher.

The first step is to bore a ⅝"-diameter hole through the through-tenon. The location of this hole is critical. Knock together the cross stretcher

woodworking-magazine.com ■ **15**

and lower stretchers then trace a line around the through-tenon where it emerges from the lower stretcher.

Now lay out the location of the ⅝" hole so ¹⁄₁₆" of it crosses over this line. This space ensures the joint will tighten up when the tusk is knocked home. Drill the hole and square out the corners with a chisel.

One face of this through-mortise needs to be angled to match the angle on the tusk. I've found a 4° angle to work nicely. To lay out a 4° angle on your mortise, simply scribe a parallel line that is ¹⁄₁₆" away from the edge of the mortise. That will give you the 4°. Then use a bench chisel to chop an angled ramp on this one face of the through-mortise. All the other faces of this mortise are left perpendicular.

Most people struggle with making the tusks. Here's the easy way: Start with a piece of oak that is ⅝" x ⅞" x 7" and cut a 4° taper on the width of the piece. Drive this overlong piece into the through-tenon until everything fits snugly and the tusk is roughly centered on the mortise. Then mark the final length of the tusk and cut it to size with a handsaw.

One Last Detail

One of the hallmarks of Arts & Crafts furniture is a small chamfer on the ends of legs, tenons and posts. I've always judged other people's work by these chamfers because they can be done quite poorly (got a belt sander?). Even when it looks like the maker wanted to take extra care, the grain can be easily torn out or splintered at the corners.

Once again, this is an area where I've experimented a lot with both hand and power techniques. And though I'll never give up my chamfer plane for long-grain chamfers, making them on end grain is a task best handled by a disc sander. (See the story "Improving Small Chamfers" on page 18 in this issue for more information.)

Assemble in the Right Order

I like to break all the long edges of my work right before assembly. It's easier to reach all the long edges with the sandpaper, and it prevents you from having sharp edges in tight corners where your sandpaper wouldn't go. Plus, it's just as fast as doing it after assembly.

Glue up the two ends of the plant stand that have lower stretchers. Paint the inside of the mortises with glue and clamp things so the open mortises face the ceiling to prevent excess glue from running everywhere.

Once the glue is dry in the end assemblies, paint glue on all the blind mortises, slip the cross stretcher in place and clamp up the remaining top stretchers and aprons. Now you can turn your attention to getting the tile in its proper place.

"The perfection of a clock is not to go fast, but to be accurate."
— Luc de Clapiers, marquis de Vauvenargues (1715 - 1747), moralist and essayist

A Raised-panel Tile?

The tile rests on a panel of secondary wood that is sandwiched between strips of wood that are fastened to the inside of the aprons. The strips of wood create a groove that the panel floats in.

Four of these strips are visible. These ¼" x ¾" x 11¾" strips rim the top of the aprons and fill in the space between the legs and aprons. Fit these strips between the legs and secure them with glue, pins and clamps.

When the glue dries, flip the plant stand on its head and fit the panel in place. You'll need to notch out its corners and allow a little expansion gap (unless you use plywood for this piece), but

Use a sliding bevel gauge set 4° off vertical to help guide your eye as you chisel out the mortise. The goal is to remove a wedge of material that is ¹⁄₁₆" thick at the top that tapers to nothing at the bottom of the mortise.

Plane down the over-long tusk until it fits snug in the through-mortise. The advantage to using a plane is that you remove a predictable amount of material with each pass – and the tusk is ready for finishing when you are done.

I wouldn't dream of cutting the tusk to length with power equipment. It's too dangerous. A backsaw and a bench hook make short work of the task.

that is easily handled by a backsaw and block plane. When the panel fits, secure it against the top strips and nail in two ¾" x ¾" x 11¾" cleats below. The cleats should properly cross the width of the panel.

Lay out your chamfers by lightly scoring the ends of your legs using a cutting gauge set to ⅛". Don't make this mark too deep or it could be visible on your completed work.

Set a miter gauge to 45° and use that to guide the leg gently to the spinning disc of the disc sander. (I have one of these sanding discs as an accessory for my table saw. It works great.) When your chamfer reaches your scribed line, back the leg away from the disc.

For the finish, I used the formula developed for the Spring 2007 issue ("Authentic Arts & Crafts Finish"). The recipe is as follows: Stain the bare wood with Olympic Interior "Special Walnut" oil-based stain. Let the wood soak for 15 minutes under the stain then wipe off the excess.

The next day, apply Watco's "Dark Walnut" Danish oil with a rag. Let it soak for 15 minutes then wipe off the excess. On the third day, apply one coat of Zinsser's Bulls Eye amber shellac. Shellac gets quite glossy, so you can add a coat of paste wax to reduce the sheen. Or you can apply a satin wiping varnish, which will give you extra protection (this project will see some water) and also reduce the sheen.

Attaching the tile is the easy part. I used a bead of tile adhesive. Draw the adhesive onto the wooden panel then press the tile into place. Take care not to use too much adhesive because it can easily squirt out from below the tile and make a mess of things on your finished project. Allow it to sit overnight. If you expect the plant stand to see lots of overflow, consider grouting around the edge of the tile as well.

This project will not end up in my home (we seem to kill all forms of foliage), but it will have my name on it. So if there are ever jetlagged woodworkers poring over this project, they'll know who got the details of this piece just right. **WM**

— *Christopher Schwarz*

After you clamp up the ends of the plant stand, inspect the open mortises. It's possible that excess glue ran all over the open mortise. If it dries there, it could interfere with your final assembly. Tease it out (I use a coffee stirring stick).

Take care when installing the strips at the top of the aprons. You want the strips and the apron flush, and you don't want unnecessary glue squeeze-out. Cleaning up this seam is tough thanks to the top stretcher.

Nail, but don't glue, the cleats in below the panel. If the tile ever breaks it will be easier to repair if you can pry off the cleats, remove the panel and replace the tile.

Improving Small Chamfers

While the definition for this edge treatment is short and simple, the methods used to create end-grain chamfers are many and varied.

Sharp corners and edges on a project present a problem. A sharp edge is less likely to hold stain, it can catch your clothing as you walk by and it will undoubtedly be the first area that shows wear. This is why you should always "break" the edges of your work before moving on to the finishing stages.

Break the edges with sandpaper and you simply create a minute roundover profile. However, a more prominent edge treatment, and the method used on the tops of the legs on the "Gustav Stickley Plant Stand" (see page 10 in this issue), is a small chamfer.

A chamfer is a flat surface that connects two faces. Chamfers are generally cut at a 45° angle to those faces, but not always.

How a woodworker creates a chamfer is often a reflection of his or her style of woodworking. If you're a hand-tool aficionado, you're less likely to turn to a router or router table to cut a chamfer. On the other hand, if you are a power-tool builder, I doubt you would grab a chisel to do the work. While a chisel and a router are both valid methods for creating chamfers, rasps or a disc sander are also popular choices.

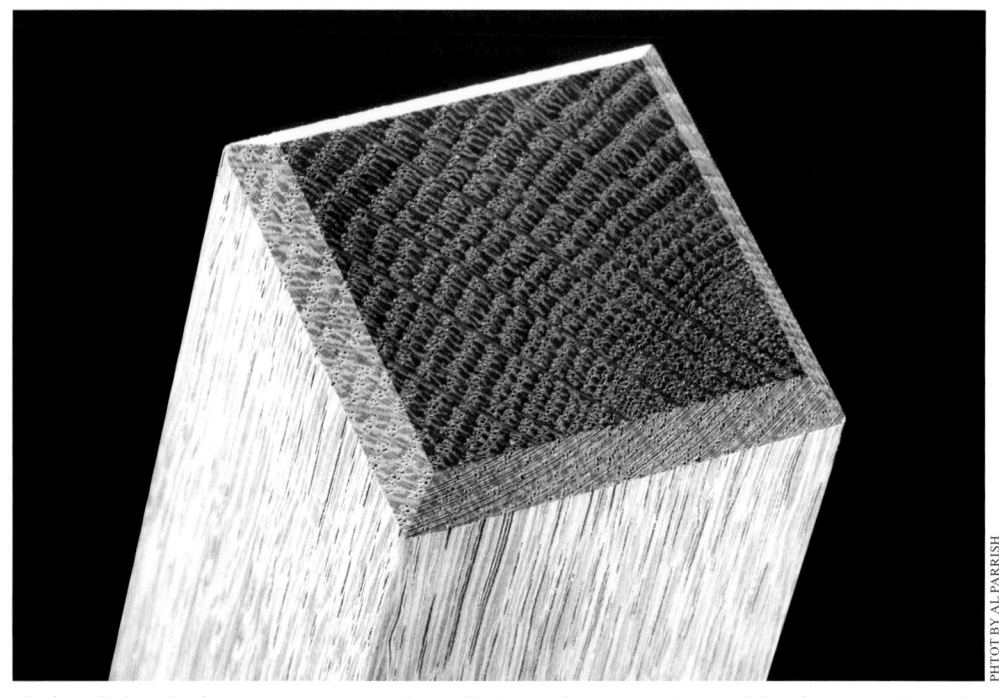

Hand-tool Chamfers

Small chamfers can be cut by hand with a few different tools. If you're a hand-tool devotee, you might immediately think handplane. But for an end-grain chamfer this small, I would pass on attempting it with a plane. There just isn't enough surface area on which the plane's sole can ride and accurately cut.

If you have a well-developed eye and can follow lines on your project, a chisel might be your best solution for small chamfers. Some hand-tool woodworkers turn to a rasp (another option that requires a keen eye). Both of these methods have advantages and disadvantages.

Each method begins with marking layout lines for the chamfered area. The tool of choice is a marking gauge. Set the gauge to the appropriate size, then mark the surfaces to define the chamfers. In the plant-stand article, the marking gauge is set to 1/8". Score the lines lightly around the faces of the leg and again on the top end of each leg. You want enough of a mark to follow, but you don't want it to show in the completed chamfer.

Chamfer by Hand – Chisel

To attempt this technique, the cutting edge of the chisel has to be sharp. A dull tool makes this task all that much harder. The aim is to take small cuts, working in from the corners to the middle.

Trim the waste from the corner toward the

Ideal small chamfers have a consistent profile on all edges – the corners align and the slopes match – and the appearance is "crisp." Discover a better technique to create this simple, classic edge treatment.

How you mark out your chamfer lines depends on the type of work you plan to do. Add lines to the end grain only if you plan to chamfer with hand tools.

Dull tools waste your time and materials. These damaged corners and rough chamfers are the product of a dull router bit.

Slicing chamfers with a chisel requires you to work in from the ends and slightly uphill to create a crest at the center of the cut. Once the ends are at your lines, remove the center to complete the chamfer.

Be patient and diligent as you work the chisel. Gently peel away the waste until the chamfer is flat. Steady hands reduce sanding.

Flake-out at a corner is a result of an inadvertent slip of the hand or improper technique. If this happens, you should start over.

center of the leg and always try to maintain a slight upward slope on the cut. Try to form a molehill, not a mountain, as you work. Once you reach the layout lines at your corners, it's simply a matter of slicing away the center until the chamfer is flat and straight.

Take a good look at this technique and you'll find the "cons" outweigh the "pros" in big way. This technique is good because it's completed with a single tool – although you'll have to sand the chamfer after it's cut, unless you have incredible control with your chisel.

On the downside, not only do your tools have to start sharp, they have to stay sharp throughout the process. Also, different woods influence the work. It's tougher to chamfer oak with a chisel than white pine. And finally, if you do make a cut from edge to edge across the leg, you're all but sure to knock off the trailing corner. Once that's gone, there's no coming back. It's time for a new leg.

Chamfer by Hand – Rasp

Possibly the easiest method for creating small chamfers by hand is to use a rasp. While this too is a one-tool operation, this method requires a certain amount of skill as well.

How a rasp is used is not the issue. That's easy. Grab the handle and start moving the tool back and forth. But if that's all you think about while you work, you're going to create a shape that more resembles a roundover than a chamfer. Achieving a flat surface that terminates at both layout lines takes patience and a bit of self-control.

Use a less-aggressive rasp to cut your chamfer, work diligently across the entire width of your leg and take your time as you work. If you hurry you're liable to remove the tool from the edge during a backstroke. Then, as you re-engage the rasp with the wood, you're likely to dig into the side of the leg causing irreparable damage. (If you use a wide tool, you're less likely to have this happen.)

The trick to get accurate and crisp chamfers with a rasp is to work to both layout lines and remove the majority of the waste area. Then hold the tool at a 45° angle and take the last few strokes to create the desired flat surface. (Due to the coarseness of a rasp, you'll need to finish the chamfer with a very smooth file or sandpaper backed by a wood block.)

Power-tool Chamfers

Turn to power tools and you'll find two easy-to-use techniques for cutting small chamfers: a router table and disc sander. The setup for these techniques is distinctly different, but the outcome with both is quick, accurate and repeatable. And with each, sharp cutting tools (be it a router bit or sandpaper particles) is paramount.

The only method used to cut chamfers where infinite angles are not easily possible is when working at a router table using a chamfer router bit. The choice is limited by the availability of router bits – unless you manipulate the router table surface or have a specially designed carriage built into your router table. In all, I'm aware of five additional angles, over and above the traditional 45° angles, that are possible with standard router bit designs. This method also eliminates the need for layout lines because once the router table is set and the bit positioned, all cuts are created equal.

Install a chamfer bit into your router, then position the bit and fence for the cut. To match the chamfer on the sample leg, raise the bit $1/8$" above the tabletop and position the fence to just capture the bit's bearing.

Because the edges of the leg's top are short, there are two acceptable approaches to make these router cuts – both require the use of a push stick (a proper push block or backer block makes this task safe). The leg can either be vertical when fed over the bit, or it can be laid flat with the end facing the fence.

With leg stock vertical, there is little table support under the leg. A push block is a necessity to accomplish your task.

Stock support increases when the leg is laid flat on the tabletop, but even in this position the operation requires a push block.

Profiles of chamfers made using router bit angles other than 45° differ depending on whether the leg stock is run vertical or flat to the table. Here you can see the different chamfers that were cut with a 30° chamfer bit.

Which approach you select is your decision – except when you're not using a 45°-chamfer angle. At that time you need to decide which approach produces the chamfer angle you're looking for. (See the photo at top right.)

The jury is out on which approach to use if you're working with a 45°-chamfer bit. Regardless of how you position the stock, vertical or laid flat, the resulting chamfers match. Some woodworkers find feeding vertical leg stock over a bit is awkward. Others don't. Try the two approaches to determine which you're most comfortable using.

A chamfer cut at a router table is very crisp (the result of a sharp bit) and is easily repeated on any number of legs. One issue that may arise is machining marks caused by well-worn router bits. These marks tend to be magnified when stained, so check the chamfer and make sure to sand the flat surfaces carefully.

Disc-sander Chamfers

Because the chamfers are small, a disc sander, whether a stationary tool or simply an accessory on your table saw, is a viable option. I would steer you away from this technique if the chamfers are large, long (wider than a sanding disc) or oriented to long grain instead of end grain. But for our project, this method is a good one.

Begin by marking layout lines around the faces of the leg. Next, set a miter gauge at an appropriate angle – here again you have infinite angles available. Position the gauge at the sander so the end of the leg makes contact on the downward cutting portion of the spinning disc.

This technique requires you to do two things at once (similar to rubbing your head while patting your stomach). If you simply move the leg stock against the disc, the chamfer is cut, but the charred-from-burning color is not pleasing. To cut a clean chamfer, push the leg in toward the sanding disc as you move the workpiece across the disc.

Work to your layout lines, then rotate the stock and cut the next chamfer. This is a quick technique and your chamfer is crisp, clean and ready for finish. The downside is that you control the depth of cut. It's easy to overfeed the leg and there is no easy way to set stops.

I'm a power-tool woodworker – so you can guess which methods I like best. Maybe it would be best to combine the repeatable results from a router table with the perfectly sanded outcome from a disc sander to create the ultimate small chamfer. Is that being too particular? **WM**

— *Glen D. Huey*

"I will not give away my hard-earned skills to a machine. It's a bit like robbery with violence, for (machines are) not only intended to diminish my bank balance, but also to steal my power."

— John Brown (1932 - 2008)
Welsh stick chairmaker

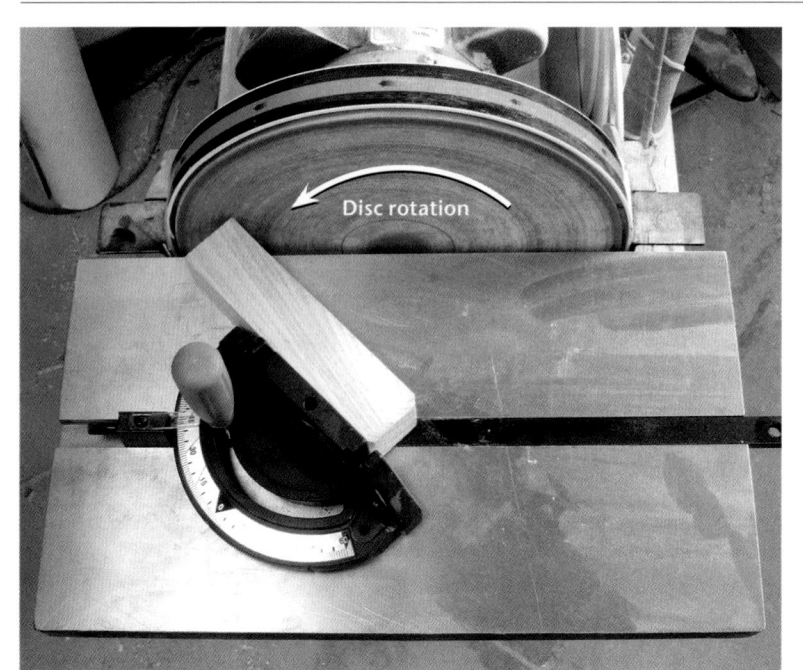

The rotation of your disc sander plays a big part in the setup. It's vital that you introduce the leg stock on the downward portion of the disc. Move across the disc as the chamfer is being cut to reduce burning the surface. A light touch is needed.

Glossary

"The right word may be effective, but no word was ever as effective as a rightly timed pause."
— Mark Twain (1835 - 1910), American author

Woodworking's lexicon can be overwhelming for beginners. The following is a list of terms used in this issue that may be unfamiliar to you.

boiled linseed oil (n)
Linseed oil is a traditional finish and shop lubricant (it was used to grease the soles of handplanes). Extracted from the flax plant, raw linseed oil will take weeks or months to dry when it comes in contact with oxygen. Historically, linseed oil was heated to help it accept a lead drier to make it dry faster. Today, linseed oil is treated with modern driers, yet it is still labeled as "boiled linseed oil." As a finish, boiled linseed oil is simple to apply, but it offers little protection and must be renewed regularly or the project will look dull and lifeless.

build up (v) or buildup (n)
When adding a film finish to a project, several layers are required for the film to protect the wood and look acceptable. In finishing parlance, it is said that you need to "build up" a finish. The expression is also used as a noun to convey that you have added too many layers of finish: "You have too much buildup and your finish looks like plastic."

expressed joint (n)
Where the structural details of a joint are allowed to show in finished work. Typical expressed joints include through-dovetails and through-tenons. In much high-style work, woodworkers sought to hide the structure of all joints. In modern work since 1900, expressed joinery can be used as an outward display of build quality.

flash off (v)
An expression used in finishing. When the topmost layer of a wet finish turns from shiny to slightly dull, it is said to "flash." When it has flashed, it is not dry but has begun to set up. When many finish products flash, that usually is the time to wipe them down to remove the excess.

Forstner bit (n)
Invented in 1874 by Benjamin Forstner, this style of boring bit is used to create clean, flat-bottomed holes with very little penetration by the central spur. This makes them ideal for stopped holes compared to the traditional auger, which has a long lead screw. Forstner bits also offer the woodworker the ability to overlap holes without the bit wandering, which is difficult to achieve with twist or brad-point bits.

Morris chair (n)
A style of chair named after William Morris, the founder of the English Arts & Crafts movement. Despite the name, the chair was not invented by Morris, but by one of his associates. The Morris chair is characterized by an adjustable back and is widely considered the spiritual progenitor to the La-Z-Boy chair.

Stick chair

stick chair (n)
A style of chair where the strength of the chair is contained in its solid-plank seat. The legs are drilled and wedged into the seat, as are the spindles that support the arms and crest rail. Stick chairs are distinct from frame chairs (e.g. ladderback chairs), which derive their strength by a series of intersecting posts and rungs. The seat on a frame chair is traditionally woven or loose.

tack rag (n)
A cloth that has been impregnated with resin or a varnish-like material. The rag is used to remove loose dust from projects after the finish has been sanded.

tear-out (n)
When small chunks of grain have been torn from a board, creating an undesirable gash. Tear-out typically occurs when a cutter encounters a section of grain that allows the cutter to get under the grain and lever the fibers upward. This forces the actual cutting action to occur in front of the cutter, instead of right at the knife. When this occurs the wood tears instead of being cleanly sliced away. **WM**

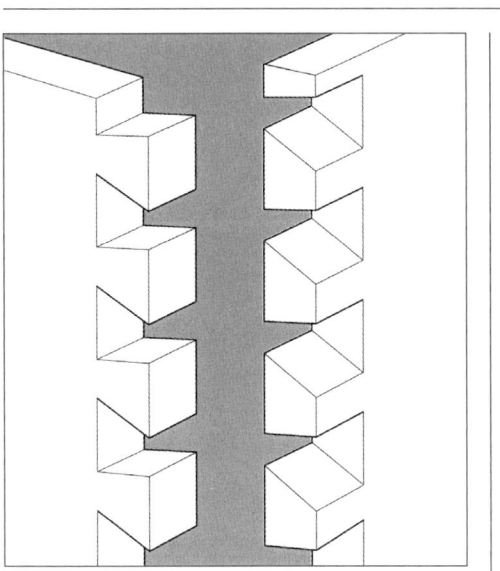

Through-dovetail joint

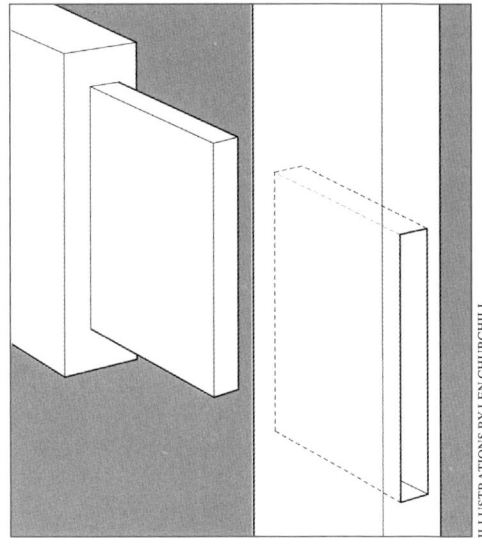

Through mortise-and-tenon joint

Hanging Shelves

This simple project with authentic details provides practice with little risk, and a handsome and useful display.

Hanging shelves are one of the most adaptable projects in woodworking. A small shelf can fill a need in the kitchen or bath, while a larger one can hold books in the den, or a collection of tools in the shop. The method of making them provides an opportunity to develop skills and use leftover material. It's all a matter of scale.

The illustration at right shows some variations in size and shape, and the techniques for making the shelves (and attaching them to the wall) are a good way to practice your joinery. If the project turns out well, put it in the living room. If the end result contains flaws, find a dark corner in the guest bathroom or a dusty place in the shop.

Size the components based on the overall size and the intended purpose. I wanted a small set of shelves for spices in the kitchen or small cosmetic items in the bath. These shelves are 4" deep and the overall height is 20". While sketching, I settled on an overall width of 13¾". I milled the ash boards I had to a thickness of ⅝" to maintain an overall sense of proportion.

I milled all of the stock to 4" wide and cut the parts to the lengths given in the list. All of the shelves finish ⅛" narrower than the sides, but I waited until after making the through mortise-and-tenon joints to reduce them in width. This left a little leeway for fitting the joints.

With both side pieces next to each other on the bench, I oriented them with their most attractive surfaces facing out, and I laid out the locations for the through-mortises. I used a wheel marking gauge to incise the edges of the mortise locations. This gives a more precise location than a pencil line, and when it comes time to clean up the edges of the mortises, it's easy to see where to stop.

A simple set of hanging shelves is enhanced with decorative joinery, hidden shelf supports and a hanging method that shows no fasteners.

Method to Make Square Holes

I decided to forego using a hollow-chisel mortiser or a router with a jig to make the through-mortises. The small size and location across the width complicated the setup for either of these options. Instead, I removed most of the waste with a ⁵⁄₁₆"-diameter Forstner bit in the drill press. I set a fence on the drill press table to center the bit in the mortise at the top of the sides vertically, and drilled a series of overlapping holes.

"In theory, there is no difference between theory and practice. In practice there is."

— Yogi Berra (1925 -)
former Major League Baseball player and manager

After resetting the fence, I drilled another series of holes to locate the bottom mortises. Making the mortises this way involves some risk of tearing out the wood on the back of the joint. This can be minimized by knifing in the layout lines on both sides of the joint, and using a piece of scrap wood below the work when drilling and paring.

Using a ¾"-wide chisel, I pared away the scallops that remained where the holes overlapped. As the scallops disappear, and the paring cuts get closer to the edge of the mortise, it takes more effort to make these cuts. I positioned my shoulder directly over the chisel so I had extra leverage as I pushed down. It's also easy to sight along the back of the chisel to be sure it is vertical from this position.

After working the wide top and bottom edges, I used a ¼"-wide chisel to pare the ends of the mortises down to the lines. A cut in this direc-

Hanging Shelves

NO.	PART	SIZES (INCHES)			MATERIAL
		T	W	L	
❏ 2	Sides	5/8	4	20	Ash
❏ 2	Fixed shelves	5/8	3 7/8	13 3/4	Ash
❏ 2	Adjustable shelves	5/8	3 7/8	12 1/4	Ash
❏ 1	Cleat	5/16	1 1/4	12 1/4	Ash
❏ 2	Cleat	5/16	5/8	12 1/4	Ash*

* 45° bevel on edge, one piece attaches to wall, the other to the top shelf

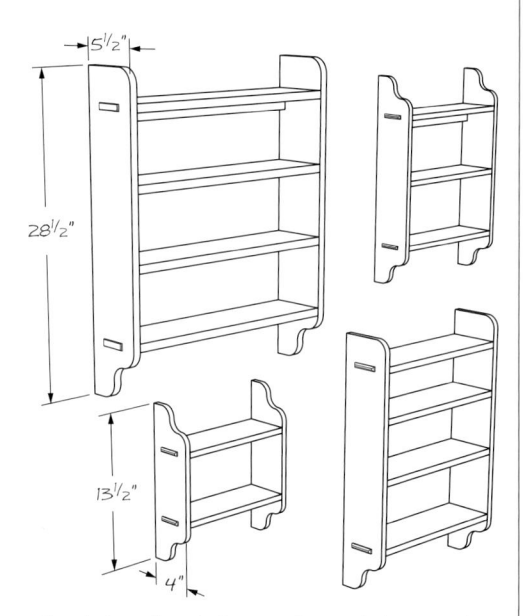

Simple hanging shelves can be made in a number of sizes and shapes. You can hone your skills and fill a need at the same time.

tion is trickier to control, even though the effort to make the cut is easier. These cuts go with the grain, so taking too big a bite can cause the wood to split along the grain.

I stopped paring when the cuts got close to the layout lines and switched from a chisel to a rasp for the wide parts of the joint, and a small flat file for working the ends. This gave me more control and a better surface for the last few cuts that define the mortise.

With one hand above and the other hand below the work, hold the rasp vertically and watch the flat side of the rasp and the layout line as cuts are made on the down stroke. Use the same technique with the file to create a crisp line and corner on the end of the mortise. Use a small adjustable square frequently to check the joint.

In addition to the lines on the finished face being straight and square to each other, I also

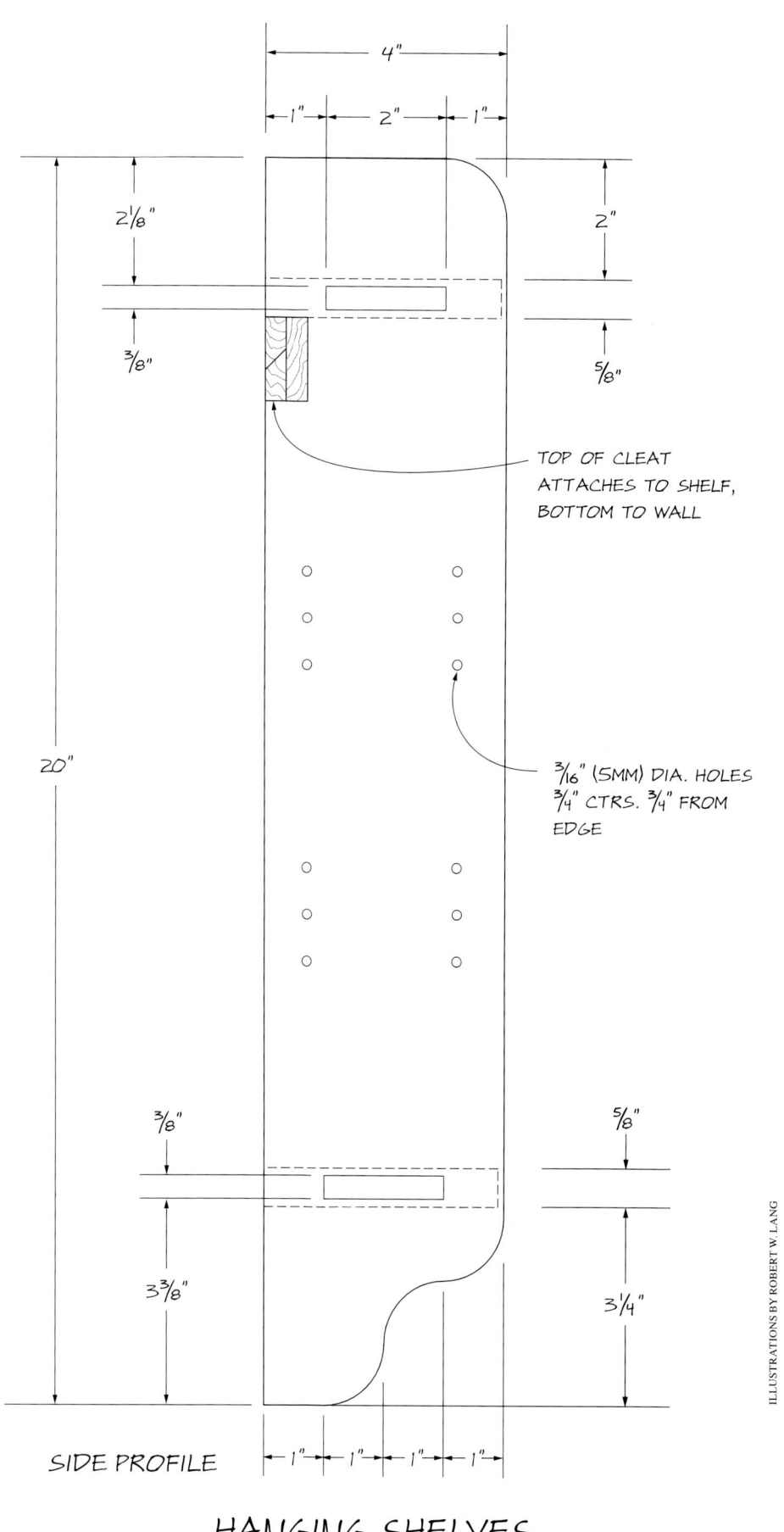

TOP OF CLEAT ATTACHES TO SHELF, BOTTOM TO WALL

3/16" (5MM) DIA. HOLES 3/4" CTRS. 3/4" FROM EDGE

SIDE PROFILE

HANGING SHELVES

ILLUSTRATIONS BY ROBERT W. LANG

woodworking-magazine.com ■ 23

After paring close to the layout lines, a hand-cut rasp is used to remove the last bit of material, leaving a straight and crisp line.

A small flat file is ideal for perfecting the ends of through-mortises.

checked that the walls of the mortise were square to the face of the board. If there is some variation, it should be held to the inside face of the board. The joint will still function if the mortise isn't perfect, but to look good it must be a tight fit on the show side.

Tenons to Fit

On a good day, all the mortises will be the same size. I used a pair of fractional dial calipers to check before cutting the tenons. Just as there are many ways to make the mortises, there are a number of methods to make the tenons. I set up a 1"-diameter straight bit in the router table, with the edge of the bit $^{13}/_{16}$" from the edge of the fence. I set the height of the bit lower than I needed to keep from overcutting the tenon cheeks.

Using a square scrap of wood as a push block, I ran the end of a shelf along the fence and over the bit. I then flipped the board over to cut the other side. Using the calipers, I measured the resulting tenon to compare it to the mortise size. This method of trial and error ensures that the errors land in scrap wood and don't result in a skinny tenon. I made slight adjustments to the bit height to make the tenons a few thousandths of an inch bigger than the mortises.

I fit the tenons for height first, placing a corner into the mortise and removing small amounts of material with the rasp held flat across the tenon cheek. When I could force each corner into the mortise, I placed the shelf vertically on the side, lined up the edges of the shelf and side, and marked the ends of the tenon directly from the mortise.

I used a dovetail saw to remove the excess material from the tenon, cutting close to, but just outside the pencil line. Again, this keeps any error manageable without ruining the part. After sawing, I used a chisel, then a rasp, to work the tenon down to the finished size. Before giving the tenon a test fit in the mortise, I put a small chamfer on the ends of the tenon with a rasp. I also put a very light chamfer around the inside edge of the mortise. These chamfers help get the joint assembly started, and they keep damage to a minimum as the tenon comes through the show side of the mortise.

In theory, the joint should come together with hand pressure. I aim for that, but it almost always takes a few tries to get the fit just right. I push until the tenon gets stuck, then take the joint apart by tapping on the inside of the mortised piece with a dead-blow hammer. Tight spots will show as shiny areas where the two pieces rubbed each other. If you have trouble seeing them, rub the tenon with a soft pencil and push it into the mortise as far as you can. When you take the joint back apart, you can see where the graphite has rubbed off.

If the wood is hard, you can get away with lightly tapping around the mortise to get the joint together. The wood will make a different tone in tight areas than it will in loose ones. It takes some experience to know where to hit and how hard to hit. The risk is splitting the wood, and it doesn't really work to beat on it until something breaks, then beat it a little less.

I make most of the adjustments to the tenon, unless I discover a high spot within the mortise. This is a process of testing the fit, taking the joint apart, making a few strokes with the rasp then testing the fit again. I switch to a card scraper at the very end, aiming for a finished surface on the exposed part of the tenon as the final fit is reached.

Holding the rasp at a 45° angle quickly brings the chamfered ends down to the layout line.

Turning the Corner

When the joint finally goes together, I find something – either a metal straightedge or a scrap of wood that is as thick as half the exposed portion of the tenon. In this piece, the end of the tenon protrudes $3/16$" beyond the face of the side, so I laid a $3/32$"-thick straightedge against the side, and marked around the tenon with a pencil. This established the limit of the chamfers on the tenon ends, which I cut with a rasp.

Before disassembling the sides and shelves, I marked the edges of the shelves so that I could trim them to be flush at the back, and $1/8$" in from the front edge of the sides. I made the rip cuts on the table saw, then I used a block plane to remove the saw marks and chamfer the shelf edges.

With the joints fit, I used double-sided tape to temporarily hold the two sides together, oriented with the outside faces out and both front edges together. I then laid out the curved profiles at the top and bottom. I used my adjustable square to draw a grid on one side, and a compass set to a 1" radius to mark the curves.

I cut the curves at the band saw, and removed the saw marks with an oscillating-spindle sander. The sander is nice to have, but these edges can also be cleaned up with the curved side of the rasp, followed by a card scraper.

Room for Adjustment

After taking the sides apart, I laid out the holes for the adjustable shelf pins. I marked the holes on $3/4$" centers, $3/4$" in from the front and back edges. I spaced the sets of holes so that the shelves would divide the space in thirds when the shelf pins were in the center holes of each group of three. After marking, I drilled the $3/16$"-diameter holes at the drill press. I used small brass shelf pins, with a 5mm shank. This was a tight fit in the $3/16$" holes, but it worked.

I didn't want the shelf pins to be visible, so I used a $3/8$"-diameter core box bit to cut two stopped grooves in the underside of each end of each shelf. I set up the bit in the router table, with a square block extending from the fence to guide the edge of the shelf as I pushed the shelf into the bit and against the fence.

After sanding all the parts with #120 grit with a vibrating sander, then with #180 grit by hand, my shelf was ready to assemble. Before assembly, I brushed yellow glue on the end-grain surfaces of the mortise and the shelf. After letting this dry for 10 minutes, I started the tenons in the mortises, and brushed glue on the cheeks of the tenons. I was frugal with the glue so that there wouldn't be any squeeze-out to clean up.

With all the tenons in place and the glue applied, four bar clamps brought the assembly together. I removed the small amounts of glue squeeze-out with the back of a sharp chisel and a damp rag, and then I let the work sit in the clamps overnight. After removing the clamps, I lightly chamfered the edges of the sides and shelves with a fine rasp and a piece of #120-grit sandpaper.

To hang the shelf from the wall, I milled some scrap stock to $5/16$" thick. After establishing the length to fit within the sides of the shelves, I ripped one piece of this thin stuff to $1 1/4$". I set the blade of the table saw to cut a 45° bevel and the fence to rip two pieces $5/8$" wide. I glued one of these angled pieces to the flat piece, as seen in the photo below right.

When the glue dried, I planed the edge where the two pieces met flush, and glued this assembly to the bottom back edge of the top shelf. I set the other angled piece aside to screw to the wall. The angled edge attached to the shelves drops over the angled edge of the piece attached to the wall. This provides a secure connection, and the only thing visible from the front of the shelves is the face of the piece below the top shelf.

I hand-sanded all the pieces with #180-grit Abranet (an abrasive mesh) before staining. I applied a heavy coat of Olympic "Special Walnut" oil-based stain with a rag, let it sit for 10 minutes then wiped off the excess. For a topcoat, I sprayed semi-gloss lacquer from a can, sanding between coats as described in the article on page 30.

A small simple project such as this is a good way to spend some time in the shop, and have something useful and attractive to show for it. **WM**

— *Robert W. Lang*

Supplies

Rockler
800-279-4441 or rockler.com

1 ■ brass shelf pins
   #22252, $3.99 pkg. of 16

Price correct at time of publication.

Stopped grooves made at the router table with a core box bit hold the shelves securely and conceal the shelf pins.

The completed through mortise-and-tenon joint is incredibly strong, and it adds a decorative accent to a simple project.

A hidden French cleat slips over a matching angled cleat to hold the shelf to the wall.

Saddle Squares

This little slip of a layout tool is an excellent way to transfer layout lines around corners.

There haven't been too many innovations in the last couple centuries when it comes to the basic cadre of layout tools. But a little more than a decade ago, Bridge City Tool Works introduced the "saddle square" as a "straightedge for corners" to more accurately mark lines around corners, according to Bridge City's founder John Economaki. For the relatively few woodworkers who have used one, this handy little tool has changed layout immeasurably for the better.

Transferring a line from one surface to an adjacent surface with a combination square or try square is never easy because you have to move the tool to do it. (Try to quickly wrap a line around a piece of stock with a combo square, and you'll see how easy it is to muck it up.) A saddle square allows you to keep the tool tightly in contact with both stock faces as you make the mark, cutting down on the possibility for error.

Both Bridge City and Veritas (the toolmaking arm of Lee Valley Tools) now offer two sizes of commercially made saddle squares, but we found that in a pinch, a well-made butt hinge (without balls or finials) also works well (just be sure to choose one with no hinge slop). Actual saddle squares are, however, more handy because they can mark longer distances, and they're easier to hold to the work with one hand (the articulated Bridge City versions are tightly joined, so they don't easily slip in use).

Saddle squares are designed to transfer layout lines from one face of a board to a second adjacent face, without moving the tool. A well-made hinge works, too, though the legs may prove a bit too short in some layout situations.

For looks, I prefer both of the Bridge City versions, but in ease of use, I found the ridges on the faces of the Veritas versions, as well as the wider faces, allowed me to more easily hold the tool to my work. However, the Veritas saddle squares work only on 90° corners, so if you're a chairmaker, or commonly work with angles other than 90°, consider the Bridge City tools (or a good hinge).

I've also found the saddle square a must-have at the table saw for cutting my work to size. Sure, I could lay my tape measure along the edge of a board and mark the cut, but sometimes it's hard to balance the tape or a rule on thin stock. It's easier to mark the workpiece face, then transfer the mark around the edge and "show" that mark to a sawtooth to accurately set the saw's rip fence or the stop on a crosscut sled.

For the time it saves on layout and the little space it takes up, we think a saddle square is a must-have tool. **WM**

— *Megan Fitzpatrick*

In this panel glue-up, you can see the the board lengths aren't equal. In this scenario, it's hard to balance a measuring tool on the end to mark the width. With a saddle square, it's simple to mark the face and accurately transfer the line around to the edge, then line up the blade to the mark.

"Though he may not always recognize his bondage, modern man lives under a tyranny of numbers."
— Nicholas Eberstadt (1955 -)
American political economist and demographer

Saddle Squares

BRIDGE CITY
SS-2 Brass and Rosewood Saddle Square

This was the first saddle square on the market, and in addition to its usefulness, it's nice to look at. Articulation allows for tight work on non-90° corners. The version with two 2"-long legs is ideal for typical layout work and takes up little space in your shop apron.

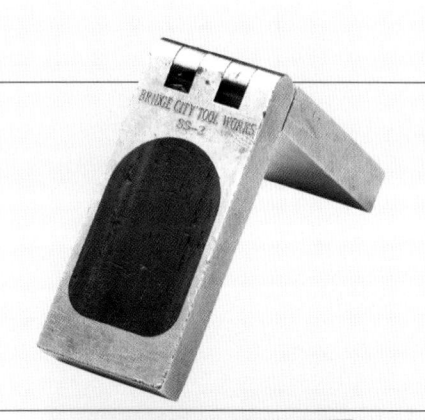

Bridge City Tools ■ 800-253-3332 or bridgecitytools.com
Retail Price ■ SS-2 (2" x 2" legs), $69
(2" x 4" legs), $72

BRIDGE CITY
SS-2X4 Aluminum Saddle Square

This aluminum version from Bridge City is a less expensive option than the company's brass and rosewood tool, and is available only in the 2" x 4" size. The matte black finish is sleek looking, and it's grabby on your fingers as well as on your work. Articulation allows for tight work on non-90° corners.

Bridge City Tools ■ 800-253-3332 or bridgecitytools.com
Retail Price ■ $44

VERITAS
Saddle Square

This inexpensive anodized aluminum saddle square has $1\frac{1}{4}$" x $2\frac{1}{4}$" legs, and is machined square with no articulation; that makes it useful only for 90° work (which is 98 percent of what most woodworkers routinely do). Also, the larger face makes it a little easier to hold to the work than the Bridge City versions. While this Veritas tool is not as snazzy looking, it's functional and inexpensive.

Lee Valley Tools ■ 800-871-8158 or leevalley.com
Retail Price ■ $14.50

VERITAS
Large Saddle Square

This larger version of the Veritas saddle square has $1\frac{3}{8}$" x $3\frac{3}{8}$" legs, which accommodates a standard 2x4 for stud-wall layout; the slot through the center makes it easy to mark a stud's center. It's also useful for marking lines on larger stock for woodworking projects because of its one long leg.

Lee Valley Tools ■ 800-871-8158 or leevalley.com
Retail Price ■ $16.50

Butt Hinge

An inelegant but readily available solution is to find a well-made hinge in your stock of odd hardware. Just make sure there's no slop in the leaves (and you might want to check the hinge against a square you know is accurate before using it for layout).

Any hardware store
Retail Price ■ varies

A Super Smooth Surface

Fillers level open-grain wood in a single step and save time.

Some woodworkers like the look and feel of grain on their projects while others strive for a super smooth surface. Be it high sheen or dead flat, a super smooth surface requires work during the finishing stage of your project.

Chances are your normal finishing supplies or methods of work won't produce a smooth finish unless you're working on closed-grain woods such as maple or cherry. With these woods, it's possible to fill pores and level the surface using most topcoat materials while sanding between layers until you achieve a smooth surface.

On the other hand, open-grain woods, such as walnut, mahogany or oak, need additional work to attain super smooth status. The grain must be levelled by filling the pores. Depending on your final finishing approach – staining the project or simply leaving the wood natural – you have a few options.

If you plan to finish your project without stain, then sandpaper and oil might be your best choice. If you plan to enhance the color with stain, you can use excessive coats of finish. Given enough time to apply then sand off topcoat material, you can eventually fill even the most open-grained hardwoods. Or you can use grain filler.

Grain filler, sometimes called pore filler or paste wood filler (but not wood putty), is a combination of filler material, binder and usually some type of colorant.

Silica, calcium carbonate or clay is usually the filler material. The binder is either oil or varnish in oil-based filler, or glycol if it's water-based.

As for a colorant, most oil-based fillers have a colorant added – even those listed as "natural." Oil-based fillers can be shaded with compatible stains or concentrated colors as can water-based fillers, but water-based fillers are also available as "clear." When clear filler dries, the filler material becomes translucent and does not affect the final finish appearance, as color-added fillers do.

Stain-free Projects

On a project where you need to fill the pores and stain is not required, I suggest a coat of boiled linseed oil (BLO). Then sand the piece with #400-grit silicon-carbide sandpaper while the oil is wet. This action mixes wood dust from the project into the oil to create a slurry. That slurry, in turn, fills the open pores. This process is quite effective, but it might require you to add a couple extra layers of finish to make the surface super smooth.

Yes, the addition of BLO will affect the finish appearance. If you want to lessen the yellowing brought on by BLO, use tung oil. And if tung oil is still a bit more yellow than you wish, switch to a clear water-based filler.

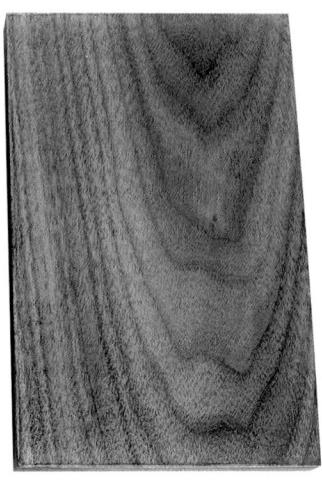

To achieve a super smooth finish, open-grain wood has to be filled and there's more than one choice for filler. The product, and the method used to apply that product, directly influence the final appearance.

After a coat of sealer and a light sanding, non-filled areas stand out due to sanding dust left in the still-open pores. The left-most sample began as raw wood while the center sample has an oil/sanding filler. The right-most sample, the piece clearly more filled than its counterparts, has two coats of water-based filler added.

"It often requires more courage to dare to do right than to fear to do wrong."
— Abraham Lincoln (1809 - 1865)
16th president of the United States

Stained Projects

Apply color-added filler directly on your project and the filler is essentially a stain. Unless you experiment with fillers as stain and are happy with the results, I suggest you first stain and seal the wood (for which I like shellac). As you sand the sealer coat, you fold any peaks of sealer into open pores. That helps fill the pores so less filler is needed to level the surface. Then add paste filler.

It's at this point in the finishing process that you need to decide on the final appearance you want. Are you looking for a clear filler to keep the appearance as-is? If so, water-based filler is your only choice. Would natural or light-colored filler work with the stain you've selected? Or, would a dark-tinted filler add to the overall look of the project when complete? In either case, you have the option of oil-based or water-based fillers.

I prefer dark-colored filler for most projects. In the same vein as filling nail holes, many hardwoods darken in time while the color of the filler remains constant. Any differences in the two shades are amplified as the piece ages. One caveat to this is walnut. Walnut lightens with age, so you need to evaluate the stain color in order to reach a decision. However, if you're not staining walnut, you should use the oil/sanding method described above.

Oil-based vs. Water-based

Perhaps the most important question to ask is whether water-based filler or oil-based filler is better. There are pros and cons with each of these two varieties of fillers.

Water-based is easy to apply and cleanup is a breeze. Simply wipe the filler on using a circular motion to help force particulate into the pores, wipe off any excess and let it dry. Keep a close eye on this step because sometimes water-based fillers dry too fast. I needed to apply a second coat of filler to completely fill the pores of both walnut and mahogany when using a water-based filler.

Once it's dry, you'll need to sand the filler to level the surface. With sanding comes the risk of sanding through the filler and stain, exposing bare wood. If that happens, start over.

I prefer oil-based filler if I plan to fill open-grain hardwoods. Application of oil-based products is more involved than water-based products because there's an additional step. First, wipe or brush oil-based filler onto a previously sealed and sanded wood, again using a circular motion. Because oil dries more slowly than water, you need to keep an eye on this filler until the sheen flashes off to a dull haze. At that time, scrape the excess filler from the surface, then wipe with a coarse cloth – burlap is an excellent tool. Wipe across the grain, not with the grain. When you wipe with the grain there's a chance to pull filler from filled pores and then you'll have to apply it again.

Allow the oil-based filler to dry before you add a sealer coat or other topcoats.

For my test, one application of oil-based filler significantly filled the pores on both walnut and mahogany.

Once the grain is filled to a level surface, it's on to your topcoat. If you select a water-based filler, there should be zero compatibility issues. However, if you use an oil-based filler, lightly sand the surface with an abrasive pad to remove any airborne dust particles. Then, due to compatibility issues with some topcoats, apply a sealer over the filled surface. For me, another coat of shellac is the best choice, after which any finish is OK. (If filler is allowed to thoroughly and completely dry, a sealer coat over the filler can be skipped, but I prefer to play it safe.)

If a super smooth surface is what you yearn for, give filler a try. It works. But a word of caution: If you're looking for a "piano" surface – that super-high-gloss sheen – you'll still have to apply a significant number of topcoats to achieve a level surface that won't show grain in reflected light. That's why most furniture is finished with a dull or hand-rubbed finish. A dull finish does not reflect light as much, so hiding minute imperfections is possible.

As with all finishing techniques, it's best to practice on a piece of scrap from your project lumber to assess the end result. **WM**

— *Glen D. Huey*

Water-based filler dries very quickly. Here you can see swirls from the application of the product. Make sure to wipe excess water-based filler from the project while moving with the direction of the grain.

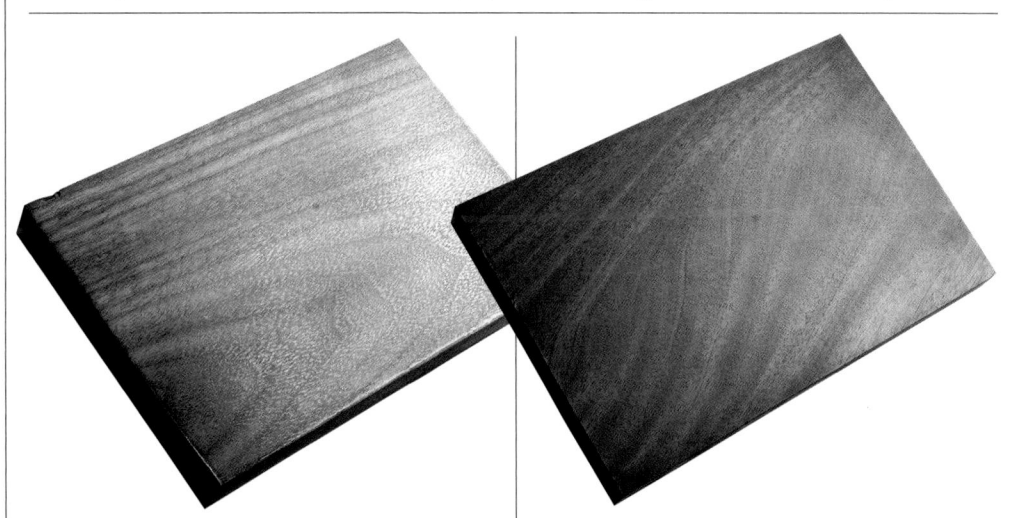

This sample of walnut was filled with an oil/sanding dust filler, followed by three layers of sanded shellac. Holding the piece under a raking light shows that more work is needed to gain a super-smooth surface – dull areas are level and shiny areas (white areas under reflected light) are yet to be filled entirely.

A dark-tinted oil-based grain filler levels the surface in a single step and adds a deep tone to the overall finish. This is especially nice when you wish to add age to a finish such as on reproduction furniture.

Sanding Finishes

The opportunity to make or break the look of your project. We look at the techniques and some new materials.

As the completion of a project approaches, the temptation to rush and be done with it is strong. But the final steps of applying a first-class finish are as important as the first steps of laying out and building. Careless work at this point can compromise the final appearance, or create problems that may take an enormous amount of time to correct – or both.

Sanding between coats of finish is often glossed over in books and magazine articles. Many woodworkers don't understand what they are sanding, why they are sanding or how to do it efficiently and effectively. The goal is a smooth and flawless surface. But the goal of perfection is elusive, and a surface that looks and feels smooth and flawless is a reasonable compromise.

There are two types of finishes that need to be sanded between coats: reactive finishes (lacquer and shellac, for example), where the solvent of a fresh coat partially dissolves the finish beneath it; and non-reactive finishes (such as varnish), where the solvent has no effect on underlying coats.

The techniques for sanding are much the same, but leveling one coat of varnish before applying another requires a more thorough and careful approach. Oil finishes can be wet-sanded during application and wiped dry. If any oil dries on the surface, it should be sanded between coats.

"You throw the sand against the wind and the wind blows it back again."
— William Blake (1757 - 1827)
English poet, painter and printmaker

Careful sanding between finish coats will make the difference between a tolerable finish and a great one. You don't need to worry about following the wood grain, but there are plenty of other things to consider: the right abrasive, the proper technique, and getting rid of dust and other debris.

In a perfect world, gravity would let a finish flow out to a perfectly level surface before a finish could dry. And in this imaginary perfect world, all surfaces would be horizontal. In reality, however, the pores in the wood and uneven application from a brush, rag or spray gun all prevent any finish from becoming absolutely level before the finish dries, no matter how careful the finisher may be.

In addition, dust and other airborne objects will find their way to the surface, even in the cleanest of finishing rooms. The goal of sanding between coats is to remove – or at least disguise – these imperfections, leaving a smoother and flatter surface with each subsequent coat.

Given enough time and many coats of finish, a nearly perfect, high-gloss finish can be achieved. Not every project is a grand piano, however, and for most work a lower sheen that shows evidence of the pores of the wood is desired. This sort of finish doesn't take long, and can be achieved in a few coats with the right technique.

Sanding a finish is an exercise in restraint, particularly if there is a layer of stain between the finish and the wood. You want to level the surface without removing any color. Preparation before staining will eliminate most of that risk. Use a plane, scraper or sanding block to ensure level, flat surfaces.

Avoiding Low Places

A common mistake on raw wood is to sand low spots. If you have a dent or a dip, sanding directly on it won't help; you need to sand everything else down to that level. After sanding all the flat surfaces, lightly go over the edges, breaking any sharp corners. This will keep the stain and any following coats from building up at the edges.

Finish sanding is also an exercise in patience. Lacquer, varnish and shellac will be dry to the touch long before they are completely dry. You can sand these surfaces when they are dry to the touch, but just because you can, doesn't mean that you should. These coatings will tend to pill up if you don't wait overnight before sanding.

Few woodworkers are that patient, and one of the attractions of these finishes is the fact that you can apply several coats in a short period of time. Many products developed for sanding finishes have been engineered to minimize pilling in uncured finishes, but some of these introduce other problems.

Minimize the Risk

White colored, stearate-coated papers are lubricated to keep from loading the paper with sticky sanding residue, but this lubricant can interfere with the adhesion of subsequent coats in some finishes such as water-based lacquer.

Sanding with a sheet abrasive alone is the riskiest approach, and it requires a light and careful touch around the edges. Grain direction doesn't matter, because you are sanding a film rather than the wood below it. The direction of your fingers in relation to the paper is more important. Keep the motion of the paper at a right angle to your fingers to even out the pressure and avoid introducing finger-shaped grooves.

A sanding block will even out pressure from your hand, but a rigid block can cause problems. If the finish starts to pill below a hard block, it can leave a groove or even tilt the block so its hard edge sands through the stain at another point. A good sanding block has some give to it. Traditionally, a layer of cork on a block of wood is used.

A recent addition to the sanding arsenal is the sanding sponge, and this is my weapon of choice for finish sanding. It is the right combination of stiffness to keep flat surfaces flat, with enough give to go around corners and over bumps. It can also reach to sand faces on an inside corner simultaneously, as seen in the photo below.

If the finish starts to pill and build up on the abrasive surface, it can be knocked loose by tapping the sponge on a hard surface, or by rinsing it under running water.

There are two other useful abrasives that are easily cleaned, and these also provide space for the little goobers of finish to go while sanding.

Non-woven nylon abrasive pads don't work as quickly as sandpaper or a sanding sponge, and they need to be held and moved correctly on a flat surface. But they are great when you need to wrap them around a corner, or scrunch them into a moulding profile. If the pad begins to load up, it can be cleared by shaking it or snapping it, and it can be rinsed in water or a solvent.

A New Favorite

The other new and notable abrasive is Abranet, recently introduced by Mirka. Abranet comes in sheets and disks, but it isn't sandpaper. It is abrasive-impregnated mesh. As you sand with it, the dust and residue can move through the open spaces in the mesh. Mirka makes some sanding blocks designed to be used with Abranet that connect to a vacuum hose – an effective, inexpensive and almost dust-free sanding solution.

Abranet lasts a long time, and if a slightly sticky finish begins to fill the spaces in the mesh, you can clear them easily. Grab each side of the sheet, bring the edges together and quickly snap them apart. If that trick doesn't work, you can blow compressed air from the back side of the sheet. If all else fails, rinse the sheet in solvent.

After sanding, the fine powdery dust must be removed before applying the next coat of finish. Compressed air can be used, provided that there isn't so much dust that it will form a cloud that will settle back on the surface. The residue can be vacuumed off with a brush attachment, but the bristles should be short and soft. The vacuum is more effective than blowing, but will take longer and require more attention to make sure no areas are missed.

The alternative to an air attack is wiping the sanding residue away. A soft cotton rag can work, but it does a much better job if it is dampened with a solvent, such as mineral spirits or paint thinner. Commercially made tack rags are sold as the ideal solution, but I don't buy that argument.

The quality of the cloth, and the sticky stuff that attracts the dust can vary widely. A good tack rag will pick up dust without leaving anything behind. A bad one can be stiff enough to cause scratches, or leave a residue that prevents the next coat of finish from adhering. **WM**

— *Robert W. Lang*

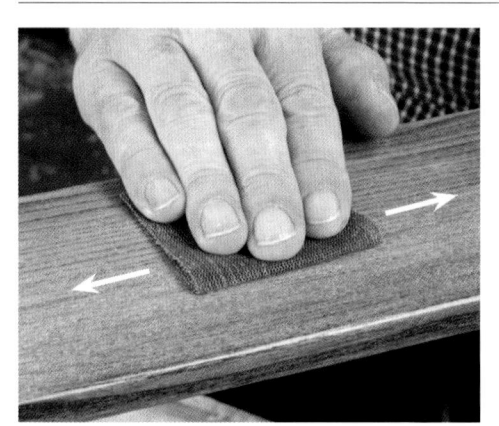

Supplies

Mirka Abranet
amazon.com

On flat surfaces, grain direction does not matter, but it is important to move at a right angle to the direction of your fingers. Going the same way can produce grooves in the surface.

Sanding sponges are an excellent balance of a flat surface that gives enough to gently handle corners and edges.

Sponges are also good for getting at both sides of an inside corner.

A nylon pad and a gentle touch can sand an outside corner without going too far.

Abranet is mesh, so dust has a place to go. If it clogs, it can be cleaned with a blast of air.

End Grain

Reviving Techniques Forgotten (and Gross)

Hock up a loogie and start saving your earwax.

With a sound like a cat retching up a hairball, I reached deep inside myself to call forth enough spittle in my mouth to do the job.

I looked at the sharpening stone. I looked at my plane iron. Then I shook my head and deposited the contents of my mouth on the stone. Yes, this might be a little graphic for a family magazine, but it's all in the name of honest historical discovery, I assure you.

I spread the loogie on the stone and started to hone the plane iron, but not in the way that you think. Instead of planting the stone on the bench and holding the plane iron with two hands (or a honing guide), I did something you never see in woodworking magazines: I held the tool with my right hand, the stone with my left and rubbed them together.

At that moment I thought I had really gone too far with this experiment. After a dozen strokes, however, it didn't feel so weird and so I got brave enough to take a peek at the bevel of the tool.

It was surprisingly shiny and consistent – not at all what I expected from this 17th-century hotdogging sharpening technique.

You see, for the last year I've been reading and trying to update the first-ever woodworking book in English: Joseph Moxon's "Mechanick Exercises." I've read the section called "The Art of Joinery" more than a dozen times now, and I can tell you that it's like visiting another country.

Lots of things are familiar (like finding a Starbucks while visiting London), but plenty of techniques seem crude or just plain wrong (like eating at a Burger King on the Champs Elysées). Exhibit A of the weird is the sharpening instructions offered by Moxon, who was a printer and globe maker by profession, not a woodworker.

After my surprising success with this oddball method, I was emboldened to try some of the other things in the book.

Such as planing miters. This technique is a lot like the sharpening technique in that you hold the work in one hand and the tool in the other. Except for large pieces of work, Moxon instructs you not to clamp things in your workbench's vise. Instead, you hold your plane upside down in your left hand and thrust the miter over the tool's sole with your right.

Again, I didn't think I had the manual dexterity to pull this off. So I took a fairly soft wood (poplar) and marked and sawed a miter on the end with a carcase saw. I left a little bit of my knife line. Then I gave the technique a whirl.

Again, I was surprised. A well-sawn miter is fairly easy to true this way (with a little practice). I even checked my work with a miter square to confirm that I was indeed at 45°.

With other techniques I didn't have to overcome my fear, I instead had to overcome the 17th-century English. Moxon's instructions for mortising have you work from the ends of the mortise to the middle. But it was unclear (to me) at which end of the mortise you start. And this greatly affects how the chisel works because of the direction you are told to face the tool.

So I tried starting at the far end. No good. That mortise would never be clear of chips (good thing it was practice wood). The I reversed the order of my steps and everything fell into place. I made a tidy mortise in no time flat.

Score: Moxon, 3; Moderns, 0.

In addition to the practical advice, Moxon also sheds a little light on some of the practices that were common in English workshops, such as pouring low-alcohol beer into the hide glue to make it work better. Moxon says that's not a good idea so I'll skip that experiment, but there is one little trick I would like to try some day.

In Moxon's section on house carpentry, he discusses a prank that masters would play on their apprentices. The masters would coat nail heads with earwax so the apprentices' hammers would slip off the nails. I think this would be a hilarious practical joke to play on my shop mates (especially after they thought the spit on the sharpening stone was a joke).

But it's going to take me a long time to save enough earwax to coat the heads of a strip of 18-gauge pneumatic nails. WM

— *Christopher Schwarz*

Extras

"The secret to success is constancy to purpose."
— Benjamin Disraeli (1804 - 1881)
British statesman and author

Visit the New & Improved Woodworking-Magazine.com

Woodworking-Magazine.com has been upgraded to include … wait for it … *Woodworking Magazine* articles!

In addition to an ever-growing database of articles from back issues of the magazine, you'll also find direct links to the newest additions to the editor's blog, CD compilations, books and more.

Plus, the new site is tied into our sister publication's site, PopularWoodworking.com, so you'll be able to easily find all the woodworking information and resources you need.

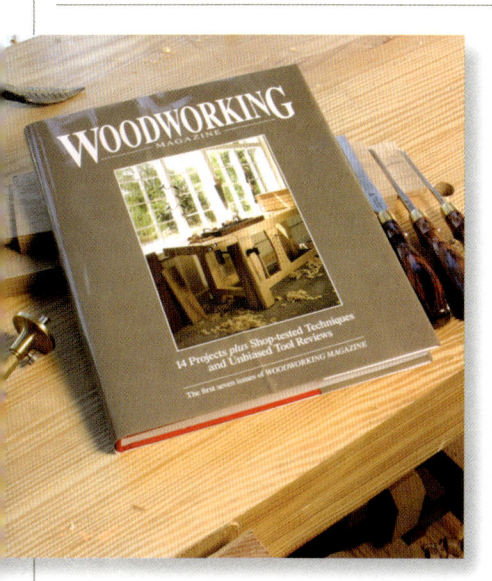

Woodworking Magazine – The Hardbound Book (And a New One on the Way)

Although we offer digital versions of all issues of *Woodworking Magazine,* we have an affection for the printed word. So, we collected the first seven issues of the magazine and bound them into a book (now in its second printing).

Woodworking Magazine – The Book, Issues 1-7 is available on our web site (woodworking-magazine.com/books) for $34.95 (includes domestic s&h). It's a perfect way to ensure your collection will last for years to come (and a great gift for fellow woodworkers).

And, we're working on a new book that will collect issues 8-12. Look for it on our web site in 2009!

New! The First 8 Issues of *Woodworking Magazine* Now Available On CD

We sold out of our older CD, so we've revised the new printing to include issues 1-8! This easy-to-navigate and searchable CD collection gives you instant access to the first eight issues of *Woodworking Magazine* – including the first three issues that are sold out. Here's just a sample of what you'll find:

- **SolidWorks 3D Drawings:** You'll find "live model" drawings for many of the projects – drawings you can rotate in every direction to see all sides of the project in its assembled form. You can even pull individual parts off and rotate those around to look at all the joinery by zooming in and out. (The software to "read" these files is free – and there's a link to download it.)
- **Help With Tools and Supplies:** Buying the tools we recommend or the supplies you need for a project is simple with the enhanced CD. Click on a supplies box and you'll be whisked to the company's web site where another couple clicks will let you purchase the items you need.
- **Find the Information You Want:** All of the files are fully searchable so you can find that trick, technique or quote you're looking for.
- **It's Great for the Shop:** You'll no longer have to worry about spilling varnish on your printed copy of the magazine – simply print out the drawings you need and head to the shop.

Order your copy of this exclusive disc now at woodworking-magazine.com or call 800-258-0929 (ask for disc #Z2983; just $24.95, including s&h!).

IMPORTANT SAFETY NOTE

Safety is your responsibility. Manufacturers place safety devices on their equipment for a reason. In many photos you see in *Woodworking Magazine,* these have been removed to provide clarity. In some cases we'll use an awkward body position so you can better see what's being demonstrated. Don't copy us. Think about each procedure you're going to perform beforehand. Safety First!

CONTACT US

We welcome letters from readers with comments about this magazine, or about woodworking in general. We try to respond to all correspondence. To send us a letter:
- E-mail: letters@fwpubs.com
- Fax: 513-891-7196
- Mail carrier:
  Letters • *Woodworking Magazine*
  4700 E. Galbraith Road
  Cincinnati, OH 45236

Number 12, Winter 2008. *Woodworking Magazine* (ISSN 1941-5834) is published 4 times a year in March, May, August and December by F+W Publications, Inc. Editorial offices are located at 4700 E. Galbraith Road, Cincinnati, Ohio 45236; tel.: 513-531-2222. Unsolicited manuscripts are not accepted. Subscription rates: A year's subscription (4 issues) is $19.96 in the U.S., $24.96 in Canada, and $29.96 elsewhere. Produced and printed in the U.S.A.

Wood Types

Winter 2008

Understanding Wood: Four Structure Types

All hardwoods have vessels (little pipelines) that are used in sap production. The size and distribution of these vessels vary among species; some are visible to the naked eye. When the vessels are cut across the end grain, they're often referred to as pores, thus hardwoods are known as "porous woods" (see below for further classification). The size, number and distribution of the vessels affect the appearance and uniformity of hardness in a particular wood. Softwoods, which don't have pores, are known as "non-porous woods."

Ring Porous

In some species (e.g. oak and ash), the largest pores are in the earlywood while those in the latewood are more evenly distributed and uniform in size. These woods typically have distinct figures and patterns, and the uneven uptake of stain (the large pores soak up more color) make the figure more pronounced. These are also known as open-grain woods.

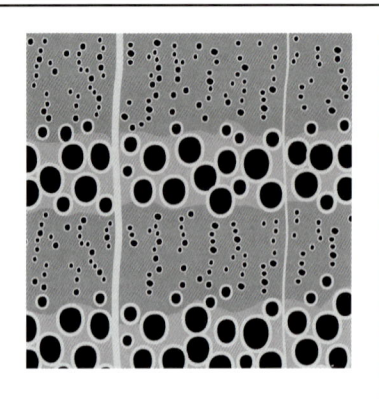

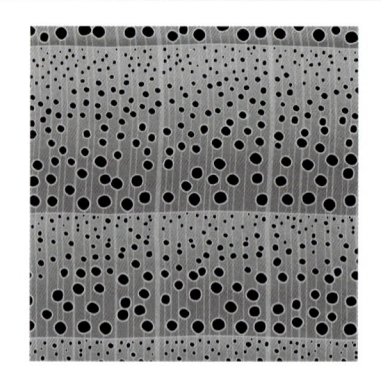

Semi-Ring Porous or Semi-Diffuse Porous

In some species (e.g. black walnut and butternut), pores are large in the earlywood and smaller toward the latewood, but without the distinct zoning seen in ring-porous woods. Also, some species that are usually ring-porous (e.g. cottonwood) occasionally tend toward semi-ring porous.

Know the Parts of Softwood and Hardwood

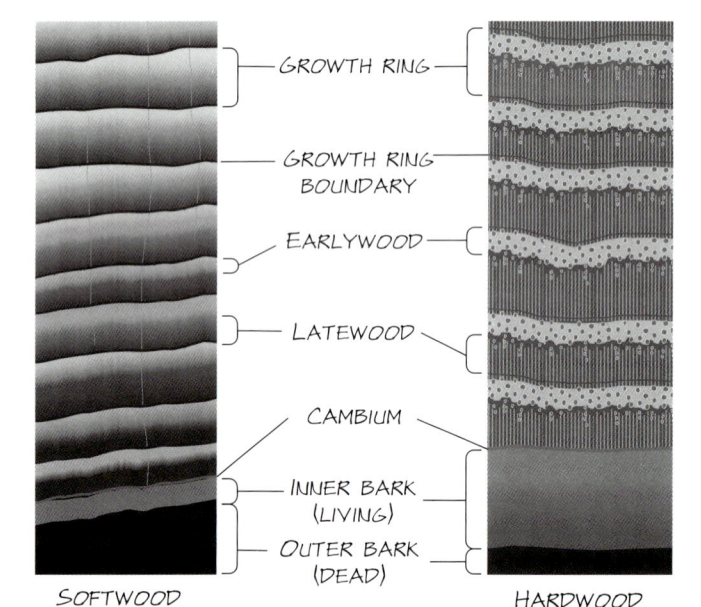

- Growth Ring
- Growth Ring Boundary
- Earlywood
- Latewood
- Cambium
- Inner Bark (Living)
- Outer Bark (Dead)

Softwood | Hardwood

Diffuse Porous

In some species (e.g. maple, cherry and yellow poplar) the pores are distributed fairly evenly across the earlywood and latewood. Most domestic diffuse-porous woods have relatively small-diameter pores, but some tropical woods of this type (e.g. mahogany) have rather large pores. These woods usually have even uptake of stain (there seems to be no scientifically proven explanation of the cause of blotching). These are also known as closed-grain woods.

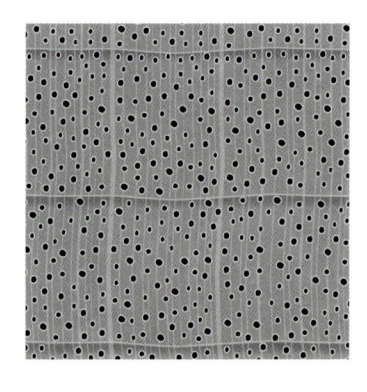

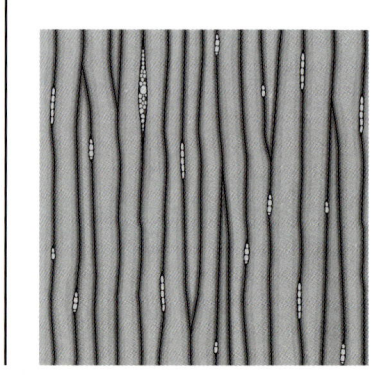

Non-Porous

Softwoods don't have vessel cells (water is conducted in the living tree in tracheid cells). Different softwoods have different growth-ring characteristics however. In white pine, the rings are non-distinct, and stain uptake is fairly even, as in diffuse porous woods. In yellow pine, where the rings are clearly visible, stain uptake in earlywood is more pronounced than in latewood, as in ring-porous woods.

Illustrations by Mary Jane Favorite, based on photographs from R. Bruce Hoadley's "Understanding Wood"